THE JESUITS AND GLOBALIZATION

THE JESUITS AND GLOBALIZATION

Historical Legacies and Contemporary Challenges

Thomas Banchoff and José Casanova, *Editors*

Georgetown University Press
Washington, DC

© 2016 Georgetown University Press. All rights reserved. No part of this book may be reproduced or utilized in any form or by any means, electronic or mechanical, including photocopying and recording, or by any information storage and retrieval system, without permission in writing from the publisher.

Library of Congress Cataloging-in-Publication Data

Names: Banchoff, Thomas F., 1964- editor. | Casanova, José, editor.
Title: The Jesuits and globalization : historical legacies and contemporary challenges / [edited by] Thomas Banchoff and José Casanova.
Description: Washington, DC : Georgetown University Press, 2016. | Includes bibliographical references and index.
Identifiers: LCCN 2015024223 | ISBN 9781626162877 (hardcover : alk. paper) | ISBN 9781626162860 (pbk. : alk. paper) | ISBN 9781626162884 (ebook)
Subjects: LCSH: Jesuits. | Jesuits--Education. | Globalization. | Globalization--Religious aspects--Catholic Church.
Classification: LCC BX3702.3 .J47 2016 | DDC 271/.53—dc23
LC record available at http://lccn.loc.gov/2015024223

∞ This book is printed on acid-free paper meeting the requirements of the American National Standard for Permanence in Paper for Printed Library Materials.

16 15   9 8 7 6 5 4 3 2 First printing

Printed in the United States of America

Cover design by Pam Pease

The cover image is a combination of two public domain images: a quasi-traditional version of the IHS emblem of the Jesuits by Moranski and the inset map *Orbis Terrarum Nova et Accuratissima Tabula* by Pieter Goos (17th century).

CONTENTS

Preface vii

Introduction: The Jesuits and Globalization   1
THOMAS BANCHOFF AND JOSÉ CASANOVA

Part I: Historical Perspectives

1   The Jesuits in East Asia in the Early Modern Age: A New "Areopagus" and the "*Re*-invention" of Christianity   27
M. ANTONI J. UCERLER, SJ

2   Jesuit Intellectual Practice in Early Modernity: The Pan-Asian Argument against Rebirth   49
FRANCIS X. CLOONEY, SJ

3   Global Visions in Contestation: Jesuits and Muslims in the Age of Empires   69
DANIEL A. MADIGAN, SJ

4   Jesuits in Ibero-America: Missions and Colonial Societies   92
ALIOCHA MALDAVSKY

5   The History of Anti-Jesuitism: National and Global Dimensions   111
SABINA PAVONE

6   Restored Jesuits: Notes toward a Global History   131
JOHN T. MCGREEVY

7   Historical Perspectives on Jesuit Education and
    Globalization   147
    JOHN W. O'MALLEY, SJ

Part II: Contemporary Challenges

8   The Jesuits and the "More Universal Good": At Vatican II
    and Today   169
    DAVID HOLLENBACH, SJ

9   The Jesuits and Social Justice in Latin America   188
    MARIA CLARA LUCCHETTI BINGEMER

10 Global Human Development and the Jesuits in Asia   206
    JOHN JOSEPH PUTHENKALAM, SJ, AND DREW RAU

11 Global Human Mobility, Refugees, and Jesuit Education at
    the Margins   224
    PETER BALLEIS, SJ

12 Jesuit Higher Education and the Global Common Good   239
    THOMAS BANCHOFF

13 The Jesuits through the Prism of Globalization, Globalization
    through a Jesuit Prism   261
    JOSÉ CASANOVA

List of Contributors   *287*
Index   *289*

PREFACE

We are in the midst of a phase of globalization both promising and perilous, marked by a diffusion of power away from the West, far-reaching social and technological transformation, and new patterns of transnational cooperation and conflict.

Is the experience of the Jesuits as global missionaries and educators for almost five centuries relevant to the challenges we face today? Does their characteristic way of proceeding, which combines strong convictions with an openness to intercultural encounter, hold lessons for an increasingly multipolar and interconnected world?

These questions led us to undertake a three-year project on the Jesuits and globalization, based at the Berkley Center for Religion, Peace, and World Affairs at Georgetown University, that has culminated in this book.

A political scientist and a sociologist, we have partnered with leading historians and theologians, Jesuit and lay, to explore the historical legacies and contemporary significance of the Society of Jesus, the most global community within the world's oldest and most influential transnational organization, the Roman Catholic Church. The Jesuits were founded in 1540, in the midst of the first age of global exploration. They were suppressed in 1773 and reestablished two centuries ago, in 1814, at the outset of a new wave of European global expansion. And in the half century since the close of the Second Vatican Council in 1965, they have ridden a third wave of globalization, with its unprecedented revolutions in information, communications, and transportation technology.

At three workshops—in Washington (April 2013), Oxford (October 2013), and Florence (May 2014)—our authors' group shared preliminary arguments and broadened our original interest in the Jesuit way of proceeding to encompass a wider set of questions about the significance of globalization for the Jesuits and the significance of the Jesuits for globalization. Our inquiries have crossed different global eras, covered multiple world regions, and touched on topics ranging from mission and dialogue to education and the common good. In December 2014 the project culminated in a capstone conference in Rome to mark the bicentennial of the reestablishment of the Society.

We would like to extend our deepest thanks to the contributors and to President John J. DeGioia of Georgetown University, who has generously supported this project from the outset. Drew Rau provided expert editorial assistance at all stages of manuscript preparation, and Philip Endean, SJ, and Colin Steele provided vital feedback at critical stages. Erin Coleman and the rest of the Berkley Center staff offered first-rate organizational support for our series of workshops. We would also like to express our gratitude to Fr. François-Xavier Dumortier, SJ, rector of Gregorian University and our host for the 2014 conference in Rome. The Gregorian is the oldest Jesuit university in the world, and Georgetown is the oldest in the United States. It is fitting that two partners in the global Jesuit network should collaborate on a project like this one.

       Thomas Banchoff and José Casanova
       Washington, DC

INTRODUCTION

THE JESUITS AND GLOBALIZATION

THOMAS BANCHOFF AND JOSÉ CASANOVA

Since its inception in the mid-sixteenth century, the Society of Jesus has been closely connected with processes of globalization. During the early modern era, following the Iberian colonial expansion, the Jesuits became pioneer globalizers by founding missions and educational institutions all over the world. Along the way they developed a particular "way of proceeding" that was often characterized by flexible accommodation to local circumstances that combined a commitment to the Gospel with an affirmation of the positive characteristics of the cultures they encountered. In the early modern phase of globalization, into the 1700s, no other group contributed so much to global connectivity and, through their correspondence and cultural and political influence, to a global consciousness linking the four quadrants of the world. Over time, however, the Jesuits' influence, initiative, and open and pragmatic way of proceeding also provoked much resistance and controversy. The mid-eighteenth century saw their expulsion from every Catholic kingdom and the final suppression of the Society of Jesus by the pope in 1773.

In the decades after the reestablishment of the order in 1814, Jesuit missionaries and educators reengaged their global enterprise in new ways. The United States served not only as a place of refuge for many expelled Jesuits but also as a springboard for their renewed global religious, cultural, and educational mission. While the Jesuits made progress in the reestablishment of a worldwide network of schools and missions, their strong defense of the papacy and their militant opposition to the emerging forces of liberalism and secularism in Europe and Latin America reawakened a virulent anti-Jesuitism that led to their repeated expulsion from multiple countries.

In the wake of two world wars, decolonization, and the Second Vatican Council (1962–65), the Society of Jesus renewed its global commitment in a new idiom, emphasizing the promotion of justice and the universal common good as part of the service of faith. A half century later in an era of accelerating globalization, Jesuits are following the lead of Pope Francis, one of their own, in exploring new ways to spread the Gospel, accompany the poor and excluded, promote education, and support a shift from what Francis calls a "globalization of indifference" to a globalization of fraternity.[1]

On the occasion of the bicentennial of the reestablishment of the Society of Jesus, this book brings together experts across disciplines to address two core questions: What does the experience of globalization tell us about the Jesuits? And what does the experience of the Jesuits tell us about globalization? We aim not to offer a global history of the Jesuits or a linear narrative of globalization but instead to examine the Jesuits through the prism of globalization and globalization through the prism of the Jesuits in a way that may contribute to a more critical and reflexive understanding both of the Jesuits' history and of our contemporary human global condition. Through a threefold focus on the themes of global mission, education, and justice, we address the complex paths and the intercultural encounters that have led to the present. We also explore the challenges and opportunities of the contemporary phase of globalization—both for the Society of Jesus and for a deeper understanding of the global present and future.

Dynamics of Globalization

The term "globalization" only came into broad usage during the late twentieth century as academic disciplines and media commentators grappled with accelerating transnational flows of people, ideas, goods, and capital enabled by ongoing revolutions in information, communications, and transportation technologies. The first extended debates about globalization took place within the social sciences, particularly within sociology and economics, in the 1990s. Anthropology, political science, and international relations soon joined the fray.[2] More recently historians and particularly the new fields of world history and global history have entered the debates, adding more empirical discernment and historical depth to the discussion.[3] Over time the two initial opposing positions in the globalization debate—one insisting it is a new phenomenon; the other, that it has long been with us—have given way to more careful and discriminating analysis. Calls for "the globalization of history" and "the historization of globalization" have highlighted the need for clearer distinctions not just among different phases of globalization but also among different dynamics of globalization across time and space.

Historical processes of globalization are neither constant nor continuous nor unidirectional, and they have always affected various parts of the world in quite different ways. One should avoid the temptation to reconstruct world history as the inevitable formation of ever-wider and interconnected human webs leading to the emergence of a global network society encompassing all peoples, societies, and cultures of the earth.[4] Any approach to globalization is also complicated by the shifting relationship between what might be termed its "subjective" and "objective" dimensions. *Objective processes of globalization*, mediated by changes in communications and transportation technology, involve the movement of people, ideas, goods, and capital across greater expanses of space. The *subjective dimension of globalization* refers to the growth in global consciousness—that is, to the increasing reflexive awareness of humanity as a species sharing the same history and the same planet. In this respect, following the theorist Roland Robertson, one could define *globalization* broadly as the set of processes involving the world becoming a single place with increasing global connectivity and global consciousness.[5]

The deep historical roots of the subjective dimension of globalization are of particular importance in the Jesuit story. They can be traced back to the concurrent emergence of projects of "universal" kingdoms or empires as well as of "universal" ethical and religious visions in various parts of Eurasia during the so-called Axial Age, around the middle of the first millennium BCE. The German philosopher Karl Jaspers coined the term "Axial Age" after World War II to denote the epoch in human history when classic texts of ancient civilizations—including those in the canons of Confucianism, Buddhism, Hinduism, Judaism, and Greek philosophy—appeared around the same time.[6] This period constituted a turning point for global humanity because a strong idea of "transcendence" first emerged and with it the very condition necessary to gain some reflexive distance from "the world" and to ground universal ethical or religious visions and even the projects of "world empires."[7] The subjective dimension of imagining a single humanity sharing one earth, an idea that would later shape the missionary impetus of Christianity and Islam and the self-understanding of the Society of Jesus, was first anticipated in and through the axial breakthroughs.

For many centuries this utopian or eschatological anticipation of globalization lacked any objective or material base. Until the age of European colonial expansion inaugurated in the sixteenth century, the global horizon of the world's great philosophical and religious traditions had very clear territorial limits, set both by the particular political, social, and economic regimes in which they were civilizationally and territorially embedded and by the geographically circumscribed limitations of existing means of transportation and communication. Between the eighth and the fifteenth centuries, the world of Islam and the Mongol Empire were catalysts and carriers of powerful trans-regional dynamics encompassing much of Afro-Eurasia and entailing increasing interconnectivity and parallel political, economic, and cultural transformations.[8] But this incipient globalization was limited to the "Old World," given the limitations of maritime technology.

Three Phases of Globalization: Early Modern, Modern, and Contemporary

In the literal sense of the term, globalization proper begins with the "discovery" of the "New World," the circumnavigation of the globe, and the ensuing European global colonial expansion—a phase that coincides with the founding of the Society of Jesus in 1540 and its rapid international outreach. This "first globalization" was global in that it incorporated the new Columbian exchange formed by the transatlantic triangle of Europe, Africa, and the Americas, as well as the new transpacific realm linking for the first time Eurasia, Oceania, and the Americas.[9] Afro-Eurasian exchanges continued and intensified but now became linked to the transatlantic and transpacific networks. This was the first truly worldwide human web, different both from the preceding trans-regional dynamics and from the subsequent phase of Western hegemonic globalization that would follow in the nineteenth and twentieth centuries. What is striking in retrospect, and is often obscured by the intervening centuries, is the cultural and political pluralism that persisted in the early modern period. While Spanish, Portuguese, and other European expansion subjugated indigenous peoples in the Americas, in other parts of the world, powerful empires with their own economic, social, cultural, and religious bases, including the Turkish Ottoman, Indian Mughal, and Chinese Qing empires, persisted.

A second, modern phase of globalization can be dated to the turn of the nineteenth century and two powerful political and technological transformations. The American and French Revolutions ushered in an era of energetic and expansionist nationalism in the North Atlantic while successive industrial revolutions and their transformative military, transportation, and communications technologies enabled a more aggressive phase of European and American imperialism. It is certainly true that characteristics of the modern phase of globalization—particularly the spread of the world capitalist system and the internationalization of the system of sovereign territorial states inaugurated with the Peace of Westphalia in 1648—had their origins in the early modern period. What was new was the near-universal reach of Western power, driven by nationalist ambition and technological superiority. By the end of World War I, the Chinese and Ottoman empires had collapsed, and the North Atlantic powers dominated most of Africa and Asia. Western global influence persisted into the mid-twentieth century, even through two destructive world wars and the rise of the Soviet Union and communist China. In comparison to the early modern period, the modern phase of globalization saw the deep expansion of Western influence, which reduced but never eliminated cultural and political diversity worldwide.

The roots of the contemporary phase of globalization can be traced to the emergence of the United Nations and the breakup of the remaining Western colonial empires in the post–World War II decades. However, its distinctive characteristics—a deeper technological connectivity, the relative decline of the United States and Europe, and a greater political, cultural, and ideological pluralism—took clear shape only in the 1980s. Since then an ongoing communications and transportation revolution has spurred the deeper integration of the global economy and brought more people across more regions into contact than at any point in history. Thanks to global media and to the Internet in particular, the subjective dimension of globalization, the awareness of living within a global frame, is much more pronounced than in the first two phases of globalization. While the United States remains the single most powerful state in the world system, the collapse of the Soviet Union and China's economic opening have not spurred convergence around the model of Western liberal democracy. On the contrary, the persistence of political autocracy in Russia and China and the rise of political Islam have generated greater degrees of global ideological and political conflict. And the differential growth of economic power—evident in the rise of China, India, Brazil, and other countries—has driven a trend toward multipolarity.

The distinction among these three phases of globalization—the early modern, modern, and contemporary—is necessarily somewhat arbitrary.[10] The transitions emphasized here—from early modern European, with its global cultural and political diversity; to the modern, marked by the peak of Western influence within the world system; and to our contemporary shift toward a more pluralistic and multipolar world—contradict any simple linear scheme. For example, despite the indisputable fact that Western modernity in the nineteenth and twentieth centuries was inherently globalizing—marked by the economic, political, and cultural expansion of European and American power and practices around the world—contemporary globalization is not simply, as per Anthony Giddens, "a consequence of modernity," or an enlargement of modernity, from society to the world.[11] Globalization today is marked by a diffusion of power beyond the West and by a political, cultural, and religious pluralism that has more in common with the diverse historical processes of globalization in the early modern period, before European hegemony, than with the modern period.[12]

While necessarily arbitrary in certain respects, this threefold periodization provides an excellent framing for an exploration of the Jesuits and globalization. The early modern period coincides with the Jesuits' founding, initial international expansion, and eventual suppression; the modern period overlaps with the period between the reestablishment of the Society of Jesus and the Second Vatican Council; and the transition from the modern to the contemporary phase of globalization tracks the decades between the Council and the papacy of Francis. The next sections sketch the arguments that the contributors present across all three periods, with a focus on three central areas of Jesuit concern: mission and dialogue, education and the human person, and justice and the common good. In the process they provide an initial exploration of two central questions addressed across the chapters: What does the experience of globalization tell us about the Jesuits? And what does the experience of the Jesuits tell us about globalization?

The First Jesuit Centuries: Riding the Wave of Early Modern Globalization

The foundation of the Society of Jesus coincided with the first, early modern phase of globalization. Ignatius of Loyola (1491–1556), who hailed from the Basque Country of Spain, experienced a vision of Christ while recovering from battle wounds in 1521 and resolved to give his life over to the Lord. While studying at the University of Paris, he gathered a circle of companions who were captivated by his spiritual insights and practices, which drew on the tradition of personal piety inspired by Thomas à Kempis's *Imitation of Christ*, among others. Later codified in the *Spiritual Exercises*, Ignatius's approach called for unconditional service to the Lord, in the world, for the salvation of souls. In 1540 he and his companions received papal approval for their Society of Jesus, which quickly grew and expanded into ministries for the poor and for education. They were particularly active in Italy, Spain, and Germany, where they became associated with the Counter-Reformation.

From the outset Ignatius and his followers had a global, missionary orientation. As expressed explicitly in the "Formula of the Institute of the Society of Jesus," the 1540 foundational charter of the order, the Jesuits took an oath "to travel to any part of the world where there was hope of God's greater service and the good of souls" to minister to "the Turks or any other infidels, even those who live in the regions called the Indies, or . . . any heretics whatever, or schismatics, or any of the faithful."[13] Global mobility was culturally encoded, as it were, into the makeup of the Jesuit order from its inception. A few decades after their official foundation, the Jesuits had established missions throughout the world—in Goa, Malacca, the Moluccas, the Philippines, Macau, Japan, and China in Asia; in Ethiopia, the Congo, Angola, and Mozambique in Africa; and throughout the Portuguese and Spanish empires in the Americas—and rapidly grew and expanded throughout Europe, including in the Polish-Lithuanian Commonwealth and onto the Missio Moscovitica. The Jesuits spearheaded the Counter-Reformation and established colleges, their main institutional innovation, everywhere. Indeed, no other group took the globe as eagerly as the focus of its activities, with the Jesuits taking inspiration from Jerónimo Nadal's famous slogan, "The world is our home."[14]

In the age of "gunpowder empires," Jesuits sailed around the world with conquistadores, traders, and colonial administrators. Francis Xavier (1506–52), a friend of Ignatius's and a paradigmatic Jesuit missionary, was sent to Asia by request of King John III of Portugal even before Pope Paul III had approved the new order. Colonial administrators sponsored many of the Jesuits' missions. The vast Jesuit Portuguese Assistancy undoubtedly constituted the core of the global Jesuit enterprise.[15] From its beginning the Jesuit global *empresa*, besides its religious missionary connotation, also had a very worldly and secular one, that of an economic and political enterprise. The Jesuits' concurrent presence at the courts of Moscow and Beijing explains how they could have mediated the Sino-Russian Treaty of Nerchinsk (1689), helping to draft the two official Latin copies of the first international treaty that set the territorial borders of the Chinese and Russian empires.[16] Not surprising, the Jesuits have been analyzed as the first "multinational corporation" and maligned as the first "international" secret organization bent on global political power.[17]

Yet as the contributors to this volume emphasize, the Jesuit global missionary enterprise ought not be reduced to the globalizing logic of the emerging world capitalist system or to a rigid missionary impulse to spread the Gospel.[18] The Jesuit globalizing mission or impulse always had a surplus that exceeded, transcended, and, at times, even contested prophetically the dominant logic of capitalist expansion and state territorial colonial power.

This was most evident in the missions to China and India, where Jesuits showed dexterity in engaging with local religious, social, and political systems on their own terms. While adhering unswervingly to their Gospel command to win souls for Christ, Alessandro Valignano in Japan, Matteo Ricci in China, and Roberto de Nobili in India, among others, developed a distinctive way of proceeding that involved dialogue, the patient mastery of languages, and cultural and scientific exchanges not just in the pursuit of narrow missionary aims but also in recognition of a common humanity. Valignano's method of accommodation, elaborated throughout his writings, demanded that European Jesuits adopt local customs and habits as a condition for Christianity to take root and become inculturated in Japan and China.[19]

The historical chapters by Antoni Ucerler, Francis Clooney, and Daniel Madigan examine critically the very diverse early Jesuit encounters with the leading traditions of Asia—and in particular with Confucianism, Buddhism, Hinduism, and Islam—and reach different conclusions about the scope and significance of the Jesuit way of proceeding. In "The Jesuits in East Asia in the Early Modern Age: A New 'Areopagus' and the 'Re-invention' of Christianity," Ucerler makes the case for far-reaching cultural accommodation in Japan and China. His main thesis is that the Jesuits' schooling in Renaissance humanism, with its high estimation of the cultures of pagan antiquity and training in classical rhetoric, as well as their theological understanding of the Pauline mission to the Gentiles, led early Jesuits to understand their missionary work in East Asia as a re-enactment of the apostolic experience of the primitive Church. Inculturation implied a form of recurring historical reincarnation of the universal Christian kerygma in new and diverse cultural settings, reminiscent of the inculturation of Hebrew Christianity in Hellenic and Roman antiquity, in a process that entailed deep theological, metaphysical, and epistemic transformations.

Ucerler further argues that rather than being an idea generated by European missionaries enacted upon passive Asian subjects, inculturation was often the result of a pragmatic interactional process. In fact, he writes, "the initiative for cultural accommodation often came from members of the local cultural elites who helped the Jesuits understand the cultural, social, political, linguistic, and religious contexts in which they were operating," impressing upon them "the urgent need to engage the local culture *on its own terms* if they wished to make any significant progress." In Japan the decision to promote the formation of a "native" clergy and the admittance of Japanese into the Jesuit order led to the establishment of a Jesuit novitiate and a college of higher learning in Funai. Valignano soon recognized the need to adapt the educational guidelines of the *Ratio studiorum* (*Plan of Studies*) to Japanese circumstances and to blend the teaching of Western and Eastern classics—an early intercultural experiment in humanities education. In China Ricci's method of accommodation went even further. He developed what Ucerler calls "a new Chinese rhetoric of pre-evangelization" to persuade the Chinese literati, through dialogue and scholarship, that "Christianity, far from being an alien doctrine brought to China by foreign barbarians, represented the fulfillment of Confucian philosophy in that it provided a more authentic reinterpretation of its central tenets." The parallel incorporation of Confucian rites into some Christian practices entailed an ambiguous but productive distinction between the one true Catholic faith to be upheld, idolatrous beliefs and customs to be rejected, and virtuous civic practices to be accommodated. As in Japan, the Jesuits' experience of globalization in China deepened their own understanding of their missionary vocation, as it had for the apostle Paul, because it involved bringing the Christian message to different cultures in a pragmatic spirit.

Francis Clooney's chapter, "Jesuit Intellectual Practice in Early Modernity: The Pan-Asian Argument against Rebirth," explores some of the limits of the Jesuits' way of proceeding in their encounter with Hinduism in particular. During the early modern period, Jesuit missionaries in South and East Asia made impressive efforts to engage Hindu and Buddhist elites in debates about the transmigration of souls, a doctrine that contradicted core Catholic beliefs about the immortality of the soul and the resurrection of the body. The comprehensive Jesuit apologetic against rebirth, articulated in different fashions by Xavier, Valignano, Ricci, and de Nobili, does demonstrate the real measure of the Jesuits' resolve and capacity to engage a variety of new cultures, their great capacity for quickly learning new ideas in new languages, and their faith in the power of rational argument. At the same time, as Clooney argues, it suggests the limits of their ability and willingness to engage beliefs and ideas that were genuinely different from their own.

Interestingly the limits of the Jesuit approach to interreligious dialogue in the early modern period were not always, or even primarily, theological. Clooney demonstrates how, in their critiques of Asian doctrines generally and rebirth in particular, the Jesuits did not refer to the Bible, to divine revelation, or to positive Christian faith doctrines. Instead, they couched their rhetorical arguments in solely philosophical terms, premised on the notion that any reasoning person could reach conclusions concerning the sole birth of the "soul" and the impossibility of rebirth on purely logical grounds without the help of revelation. Clooney's analysis probes how the limitations to the Jesuit way of proceeding were not so much grounded in

Christian-theological doctrine but in epistemic-metaphysical assumptions about the self, free will, justice, and subjective moral responsibility that were deeply embedded in the entire Western philosophical tradition that the Jesuits took for granted. In this case, the encounters of early modern globalization reinforced existing cultural divides.

Daniel Madigan's chapter on the Jesuit engagement with the world of Islam probes even more strikingly the limits of the Jesuit method of accommodation. It shows that in their dealings with Muslim "infidels" in South Asia during the rule of Emperor Akbar (1542–1605), Jesuit missionaries could not free themselves from the traditional negative religious taxonomy that was centered on Roman Catholicism as the one true faith and considered any deviation from it a dangerous error. Madigan argues that in their missions abroad and in their theological writings, "Jesuits have very often shared the negative view of Islam that they inherited from the Church's long history of polemics, that they imbibed from the cultures and polities in which they lived, or indeed that they may have drawn from Ignatius's own rather ambivalent attitude toward Muslims." One cannot find precursors to the contemporary interest in Christian-Muslim dialogue in the global Jesuit encounters with Islam in the early modern era.

This negative approach was not limited to Islam but extended, in different registers, to all of what are now called the "Abrahamic faiths," including non-Catholic Christianity. In early modern Jesuit encounters with Muslims, Jews, and Protestant "heretics," or even Eastern Christian "schismatics" in Ethiopia, India, or Eastern Europe, one can hardly find any trace of the Jesuit way of proceeding in accommodating differences. In important respects the "Otherness" of China and India and the newly discovered "pagan" cultures of the Eastern and Western Indies created more of an opening to accommodation, because they could be approached as cultures and not as competing religious systems. Madigan's discussion of the Jesuits and Islam suggests the greater facility of inculturation into unknown cultures that share no long histories of mutual prejudices or theological entanglements. By contrast, he points out that it is difficult to conceive of inculturating into what we perceive as a heretical form of our own tradition.

The impacts of global encounters on the Society were very different in the context of the Spanish and Portuguese empires in the New World. As they did in Asia, some Jesuit missions evidenced an openness to native cultures. In his *Natural and Moral History of the Indies* (1590), for example, José de Acosta not only described the new cultures in the Americas but also advised adopting an openness to the differences they presented and an accommodating attitude. But as Aliocha Maldavsky points out in her chapter, "Jesuits in Ibero-America: Missions and Colonial Societies," a crucial variable in the early modern Jesuit encounters with other cultures was the extent to which they could free themselves from their colonial sponsors, whether Portuguese or Spanish, and enter into more equal and non-hegemonic relations with the Other while relatively free or seemingly unencumbered by Western colonial baggage.

The Jesuits were rather latecomers in the Iberian colonial enterprise, and they had to find their own niche in a mission of Christian evangelization that the older mendicant orders, the Franciscans and the Dominicans, had pioneered. Maldavsky examines four of these Jesuit niches: urban colleges and Jesuit residences, indigenous parishes, rural missions, and the indigenous "reductions," or settlements that the Society managed at the borderlands of the Iberian empires. The analysis stresses the interplay of local settlement and global mobility, the embeddedness of the Jesuit missions in colonial coercion and political control, and their accommodation not only to native cultures but also to emerging colonial societies. In contrast to China, Japan, and India, where early colonial empires never gained a firm foothold, Jesuit global encounters in Latin America were mediated by political power structures that limited their freedom to maneuver but also provided flexible spaces for cultural accommodation and institutional growth.

As examples from Asia and the Americas demonstrate, the experience of early modern globalization presented both challenges and opportunities for the Jesuit order. Its work of mission and dialogue was enabled by Ignatius's pragmatic way of proceeding and the global vision articulated in the *Spiritual Exercises*, through which he encouraged the exercitant to imagine people across "the face of the earth, in such great diversity in dress and in manner of acting. Some are white, some black; some at peace, and some at war."[20] But it was also constrained by inherited Western philosophical and religious categories, which set limits on dialogue, and by the growing secular power of states and empires that restricted Jesuit freedom of maneuver.

The wider global significance of the Jesuit experience during the early modern period is most evident in the area of education and scholarship. Although not envisioned as part of the Society's original foundational mission, after the founding of the first Jesuit school in Messina in 1548, education became the primary and premier ministry of the order. As John O'Malley highlights in his chapter, "Historical Perspectives on Jesuit Education and Globalization," the Jesuit model of education emerged from the melding of three separate currents: the Aristotelian philosophical-scientific synthesis institutionalized by the medieval university, the classical tradition of humane letters that crystallized in the Renaissance humanist college, and the Christian tradition of "spiritual conquest" through conversion of the Other. By the time of the suppression, some seven hundred Jesuit schools and universities operated in Europe and around the world. The combination of the ideal of missionaries on the move with that of resident schoolmasters proved an effective way to share Western learning and to win converts.

It also sparked an infusion of scholarship about foreign languages, cultures, and practices back into Europe, contributing to a greater awareness of global humanity. As O'Malley points out, it was Jesuits on foreign missions, many of them engaged in schools, who produced grammars and dictionaries while following Ignatius's injunction to learn local languages and engage more deeply with alien cultures—knowledge that they shared through scholarship and correspondence. The virtuous feedback between the global network of Jesuit colleges and the global network of missions shaped the Jesuits as pioneer globalizers of the early modern era, creating the conditions for what, according to Steven Harris, could be called "the global Jesuit geography of knowledge."[21]

In the early modern period the Jesuits both thought globally and acted globally, constituting perhaps the first self-conscious global network. Historically with their final defeat in the Rites Controversy at the beginning of the eighteenth century, when the Vatican rejected the strategy of cultural accommodation in China and India, the Jesuits' way of proceeding lost ground. Their ethical contextualism was ridiculed as opportunistic casuistry.[22] Critics within the Church, particularly the Dominicans and the Franciscans, accused the Jesuits of using a cunning strategy of relativist "accommodation" that compromised the universality of Christianity. The Eurocentric perspective and uniform Romanization prevailed within the Church. Externally the transnational papal order also lost the battle against the triumphant Westphalian model of sovereign territorial states and against the absolutist Catholic kings who one after another expelled the Jesuits from their realms and conspired with Pope Clement XIV to dissolve the order in 1773.

The expulsion of Jesuits from the Spanish and Portuguese empires and the suppression of 1773 had complex political causes. Sabina Pavone's "The History of Anti-Jesuitism: National and Global Dimensions" offers an interpretative key to understanding the confluence of anti-Jesuit currents that led to the papal suppression. She groups the sources of anti-Jesuitism into four main analytical types—"religious-political," "ecclesiastical," "Jesuit," and "Enlightenment" anti-Jesuitism—although in fact she shows how they tended to overlap and grow together almost from the very founding of the Society. Ultimately the frequent juxtaposition of two seemingly opposed tropes frequently used against the Society of

Jesus from its beginnings—that of being "a state within the state" and "a world empire"—captures best the interstitial and ambiguous position of the transnational order both within the Westphalian system of nation-states and within the competing imperial projects.

Throughout the early modern phase of globalization, when Jesuit influence was at its peak, the order's growth and direction was shaped by its global encounters. The Jesuits impacted the wider course of globalization by becoming key players in the colonial enterprise and through their role, as missionaries and educators, in generating pathbreaking scholarship on geography, native languages, history, and culture that shaped the Europeans' understanding of an emergent global order. However, their efforts to bring Christianity to powerful empires in India, Japan, and China tested the Jesuit way of proceeding, demonstrating the difficulty of cultural accommodation as a means to spread the Gospel. Only in Ibero-America, where Spain and Portugal destroyed existing empires, were Jesuits able to advance the missionary enterprise and engage more deeply with native populations. Two key dimensions of their global enterprise—their efforts toward cultural accommodation in Asia that ignited the Rites Controversy and their extensive social and political influence in the Americas—sparked opposition both in the Church and across states that contributed to their suppression.

From Reestablishment through Vatican II: Globalization's Modern Phase

Suppression proved a catastrophe. The Society was stripped of its property, including its network of schools, most of which were transferred to other ecclesiastical or secular authorities. The Jesuits could remain priests but were subordinated to their local bishops. Only in Prussia and Russia, whose non-Catholic leaders largely ignored Clement XIV's suppression order, did the Jesuits maintain some continuous existence. Not until the changed political climate after the defeat of Napoleon and the restoration of monarchies in France and across Europe did Pope Pius VII reestablish the Society of Jesus in 1814. Amid the growth of secular politics and increased challenges to papal authority, the pope had good reasons for turning to the Jesuits, who remained eager to offer their services for the Church's cause. What followed was not an immediate renaissance but a gradual consolidation as the Jesuits were permitted to operate in more and more countries over time. By the early twentieth century, their numbers grew from less than a thousand aging members at the time of the reestablishment to more than seventeen thousand, not far from pre-suppression levels.

The rebirth of the Jesuit order in the nineteenth century coincided with the second, or modern, phase of globalization that was marked by a new wave of migration from Europe and the imperial expansion of Europe and then the United States. "The first and most basic impetus behind Jesuit globalization," John McGreevy notes in his chapter, "was one of the great migrations of modern history, the decision of sixty million Europeans to leave the continent over the course of the nineteenth century." Jesuits also participated in a new wave of European colonial expansion, which was made possible by an ongoing industrial transformation and revolutions in transportation and communications that translated into Western economic and military hegemony. Like other Christian missionary organizations, the Jesuits followed the European powers into sub-Saharan Africa, which was completely colonized by the end of the nineteenth century. And they established a presence in the Middle East and South Asia, mainly under British and French protection. Japan and, to a lesser extent, China resisted Western military encroachments, placing a limit on the penetration of missionary activity, including that of the Jesuits.

In these colonial contexts during the nineteenth and early twentieth centuries, the Society of Jesus did not display its earlier embrace of intercultural encounter as a hallmark of the traditional way of proceeding. With few exceptions, the Jesuits aligned themselves with the status quo of Western subjugation of colonial peoples. To some degree this position was in line with the nationalist and militarist spirit of the times, to which the Jesuits were not immune. But in Europe it was also linked with a reactionary and antirevolutionary stance that grew out of the trauma of the French Revolution and concern about further encroachment on papal power. Popes from Gregory XVI through Pius IX, battling to maintain their territory and autonomy in the wake of new revolutionary convulsions in 1830 and 1848, unleashed a series of encyclicals against modernity and the dangers of the Enlightenment and secular thought. Pius IX's 1864 *Syllabus of Errors* was the most famous. Successive Jesuit superior generals took up this antimodern siege mentality, which militated against cultural or religious accommodation both in Europe and in Jesuit missions worldwide. This stance contributed to hostility from secular governments and, in many cases, to expulsions around the world. As McGreevy notes, "Between 1840 and 1901, the Jesuits were expelled, often multiple times, from Switzerland, various parts of modern-day Italy (including Rome, Piedmont, and Naples), New Granada (modern-day Colombia), Uruguay, Ecuador, El Salvador, Costa Rica, Peru, Austria, Spain, Germany, Guatemala, France, and Nicaragua. In Mexico a liberal government expelled 'foreign-born' Jesuits."

The Jesuits in the United States represented a partial exception to this overall pattern. With a focus on the American experience, McGreevy reconstructs the process through which many Jesuits ended up in the United States, through migration or as a result of expulsions, and flourished within the country's more open society even in the face of entrenched anti-Catholic prejudice. With America as a base, many reengaged internationally as missionaries and schoolmasters in response to central direction from Rome. At a time when the Jesuits could hardly be viewed as a pioneering avant-garde of globalization but rather saw themselves and were viewed by others as a reactionary rear guard countering the spread of nationalism and liberalism, they also began to emerge as a truly transnational papal order that was enabled by ongoing revolutions in communications and transportation technology. Paradoxically, McGreevy points out, even in the high age of capitalist and Western imperial globalization, "some of the most global citizens of the nineteenth century were not cotton exporters developing global markets or physicians tracking the spread of disease. Instead, they were Jesuits."

The chapters by both O'Malley and Thomas Banchoff highlight the educational dimension of the Jesuit renaissance in the United States and its radiation around the world. As O'Malley points out, the rapid expansion of Jesuit colleges and universities in the United States—twenty-two existed by the turn of the twentieth century—showed the adaptability of the model of the *Ratio studiorum* in a context of rapid demographic, economic, and cultural change. In a country that placed a premium on social mobility, colleges gradually reduced required courses in philosophy and the humanities to make room for the natural and social sciences. In his chapter on "Jesuit Higher Education and the Global Common Good," Banchoff argues that the pragmatic growth of Jesuit colleges into universities with schools of law, medicine, and business, in response to a dynamic society around them, adapted a long tradition of civic engagement to modern circumstances. Similar adaptation took place in other parts of the world but not with the pace and scope of the changes seen in the United States.

At the height of the second Industrial Revolution, around the turn of the twentieth century, new currents in the Jesuit approach to social and political issues presaged a turn to "the promotion of justice" as a core element of the global Jesuit mission since Vatican II. One trend was the rise of Catholic social teaching, which took a structured form with the publication of Pope Leo XIII's encyclical *Rerum novarum* (1891). Many Jesuit missionaries, scholars, and teachers gravitated toward the ideas of solidarity and social justice, which resonated with the ideals of charity and the common good that were first expressed in the "Formula of the Institute," the Society's founding document. In response to the plight of the burgeoning urban poor in industrializing societies, successive superiors general supported the creation of social institutes both to promote understanding of new economic and social dynamics and to minister to workers and their families. Jesuit scholars influenced the further elaboration of Catholic social thought in Pius XI's encyclical *Quadragesimo anno* (1931), published during the Depression. As Banchoff points out in his chapter, more than a decade before the watershed of Vatican II, Jean-Baptiste Janssens in 1949 was the first superior general to connect the social justice imperative with the Jesuits' global engagement. According to Janssens:

> In regard to our missions however I cannot refrain from stressing not only the necessity of teaching the true social doctrine, but even more of promoting social works and a public order that is in conformity with justice and human dignity. For there is a danger, since we are not aroused by what has become customary, that we shall hardly notice to what degree most of the natives are deprived of the condition of life that befits a human being and a Christian. . . . For it is not merely souls but men that we must love in Christ.[23]

In the period between the reestablishment of the Jesuit order and Vatican II, globalization shaped the Jesuit order in several ways. It provided a new outlet for missionary activity; it enabled the creation of a more centralized international structure, directed from Rome, and the movement of Jesuits around the world at a greater pace; and, in the experience of the laboratory of the United States, it facilitated the growth and expansion of educational institutions and the export of new models around the world. The impact of the Jesuits on globalization over this period is less easy to demonstrate. In their conservative stance, the Jesuits accommodated to the political status quo through most of the nineteenth century, partly as a survival strategy amid reconstruction but also out of conviction. From around the turn of the century, amid the economic, social, and political dislocation of the Industrial Revolution, the Depression, and world war, the Jesuits played an important role in the development of Catholic social teaching and movement toward the idea of universal human dignity as the foundation for justice at a global level.

The Jesuits and Globalization in our Contemporary Era

The contemporary phase of globalization has its roots in the postwar decades with the rise of US hegemony, the construction of the United Nations system, and the dissolution of Europe's remaining empires. Under

US leadership a global human rights regime came into being, expressed in the UN General Assembly's Universal Declaration of Human Rights (1948). In part a weapon against the Soviet Union and its allies during the Cold War, the idea of universal human rights deepened the subjective dimension of globalization, the awareness of being part of a common humanity. And it was increasingly complemented by objective technological forces drawing the world together—an emergent reality evoked by Marshall McLuhan's use of the term "global village" (1962) and by William Anders's *Earthrise* (1968), the first photograph of Earth taken from space. While the contemporary phase of globalization accelerated with the information and technological revolutions of the 1980s and 1990s and the rise of the Internet, it had its roots in the postwar decades.

The Catholic Church's opening to the modern world at Vatican II unfolded in this new global context. It involved three related shifts: an embrace of human rights and religious freedom, an opening to interreligious dialogue, and an increasingly global frame for Catholic social thought and practice. As David Hollenbach illustrates in his chapter, American Jesuit John Courtney Murray played a decisive role in the Church's final embrace of religious freedom and liberal democracy in one of the Council's key declarations *Dignitatis humanae* (1965). Drawing on the American experience while at the height of US global power, Murray argued that the best way to advance both religion and justice was to provide constitutional guarantees of the free exercise of faith both in conscience and in action. His argument ultimately helped to persuade the Council fathers to abandon any official preference for regimes that favored Catholicism over other faiths, the basic stance that the Church had taken since the era of emperor Constantine in the fourth century.

Vatican II was also an opening to the religious Other and to the whole world—religious and secular—as a frame of reference. The declaration *Nostra aetate* (1965) broke new ground by embracing dialogue with Judaism, Islam, and other religions in a spirit of mutual recognition and respect. Other Council documents highlighted the importance of social justice on a global scale, encompassing all humanity across cultural, social, and national boundaries. The Pastoral Constitution on the Church in the Modern World, *Gaudium et spes* (1965), opened with a declaration of global solidarity: "The joys and the hopes, the griefs and the anxieties of the men of this age, especially those who are poor or in any way afflicted, these are the joys and hopes, the griefs and anxieties of the followers of Christ."[24]

Fr. Pedro Arrupe, elected superior general in 1965 as the Council was ending, adopted the global opening of Vatican II, linking it to the original charism of Ignatius and his companions. Under Arrupe's leadership, the

Jesuits took up the themes of human rights, social justice, and interreligious dialogue as central to their mission. The Thirty-Second General Congregation in 1974–75 was a turning point. Its famous Decree 4 committed the Society to "the service of faith, of which the promotion of justice is an absolute requirement."[25] Two decades later the Thirty-Fourth General Congregation in 1995 emphasized the importance of interreligious dialogue, going beyond *Nostra aetate* in an openness to other traditions as part of God's plan for human salvation. Arrupe and his successors invoked the spirituality of St. Ignatius, with its emphasis on reflective action in the world, and built on the work of Jesuits who had embraced Catholic social teaching and universal human rights in earlier generations. The new emphasis on social justice and interfaith encounter broke with the order's previously predominant political conservatism and religious exclusivism, earning the enmity of many Church conservatives.

As the Society of Jesus itself became more global over this period—a decline in its ranks in the West was partly balanced by a growth in vocations in the developing world—a truly transnational conversation about mission, dialogue, and justice could unfold for the first time in the Jesuits' history. As Hollenbach emphasizes, Jesuit transnational collaboration spurred new theological and social analysis of the relationship between promoting justice, overcoming poverty, and changing the dynamics of global economic interaction. In Africa, for example, the Cameroonian Jesuit Engelbert Mveng wrote passionately about the need to overcome the consequences in Africa of the slave trade and colonization by European nations. Mveng called these consequences "anthropological poverty," or the deprivation not only of material well-being but also of the people's history, language, culture, faith, and, indeed, their very humanity. Elsewhere Jesuit pioneers in interfaith dialogue have included Aloysius Pieris in exchange with Sri Lankan Buddhism and Michael Amaladoss with Indian Hinduism.

Latin America provides a powerful example of a regional dynamic within the Society of Jesus and its wider global impact. In her chapter Maria Clara Lucchetti Bingemer shows how colonial legacies, economic and social conditions, and the determined leadership of Latin American bishops in the aftermath of the Second Vatican Council shaped a "preferential option for the poor" of great relevance to the global Church. The flowering of liberation theology in the 1970s, in dialogue with Marxism, generated divisions within the Church and a rebuke from Rome. While the most famous Latin American liberation theologians were not Jesuits, Latin American Jesuits corporately served as a supporting community and think tank for the movement. An initial impetus was a meeting between

Arrupe and Jesuit major superiors in Rio de Janeiro in 1968. His successor as superior general, Peter-Hans Kolvenbach, later acknowledged that "it is Latin America that has opened the eyes of all Jesuits to the preferential love for the poor and to the fact that the true, integral liberation of men and women must take priority as the focus of the mission of the Society of Jesus today."[26]

The new priority had deep implications for the two main Jesuit ministries—mission and education. This was nowhere more evident than in the transformation of the University of Central America in El Salvador under the leadership of the philosopher-theologian Ignacio Ellacuría and his Jesuit community, most of whom were assassinated by the Salvadoran Army during the country's civil war in 1989. Their martyrdom served as the ultimate witness to their commitment to what Ellacuría called a liberating "civilization of poverty" in opposition to the oppressive civilization of wealth. He was a deep mystical thinker, a contemplative in action, who was firmly anchored in Ignatian spirituality and supported by his friendship with the also martyred archbishop Óscar Romero. The life and legacy of Ellacuría continue to inspire Latin American Jesuits to work for peace, justice, and development well into the era of Pope Francis.

The chapter by John Joseph Puthenkalam and Drew Rau sheds light on the social engagement of the Jesuits in India, with the largest province in Asia. They track the Jesuits' response to the forces of globalization impacting the region—that is, their critique of economic and social inequality around the world and their productive contributions to the idea of global human development. The history of Jesuits in Social Action, an initiative founded in 1973 in India to fulfill the order's new emphasis on promoting justice, illustrates a practical response to the challenges of globalization. Today India occupies a critical position at the intersection of the Jesuits and globalization. The country's impressive economic growth and democratic institutions have made it a key player in the global order. And it has displaced the United States as the country producing the most Jesuits, many of whom are engaged in missionary, educational, and additional pastoral work in other parts of the world.

Two of the chapters move beyond specific regions to explore how the Society of Jesus has grappled with the wider challenges of globalization. Peter Balleis focuses on migration, refugees, and the Jesuit mission in a global context. He shows how during two previous waves of globalization—in the sixteenth and seventeenth centuries and again in the nineteenth century—human mobility on a global scale shaped the internal composition of the Jesuits and their understanding and practice of a vocation to serve the poor and others on the margins of society. In our contemporary era of globalization, the Jesuit Refugee Service, founded at the behest of Arrupe in 1980, has collaborated with a range of other humanitarian actors and addressed the needs of millions displaced through war and civil conflict. During the first trip of his pontificate in 2013, Pope Francis dramatically illustrated the idea of accompaniment, with deep roots in Jesuit spirituality, when he visited the island of Lampedusa and drew attention to the suffering of refugees trying to make their way to Europe.

Banchoff's chapter, "Jesuit Higher Education and the Global Common Good," shows how the global and civic dimensions of the Jesuit educational enterprise have evolved into our contemporary era. Across successive waves of globalization the Jesuits have maintained an extensive international network committed to the care of souls and the cultivation of skills and knowledge to benefit the common good. In the fifty years since the Church's opening to the modern world at Vatican II, most of the more than 150 Jesuit institutions of higher learning have aspired not just to pursuing academic excellence, *cura personalis*, and the service of faith but also to promoting justice around the world. This new orientation of Jesuit higher education to the *global* common good, not uncontested, has generated opportunities for deeper international collaboration among Jesuit colleges and universities that is often difficult to realize in practice.

In our contemporary era what does globalization tell us about the Jesuit experience, and what does the Jesuit experience tell us about globalization? The main lines of Jesuit global development over the past several decades—its embrace of the promotion of justice, human rights, and interfaith dialogue—constitute a positive response to the onset of the contemporary phase of globalization after World War II and its acceleration since the 1980s. Pedro Arrupe lived and worked in a constructive reaction to the scale of human suffering at mid-century—he himself was a witness to the cataclysm of the atomic bombing of Hiroshima—and his legacy is mediated by the teaching of Ignatius in striving to do more for the common good and the greater glory of God. Globalization not only impacted the mission and identity of the Society of Jesus, reawakening the global frame of reference present to Ignatius and his first companions, but also enabled new forms of transnational interaction within the order and the internationalization of its perspectives on the world.

The experience of the Jesuits also sheds light on the current phase of globalization. The Society of Jesus has explored, as in the early modern period, the possibilities of deeper cultural encounter in a pluralistic age. Against the expectations of many, the collapse of the Soviet bloc, the progressive opening of China, and the politics of the developing world have not led to any convergence around the Western model of free markets and liberal democracy. The rise of violent political extremism and political disintegration in the Middle East in the wake of the wars in Afghanistan and Iraq and the Arab uprisings attest to the persistence of deep political, religious, and ideological conflict even as information and communications technologies draw the world closer together. In our contemporary era the international Jesuit educational network, with its global and intercultural orientation, illustrates possibilities for meaningful dialogue and collaboration for the global common good. And the work of the Jesuit Refugee Service shows how religious organizations can partner with secular partners to serve the marginalized.

One should not overestimate the impact of the Society of Jesus on globalization today or into the future. In the papacy of Francis, a Jesuit deeply formed by Ignatian spirituality, one can see a powerful expression of both the service of faith and the promotion of justice on a worldwide scale. The Jesuit network remains influential in many parts of the world, even though it is much smaller, less centralized, and less connected to political and economic elites than it was during the pre-suppression centuries. As Francis has pointed out, it may be a blessing to operate at the peripheries and not at the centers of globalization. Today, more than ever, the mission of the Jesuits—and of the Church—is focused less on instruction and conversion and more on listening and serving while accompanying the people at the margins, those who are most negatively affected by contemporary processes of globalization, and advancing the globalization of fraternity.

What are the implications of the Jesuit experience across the centuries for our theoretical understanding of globalization? In conversation with the other contributors, José Casanova's concluding chapter looks at contemporary social scientific theories of globalization through the prism of Jesuit history and at Jesuit history through the prism of globalization. In their complex history, in their global consciousness, and in their global practices, the experience of the Jesuits supports those theories of globalization that emphasize the simultaneous and seemingly contradictory dynamics of homogenization and heterogenization and the interweaving of the global and the local. In the eye of successive global storms, the Society has illustrated the unexpected turns, zigzags, and contingent dynamics of the processes of globalization from the sixteenth century to the present. The history of the Jesuits confounds and complicates simple, unambiguous narratives and one-dimensional, unilinear theories of globalization. Their present and future trajectory, too, will be bound up with humanity's global fate.

Notes

1. Pope Francis, "Message of His Holiness Francis for the Celebration of the World Day of Peace," December 8, 2013, sec. 1, https://w2.vatican.va/content/fran cesco/en/messages/peace/documents/papa-francesco_20131208_messaggio-xlvii -giornata-mondiale-pace-2014.html.

2. Immanuel Wallerstein, "The Modern World-System as a Capitalist World Economy," in *World-Systems Analysis: An Introduction* (Durham, NC: Duke University Press, 2004), 23–30; Leslie Sklair, *Globalization: Capitalism and Its Alternatives* (Oxford: Oxford University Press, 2002); and John W. Meyer et al., "World Society and the Nation-State," *American Journal of Sociology* 103, no. 1 (July 1977): 144–81.

3. Jürgen Osterhammel and Niels P. Petersson, *Globalization: A Short History*, trans. Dona Geyer (Princeton: Princeton University Press, 2005), vii; and Jerry H. Bentley, "Globalizing History and Historicizing Globalization," in *Globalization and Global History*, ed. Barry K. Gillis and William R. Thompson (New York: Routledge, 2006), 18–31.

4. John R. McNeill and William H. McNeill, *The Human Web: A Bird's-Eye View of World History* (New York: Norton, 2003); and Manuel Castells, *The Rise of the Network Society* (Malden, MA: Blackwell, 1996).

5. Roland Robertson, *Globalization: Social Theory and Global Culture* (London: Sage, 1992).

6. Karl Jaspers, *The Origin and Goal of History* (New Haven: Yale University Press, 1953).

7. For contemporary debates on the Axial Age, globalization, and the related theory of multiple modernities, cf. Shmuel N. Eisenstadt, ed., *The Origins and Diversity of Axial Age Civilizations* (Albany: SUNY Press, 1986); Johann P. Arnason, Shmuel N. Eisenstadt, and Björn Wittrock, eds., *Axial Civilizations and World History* (Leiden: Brill, 2005); Robert N. Bellah, *Religion in Human Evolution: From the Paleolithic to the Axial Age* (Cambridge, MA: Harvard University Press, 2011); and Robert N. Bellah and Hans Joas, eds., *The Axial Age and Its Consequences* (Cambridge, MA: Harvard University Press, 2012).

8. Johann P. Arnason and Björn Wittrock, eds., *Eurasian Transformations, Tenth to Thirteenth Centuries: Crystallizations, Divergences, Renaissances* (Leiden: Brill, 2011); Amira K. Bennison, "Muslim Universalism and Western Globalization," in *Globalization in World History*, ed. A. G. Hopkins (New York: Norton, 2002), 73–98; Janet L. Abu-Lughod, *Before European Hegemony: The World System, A.D. 1250–1350* (New York: Oxford University Press, 1989); K. N. Chaudhuri, *Asia before Europe: Economy and Civilisation of the Indian Ocean from the Rise of Islam to 1750* (Cambridge: Cambridge University Press, 1990); Jerry H. Bentley, *Old World Encounters: Cross-Cultural Contacts and Exchanges in Pre-Modern Times* (New York: Oxford University Press, 1993); and Robert Tignor et al., *Worlds Together, Worlds Apart: A History of the Modern World from the Mongol Empire to the Present* (New York: Norton, 2002).

9. Geoffrey C. Gunn, *First Globalization: The Eurasian Exchange, 1500–1800* (Lanham, MD: Rowman & Littlefield, 2003); Alfred W. Crosby, *The Columbian Exchange: Biological and Cultural Consequences of 1492* (Westport, CT: Greenwood Press, 1972); and Eric Wolf, *Europe and the People without History* (Berkeley: University of California Press, 1982).

10. Robertson, *Globalization*; Roland Robertson and Kathleen E. White, eds., *Globalization: Critical Concepts in Sociology*, 6 vols. (London: Routledge, 2003); and Martin Albrow, *The Global Age: State and Society beyond Modernity* (Stanford: Stanford University Press, 1997).

11. Anthony Giddens, *The Consequences of Modernity* (Stanford: Stanford University Press, 1990).

12. Abu-Lughod, *Before European Hegemony*; and C. A. Bayly, *The Birth of the Modern World, 1780–1914: Global Connections and Comparisons* (Malden, MA: Blackwell, 2004).

13. As quoted in John W. O'Malley, SJ, *The First Jesuits* (Cambridge, MA: Harvard University Press, 1993), 5–6.

14. John W. O'Malley, SJ, "To Travel to Any Part of the World: Jerónimo Nadal and the Jesuit Vocation," in *Saints or Devils Incarnate? Studies in Jesuit History* (Leiden: Brill, 2013), 147–64.

15. Dauril Alden, *The Making of an Enterprise: The Society of Jesus in Portugal, Its Empire, and Beyond, 1540–1750* (Stanford: Stanford University Press, 1996).

16. Joseph Sebes, SJ, *The Jesuits and the Sino-Russian Treaty of Nerchinsk (1689): The Diary of Thomas Pereira, S.J.* (Rome: IHSI, 1961); and Jan Joseph Santich, OSB, *Missio Moscovitica: The Role of the Jesuits in the Westernization of Russia, 1582–1689* (New York: Peter Lang, 1995).

17. Sabina Pavone, *The Wily Jesuits and the* Monita Secreta: *The Forged Secret Instructions of the Jesuits; Myth and Reality* (St. Louis: Institute of Jesuit Sources, 2005).

18. See also Luke Clossey, *Salvation and Globalization in the Early Jesuit Missions* (New York: Cambridge University Press, 2008); and Immanuel Wallerstein, *The Modern World-System I: Capitalist Agriculture and the Origins of the European World-Economy in the Sixteenth Century* (New York: Academic Press, 1974).

19. Josef Franz Schütte, SJ, *Valignano's Mission Principles for Japan,* trans. John J. Coyne, 2 vols. (St. Louis: Institute of Jesuit Sources, 1980–85).

20. Ignatius of Loyola, *The Spiritual Exercises of St. Ignatius*, trans. Louis J. Puhl, SJ (Chicago: Loyola Press, 2010; original 1548), no. 106.

21. Steven J. Harris, "Mapping Jesuit Science: The Role of Travel in the Geography of Knowledge," in *The Jesuits: Cultures, Sciences, and the Arts, 1540–1773*, ed. John W. O'Malley, SJ, et al. (Toronto: University of Toronto Press, 1999), 212–40.

22. Blaise Pascal's *Provincial Letters* (1657) offers the most famous and influential critique of Jesuit casuistry. For an easily available reprint of the original English version, see *Pascal: The Provincial Letters*, trans. Thomas M'Crie (Charleston, SC: Forgotten Books, 2008).

23. Jean-Baptiste Janssens, SJ, "Instruction on the Social Apostolate: To All

Jesuit Provincials," Rome, October 10, 1949, no. 24, http://www.sjweb.info/sjs/documents/Janssens_eng.pdf.

24. Paul VI, *Gaudium et spes* (Pastoral Constitution of the Church in the Modern World), December 7, 1965, sec. 1, http://www.vatican.va/archive/hist_councils/ii_vatican_council/documents/vat-ii_const_19651207_gaudium-et-spes_en.html.

25. Thirty-Second General Congregation of the Society of Jesus, Decree 4, "Our Mission Today: The Service of Faith and the Promotion of Justice," 1975, no. 2, http://www.sjweb.info/documents/sjs/docs/D4%20Eng.pdf.

26. From Kolvenbach's sermon in Caracas, Venezuela, on October 12, 1984, quoted in Kevin M. Cahill, MD, *To Bear Witness: A Journey of Healing and Solidarity, Updated, Revised, and Expanded Edition* (New York: Fordham University Press, 2013), 90.

PART I

HISTORICAL PERSPECTIVES

1

THE JESUITS IN EAST ASIA IN THE EARLY MODERN AGE
A New "Areopagus" and the "*Re*-invention" of Christianity

M. ANTONI J. UCERLER, SJ

When we speak of the Christian faith in a global context, whether it be five hundred years ago or in the present day, we are faced with a seemingly irresolvable and ever-fluid tension between the universality of Christianity's claims and the myriad cultural realities that define it locally *over time* and that provide the context for its historical development. This was the crux of the problem the Jesuits faced as they accompanied the Portuguese and Spanish merchants and colonial administrators on their voyages into the Atlantic and Pacific worlds. The age of maritime exploration—or "Age of Discovery," as the Iberian empires referred to their own exploits—was, for better or for worse, the *first age of globalization* and the first sustained encounter with the Other, and its consequences would last for centuries thereafter.

Jesuit Pioneers in East Asia

What role(s) did the Jesuits play in these encounters, and what does their correspondence reveal about their mind-set? What did those first Jesuits who set out for East Asia, including Francis Xavier (1506–52) and his successors, Alessandro Valignano (1539–1606) and Matteo Ricci (1552–1610), hope to accomplish as they left Europe thousands of miles behind them, never to return to their native shores? To understand their way of proceeding (*modo de proceder*) across cultures, we must explore the nature of the Jesuit missionary enterprise (*empresa*)—a word with both religious and secular connotations—and the means they employed to introduce

Christianity to ancient civilizations that had never heard of the Christian faith.

Was there a master plan or strategy? Were all the missionaries in agreement as to the best way to proceed, or were there differences of opinion among them? If there were disagreements, were they minor, or did they reveal fundamentally divergent or even incompatible ideas as to how Christianity was to be transmitted to a non-Christian people? Were the beginnings of Christianity in Japan and China both as a faith, with its specific doctrines, and as an organized religion, with its particular institutions and external forms of expression and religious practice, simply the imposition of an alien religious and cultural phenomenon by uninvited Western intruders upon unsuspecting East Asian peoples? Or did Christianity, in the process, take root and become a Christianity—at least in part—"Made in Japan" and "Made in China" rather than just being imported or transplanted into those countries?

What soon emerges from an examination of the Jesuits' correspondence, and from other historical records, is that from the outset there was no clear agreement among the Jesuits regarding the best way to preach the Gospel. In fact, it took them at least several decades to formulate and refine their vision, and in the interim, they engaged in a great deal of experimentation as well as trial and error. One only need recall the misunderstanding that resulted in Japan when Francis Xavier initially adopted Dainichi Nyorai (Mahāvairocana), an Esoteric Buddhist term, in the belief that it could adequately express the concept of the Christian God. As he had arrived from India, the Japanese initially believed that Xavier belonged to an unfamiliar Buddhist sect and was bringing them a new teaching from within that tradition.[1]

In the second generation after Xavier, in 1573 Jesuit superior general Everard Mercurian (1514–80) appointed Alessandro Valignano to act as his visitor, or delegate, for all the missions of the East Indies, which stretched from the eastern coast of Africa all the way to Japan. Valignano's impact would be most strongly felt in India, Japan, and China. To begin a new mission in the Middle Kingdom, he sent two fellow Italians, Michele Ruggieri (1543–1607) and Matteo Ricci (1552–1610), to Macau to study the language.

The approach he encouraged Ruggieri and Ricci to adopt in the Middle Kingdom was what we today refer to as "cultural accommodation" or "inculturation"—a method that, in great part thanks to him and to his successors, we now take for granted. At the time, however, it was far from being the obvious or even "safe" (i.e., orthodox) choice. A common misconception about cultural accommodation is that it was purely the invention of European missionaries, whereby those who were receptive to the Christian message remained passive subjects. But in both Japan and China, the initiative for cultural accommodation often came from members of the local cultural elites who helped the Jesuits understand the cultural, social, political, linguistic, and religious contexts in which they were operating. It was frequently these Japanese and Chinese interlocutors who impressed upon the Jesuits the urgent need to engage the local culture *on its own terms* if they wished to make any significant progress.[2]

Cultural Accommodation and the "Jerusalem Compromise"

Valignano's letter from Goa to Claudio Acquaviva (1543–1615), who succeeded Everard Mercurian as Jesuit superior general in 1581, is worth quoting in extenso as it clarifies this point. Writing in 1595, with more than twenty years of experience in Asia behind him, Valignano recounts how Ōtomo Sōrin (1530–87), the lord of Bungo in Kyushu who was known as Don Francisco after his baptism, and a number of other Japanese Christian lords had insisted that the Jesuits respect Japanese customs. Valignano makes no effort to hide the irritation these Japanese warlords expressed to him about his fellow missionaries' demeanor:

> They said that the way of proceeding in our houses was so different and contrary to what was appropriate in Japan that they never came to our residences without leaving very upset, and that this unease was shared by all the [samurai] lords and [Japanese] Christians. . . . And he also told me that if we wanted to attempt to convert Japan, we would have to master the language and live according to [Japanese] norms of civility (*policía*). Moreover, [he noted that] it could only be taken as a sign of diminished intelligence to imagine that a handful of foreigners could possibly induce the samurai and their lords to abandon their own time-honored customs and civilized forms of courtesy in order to accommodate themselves to our foreign ways . . . which appeared to the Japanese to be most barbaric and lacking in civility.[3]

But the problem that Valignano and his fellow Jesuits faced did not simply involve making superficial changes to their outward behavior. From a theological perspective, the key question was, what form should or could Christianity take outside of Europe? And to use Aristotelian categories familiar to them, they had to consider what was *essential* and what was *accidental* to their preaching. In theological terms, it meant interpreting anew the problem of preaching a God who Christians claimed had entered human history at a particular time and place. But what exactly did that mean in sixteenth-century East Asia?

The Jesuits in Japan and China became acutely aware of the difficulty of explaining the Incarnation and the Cross of Christ, "a stumbling-block to Jews and foolishness to Gentiles" (1 Corinthians 1:23). Why should a samurai or a Ming dynasty mandarin believe that a Jewish carpenter had risen from the dead? And what good could come from a faith that took as its symbol the dead body of an executed prisoner from some far-off land? As far as the Chinese were concerned, the very existence of a place named "Israel" was dubious at best and, in any case, quite irrelevant to their worldview.

The Jesuits knew that their faith was to make no distinction between "Jew or Greek" (Galatians 3:28), but that was easier said than done. The early Church had had to face a serious dilemma. How could the Jesuits translate the apostles' faith in Jesus's identity as the Messiah and hence the fulfillment of the promises of the Hebrew Scriptures into terms that were comprehensible to the pagan cultures of Greece and Rome? Simply put, the heart of the matter was in determining *what was essential to the kerygma and what was not*. The crucial turning point for the early Church came at the Council of Jerusalem, where Peter acknowledged Paul's arguments and agreed that strict adherence to Jewish customs and rituals could not be demanded of all new believers. The revolutionary compromise was to ask the non-Jewish converts to abstain from sexual immorality and idolatrous behavior without asking them to give up their "foreign" identities and become Jews (Acts 15:20).

It was the Jesuits' understanding of the "Jerusalem compromise" that inspired them to speak of their work in Japan and China as that of apostles in a new "primitive Church."[4] While they never used the particular expression "Jerusalem compromise"—which is my own turn of phrase—in their own writings, we find this idea implicitly present in the conclusions that they drew from their own experiences in East Asia and the policies that they formulated in the light of the great Pauline experiment of the first century.

How would one define the outer boundaries of the Jerusalem compromise in this case? In Japan, it would involve discussing and debating at length issues very similar to those faced by the early Christian communities of the first century: What constituted idolatry? What was permissible with regard to Buddhist rituals, which Christian samurai were often expected to attend as retainers of their non-Christian overlords in Warring States Japan? The same questions would emerge dramatically almost a century later in China regarding the Chinese rites performed at Confucian temples and with family tablets erected to commemorate deceased ancestors. Was participation in such local rituals a form of idolatry and therefore a legacy of original sin? Or could these rituals be seen as bearing the seeds of divine grace working in and through a common human nature projected toward what was good and true?[5]

Thus even if the Jesuits realized early on that it was neither possible nor desirable to impose a completely European version of Christian culture in Asia, they could not simply adopt a tabula rasa approach and thereby ignore fifteen hundred years of Christian cultural history. After all, the canonical books of the New Testament and many Christian dogmas had been defined at ecumenical councils in Greek and Latin, or other ancient languages, including Syriac and Armenian. The Jesuits knew that just as the first Greek and Roman converts had needed to learn about their Jewish brethren, the same was true of their Asian interlocutors in the sixteenth and seventeenth centuries. But just as Paul had challenged Peter not to try to force converts to become Jewish from a cultural or even a religious standpoint, so too the Jesuits in Japan and China struggled to find ways that would avoid imposing a European cast onto their own converts.[6]

A New Missionary Rhetoric for a New "Primitive Church"

The Jesuits drew on another feature of the primitive Church when they reflected on the scene of the Pentecost (Acts 2:1–13), where everyone present heard the Gospel *in their own language*—that is, in words that were intelligible and that resonated within their respective cultures. Thus the Jesuits searched for the *right words*, for a language that would be comprehensible to peoples who did not live within the cultural confines of the Judeo-Greek and Roman worlds. It was as if a process of "incarnation" had to take place once again. *Christianitas*, defined as a broad nexus of Christian faith and cultural expressions, had to be "*re*-invented" and its geographical and mental borders broadened and extended to include the ancient traditions of Asia. What followed was the Jesuits' heavy investment of time and energy in the study of Asian languages, an exercise informed by their training in classical rhetoric.

As John O'Malley has argued in his writings, the rhetorical mind-set was one that permeated the Jesuits' approach to apostolic engagement. To be persuasive—as Ignatius of Loyola had instructed the fledgling Jesuit order to do in its *Constitutions*—one had to accommodate oneself to different times, places, persons, and circumstances. Jesuit accommodation was born out of Renaissance humanist culture and found concrete expression in movements such as the *devotio moderna*, which called for a piety that not only appealed to the mind through scholastic arguments or deductive proofs but also sought to move the hearts of believers, spurring them to lead fervent Christian lives.[7] This emphasis played out in a number of traditional Jesuit ministries such as preaching and became an integral part of their educational goals as they became codified in the *Ratio studiorum* (*Plan of Studies*), which was compiled and then revised in 1586, 1591, and 1599. This document served as their blueprint for establishing schools, beginning with the Roman College. They took this education, training, and cultural worldview with them when they boarded their ships bound for the East.

This education predisposed the Jesuits to adapt to the local realities they encountered in East Asia. Valignano gave the tradition a new twist when he brought together Quintilian's *ars bene dicendi*, or the "art of speaking well," and the paradigm of a new *ecclesia primitiva*. As he stated succinctly, "The Lord does not come to the aid of the Japanese Church with miracles, unlike in the primitive Church; thus, interior virtue must be accompanied by *exterior forms of persuasion*—wherein the [Japanese] Bonzes excel."[8]

In Valignano's detailed report to Rome to inform the superior general of the resolutions he had compiled for the governance of the mission, he notes how, "in the opinion of the majority, the only way to ensure the survival and development of the Church in this country was to promote the formation of a native clergy and the admittance of Japanese young men into the Order." They needed proper training in both religious subjects and the humanities. In his view it was "the only remedy for the conversion and conservation of the Japanese mission. . . . There is no other way to sustain the mission without this means [of education]."[9] As a result of these deliberations, in 1580 Valignano established a Jesuit novitiate, two schools (*seminarios*), and a college of higher learning (*collegio*).

In practice the program at the seminarios included teaching the students to read and write in both Latin and Japanese, as well as training them in the etiquette, customs, and ceremonies, or *katagi* (old Portuguese: *catangues*), of Japan. Moreover, the entire program was to be informed by a pursuit of *buenas costumbres* (virtuous conduct) and *buena doctrina* (proper religious education).

The aim of the collegio in Funai, however, founded in the domain of the Christian lord (Don Francisco) Ōtomo Sōrin (and later transferred to Amakusa and Nagasaki), was to provide a higher level of studies in not only European but also Japanese humanities. It also offered studies in philosophy and theology for those who were training for the priesthood and had already completed their basic studies at the seminario.

Being a pragmatist Valignano knew that the curriculum had to be adapted and could not simply be taught in the same way as it had been at the Roman College, or at the Jesuit colleges at Évora or Coimbra, or at the Universities of Paris, Alcalá, and Salamanca. Valignano decided to combine Western classical texts with those that were part of the Eastern tradition. He refers to the latter as *gakumon* (the Japanese word for scholarship or higher learning).

He also wrote to Europe requesting that a compendium of philosophy and theology be composed especially for the college in Japan, but it never materialized. In the end Pedro Gómez, the vice provincial of Japan from 1590 to 1600, wrote a textbook in 1593–94 for use at the collegio. Gómez had taught the entire curriculum of humanities at Coimbra under the guidance of Pedro da Fonseca (1528–99), the "Aristotle of Portugal," before coming to Japan. He based his own compendium on the Roman Catechism published in 1566 in the aftermath of the Council of Trent, but he adapted its content to the Japanese context and presented many parts in a dialogical format. In 1595 a team of converts translated his text, originally composed in Latin, into Japanese.[10]

Unlike the Roman Catechism, the main thrust of Gómez's work was not that of refuting heresy and defining orthodoxy. Instead, as the Japanese historian Obara Satoru has pointed out, "[His] main consideration was to tie Christian dogma with the issues of morality and the inner life" rather than "to engage in the abstract refutation of heresy."[11] This explains the emphasis on praxis and the detailed exposition of "Christian virtues and their opposite vices"—an emphasis we do not find in the Roman Catechism. Gómez clearly felt free to follow a different line of argumentation as his principal aim was also different from that of the Roman Catechism.

Though Gómez used classical literary and patristic texts from the Latin tradition, he replaced the study of Greek with that of classical Japanese and Chinese texts, many of which were published on the Jesuit mission press between 1590 and 1620. In fact, to further his educational goals, he arranged to acquire a fully working Gutenberg handpress, for which movable type was cast, thus enabling the first instance of printing with Japanese characters.[12] In a letter written to the Jesuit authorities in Rome in 1613, Diogo de Mesquita, the Portuguese Jesuit who had originally acquired the press in Lisbon in 1586, sums up succinctly and eloquently the important function the press played over the years in the life of the Japanese mission: "During these persecutions, especially when priests cannot travel freely through the territories of Christians whose lords are pagans, it is impossible to exaggerate the wonderful results obtained by these books . . . for *they serve as preachers* to the Christians [my emphasis]. With this aid both the persecuted and those who do not suffer persecution are equally confirmed in their faith and their [Christian] customs."[13]

In China circumstances were quite different. The country was united under the emperor and governed by a vast cohort of officials across the country who were accountable to the imperial court in Beijing. As a result, in contrast to the reliance of the Jesuits in Japan on local warlords who offered protection, the Jesuits in China depended on the good will of provincial governors and mandarins, in whose hands the Jesuits had to place their fates. The latter group, however, could be influenced by the local literati, many of whom befriended the Jesuits and became their advocates and informal patrons. Among those who were key converts and allies in the early years of the mission, a few exceptional figures stand out, including Xu Guangqi (1562–1633), Yang Tingyun (1562–1627), and Li Zhizao (1565–1630). These learned individuals supported and educated Ricci and his successors as to how they should engage with the Chinese elites and how they could navigate the complicated protocols that governed their relationships with local officials. Many of them also lent both credibility and authority to the foreign Jesuits' writings, whether composed directly in classical Chinese or translated, by writing prefaces to their works according to Chinese scholarly custom. Those of financial means often also paid for the printing of these books. Unlike Warring States Japan, China had a well-established network of small print shops throughout the country whose printers catered primarily to scholars and those aspiring to official positions in the bureaucracy, the pursuit of which involved studying the classics and their commentaries in preparation for the imperial examination.[14] Although it was not possible for the Jesuits to establish schools in China as they had in Japan, they sought in both countries to transmit the Christian message through the medium of print.[15]

Ricci and his successors soon realized that in a land where the spoken word was not held in as high regard as the written one, the composition of scholarly books in Chinese was the primary rhetorical means by which to reach out to the mandarin class. From Beijing in 1608, Ricci penned a letter to the superior general of the order, Claudio Acquaviva, and explained why he considered this to be so important: "I do everything so that our Fathers study very well the books of China and learn how to compose in Chinese; for if the truth be told—which may be hard to believe—one accomplishes more in China with books than with mere words."[16]

These intellectual endeavors in China would soon include scientific pursuits at the service of the court. Calendar reform was considered paramount for the continued legitimacy of the reign of the "Son of Heaven" and the ruling dynasty, and this task required up-to-date knowledge of astronomy and mathematics, for which the following generation of Jesuit missionaries would become famous. Among them were Diego de Pantoja (1571–1618), Giacomo Rho (1593–1638), Johann Adam Schall von Bell (1592–1666), Ferdinand Verbiest (1623–88), Jean-François Gerbillon (1654–1707), and Joachim Bouvet (1656–1730), to name but a few. The last two had been sent by Louis XIV of France and were retained at court by the Kangxi Emperor (1654–1722), who reigned from 1661 until his death.[17]

For the Jesuits in East Asia, the proclamation of the Gospel required cultural and linguistic mediation—that is, a multifaceted process of *re*-inventing the Christian message, with "invention" here being understood according to its Latin root, *inventio*, as a technical term signifying the "discovery" of persuasive arguments with which to move the hearts and minds of one's audience.[18] Here the *ars bene dicendi* and the *ars bene evangelizandi* (the art of evangelizing well) were very closely connected. Before one could begin to construct complex theological arguments, one needed to discover (*invenire*) the appropriate individual words, images, metaphors, and allusions with which to express the faith. But seeking such persuasive arguments was not simply an exercise in external eloquence. The search for the right words with which to make the Christian kerygma comprehensible was a reenactment of the original incarnation of that message. It reflected the apostle Peter's exhortation to be always prepared "to make your defense to anyone who demands from you an account of the hope that is in you" (1 Peter 3:15).

The Jesuits believed that if it had been possible to find seeds of divine grace in the polytheistic and otherwise pagan cultures of Greece and Rome, then traces of the same Holy Spirit could be found in the highly sophisticated civilizations of China and Japan. In his letter from Kagoshima written on November 5, 1549, Xavier had referred to the Japanese as "the best people yet discovered." Valignano would expand on this assessment in his *Sumario de las cosas de Japón* (*Summary of Things Japanese*) of 1583, in which he described the people as follows: "Of all peoples in the East, until now we have seen that only the Japanese are moved to become Christians of their own free will, convinced by reason and desirous of their own salvation."[19] He would soon express a similar opinion when speaking of China and Chinese civilization.

Ricci echoed similar sentiments in a letter that he composed from Beijing on February 15, 1609, to his fellow Jesuit Francesco Pasio:

> In ancient times they [i.e., the Chinese] followed the natural law more faithfully than in our own countries. And 1500 years ago, this people

was not inclined to the worship of idols; and those they did adore were not like the evil idols worshipped by the Egyptians, Greeks or Romans, but rather men whom they considered virtuous, and who had performed many good deeds. On the contrary, the books of the literati, which are the most ancient and authoritative among their writings, do not adore anything but heaven and earth and the Lord of both. And if we examine these books, we will find little therein against the light of reason and much that is in conformity with it . . . and we can hope in Divine mercy that many of their ancient sages were saved by their observance of the natural law with the help that God would have given them on account of their goodness.[20]

In Ricci's words we can hear echoes of Paul's letter to the Romans: "For it is not the hearers of the law who are righteous in God's sight, but the doers of the law who will be justified. When Gentiles, who do not possess the law, do instinctively what the law requires, these, though not having the law, are a law to themselves. They show that what the law requires is written on their hearts, to which their own conscience also bears witness" (Romans 2:13–15).

Theological Imagination and the Challenges of a New Asian "Areopagus"

What distinguishes the early Jesuits in Japan and China as theologians was their willingness to take an approach similar to that of the apostle Paul, who declared to the learned Greeks gathered at the Areopagus in Athens that he could announce to them the identity of the unknown god whom they worshipped in their pantheon:

> For as I went through the city and looked carefully at the objects of your worship, I found among them an altar with the inscription, "To an unknown god." What therefore you worship as unknown, this I proclaim to you. The God who made the world and everything in it, he who is Lord of heaven and earth, does not live in shrines made by human hands, nor is he served by human hands, as though he needed anything, since he himself gives to all mortals life and breath and all things. (Acts 17:23–25)

Paul speaks at the Areopagus of the "Lord of heaven and earth" (οὐρανοῦ καὶ γῆς . . . κύριος) whom the Greeks do not know. It is no coincidence that Ricci would choose *The True Meaning of the Lord of Heaven*

(*Tianzhu shiyi*) for the title of his Chinese catechism, which was composed in dialogic format.[21] This text, which Ricci began editing in 1595 and later published in 1603, was influential not only in China but also in Japan and in Korea, where the intellectual elites read classical Chinese. An edition specifically destined for Japan and the Japanese bonzes was reprinted in 1605 in Guangzhou (Canton). It was based on a natural theology that progresses toward the idea of divine grace working in creation. It took as its initial intellectual point of reference Alessandro Valignano's earlier *Catechismus Christianae fidei*, which was published in Lisbon in 1586.[22] And as the Christian faith would revolutionize the meaning of the word θεός in Greek, so too Ricci hoped that his efforts would have a similar transformative impact on the concept of *tian*, or "heaven," in Chinese philosophy and religion.

But similarly to Paul, whom Ricci adopted as a model and who had not accepted Greek polytheism, so too Ricci was not willing to accept everything in Chinese thought. Ricci did, in fact, reject the tenets of the neo-Confucian school founded by Zhu Xi (1130–1200), whose interpretations of the classics were very influential during the late Ming period. They interpreted tian as an "ultimate principle" (*li*) and as an impersonal force or energy (*qi*) that formed and governed the universe. Not surprising, on the one hand, Ricci considered such a way of comprehending "heaven" as leaning toward pantheism and therefore eminently atheistic. He was convinced, on the other hand, that Confucian thought had never been atheistic and that neo-Confucianism represented an aberration and inauthentic interpretation of this foundational philosophy in Chinese society. His "revisionist" solution was to call for a return to what he envisioned as the "original" and thus more "orthodox" form of Confucianism as it found expression in the writings of the ancient Chinese sages. Ricci viewed their practices as an imperfect ethical theism not unlike the school of Stoicism in the West.[23]

Ricci believed that in the early classics he had identified the presence of a personal god, whom he referred to as "Lord of Heaven" (*Tianzhu*). On this basis he attempted to persuade the Chinese literati that Christianity, far from being an alien doctrine brought to China by foreign barbarians, represented the fulfillment of Confucian philosophy in that it provided a more authentic reinterpretation of its central tenets than that offered by the "heretical" school of Zhu Xi, Wang Yangming (1472–1529), and other neo-Confucian scholars of his own age. Moreover, he believed that what he was attempting to do reflected more accurately the wisdom and traditions of the "golden age" of Chinese philosophy under the Zhou dynasty (1046–256 BCE), whose sages had written about and worshipped a transcendent personal force in the universe consistently referred to as "Lord on High" (*Shangdi*).[24]

With these reflections, Ricci situated himself in the midst of the various philosophical and religious debates that occupied the Chinese scholars with whom he chose to engage—once again not unlike Paul at the Areopagus. On the one hand, he came to share the disdain many Chinese literati of his day had for Buddhist and Daoist monks. The mandarin class generally considered these monks insufficiently learned at best and outright ignorant at worst. Ignatius Qu Rukui (Taisu, 1549–1611), one of the first literati to embrace Christianity as a result of his conversations with Ricci, summed up the purpose and method of evangelization as envisioned by his friend and mentor in his new faith as to "reject Buddhism and come closer to Confucianism" (*qi Fo jin Ru* 棄佛近儒). Taisu had written the preface to Ricci's famous *Jiaoyoulun* (Treatise on friendship) in 1599 and was baptized in 1605. This new stance favoring Confucian thought and customs soon led to irreconcilable differences between Ricci and Michele Ruggieri, his fellow Italian and Jesuit. In the preface to the first Chinese catechism that Ruggieri composed and published in 1584, the "True Record of the Lord of Heaven," he had referred to himself as "the monk from India" (*Tianzhu guo seng* 天竺國僧).[25]

As Ricci walked the fine line between a sympathetic interpretation of the Chinese classics and a polemical rejection of many of its tenets that he found incompatible with the Christian faith, he made strenuous efforts to formulate what we might call a "new Chinese rhetoric of pre-evangelization." He wrote not only a coherent discourse that was comprehensible to the Chinese but also something much more: a proclamation of the Gospel that was rooted in and based on a tradition and a terminology that was already an integral and indelible part of their own history and culture.

Perhaps then we can say that Ricci was not attempting to plant the Gospel in China as if it were a mature and fully grown tree that had been nurtured in a foreign and unknown land and then suddenly uprooted and forcibly transplanted into Chinese soil. Ricci rather assumed a challenge and a risk—but one that he firmly believed was possible and worthwhile—in seeking to discover the seeds of the Gospel already present in China and then to cultivate and nurture them. He believed that these seeds had been present *ab antiquo* through the natural law and the action of the Holy Spirit in the fertile soil of Chinese culture and that they could grow in such a way as to bring the "Good News" of Christ to all the inhabitants of the Middle Kingdom.

Some critics, both past and present, have denounced Ricci's project as doomed to failure on account of the perceived implausibility of connecting early Confucianism and Christian thought. Yet this critical assessment, while technically accurate in many respects, would appear to miss the mark. Ricci was not claiming a historically tangible connection between the two; rather, his method is rather reminiscent of the medieval tradition of the four readings of Scripture: historical, allegorical, tropological (moral), and anagogical. Ricci's linking of ancient China's Shangdi to his own translation of Tianzhu seems close to the allegorical (nonliteral) or typological reading, which focused on finding the meaningful connections between the Old and New Testament narratives. Ricci was trying to establish a link between the old Chinese tradition of Shangdi and its "true meaning" and the new fulfillment in faith in Christ as expressed in the word "Tianzhu." He was also concentrating on the moral dimension of that understanding of a supreme being. In this exercise, he was not dabbling in philosophical relativism or religious syncretism. Rather he was returning to Paul's idea of explaining the identity of the unknown god in the pantheon of Athens, thereby acknowledging the presence of a legitimate natural form of worship, whose deeper meaning and historical significance he was trying to uncover and highlight.

Ricci's hybrid methodology was also in keeping with the famous "thought experiments" that are a defining characteristic of the *Mengzi*, the book by Mengzi (372–289 BCE) or "Mencius" as he came to be known in the West thanks to the Jesuit Latinization of his name. Mencius employed an abundance of agricultural imagery and metaphors, such as the four "sprouts," "seeds," or "beginnings"/"principles" (*duan*) of human nature, to explain his theory on the original goodness of every human being (*Mengzi*, 2A.6 and 6A.6).

Not everyone was willing to give the Jesuits the benefit of the doubt with regard to their own version of theological thought experiments. Several decades after both Valignano and Ricci had departed from this world, the debate over the Chinese rites began to intensify. But the crisis did not develop all at once. The Sacred Congregation for the Propagation of the Faith (Propaganda Fide), which Gregory XV had established in 1622 to support missionary activities around the globe, issued an unequivocal statement in 1659 that reflected the "rhetoric of the Areopagus" approach, if we may call it that, that the early Jesuits in Japan and China had adopted: "What could be more absurd than to bring France, Spain, Italy or any other European country over to China? It is not your country but the faith you must bring, that faith which does not reject or belittle the rites or customs of any nation as long as these rites are not evil, but rather desires that they be preserved in their integrity and fostered."[26]

The proviso "as long as these rites are not evil" reminds us once again of the Council of Jerusalem's proviso with regard to avoiding immoral behavior and idolatry. But the devil was in the details rather than in general principles and formulations. Fifty years later this opinion was reversed, leading to Clement XI's condemnation of the Chinese rites in 1704 and again in 1715. The Jesuits' argument that these customary rituals performed on behalf of one's ancestors fulfilled a social rather than a religious function failed to convince the highest authorities in Rome. Benedict XIV subsequently reaffirmed the Church's rejection of these hybrid rites and rituals in 1742. It took nearly two hundred years, but in 1939 Pius XII finally lifted the ban on Chinese Christians' participating in what the Church no longer considered as religious but civic—and therefore not idolatrous—rituals.

The Transition to Modernity

As we view the efforts of the early Jesuits in East Asia and try to explain and make sense of their modus operandi in the early modern phase of globalization, we see that they combined a Pauline theology with the humanist educational ideals of *eloquentia perfecta* in which they had been trained. This movement to rediscover and revalue the ideals of classical Greek and Latin culture in the European secular sphere, and the parallel efforts of Christian thinkers such as Erasmus and the adherents of the devotio moderna movement, coincided historically with the Jesuits' presence among the "newly discovered" peoples beyond the confines of Europe. In this sense they were truly men of their times and very much in touch with the latest developments in their own culture. In Asia they encountered civilizations that they came to identify as the new Greeks and Romans of their age; and for their *compositio loci*, they chose to perform a grand experiment—that is, to attempt to merge the Pauline scene of the Areopagus with the realities of Ming China and Warring States Japan. Their memory and "re-imagination" of the primitive Church of the first century became their new theological commonplace.

One of the first prominent Japanese Christians of the modern age to struggle with this issue of the Christian faith wrapped up in European cultural layers of *Christianitas* versus being true to one's own Japanese—samurai—identity was Uchimura Kanzō (1861–1930), who created a "non-church" (*mukyōkai*) movement at the turn of the twentieth century.[27] Born just before the Meiji Restoration of 1868, he experienced firsthand Japan's turbulent transformation from a feudal society under the Tokugawa shoguns to a constitutional monarchy and rising world imperial power in the Western mold. A man of extraordinary openness and erudition who spent time living and working in the United States, he nevertheless refused to give in to the idea that he had to capitulate emotionally and spiritually and become European or American in his outlook to be an authentic Christian. He had the following to say about the relationship between his faith and his national identity:

> I love two J's and no third; one is Jesus and the other Japan.
> I do not know which I love more, Jesus or Japan. . . .
> Jesus and Japan; my faith is not a circle with one center; it is an ellipse with two centers. My heart and mind revolve around the two dear names. And I know that one strengthens the other; Jesus strengthens and purifies my love for Japan; and Japan clarifies and objectivises [sic] my love for Jesus. Were it not for the two, I would become a mere dreamer, a fanatic, an amorphous universal man.[28]

A generation later Endō Shūsaku (1923–96), the renowned Japanese Catholic novelist, referred to his own peculiar experiences of growing up as a Christian in Japan. Nominated several times for the Nobel Prize for Literature before his death at the age of seventy-three, he admits to struggling for decades with his dual identity as a Japanese and as a Christian. Baptized at the age of eleven, he felt that Christianity was similar to an "ill-fitting Western suit."[29] While he could tolerate such a garment, he could never wear it comfortably as it was not originally part of the Japanese wardrobe.

Referred to at times as the Graham Greene of Japan, Endō explored many of his personal doubts in his writings. Published in 1966, his most famous novel, *Silence* (*Chinmoku*), recounts the inner struggle of a Portuguese Jesuit in the mid-seventeenth century who is forced to witness the torture of Christians until he himself apostatizes to save them. The novel's historical context is based on the true story of the apostasy in 1633 of Cristóvão Ferreira (c. 1580–1650), the Jesuit provincial superior of Japan, and the Jesuits who were subsequently sent to Japan to persuade him to return to the fold and thus redeem him. Their mission was to atone for his sin with their own deaths. But rather than meeting a glorious martyrdom, the novel's central character, Sebastião Rodrigues, who resembles the historical figure of the Italian Jesuit Giuseppe Chiara (1602–85), is confronted with the dilemma of unbearable human suffering and cruelty without respite or divine intervention. He is on the brink of losing his self-identity, his soul, and, to a certain extent, his mind until he realizes that God's mercy penetrates even the depths of his own despair. That same divine mercy goes beyond his ideas about himself and calls him paradoxically to perpetrate an act of apostasy precisely out of love for Christ and his fellow Christians.[30] A complex and intriguing exploration of faith and its outer boundaries, Endō's novel initially received very mixed reviews among his fellow Japanese Catholics.

To clarify what he was trying to say, Endō wrote a prequel to the story in the form of a play that recounts the capture and interrogation of Japanese Christians and Cristóvão Ferreira by the infamous "religious inquisitor" (*shūmon aratameyaku*) Inoue Masashige (1585–1661). In the play titled *The Golden Country* (*Ōgon no kuni*), Inoue mocks with feigned pity both the Japanese Christians and foreign missionaries for their deluded belief that Christianity was a "seed" that could actually "take root" in Japan. He tells Ferreira that "it wasn't by me that you were vanquished but by this mud swamp called Japan." Addressing his assistant in another scene, he then muses, "Am I right? Or are the Christians right? Is Japan really a 'golden country' in which the seed will grow . . . or is it a swamp, as I think, a swamp in which the roots rot and die?"[31]

The ferocious persecution of Christianity in the seventeenth century has led many to conclude that the "Christian Century" in Japan amounted indeed to nothing but a colossal failure. The Edo shogunate appears to have left no stone unturned to weed out any leftover roots of the *jakyō* (evil teaching).[32] The sheer volume of anti-Christian literature compiled in the seventeenth century indicates that the authorities believed the foreign faith had permeated all strata of Japanese society and that no effort should be spared to eradicate it.[33] And yet members of the Christian community survived underground without any priests to support them for more than 250 years—a unique and unrivaled phenomenon in the history of world Christianity.[34]

In the aftermath of Commodore Matthew Perry's opening of Japan in 1853 and the signing of the Harris Treaty in 1858, the French were allowed to build a church for the foreign community in Nagasaki in 1863. Two years later, on March 17, 1865, Bernard-Thadée Petitjean (1829–84), a member of the Paris Foreign Missions, discovered the existence of a group of "Hidden Christians" in Nagasaki when they decided, at considerable risk to themselves, to come to see the church—an event that was met with astonishment both in the West and by the Japanese authorities. As the Tokugawa ban on Christianity was still in effect, authorities subsequently arrested and exiled more than 3,000 men, women, and children, many of whom lived in the village of Urakami (in the Nagasaki area), to remote locations all over Japan. They also sent 153 of them for interrogation and torture to the small town of Tsuwano in present-day Shimane Prefecture, where 36 adults and children died for their faith. It was only when news of their mistreatment reached Europe and the United States that pressure was brought to bear on the Japanese government to put an end to their plight.

US president Ulysses S. Grant (1822–85) explicitly brought up the question of continued persecution of Christians with Iwakura Tomomi (1825–83), a Meiji reformer who headed an official Japanese diplomatic delegation to the United States in 1871–72. After returning to Japan, Iwakura persuaded the government to find a way to guarantee religious freedom without further delay. It finally came about when Aoki Shūzō (1844–1914), who worked with German constitutional scholars to draft a constitution, produced an amended Governmental Code for the Japanese Empire in 1873. This took place five years after the beginning of the Meiji Restoration, which saw the establishment of a German-style constitutional monarchy in Japan following the collapse of the Edo shogunate.[35]

In China the Europeans' squabbles over the Chinese rites that prompted the Kangxi Emperor to ban Christian missionary activity in 1721, and the subsequent persecution of Chinese Christian communities, raised questions similar to those regarding Japan about the ultimate success of the mission. Prior to the ban the Kangxi Emperor had issued an edict of toleration in 1692 at the request of the Jesuit missionaries, with whom he had been very pleased. He had sent the Jesuits Tomás Pereira (1645–1708) and Jean-François Gerbillon as envoys to negotiate the Treaty of Nerchinsk between the Qing and Russia, and they played a key role in brokering the agreement in the summer of 1689.

With the modern phase of globalization in the nineteenth century came the age of Western imperialism that found concrete economic, diplomatic, and military expression in the unequal treaties that China was forced to accept. One of the direct consequences of this power play was the outbreak of the Opium Wars (1839–42 and 1856–60), which only served to humiliate China and thereby further magnify China's distrust of foreigners. The popular tendency to identify the foreign threat with Christianity culminated in the Boxer Rebellion of 1898–1901, which dealt another severe blow to the Chinese Christian community, with the crisis bringing renewed foreign intervention against the Qing dynasty and yet another cycle of antiforeign sentiment in China.[36]

Conclusion

The Jesuits were important figures in the first, early modern phase of globalization. What they achieved in Japan and China was paralleled in many other experiences of early Jesuit missionaries as they traveled the world. The Jesuits were among the world's proto-ethnologists, reporting and reflecting on the significance of their "discoveries" and intercultural encounters. As a result they were able to formulate new cultural, philosophical, and theological approaches to the Other.

In spite of their many limitations, the rich cultural legacies of the early Jesuits in East Asia are worthy of renewed scrutiny in our own time—not simply as an antiquarian curiosity from a bygone age but as an original paradigm and model of intercultural engagement. The struggle they faced in the sixteenth century is not unlike the challenge the Church continues to face today in determining how "to give an account of her [Christian] hope" (1 Peter 3:15) and how to find the appropriate means of persuasion or rhetorical commonplaces with which to bear witness to the faith in very different cultural and religious circumstances and contexts. The search for the right language, the right symbols, as well as comprehensible and meaningful metaphors, continues.

The validity of the Areopagus model of evangelization was reaffirmed by the Second Vatican Council (1962–65) and in particular in its Dogmatic Constitution on the Church, *Lumen gentium* (nos. 13–17), which has reiterated that the Holy Spirit is present and at work in *every* culture. The Council's theology has thus tried to clarify this issue by means of a Trinitarian vision, whereby the "scandal" of the Incarnation and its historical and cultural particularity is resolved in a theology of the Holy Spirit.

The question, nevertheless, of what the "Jerusalem compromise" might mean today in our own pluralistic world remains open. The theological imagination of the early Jesuits still has something eloquent to say to us today about the difficulties of translating the faith in both a *global* and a *local* context, and of expanding the contemporary cultural horizons of *Christianitas*, informed by the challenges of multiculturalism and religious pluralism even within Western societies. The important task of finding a persuasive rhetoric of evangelization that works in diverse cultural contexts remains incomplete and an ongoing process in our contemporary global era.[37] How to learn from failure while building on one's strengths and how to continue to engage with the no less complex socioeconomic, environmental, and political challenges of the present day remain open and urgent questions that the Church must continue to address in every age.

Notes

1. See Georg Schurhammer, *Das kirchliche Sprachproblem in der Japanischen Jesuitenmission des 16. und 17. Jahrhunderts: Ein Stück Ritenfrage in Japan* (Tokyo: Deutsche Gesellschaft für Natur- und Völkerkunde Ostasiens, 1928). See also Kishino Hisashi, "From *Dainichi* to *Deus*: The Early Missionaries' Discovery and Under-

standing of Buddhism," in *Christianity and Cultures: Japan & China in Comparison, 1543–1644*, ed. M. Antoni J. Ucerler, SJ (Rome: IHSI, 2009), 45–60.

2. A particularly important "turn" in the historiography of Christianity in China has been the acknowledgment on the part of Western scholars of the need to pay attention to *Chinese reactions* to the encounter. A key work that helped define this new methodology was that of Jacques Gernet, *Chine et christianisme: Action et réaction* (Paris: Gallimard, 1982). The consequences of such an approach are discussed in Nicolas Standaert, SJ, "Methodology in View of Contact between Cultures: The China Case in the 17th Century," CSRCS Occasional Papers 11, Centre for the Study of Religion and Chinese Society, Chung Chi College, Chinese University of Hong Kong, December 2002, 1–64.

3. See Alessandro Valignano to Claudio Acquaviva, Goa, November 23, 1595, in Archivum Romanum Societatis Iesu (ARSI), *Jap.-Sin.*, 12 II, fols. 315v–316r, and cited in Alessandro Valignano, SJ, *Il cerimoniale per i missionari del Giappone*, ed. Josef Franz Schütte, SJ (Rome: Edizioni di Storia e Letteratura, 1946), 23–24. All translations are my own, unless otherwise noted.

4. For Valignano's understanding of the Japanese Christian community as a new "primitive Church," see my "Valignano come storico della missione: La sua ultima parola nel Principio y progresso (1601–1603)," in *Alessandro Valignano, S.I.: Uomo del Rinascimento, Ponte tra Oriente y Occidente*, ed. Adolfo Tamburello, M. Antoni J. Ucerler, SJ, and Marisa Di Russo (Rome: IHSI, 2008), 261–78.

5. For a succinct discussion of the issue of rites and memorial tablets, see John W. Witek, SJ, "Catholic Missions and the Expansion of Christianity, 1644–1800," in *China and Maritime Europe, 1500–1800: Trade, Settlement, Diplomacy, and Missions*, ed. John E. Wills, Jr. (Cambridge: Cambridge University Press, 2011), 135–82, especially 155–60.

6. Valignano explicitly says this in chapter 10 of his guidelines for missionary policy. See *Obediências do P. Alexandre Valignano, Vizitador da Província de Japão e China, revistas e concertadas pello P. Francisco Passio, Vizitador da mesma Província, para instrucção dos Reytores, Anno de 1612*, published in part in Spanish translation in Alessandro Valignano, SJ, *Sumario de las cosas de Japón (1583): Adiciones del Sumario de Japón (1592)*, ed. José Luis Alvarez-Taladriz, Monumenta Nipponica Monographs (Tokyo: Sophia University, 1954), 9:167, paragraph 10.

7. See John W. O'Malley, SJ, "Renaissance Humanism and the Religious Culture of the First Jesuits," *Heythrop Journal* 31 (1990): 471–87; and his *The First Jesuits* (Cambridge, MA: Harvard University Press, 1993), 253ff.

8. Valignano, *Sumario de las cosas de Japón*, 241.

9. Ibid., 106.

10. I discovered the original Japanese manuscript of Gómez's compendium in 1995 in the archives of Magdalen College, Oxford. See my "Jesuit Humanist Education in Sixteenth-Century Japan: The Latin and Japanese MSS of Pedro Gómez's 'Compendia' on Astronomy, Philosophy, and Theology (1593–95)," in *The "Compendia" Compiled by Pedro Gómez for the Jesuit College of Japan*, ed. Obara Satoru, SJ, and M. Antoni J. Ucerler, SJ (Tokyo: Ōzorasha, 1997), 3:11–60. The

critical edition of the text was subsequently published by Obara Satoru as *Iezusukai Nihon Korejiyo no Kōgi yōkō*, 3 vols. (Tokyo: Kyōbunkan, 1997–99).

11. Obara Satoru, SJ, *Acceptance, Rejection and Transformation: Christianity and the Historical Climate of Japan* (Tokyo: Kirishitan Bunko, Sophia University, 1994), 43.

12. For an introduction to the work of the press, see Dorotheus Schilling, "Christliche Druckereien in Japan (1590–1614)," *Gutenberg Jahrbuch* 15 (1940): 356–95; and Diego Pacheco, "Diogo de Mesquita, S.J. and the Jesuit Mission Press," *Monumenta Nipponica* 26, no. 3–4 (1971): 431–43.

13. See Diogo de Mesquita to Claudio Acquaviva, Nagasaki, November 9, 1613, in ARSI, *Jap.-Sin.*, 36, fol. 27v.

14. For an introduction to Chinese book culture in this period, see Cynthia J. Brokaw, "On the History of the Book in China," in *Printing and Book Culture in Late Imperial China*, ed. Cynthia J. Brokaw and Kai-wing Chow (Berkeley: University of California Press, 2005), 3–54.

15. For a study of Jesuit translations into Chinese, see Ronnie Po-chia Hsia, "The Catholic Mission and Translations in China, 1583–1700," in *Cultural Translation in Early Modern Europe*, ed. Peter Burke and R. Po-chia Hsia (Cambridge: Cambridge University Press, 2007), 39–51. For the Jesuits' "apostolate of books" missionary strategy, see Nicolas Standaert, SJ, ed., *Handbook of Christianity in China*, vol. 1, *635–1800* (Boston: Brill, 2001), 600–631.

16. Matteo Ricci to Claudio Acquaviva, Beijing, February 8, 1608, ARSI, *Jap.-Sin.*, 14 II, fol. 308v.

17. The literature on Jesuit science in China is extensive. See, for example, John W. Witek, "Understanding the Chinese: A Comparison of Matteo Ricci and the French Jesuit Mathematicians Sent by Louis XIV," in *East Meets West: The Jesuits in China, 1582–1773*, ed. Charles E. Ronan and Bonnie B. C. Oh (Chicago: Loyola University Press, 1988), 62–102; Noël Golvers, *Ferdinand Verbiest, S.J. (1623–1688) and the Chinese Heaven* (Leuven, Belgium: Leuven University Press, 2003); Florence C. Hsia, *Sojourners in a Strange Land: Jesuits & Their Scientific Missions in Late Imperial China* (Chicago: University of Chicago Press, 2009); and Catherine Jami, *The Emperor's New Mathematics: Western Learning and Imperial Authority during the Kangxi Reign (1662–1722)* (Oxford: Oxford University Press, 2012).

18. See Marcus Tullius Cicero's extensive disquisitions on the topic of invention in his treatise *On [Rhetorical] Invention (De inventione)* and his book *On the Orator (De oratore)*.

19. See Valignano, *Sumario de las cosas de Japón*, 132.

20. See *Opere storiche del P. Matteo Ricci, S.I.*, vol. 2, *Le lettere dalla Cina*, ed. Pietro Tacchi-Venturi, SJ (Macerata: Filippo Giorgetti, 1913), 385.

21. For the text of Ricci's Chinese catechism, with an introduction to the text, see Matteo Ricci, SJ, *The True Meaning of the Lord of Heaven (T'ien-chu shih-i)* [*Tianzhu shiyi* 天主實義. English and Chinese], ed. Edward Malatesta, trans. D. Lancashire and P. Hu Kuo-chen (St. Louis: Institute of Jesuit Sources, 1985).

22. See Thierry Meynard, SJ, "The Overlooked Connection between Ricci's *Tianzhu shiyi* and Valignano's *Catechismus Japonensis*," *Japanese Journal of Religious Studies* 40, no. 2 (2013): 303–22.

23. For a comprehensive study of Ricci's reading of Confucianism, see Paul A. Rule, *K'ung-tzu or Confucius? The Jesuit Interpretation of Confucianism* (Boston: Allen & Unwin, 1986).

24. See Sangkeun Kim, *Strange Names for God: The Missionary Translation of the Divine Name and the Chinese Responses to Matteo Ricci's* Shangdi *in Late Ming China, 1583–1644*, Studies in Biblical Literature (New York: Peter Lang, 2004), 70:197–266. For a discussion of the early Chinese conceptions of the divine and its relation to heaven, see Ruth H. Chang, "Understanding *Di* and *Tian*: Deity and Heaven from Shang to Tang," *Sino-Platonic Papers* 108 (2000): 1–54. For a thought-provoking contemporary discussion of the place of Confucian ideas about the divine, see Weigang Chen, "Confucian Humanism and Theodicy," *Journal of the American Academy of Religion* 80, no. 4 (2012): 932–70.

25. See Ronnie Po-chia Hsia, "The Jesuit Encounter with Buddhism in Ming China," in Ucerler, SJ, *Christianity and Cultures*, 38.

26. "Instructions for Missionaries from the Sacred Congregation for the Propagation of the Faith (1659)," cited in A. Scott Moreau, Gary R. Corwin, and Gary B. McGee, *Introducing World Missions: A Biblical, Historical, and Practical Survey* (2004; repr., Grand Rapids, MI: Baker Academic, 2007), 120.

27. For an in-depth discussion of Uchimura's contribution, see Mark R. Mullins, *Christianity Made in Japan: A Study of Indigenous Movements* (Honolulu: University of Hawai'i Press, 1998).

28. From Uchimura's 1926 essay on the "Two J's," reprinted in *Sources of Japanese Tradition: 1600–2000*, vol. 2, pt. 2, *1868–2000*, comp. William Theodore de Bary, Carol Gluck, and Arthur E. Tiedemann (New York: Columbia University Press, 2006), 451–52.

29. For a study of Endō's thought as expressed in his novel *Silence*, see Emi Mase-Hasegawa, *Christ in Japanese Culture: Theological Themes in Shusaku Endō's Literary Works* (Boston: Brill, 2008), 93–137. For Endō's struggles with questions of ethnic identity and universalism, see Masamichi Inoue, "Reclaiming the Universal: Intercultural Subjectivity in the Life and Work of Endō Shusaku," *Southeast Review of Asian Studies* 34, no. 12 (2012): 153–70. For Endō's reference to an "ill-fitting suit," see p. 157.

30. For an account of Ferreira's life, see Hubert Cieslik, SJ, "The Case of Christovão Ferreira," *Monumenta Nipponica* 29, no. 1 (1974): 1–54.

31. Endō Shūsaku, *The Golden Country: A Play about Christian Martyrs in Japan*, trans. Francis Mathy, SJ (1970; repr., Singapore: Tuttle Publishing, 2003), 127 and 70, respectively.

32. This is the basic contention of Jurgis Elisonas [George Elison] in his *Deus Destroyed: The Image of Christianity in Early Modern Japan* (Cambridge, MA: Harvard University Press, 1991).

33. Besides Elisonas's work cited previously, for an analysis of anti-Christian

literature, see Kiri Paramore, *Ideology and Christianity in Japan* (New York: Routledge, 2009).

34. For an introduction to the history of this community, see Stephen Turnbull, *The Kakure Kirishitan of Japan: A Study of Their Development, Beliefs and Rituals to the Present Day* (London: RoutledgeCurzon, 1998); and Miyazaki Kentarō, "The Kakure Kirishitan Tradition," in *The Handbook of Christianity in Japan*, ed. Mark R. Mullins (Boston: Brill, 2003), 19–34. For the relatively recent discovery of secret texts used by the "Hidden Christians," see Christal Whelan, trans., *The Beginning of Heaven and Earth: The Sacred Book of Japan's Hidden Christians* (Honolulu: University of Hawai'i Press, 1996).

35. For a discussion of objections to religious freedom and how it was eventually incorporated into Japanese law during the Meiji era, see Helen Hardacre, *Shintō and the State, 1868–1988* (Princeton, NJ: Princeton University Press, 1989), 114–32.

36. For an overview, see Joseph W. Esherick, *The Origins of the Boxer Uprising* (Berkeley: University of California Press, 1987); and Victor Purcell, *The Boxer Uprising: A Background Study* (1963; repr., Cambridge: Cambridge University Press, 2010).

37. For the case of Japan, see Mark R. Mullins, "Between Inculturation and Globalization: The Situation of Catholicism in Contemporary Japanese Society," in *Xavier's Legacies: Catholicism in Modern Japanese Culture*, ed. Kevin M. Doak (Vancouver: University of British Columbia Press, 2011), 169–92.

2

JESUIT INTELLECTUAL PRACTICE IN EARLY MODERNITY
The Pan-Asian Argument against Rebirth

FRANCIS X. CLOONEY, SJ

To shed light on the place of the Society of Jesus in early modernity's era of globalization, this chapter reflects on some sixteenth- to eighteenth-century Jesuit critiques of rebirth (reincarnation, metempsychosis), drawing examples from the Japanese, Chinese, and Indian contexts.[1] The critiques themselves are not surprising, given the important differences between Christian and Asian views of life, death, and the possibility of rebirth and the long, mainstream Christian rejection of rebirth back to the early days of Christianity. Nor is the very idea of arguing matters of religious import, given the Jesuit embrace of the old Christian tradition of apologetics and similar commitments to argument on religious matters in Hindu and Buddhist Asia. What is notable, however, is the consistency of the Jesuit critique in several Asian cultures during the sixteenth through eighteenth centuries and the priority placed upon this issue.

It is difficult to determine how the common features in the Jesuit critique came about—perhaps by common training, or by the influence of one generation of Jesuits on the next, or by simply recognizing a topic objectively important across Asia—and this chapter does not answer the historical questions. However, within the constraints of a common topic, we can observe a shift over time, from direct discourse—arguments with Buddhists and Hindus about rebirth—to an inquiry among Europeans, a semblance of early Indology, regarding the Asian belief in rebirth that was driven by curiosity about the origins of a belief that some Greeks and many Asians seem to have shared. There is much evidence, particularly here, to exemplify the pan-Asian Jesuit mode and strategy of thinking and communicating. Jesuit missionary work in Asia included an intellectual program of teaching, translation, interpretation, and, as is stressed here, robust and strategic intellectual argument.

We see a Jesuit search for a vocabulary and body of concepts that would work in the various cultures and that would travel across Asia, impressing the same themes on the audiences in each case. Essential to the argumentation and to its portability is the turn to philosophy along with strategies on the foregrounding and backgrounding of Christian faith. They assume that there is not only intelligibility and room for conversation and debate across religious and cultural lines but also a real meaning to "the human" that has value across cultural and religious divides and can be appealed to as an ideal. Humans are possessed of freedom and are therefore charged with moral responsibility. Thus the inequities of the human condition can be made sense of in light of God's providence and justice without appeals to rebirth, fate, or other explanations proffered in Asian cultures and religions. What is learned from texts and what is learned from social observation are mutually confirming. As proposed such points, however valid and useful, are also Western intellectual values that as such do not, or need not be assumed to, fit easily into the Asian religious frame. For the purposes of this chapter, the key question is, what does the pan-Asian Jesuit discourse on rebirth tell us about the global religious and intellectual contribution of the Jesuits in early modernity and at the dawning of the new global culture?

This vigorous apologetic, with all its strengths and weaknesses, is intrinsic to whatever larger story we may wish to tell about the Jesuits' role in and contribution to globalization in early modernity. Consideration of rebirth and Jesuit reactions to the belief as they construed it illumines distinctive features of the early Jesuit intellectual encounter with religious Asia and the intellectual practices by which the Jesuits crafted a broad, intellectually robust discourse by which to argue against core Hindu and Buddhist beliefs, assumptions deeply settled within a variety of Asian cultures. The Jesuits' argument against rebirth makes very clear not only the real measure of their resolve and capacity to engage a variety of new cultures but also the limits on how far they reached in understanding beliefs and ideas so deeply different from their own. Like other European intellectual enterprises in early modernity, apologetics against rebirth took the Jesuits far in the minds and hearts of Asian cultures but not as far as a truly universal religious rationality or any eventual consensus on the disputed matters. Reviewing this philosophical-religious argument enables us to consider more broadly the possibilities of the overall Jesuit engagement with the religious cultures of Asia and the limits of that intellectual reach.

In examining it, we can see what happens when an orthodoxy-inspired apologetic worked out across a wide geographical area is brought into conversation with specific and substantive views from another religious tradition.

Here I propose some hypotheses concerning the Jesuit critique of the Asian cultures' view of rebirth and then illustrate them by way of examples.[2] First the Jesuit critique is couched in philosophical terms, premised on the notion that any reasoning person can argue the question of the soul's fate after death and simply by clear thinking come to conclusions on whether multiple births occur.

Second, and consequently, no reference to the Bible or Christian faith is required to make the argument against rebirth. Thus there is entirely lacking, in the examples that follow, any mention of the positive Christian doctrines related to the salvific death of Christ, Christ's dying once for all, the linear nature of salvation history, and so on. (Whether these Jesuit philosophical views presuppose a Christian worldview, couched here in philosophical terms, is another issue.)

Third, we can nevertheless glimpse in these Jesuit materials how the presumption of one birth only and the rejection of rebirth are woven into the normative Christian exposition of reality along with presuppositions about freedom and responsibility, God's justice, and the meaningfulness of human situation in the body. Similarly we may presume an implicit affirmation of rebirth is woven into Hinduism and Buddhism and broadly understood.

Fourth, this instance of interreligious argument uncovers for us the negative aspects of this ambitious Jesuit project of persuasion and conversion by means of argument. While apologetics is a venerable tradition, these early modern examples were novel applications. Unlike Christian apologists in the early Church, the Jesuits were newcomers to the cultures they critiqued, and they knew parts but not the whole as vast portions of Asian religions and cultures were yet to be understood by any European; yet still they criticized key ideas without hesitation. While they did target rebirth as central to the larger matrices of Hindu and Buddhist thought—such that the collapse of confidence in rebirth would lead to a collapse of the network of related ideas—I suggest that they did not fully anticipate how their arguments, insofar as they succeeded, would impact the entire web of values underlying these old and integral Asian ways of being. Seeking to take apart a key element in the edifice of pagan religiosity, the Jesuits were also dividing continuities—between animals and humans, the past and present—that had been taken for granted. Their attack on rebirth spread along with other modes of European intrusion on Asian cultures. When intellectual—as well as political and military, economic and cultural—forces suddenly confronted religious intellectuals, they neither expected this attack nor had ready at hand counterarguments or even proper formulations of the views and values they held or were charged with holding. Rebirth, however pervasive, had not been heavily discussed and thematized in premodern Asia. While we must appreciate the conscious efforts of many Jesuits to distance themselves from colonial power, we must also candidly admit that those cultures receiving unexpected and largely uninvited visitors from the West may not have been able to discern the Jesuits as qualitatively different from the soldiers and merchants.

The Origins of the Jesuit Argument against Rebirth

Before turning to our four hypotheses, let us recall the beginning of the Jesuit apologetic. As with many currents of Jesuit intellectual tradition, the Jesuit argument against rebirth can be traced to the first Jesuits and particularly in this case to Francis Xavier (1506–52), as reported by Fernão Mendes Pinto (1509–83), an intrepid Portuguese traveler to East Asia who wrote a vivid account of his travels. Around 1548 Francis, who had been the first Jesuit in India and had pioneered the mission in Japan, encountered a Buddhist monk (bonze) in the court of a Japanese noble. As Pinto recounts, the bonze insisted that they had met before. When Xavier insisted they had not, the bonze complained to his colleagues, "There is very little to be accomplished here since, after buying and selling with me ninety or a hundred times, he says he does not know me, which means that we cannot expect him to answer our other questions very much to the point." The bonze pressed the point that, in a previous life, Xavier had sold him silk in the town of Frenojama. Finally Xavier responded in kind to show how implausible the bonze's position was. In Pinto's words:

> Then, after paying him due respect, [Xavier] turned to the bonze and asked him how old he was. "Fifty-two," he replied. "Well then," retorted the father, "if you are only fifty-two years old, how could you have possibly been a merchant and bought merchandise from me fifteen hundred years ago? Also, since Japan has been populated for only six hundred years, as you all publicly proclaim, how can it be that fifteen hundred years ago you were a merchant in Frenojama, which at that time, as it would appear, must have been uninhabited land?"

The bonze did not relent but insisted, now giving a fuller creed of rebirth. He maintained that the world is beginningless and endless, and so too humans, who pass from body to body throughout the ages, the specifics depending on natural conditions, "as is plain to see when we are reborn of our mothers, either as males or females, depending on the conjunction of the moon at the time they bring us forth; and after we have been born here into the world, we undergo in succession a variety of these changes to which death holds us subject, due to the weak nature of which we are composed." It was Xavier's fault, he added, if he did not remember his previous births. In turn Xavier strove to demolish the bonze's "false argumentation," "by destroying it three times with words and reasons so clear and obvious, and by means of comparisons so appropriate and natural." Xavier's arguments turned out to be effective but yet unfruitful. The bonze was "left at a loss for words," but he "would not budge from his false position, so as not to lose the reputation and high regard which he thought everyone had for him."[3]

Unfortunately we are not told more of Xavier's "words and reasons so clear and obvious" and "comparisons so appropriate and natural." It is telling that Pinto, though summarizing the bonze's points, does not feel the need to give Xavier's arguments. Perhaps it is because in his mind they were obvious, self-evident to any reasonable person? We can also wonder how it is that the bonze's apparent defeat was accompanied by his resistance to making any admission of error. Was it attributable only to his concern for his reputation or also to the possibility that at another level the arguments did not touch his core beliefs and create a situation in which giving up on the idea of rebirth was the inevitable conclusion? How far could Xavier's quick and sharp comments, presumably through an interpreter, have actually reached into the psyche and heart of a learned Buddhist monk? Had arguments that could travel globally been found, or was the success more limited than Xavier and Pinto might have hoped?

In any case the Jesuit confrontation with rebirth had begun, and from the time of Francis Xavier on, the Asian religious theory of rebirth held the attention of Jesuit missionary scholars across Asia during the sixteenth to eighteenth centuries. I recently examined some of the early Jesuit views of rebirth, with a rather broad sweep of figures across Asia in the sixteenth to eighteenth centuries representing a classic mode of apologetics: Francis Xavier in India and Japan, Alessandro Valignano (1539–1606) in Japan, Matteo Ricci (1552–1610) in China, Alexandre de Rhodes (1591–1660) in Vietnam, Ippolito Desideri (1684–1733) in Tibet, and Giacomo Fenicio (1558–1632), Roberto de Nobili (1577–1656), and Jean Venance Bouchet (1655–1732) in India.[4] To give a brief feel for the arguments, I introduce here four Jesuits from the larger body of my research: Valignano, Ricci, de Nobili, and Bouchet. At the end of the chapter I refer more briefly to several nineteenth- and twentieth-century figures to indicate ways in which we might think about the early modern legacy for the Society's development after its suppression in 1773 and its reestablishment in 1814.

Alessandro Valignano in Japan

Alessandro Valignano's Japanese catechism, *Catechismus Christianae fidei*, is both a mix of positive instruction in Christian doctrine and its underpinnings and a critique of views that are incompatible. Valignano took up rebirth in chapter 4, as one of three "external" (exoteric) doctrines of Buddhism: Spirits (*kami* and *hotoke*) bestow blessings in this life and the next; humans are transformed into hotoke and, after death, experience paradises of material pleasures; and there is "the transmigration of souls and final redemption by observance of the laws of Shaka and Amida."[5] Of the last doctrine, Valignano then proposed five major criticisms, all pertaining to the relationship of the soul and the body. First, the notion that human souls could migrate into demonic or animal forms shows ignorance of human as well as divine truths (with the emphasis here on the former category). The soul is the substantial form of its body, and the relationship is unique to the human species; therefore, human souls cannot enter into a relationship with demonic or animal bodies. Second, no one can rationally hold that demons, animals, and humans have the same nature. Third, if material bodies are to be joined with spiritual souls, such bodies must be prepared by certain preparations and affections. Since animals and humans have different affections and qualities, an animal body could not be made adequate to a human soul. Fourth, animal souls are material, coming into being and perishing, and for all their activities require the animal body. Human souls are immortal and, not depending on the body for their higher functions, cannot be thought of as bound to such bodies. Fifth, whereas the human soul's intellective and appetitive functions do not need the material body, in animals these faculties do depend on bodies. Valignano concludes firmly, while appealing to the good sense of the educated Japanese, "Rebirth is therefore a doctrine that cannot be supported; it is false, inept, ridiculous, full of ignorance, and thus opposed by all learned Japanese."[6]

Since Valignano's arguments in fact already express many features recurring in the later Jesuit critiques of rebirth, I wish to comment briefly here on the style of such arguments. First, Valignano gives the impression of due diligence, seeking to get straight the arguments before critiquing them. In this effort his work reminds us of the impressive learning of the early Jesuit missionary scholars. Second, he clearly has no doubts regarding whether that rationality is universal and sufficiently common in form for him to claim that what he finds unreasonable is unreasonable also for the Japanese. Third, he has no patience with discourses that dissolve what he assumes to be the radical differences between animals and humans, and he is not sympathetic to views supportive of a real, even higher intelligence in animals. The difference between animals and humans is for him non-negotiable, whatever a Buddhist might think. Fourth, and although his arguments are couched in philosophical terms, he has no qualms about presenting the soul as having a beginning but no end. This point seems most easily to be taken as an idea arising in the Christian faith. Insofar as Hindus and Buddhists argued the doctrine of the soul, they seemed to agree that what has a beginning must have an end; only what is beginningless can also be endless. Last, if we accept the claim that the "learned Japanese" opposed the notion of rebirth, we must then wonder who is the audience for his critique. Surely not "the unlearned Japanese," to whom such elaborate arguments would seem abstruse. If the educated class is being distinguished from the monks, then the role of reasoning about rebirth in the discourse of those monks would have to be sorted out before we could conclude that a defeat in debate would mean the abandonment of the defeated belief.

While all these points require further consideration, together they point to questions we cannot avoid facing regarding the Jesuit intellectual contribution to early modern globalization: Was the spread of Jesuit learning in Asia too fast? Did the move to argument and polemic too greatly outstrip their setting down deeper cultural roots? We admire Valignano and his heirs for the speed and robustness of their learning and cannot imagine how they learned so much so quickly. But we might also hesitate regarding that speed, as it may have left Valignano ill-attuned to Asian views of the self, of humans and animals, and of the role of popular beliefs in the overall well-being of a religion.

Matteo Ricci in China

Matteo Ricci's *The True Meaning of the Lord of Heaven* offers similar arguments on reincarnation. This is unsurprising since Ricci surely knew of Valignano's work. The relevant section of the *True Meaning* is chapter 5, "Refutation of False Teachings Concerning Reincarnation in the Six Directions and the Taking of Life, and an Explanation of the True Meaning of Fasting." In turn, it is part of a longer exposition that reaches from chapter 3 to chapter 7 on human nature, the distinction of humans from both animals and God, and the obligations on humans to act in a way that leads to salvation rather than hell.[7] As free beings, humans have the freedom to make choices in this life that determine their destiny. Contrary to this, rebirth is a dangerous error because it drains such choices of ultimate value. When any given birth is cast as a matter of fate—this life is the result of a previous but unremembered life—then moral choices become impossible.

Chapter 5 critiques the belief by a series of arguments. First, no one remembers previous lives; apparent memories are due merely to the devil's trickery. Second, there is no philosophical justification for imagining that humans shift into animal bodies. Third, rebirth neglects differences among the three kinds of souls—vegetative, animal, and human—and thus mistakenly assumes that a human soul can move from a human body in one birth to an animal or plant body in another. Fourth, even were our given bodies the result of rebirth, it would hardly be a punishment for a lascivious person to descend into an animal body, for he or she could all the more shamelessly indulge in animal pleasures there. Fifth, heaven and hell are not finite spaces that could become filled up with souls of the deceased; thus, appealing to rebirth to resolve the issue of "space limitations after death" is unnecessary. Like Valignano, Ricci did not appeal to the Bible or Christian doctrine to explain or defend his position. By reason alone, Ricci shows, to his own satisfaction, that belief in rebirth is untenable, is an error that is harmful in itself, and, we presume, is a block to a proper apprehension of the truth about human nature.

We may again ask, however, whether the arguments, even if admired and linked to the respected earlier arguments of Valignano's, were really or only notionally attuned to Chinese ways of talking about such matters. Was such discourse a good example of successful "globalized" or "globalizing" communication? Or was it rather the dissemination of arguments better understood and more admired by the Jesuits than by the intended recipients?

Roberto de Nobili and Jean Bouchet in India

Roberto de Nobili's several works attacking rebirth show his deep interest in the endeavor. He addresses the theme no fewer than five times, in book chapters and then by way of a whole treatise. For this discussion, the brief treatise *Jnanopadesam* (Teaching of knowledge) may be taken as exemplary of his approach.[8] This small work condenses the first three parts of de Nobili's large *Jnanopadesam* (Catechism), and here too context is helpful. Its seventh chapter is about the creation of the "first mother" and "first father," their sin, and the resultant original sin (though these are stated without any biblical reference). The ninth chapter indicates the disposition of humans to sin; the rise, after the great flood (itself caused by human sin), of all kinds of erroneous religions; the possibility of the forgiveness of sins; and the value of instruction in the Ten Commandments. The intervening eighth chapter, devoid even of implied biblical or Christian references, critiques rebirth as a competing viewpoint that must be ruled out if further beneficial teachings are to follow. Only if there is freedom and responsibility will the subsequently mentioned obedience to the commandments take on its real force.

The eighth chapter itself opens with comments on the nature of the self as eternal but not beginningless, on the three kinds of souls—vegetative, animal, human—and on the impossibility of moving back and forth from one kind of body to another. There is no need for a theory of rebirth, and in any case such a theory cannot be reasonably sustained for many reasons. First, differences of high and low, diversity in health and happiness, wealth and power, and so on, are not punishments and rewards from previous lives; rather, it is God who is most often rewarding and punishing good and evil in this very life and after it. Second, the macrocosm (the universe) and the microcosm (each human being) both justly and necessarily include variety, for an entirely uniform world or a body without different parts could not function. Differences are natural and not a problem to be explained. Third, the differences of rich and poor, sick and healthy, and so forth, are not entirely bad, because they place people in situations where they are to help one another, and such occasions for charity are for the good of all. Fourth, it would not be fair were the body in this life to suffer for crimes the soul committed in a different body in a previous life. Fifth, there is no fate ("writing on the forehead"), as is popularly believed. If there were, then punishing people, now or later, would be unjust; fated to act in a certain way, people could hardly be held responsible for their actions. In his large *Jnanopadesam*, de Nobili proceeds to teach the full range of Catholic orthodox positions. In his view his critique of rebirth, and its inadequacy to the question of theodicy in particular, serves as a necessary background that clears the way for that orthodoxy.

While developed in terms not identical with those used by Valignano and Ricci, de Nobili's arguments proceed along the same lines.[9] He does not step back and explain why the topic is of such interest to him, but his preoccupation with it suggests again a Jesuit religious culture, now reiterated globally, in which it is possible, necessary, and valuable to debate matters of faith even while couching them in philosophical terms. Nevertheless, even as we observe the power of his arguments, we may still wonder about their intrusiveness in a south Indian religious culture that, while accepting laws of cause and effect, argued differently the consequences of that logic. So too south Indians had, and still have, particular views about the relationship of the past and present, human identity, and the relationship of humans and other forms of living existence. Singling out rebirth as a topic for debate may legitimately mark the part standing in for the whole, or it may rather be the part has been untimely removed from the full matrix of Hindu religious ideas. Since we have no reports on how the Hindu community responded to de Nobili's thought, we cannot really assess the pertinence and limitations of his arguments as received by learned south Indians and, consequently, must again wonder whether his earnest writings against rebirth were part of a successful globalization about the discourse on religion or instances of imports ahead of their time and to some extent detrimental.

Our fourth example affirms continuity in the Jesuit argument but also suggests a shift that occurs in light of Europe's, and the Jesuits', shifting interests in the eighteenth century. Shapers of Europe's knowledge of Asia, the Jesuits were also carried along by changes in that knowledge and began to use their undeniable learning in response to new questions arising outside the mission fields. Jean Venance Bouchet, working in south India a century after de Nobili, wrote a long letter in French (and thus for a European and not an Indian audience) that offered an overall exposition of rebirth.[10] In the first part he pondered the origins of the doctrine, debating whether the Greeks gave the idea to India or the Indians to Greece. In the second part he focused on the Indian teaching, drawing on popular and textual examples. Meticulous in detail, he was also clearly convinced that the Hindus had no coherent foundations on which to ground their belief in rebirth.

In the third part apologetics finally comes to the fore; here Bouchet reports on how he used the information he so meticulously reports. Popular Indian texts and ideas contradict themselves, thus undercutting belief in rebirth from within, "and so, in order to disabuse them entirely of a system that is both impious and ridiculous, we have recourse to reasons drawn from their own doctrine, their usage, and their maxims. These are the reasons by which one can make them feel the contradictions into which they have fallen, which confuse them and which constrain them from recognizing the absurdity of their beliefs."[11] Bouchet then listed five of the many internal contradictions in which he found his Brahmin interlocutors to be entangled.[12] He introduced each by summarizing what he took to be the Hindu view of the matter, claiming then to trip up his interlocutors with subsequent questions they could not answer. The result, he hoped, was that they would come to realize that their religion was a false one, based on an indefensible belief in rebirth. He ends the letter with hope regarding the conversions to come. Arguments against rebirth do not draw explicitly on

Christian doctrine, but they are expected to result in openness to Christian orthodox positions.[13]

Bouchet's approach in this letter is novel in several ways. Certainly he has a more specific grasp of a wider array of Puranic sources and draws on particular texts, which he names, such as the *Padma Purana* and *Brahma Purana*. But his discourse is *about* the Indian views on the subject and in a letter back home that is not even stylized as an address directed *to* Indians. He does allude to arguments with Brahmin defenders of rebirth, but he is primarily using his knowledge of and from India to address issues arising in the European context, in particular seeking to sort out the connection between Indian and Greek views on rebirth.[14] The missionary argument with learned Hindus was giving way to an incipient Indological discourse among learned Europeans about India. Given his erudition and honest effort to learn as much as possible about the Hindu views of rebirth, we cannot dismiss his apologetic as merely negative. And yet while retortion is a strategy that might be imagined to work in any reasoned, critical context—a pan-Asian Jesuit rhetorical tool that confounds the opponent—we cannot speculate on how his arguments came across to any given group of learned Brahmins or whether those who were confounded by them recognized any imperative to revise or drop fundamental beliefs given their inability to answer Bouchet's arguments. Again at issue is the quality of a globalizing intellectuality—that is, whether this manner of ideas and arguments deployed across Asia can be assessed as contributing successfully to a viable global network of ideas or whether it is rather to be judged as detrimental because it developed too quickly, too far removed from the realities of religion on the ground, and weighted with too many expectations regarding the success to which a debate would lead.

Developments in the Nineteenth and Twentieth Centuries

The story of the Jesuits and rebirth does not end with the suppression of the Jesuits in 1773, so a complementary step is to compare and contrast the intellectual contribution of the pre-suppression Jesuits in Asia with how they approached the same topic after the Society's reestablishment in 1814. The materials available for this purpose seem to be rather limited, however; further research is required. Nevertheless, for this work, we might look profitably to Joseph Bertrand (1801–84), a leading figure in the first decades of that return.

Here I give one example from his writing, his June 1844 letter to Gustave de Ravignan. Couched as a "response to questions posed regarding the religion of the Hindus" (translations from the French are my own),

Bertrand's main purpose is not primarily to provide information about the Hindus. Though it is descriptive of features of Hindu religion and tradition and is also critical, the letter is more basically a diatribe against Europeans enchanted with Hinduism. He mentions two common errors shared by Hindus, Buddhists, and Jains—"the absurd doctrine of pantheism" and rebirth. Hindus see the truths about creation and original sin, and the punishments and opportunities for repentance offered by God, only "from afar and through a fog." They are "poorly combined under the influence of a foolish imagination," and together "they produce the second dogma," that of "metempsychosis." Bertrand shows no interest in arguing with Hindus and gives the impression that such follies can hardly be repaired:

> I could pursue the progress of this alteration of truth and traditional dogmas, by reason—or folly—of man, blind slave of passions and the senses, taking for his guide only the dreams of his sick imagination, rolling from depth to depth along the path of the ridiculous and the absurd. But to what end? Once man is launched on this path, there is no reason to search through his errors. In light of these prodigies of human aberration, the disgust and contempt which they inspire give way only to a feeling of profound compassion for these erring spirits (*génies*) and the people they have ruined.[15]

For example:

> The Brahmins themselves deep down stick to the belief of the crowd, although they know well that the various accounts which they offer of the actions of the gods are impostures. We know well—for they will tell you, when you push them to the limit—that these are reveries invented to entertain the people. But they will not, in practice and in their souls, be any less the stupid worshippers of these idols, of Sokker (Sokanatha), of this Minaksi to whom they render these absurdities and infamies. Sometimes they manage to recognize that the divinity is one, but they do not give themselves over to these symbolic interpretations. It is possible to find some who profess these ideas. But to say that such is the religious system of the Hindus! No, it is not so! It would be better to say that the system of Dupuis is the religion of France.[16]

He says nothing more on rebirth, instead turning next to his own Christian countrymen: They deserve no compassion as they were born in the "bosom of truth." They should know better but are still enraptured by the follies of Indian ideas. The point of the letter is its polemic against Europeans who romanticize Hinduism; it suffices to identify and highlight errors.

A second nineteenth-century example might be drawn from the writings of Augustus Thébaud (1807–85), even if this American Jesuit did not work in Asia or even primarily with Asian religions. (He also served, for example, as the first Jesuit president of what is now Fordham University.) His view of Hinduism is negative, but his real and deeper premise pertains to a theory of decline from the ancient natural wisdom that the Indians (and all others) possessed in the beginning, before errors such as rebirth came to be.

In his chapter on Hinduism (or the "aboriginal religion in Hindostan"), after a brief look at the Katha Upaniṣad, Thébaud writes,

> Here, with an admirable analysis of the soul's faculties, and of the relations of the soul and body, truly worthy of the most pure primitive doctrines, we see the beginning of two great aberrations, which became the unfortunate cause of the deviation of subsequent philosophy, and the ruin of the primeval true religion. These two aberrations were: the transmigrations of the soul, and its absorption in Brahman. This was the passage from monotheism to pantheism, from which was to issue the subsequent idolatry.

He argued that there is no evidence of rebirth in the oldest scriptures, such as the Rig Veda, but then the Indian mind, lacking "a strong and exterior restraint," went astray from the truth to deviations, to "positive, unmitigated error." Like Bertrand, Thébaud pairs pantheism and rebirth as cardinal errors. Bertrand treated first pantheism and then rebirth, but here Thébaud sees the error of rebirth as preceding and preparing the way for that mistaken ideal of absorption into Brahman, since absorption is seemingly the only way beyond the cycle of rebirths. Rebirth is a downfall from the proper teaching on original sin and its consequences: "Expiation was the great moral law revealed even in Paradise, when man had to leave it. It took in Hindostan the form of the wanderings of souls from bodies to bodies, until first the idea of existence became a burden, and the wish arose to be absorbed in God, until at last philosophy should come to turn it into positive annihilation—nirvana."[17]

My hypothesis on the shift occurring in the post-reestablishment period—a hypothesis that, of course, can hardly be proven by just two examples—is that the nineteenth century witnessed an inward turn in Jesuit Indology, such as it was. It was repatriated to its European roots and answered a European set of intellectual as well as religious concerns. One needs then to wait for the work of the Jesuits in Kolkata (Calcutta) in the first half of the twentieth century, it seems, for new interest in the topic, and this time the Jesuits from the West made an effort to look for a common ground and a more constructive approach to rebirth. One might take a step further and explore twentieth-century Jesuit views, beginning with the work of William Wallace of Ireland (1863–1922) and Pierre Johanns of Luxembourg (1882–1955), and then other Jesuit scholars in Kolkata.

Wallace's work remains largely unpublished except for his extraordinary *From Evangelical to Catholic by Way of the East*, in which he makes clear his indebtedness to his study of Hinduism as one of the causes of his conversion to Roman Catholicism. In a chapter of one of his unpublished typescripts preserved in the Goethals Library in Kolkata, however, he offers a fair summary of the Hindu doctrine of rebirth, evidently with the purpose simply of making a correct and sympathetic understanding of it available.[18]

Johanns, a more published and better-known figure, was deeply engaged in the study of Hinduism and in a different manner than that of both the pre-suppression and the nineteenth-century Jesuits. In *To Christ through the Vedanta*, for instance, Johanns considered karma as transmigration in two consecutive chapters of his treatment of twelfth-century Hindu theologian Ramanuja: "Karma—Avidya—Samsara" (chapter 22) and "Karma and God" (chapter 23). In chapter 22, while treating the problem of the origins of evil, Johanns considered Plato's idea that the descent into matter is the cause of degradation, a decline that can be identified with transmigration. He notes that Ramanuja rejects the implication that the soul can fail and sin but only by offering his own unsatisfying thesis: "They have ascribed the present embodiment to the karma of a former life, and again the embodiment of the former life to the karma of a former one, and so on without end, so that they can explain any given embodiment of the series" while, unfortunately, "the series itself remains unexplained and unexplainable." Only when immersed in matter can the soul sin, but it is immersed in matter only after it has sinned, presumably in a past life. Chapter 23 begins with Johanns's insistence that the Hindu doctrine of samsara—that is, repeated implication in matter—is not the same as the Platonic theory of transmigration. Ramanuja rightly avoids the Platonic theory, Johanns says, but at the cost of being unable to explain how the soul becomes implicated in the first place: "Ramanuja cannot explain [sin's beginning], for, according to him, *the sin that connects with matter presupposes* (not only chronologically but also ontologically) *that very connection*."[19]

Yet at this point Johanns takes a turn that none of our earlier Jesuits would have taken: "The same conception, as is evident, brings also Ramanuja very near to the Christian view of sin, as the willful preferment of our selfish temporary pleasure to the will of God and to the ultimate happiness of both ourselves and the world. But we must insist on the resemblance between Ramanuja's theory of karma and the Christian doctrine of retribution."[20] Even if Johanns does not, in my judgment, fully clarify his position here, clearly he has taken the discussion in a new direction by observing that Ramanuja, even while adhering to a particularly theological version of the doctrine of rebirth, is actually thereby closer to and not further from the Christian position on sin and responsibility. A new era in the Western Jesuit discourse on rebirth had begun.[21]

Conclusion

Tracing the critique of rebirth as taken up by early Jesuit missionaries in Asia demonstrates a great confidence in the power of philosophical argumentation, eschewing explicit references to Christian faith with the aim of giving their arguments universal appeal. The critique of rebirth represents a pan-Asian discourse reaching over three centuries and a wide portion of Asia that reverberated into the nineteenth and twentieth centuries. My thesis is that tracing this discourse informs us, in a small but nonetheless reliable manner, about the place and role of the Jesuit intellectuals in a globalizing early modernity. We see their great confidence in the universality of reason and the power of philosophical argumentation. They wanted to make the case for views conformed to Christian faith without drawing on the authority of Christian faith to make their arguments. They therefore strove for a kind of philosophical detachment—ideas argued for their own sake—for the purpose of their larger missionary goal.

The sketch of key moments in the early Jesuits' critique of rebirth illustrates Jesuit argumentativeness, insistence on logical consistency, and confidence in the role of reason as the currency of exchange in global communication. For the sake of their critique, the Jesuits had to reify fluid notions of rebirth, spelling out fully positions only implicit in popular beliefs. Rebirth had first to be formulated as doctrine in order to then be criticized as bad doctrine; thus the Jesuits formalized the heterodoxy they wished to criticize. They converted oral and occasionally written Asian views, thematized or popular and dispersed; recast them as rational and doctrinal assertions claiming (even if lacking) internal consistency; and thus opened them to criticism by all reasoning persons in the new global context. That we seem not to have any record of Hindu rejoinders to the Jesuit criticisms follows logically from the Jesuit approach: If the Hindu positions had not been thematized by Hindus as arguable philosophical positions, then neither should we expect Hindu intellectuals to respond in the genre of argument the Jesuits wanted. Orthodoxy and its philosophical supports had their own style, and one effective Hindu response was simply to forgo that style and its propositional language.

Satisfied that their positions were philosophically sound and impossible to counter, the Jesuits at least hoped strongly that Hindus and Buddhists, their key belief in rebirth shattered, would become intellectually open to Christianity. But this hope seems to have been in reality largely unachieved. We have little or no evidence of Buddhists and Hindus converting due to the Jesuits' attack on rebirth, and it seems that Christian orthodoxy gained less than might have been expected from their efforts. Rebirth, as a truth imbedded in Hindu and Buddhist life, was part of a larger religious whole that as a totality was more resilient than the Jesuits had anticipated.

That the Jesuits invested greatly in argument and argued vigorously should not surprise us. Christian apologetics had many precedents in its prior history. But it is not trivial to notice that in the early modern phase of globalization, these Jesuits were applying their methods in new cultures and foreign languages, having on short notice fixed upon how to argue and what to say, in Japan and China, Vietnam and Tibet, and India. It may have been all too quick. Nor can we simply stand bemused by their aggressive reasoning. While we should rightly point to the enormous positive contributions of the early Jesuits to global interreligious learning, we ought not to minimize the limitations of their way of proceeding. Aside from the more obvious problems and damages accruing to colonialism and its imposition of the West upon the East—problems from which the Society of Jesus can never be entirely exonerated—less visible detriments also resulted from intellectual colonialism. The logic of the Jesuit attack on rebirth expressed modernity's onslaught against a traditional view of the interconnectedness of beings: Animals and humans are radically different; this life cannot be imagined to be closely connected with previous lives; and the fluid and pluralistic common beliefs about life and death are reified, placed under a harsh light, and rejected. As missionary discourse contributed to the dawning of a modernization and global Westernization that rationalized the world, it also contributed to the breakdown of older ways of thinking and fed into a secularization process that would come back to haunt the Jesuits themselves. Once a harsh intellectual light is cast upon some Asian beliefs abstracted from their living contexts, it would be all the harder for the Jesuits to plead an exemption for the beliefs of the Catholic Church.

It is fair then to wonder, even apart from our due admiration for the energy and insight of these Jesuit intellectuals, whether the cross-cultural, universalizable language of religious argument they carried with them was really as transportable as they might have anticipated. Of the ideas and beliefs that are incompatible with Christian faith, by nearly all accounts, rebirth is surely one of them. But we can hardly avoid the sense that the Jesuits, for all their intellectual impressiveness, accomplished less in their pan-Asian argument against rebirth than they had hoped. In the end they may have just been arguing with themselves.

Notes

1. For simplicity and except when quoting sources, I use "rebirth" to stand in for the related terms "reincarnation," "transmigration," and "metempsychosis."

2. There is much work to be done on the continuity and development of the Jesuit views on rebirth, particularly regarding whether the earlier Jesuit writings on the topic, in Japan and China, influenced the later writings in India and Tibet. I am also not taking on two important genealogical projects that require attention: first, cataloguing the European and indigenous Asian sources utilized by the Jesuits in their arguments and, second, tracing the lineage of a pan-Asian Jesuit conversation regarding whether and how there was some or much continuity from Valignano to Ricci and de Nobili to Gaston-Laurent Coeurdoux and beyond in the case against rebirth. Nor do I seek to discover and review indigenous rejoinders to the missionary polemic against rebirth.

3. Fernão Mendes Pinto, *The Travels of Mendes Pinto*, ed. and trans. Rebecca Catz (Chicago: University of Chicago Press, 1989), 480–81. See also Jean Venance Bouchet's eighteenth-century recollection of the same incident: "When St. Francis Xavier preached the faith in Japan, the most famous bonze of the country, finding himself with the saint in the court of the king of Bungo, spoke to him with a smug attitude: 'I don't know if you know me or, rather, if you remember me.' After recounting many extravagant scenes which one is able to see in the history of the saint's life, he added: 'Listen to me. You will hear the oracles, etc., and you will agree then we have more knowledge of things past than you, the rest of you, have of things present. You must therefore know that the world has no beginning, and that humans, properly speaking, never die; the soul simply disengages from the body where it was enclosed, and while that body rots in the ground, the soul seeks a fresh and vigorous body, in which we are reborn, sometimes in the nobler sex, sometimes in the imperfect sex, depending on the diverse constellations of the heavens and the different phases of the moon.'" In Francis X. Clooney, SJ, *Fr. Bouchet's India: An 18th Century Jesuit's Encounter with Hinduism* (Chennai: Satya Nilayam Publications, 2005), 172–73.

4. Francis X. Clooney, SJ, "The Pre-Suppression Jesuit Case against Rebirth, with Special Reference to India," in *Intercultural Encounter and the Jesuit Mission*

in South Asia (16th–18th centuries), ed. Anand Amaladass, SJ, and Ines Županov (Bangalore: Asian Trading Corporation, 2014). For a briefer form of the arguments with a new focus on the related matter of orthodoxy, see Clooney's "Arguing for Orthodoxy: Jesuit Philosophical Arguments against Rebirth in 16th–18th Century Asia," in "Christian Orthodoxy," ed. Felix Wilfred and Daniel Franklin Pilario, special issue, *Concilium* 2 (2014), 140–47.

5. I have used the 1586 Latin edition, with my own translation: Alessandro Valignano, SJ, *Catechismus Christianae Fidei in quo veritas nostrae religionis ostenditur, et sectae Iaponenses confutantur* (Lisbon: Excudebat Antonius Riberius, 1586), 81.

6. Ibid., 83–84. I also made use of the summary given in Josef Franz Schütte, *Valignano's Mission Principles for Japan*, vol. 1, *From His Appointment as Visitor until His First Departure from Japan (1573–1582)*, pt. 2, *The Solution*, trans. John J. Coyne (St. Louis: Institute of Jesuit Sources, 1985).

7. See the outline of *The True Meaning* in Matteo Ricci, *The True Meaning of the Lord of Heaven*, ed. Edward Malatesta, trans. Douglas Lancashire and Peter Hu Kuo-chen (St. Louis: Institute of Jesuit Sources, 1985), 25–31.

8. Roberto de Nobili, SJ, *Ñāṉōpatēcam: 26 piracaṅkaṅkaḷ*, ed. S. Rajamanickam (Tuttukkuti: Tamil Ilakkiya Kalakam, 1963).

9. More historical and philological study is required if we are to show that de Nobili was directly influenced in his arguments by Valignano and Ricci. We might presume that at least Valignano's Latin text was available to him, but the proof is not yet in place. Were it to turn out that there is no direct influence, that would be all the more interesting, and the intellectual culture of the Society would then seem to dispose Jesuits to "think alike" in taking up rebirth and similar issues.

10. Jean Venance Bouchet to Pierre-Daniel Huet, bishop of Avranches, 1714, in *Lettres édifiantes et curieuses, écrites des missions étrangères: Nouvelle edition*, vol. 12, *Mémoires des Indes* (Paris: J. G. Merigot le jeune, 1781), 170–255.

11. Ibid., 239.

12. Ibid., 238–48. Each point questions a particular belief. (1) If the world has no beginning, how did the cycle of rewards and punishments begin? (2) If all living persons are microcosms of the one universe, how are they all also different? (3) The rewards in this life are indulgences that in theory should be punished in a next life. (4) Does the deity Brahma or fate or the stars assign one's destiny? (5) Hindus have innumerable ways of gaining merit, so there seems to be no reason why anyone would have to be reborn. For a fuller summary of the arguments and the whole letter, see Clooney, *Fr. Bouchet's India*.

13. Ippolito Desideri, SJ (1684–1733), in *Mission to Tibet*, III.7, makes this strategic point in words that would seem to apply to the wider range of Jesuits too, even as it interestingly reports a Tibetan view as well: "The main and fundamental error from which spring all others, or better expressed, under which all the errors of the false Tibetan sect are subsumed, is the nefarious error of metempsychosis or the transmigration of souls, which the Tibetans themselves declare to be a tangled and inextricable vortex and an endless and bottomless sea

owing to the infinity of notions and fantastical difficulties of which they pretend it is composed; but, in perfect truth, it would be much more fitting to describe it as a highly intricate and inextricable labyrinth and an endless and bottomless sea owing to the vast and extremely tangled combination of errors with which that fundamental error has been blindly compounded and of which the principal and most significant are the following" (342). Desideri's overall treatment of rebirth in the *Mission* is not extensive, although it is richly intertwined with his understanding of what is distinctive to Tibetan culture and religion. Much of the treatment is descriptive and pertains to the notion of self that allows for it to have heavenly, earthly, and infernal states. In the *Mission* itself, however, he refers to his large, three-volume work in Tibetan, and in the first volume of which he refutes "the errors that make up the intricate labyrinth of belief in metempsychosis according to the system specific to this people" (192). The title of this work is, in English, "Questions to the Learned of Tibet concerning the Theory of Former Lives and Emptiness; Presented by the European Lama Called Ippolito" and is, in the view of Michael Sweet and Leonard Zwilling, the "largest and most complex of all Desideri's Tibetan works" (686n534). Even now, it is available only in the Tibetan original. All references in this note are to Ippolito Desideri, SJ, *Mission to Tibet: The Extraordinary Eighteenth-Century Account of Father Ippolito Desideri, S.J.*, ed. Leonard Zwilling, trans. Michael J. Sweet (Boston: Wisdom Publications, 2010).

14. Gaston-Laurent Coeurdoux (1691–1779), the last of the pre-Suppression figures we consider, has been amply studied by Sylvia Murr, *L'Inde philosophique entre Bossuet et Voltaire*, 2 vols. (Paris: École Française d'Extrême-Orient, 1987). His work is in continuity with scholars such as Bouchet insofar as curiosity about a topic for intellectual purposes, even apart from the practice, remains at the fore. If, from the start, the Jesuit missionary scholars balanced the gathering of knowledge and the use of that knowledge in the work of conversion—each goal serving and intensifying the other—in his work, it is the former goal, the increase of knowledge and its proper interpretation, that became the primary value and fruit of the work. We are thus moving all the closer to a more scientific knowledge dedicated to theorizing the origins and coherence of rebirth. His treatment of rebirth develops at length a comparison of Greek and Indian views, as did Bouchet but not de Nobili. But whereas Bouchet (and before him, Ricci) used this genealogy subtly to undercut the theory—as derivative, from somewhere else—Coeurdoux seems content with the more objective task of tracing the theory of rebirth to its sources and evincing a certain sympathy with the Hindu efforts to explain some of life's great and difficult mysteries from a faith perspective.

15. Joseph Bertrand, SJ, *Lettres édifiantes et curieuses de la nouvelle mission du Maduré* (Paris: J. B. Pélagaud, 1865), 1:300–301.

16. Ibid., 1:296. The Dupuis mentioned by Bertrand is probably Charles François Dupuis (1742–1829), author of the famed *Origine de Tours Les Cultes, ou la Réligion Universelle*.

17. Augustus J. Thébaud, SJ, *Gentilism: Religion Previous to Christianity* (New York: D. & J. Sadlier, 1876), 147–49.

18. I have not yet had the opportunity to study the whole typescript, and I am grateful to Felix Raj, SJ, the director of the Goethals Library, and Sunil Mondol of the library staff for making this key chapter available to me.

19. Pierre Johanns, SJ, *To Christ through the Vedanta: The Writings of Reverend P. Johanns, S.J.*, ed. Theo de Greeff (Bangalore: United Theological College, 1996), 72.

20. Ibid.

21. An additional topic, of great interest and importance, would be any historical data we can gather regarding how Asian Jesuits, in India or elsewhere, viewed rebirth, an idea that, after all, has cultural as well as theological import in Asian cultures. In this chapter, I have dealt only with Western Jesuit views of rebirth.

3

GLOBAL VISIONS IN CONTESTATION
Jesuits and Muslims in the Age of Empires

DANIEL A. MADIGAN, SJ

Much has been made of the development of a new mind-set among the Jesuit missionaries before the suppression of the Society in 1773 as they encountered new religious phenomena and sought to engage with them during the early modern phase of globalization. It is sometimes thought that the respect they came to feel for cultural and religious manifestations very different from their own eventually transformed what began as a one-way mission of Christian evangelization that assumed the exclusiveness of Christianity as "the one true religion" into a mutual intercultural and interreligious encounter that remade the missionary as much as the "native." This chapter examines that opinion more closely and focuses on the Jesuit engagement with Muslims, both in Europe and abroad, as something of an apparent exception to that principle of transformation, if indeed a principle it proves to be. It seems that with regard to Muslims, both in the pre- and post-suppression Society, Jesuits have very often shared the negative view of Islam that they inherited from the Church's long history of polemics, that they imbibed from the cultures and polities in which they lived, or indeed that they may have drawn from Ignatius's own rather ambivalent attitude toward Muslims.

The picture, however, is not uniform. A comparative study of three of the many possible figures from the early Society—Jerome Xavier (1549–1617), Bento de Góis (1562–1607), and Tirso González de Santalla (1624–1705)—can identify some of the factors at play that may have shaped their different approaches to Islam and Muslims in Europe and around the globe. It may also suggest ways in which similar elements have affected

Jesuit attitudes during successive waves of globalization since the reestablishment of the Society in 1814.

Encounters with the Mughal Empire

Of those Jesuits who went to the court of the Mughal emperors on the Indian subcontinent, Xavier and Góis are perhaps the best known, though others such as Rudolf Acquaviva and Antonio Monserrate spared no energy in the years of work that would lay a foundation for what was achieved later.[1] These figures who worked in Muslim contexts are often included in the roster of missionary legends such as Matteo Ricci, Alessandro Valignano, Ippolito Desideri, and Roberto de Nobili, and perhaps they deserve their place among them. As Francis Clooney demonstrates in chapter 2 of this volume, although the vision of those legendary figures was broad, their intellectual reach had evident limitations. In spite of their willingness to engage new cultures, their apologetics did not succeed in establishing—and convincing their interlocutors of—the validity of what they presumed to be a universal religious rationality. If those Jesuits who engaged with Hindus, Buddhists, and Confucians had difficulty, as Clooney maintains, then those who were sent among Muslims demonstrated a further shortcoming: As European Christians they were already immersed in a tradition of apologetics and polemics that had lasted almost a millennium but had achieved little success in that time.

Jerome Xavier's twenty-year mission to the Mughal court (1594–1614), which coincided with the last phase of Emperor Akbar's rule, had been prepared by two earlier Jesuit journeys. In his account of the first (1579–83), Antonio Monserrate cannot help but allow himself frequent sardonic asides about Islam and in particular about the Muslim scholars with whom the Jesuits vied for the emperor's attention and affection. Of course, he was writing his *Commentary* in 1590 with hindsight—having come to realize even during the journey that Akbar's apparent openness to conversion had not been genuine—and perhaps with a certain long-nursed bitterness, for he was finishing the account while a prisoner in Sana'a in Yemen. The *Commentary*'s translator notes that he has only slightly softened the acerbic attacks on Islam that peppered Monserrate's account without removing them altogether, because he felt that the Jesuit's evident bigotry made all the more impressive and believable whatever was positive in his description of Akbar and the Mughal court.[2]

Though the Jesuits admired Akbar as "a king of piety, integrity and prudence," they nonetheless admonished him for, among other things, having two of his sons taught by Muslim scholars: "Furthermore they warned him that some day he would be punished, because he knew well that the Musalman teaching was pernicious to the minds of men, and yet he allowed his two sons—boys of great natural ability and intellectual power—to be educated by certain old men, whose minds were filled with Muhammad."[3] They preferred to keep the education of the emperor's sons exclusively to themselves, and positions as teachers of the princes were much sought after and often granted to the Jesuits in the decades to come. Fr. Monserrate from time to time gives details of his work as a tutor to Akbar's son Murad:

> The prince's education was conducted as follows—at the beginning of each lesson he called devoutly on the names of Jesus and Mary as is the Christian custom; then he made the sign of the Cross on his forehead, face and breast; finally he paid reverence to the picture of Christ which was in his book. . . . The children were taught Christianity out of a little book of Christian doctrine and their copy-books contained pious sentiments as the examples they had to copy.[4]

One sees in their admiration for Akbar's rule and their solicitude for the education of his sons and "the children of the higher nobility" the same concern for the public good that was an essential element in the broader Jesuit commitment to education. However, at the same time, Monserrate's description shows that whatever may have been their carefully considered apologetic strategies in engaging the emperor or their Muslim opponents, in the schoolroom the Mughal youth were treated just as their Christian contemporaries in Europe were.

One does not see, however, in those Jesuits who went to the Mughal court the same kind of intellectual curiosity about religious matters that would mark the work of a Ricci or a de Nobili. They were all accomplished scholars and linguists, certainly, and keen observers. Though Monserrate's *Commentary* never reached Rome, he explained in an introductory letter to Father General Acquaviva his purpose in writing it: He wanted it to serve as a resource for the teaching of the natural history of the subcontinent, Ethiopia, and Arabia in the Society's schools. It would amplify and correct what had already been written about the history and geography of these regions in which Monserrate worked, traveled, and for a time was held captive.[5] All things considered, only a relatively small part of his work is devoted to the missionary enterprise on which they were embarked. Much of it consists of recounting the campaigns on which he accompanied the army; describing the cities, the geography, and the wildlife of the region; and documenting the political and cultural situation.

At the Mughal court, the ready answers Monserrate and Rudolf Acquaviva gave to religious questions had been the commonplaces of Christian apologetics and polemics vis-à-vis Islam for centuries. On the evidence of their own accounts, they were unable to approach the questions posed by Islam with a fresh eye. They were there to provide answers, not to ask questions. In this case, although they showed a mobility characteristic of a globalizing tendency—the objective sense of globalization, according to Frank Lechner's definition—they do not seem to have been able to escape the intellectual and theological frontiers within which they had been formed.[6] They had the opportunity at court to engage with Zoroastrians, Jains, and the still-developing Sikh tradition, yet we find they had no interest in the religious ferment of that period but only in the question of whether Akbar or his successor might formally adopt Christianity. The second mission in 1591 appears to have lacked any great desire to persevere against the consistently dashed hopes of a royal conversion and ended within a short time.

Jerome Xavier, a grandnephew of St. Francis Xavier, was the most important figure in the third mission to the Mughal court, living there from 1595 to 1614. And he was by far the most productive in terms of literary output.[7] He spent more years at court than any of his confreres and was certainly the most expert in Persian; however, one searches his works in vain for any indication that he engaged with Islam in a new way. In the dedication of his major work of apologetics—titled in its Persian form Āʾīna-i ḥaqq-numā (The Truth-revealing mirror, or perhaps The God-revealing mirror) and in its Spanish version *Fuente de Vida*—Jerome does not mince words with the emperor: "In this book we present to Your Highness the treatise on the true law that God Our Lord has revealed to the world so that humanity might be saved, and outside of which no one has salvation."[8]

The work presents itself as a dialogue among the Philosopher, the Mulla and the Father, yet it is clear that the Mulla acts only as a foil and that Islam has already been effectively dismissed as an interlocutor. The real engagement is between the Philosopher (representing Akbar), who already has a poor estimation of Islam, and the Father.[9] As was the case with his predecessors at court, Xavier was less interested in the encounter with Islam than in the attempt to win over an effectively "ex-Muslim" philosopher-king to Christianity. *Fuente de Vida* surely reflects the argumentation Xavier actually used at court, yet he could only dream of hearing from Akbar or his son Jahāngīr anything like the Philosopher's concluding speech:

I dedicate myself as a Christian and a follower of the Gospel. And I renounce from this day forward any other law. I promise to follow it and observe it all my life and to die in it. . . . Tell me what I must do and hold now that I am your disciple rather than a man who has until his old age been a teacher to so many. For I much prefer to be the disciple of a doctrine that is so elevated, so true and so powerful, than the teacher of any other, since, as the philosophers say, even the lowest of the sublime is higher than the most elevated of what is inferior.[10]

The ambiguity of the Jesuit mission to the Mughal court, observes Hugues Didier, "lies entirely in the fact that King Akbar and [his son] King Jahāngīr were more deeply interested in polemical arguments against Islam than in positive arguments in favor of Christianity."[11] Polemics the Jesuits could certainly deliver, and they were always pleased to see how well the king responded to their trouncing of their Muslim opponents in debate. We rarely hear the other side of the argument, although ʿAbdus Sattar, a longtime ally of Xavier's who had helped him greatly with some of his Persian works,[12] gives accounts of meetings in Jahāngīr's court that are quite at odds with the Jesuit version.[13] However successful the polemics may have been, the positive arguments they proposed for Christianity in the end proved unconvincing. As Clooney notes in his contribution to this volume, with regard to Jesuit arguments throughout Asia against notions of rebirth, the Jesuits themselves found their approach philosophically convincing, yet the expected conversions from Buddhism and Hinduism did not follow.

As it turns out the Jesuits were not alone in their experience of imperial favor toward religions other than Islam. It is instructive to see how similar to the Jesuit accounts of Akbar's interest in and respect for Christianity are the accounts given regarding the Parsis who went to Akbar's court. According to the very critical court chronicler ʿAbd al-Qādir Badāʾūnī, writing in 1595, the Parsi priests' explanations of the centrality of fire worship so favorably impressed the emperor that he gave orders to the same Abul Fadl whom the Jesuits considered their great ally for a sacred flame to be kept burning in the palace day and night.[14] If one also studies traditional Sikh accounts of how moved Akbar was by his visit to Guru Amar Das and by the presentations made by Sikhs at this court, a pattern begins to emerge.[15] We see how ill founded was the Jesuits' impression that their relationship to the emperor was quite particular and that Akbar and his son were on the point of conversion with most of the empire ultimately following them. In their cooler moments, they could see through the game that was being played; yet soon enough they would rise yet again to the bait.[16]

Conversions did take place, sometimes of nobles but not of the great prize Xavier and his companions sought.[17] Although they were culturally sensitive—as good sons of Ignatius, particularly sensitive to courtly culture—and although they admired Akbar, nonetheless, the theological mind-set they exhibited in Agra, Lahore, and Fatehpur Sikri was arguably little different from attitudes toward Islam that would have been found in Europe. It would be difficult to apply even to Jerome Xavier's impressive body of work Antoni Ucerler's notions of "the new Areopagus" and the "re-invention of Christianity" identified in his survey of Jesuit missions in East Asia during the early modern phase of globalization (see chapter 1).

The Journey of Bento de Góis

The famous extended journey of Bento de Góis from the western shores of the Indian subcontinent through modern-day Afghanistan to the frontiers of China provides a somewhat different example of the Jesuit approach to interreligious encounter during this period. Brother de Góis set out on his storied journey from Agra in 1602 apparently to find the answer to a question that still tantalized Europeans, though Matteo Ricci had already answered it to his own satisfaction: What was Cathay? Was it China or a different country?[18] Unfortunately Góis's diary of his five years on the road was substantially destroyed at the time of his death in 1607, so the reports written by Matteo Ricci and Fernão Guerreiro were pieced together secondhand.[19] In those letters to Rome (written to be circulated throughout the Society, as was the custom), they disguise the fact, which we know from Góis's own letters, that he undertook the journey presenting himself as a Muslim—albeit the kind of unorthodox Muslim others might well have expected to be traveling under the patronage of Akbar. Guerreiro alternatively says he went disguised as an Armenian Christian merchant—something Góis never mentions. Even as Góis passed through Lahore from Agra at the beginning of his journey, he could not go and see his Jesuit confreres because he had been ordered to maintain his disguise, which had made people think he was a descendant of Muhammad or a noble from Mecca.[20] He adds that the name Xavier gave him when he first set out was Banda 'Abdallah, a mix of Persian and Arabic that somewhat redundantly means "servant servant of God." Later he went by the name 'Abdallah 'Isawi, meaning "servant of God, follower of Jesus."[21]

This journey "in search of Cathay" should perhaps be thought of as an offshoot of the third Jesuit mission to the Mughal court and not just in the sense that reports of Christians in Cathay had reached Jerome Xavier there or that the chosen pioneer was one of the most talented and experienced of that group at court.[22] It seems possible to speculate that Xavier took the opportunity of the Cathay question to experiment with the preaching of the Gospel in a way that was not possible within the power dynamics and the political complexities of Akbar's court. Didier sees in the false report of Góis's "Armenian Christian" traveling persona a "pious lie which veils or disguises the audacity of the missionary aim of the man who had sent and formed Bento de Góis, Jerome Xavier: to proclaim Jesus Christ in a language that would be acceptable to Muslims because it would take seriously their habits of mind and their civilization."[23] Góis walked a fine line that the Jesuits at court had never attempted. They knew very clearly where the line between Muslim and Christian lay, and there was no question of blurring that. Though the emperor's moods may have shifted, the fathers could be reasonably certain of his protection, because he had repeatedly invited them to his court and insisted on keeping them there.[24] Bento de Góis, however, did not have the same security, and his identification with Akbar could have been as much a liability as an advantage, given the resistance to the emperor's reforms and the rumors of his apostasy. Góis constantly straddled the categories of Muslim and Christian: with the patronage he had from Akbar, with his clothing, with his names, with the languages he used (Turkish and Persian), and most of all in what we know of his discourse.

We should beware, nonetheless, of projecting onto sixteenth- and seventeenth-century India and Central Asia the reified notions of Islam that have become current since the nineteenth century. The much more fluid sense of what constituted being a Muslim in the seventeenth century allowed for Góis to be acclaimed as such by the local king in Chalīs after defending his faith in Jesus and on another occasion by one of the king's 'ulema who had witnessed the brother's fearless confession of Jesus.[25] Matteo Ricci even uses the term "muslim" when recounting the story, though he does so in an Italian approximation (*misermani*) of the Persianized form (*musulmān*) of the Arabic word (*muslim*, pl. *muslimūn*)! He explains to his European readership that among the Saracens, the word means "believer" or "belonging to the true religion." One wonders whether musulmān and muslim would have seemed particularly significant terms to Ricci, given that those words probably had not become broadly used in European languages until much later. He could thus say that Brother de Góis was praised as a veritable Muslim without fear of scandalizing his audience.[26]

Until the time of his death, Góis seems to have been identified by many as a Muslim, though Xavier himself writes that he had a letter from Góis from Yarkand in which he says that even though he is known as a Christian, he has not been treated badly.[27] Didier claims that his activity on his journey—what he calls the "Irano-Islamization" of Christianity and thinks was masterminded by Xavier—should be seen as symmetrical with the sinicization of Christianity that Ricci and others were attempting in China.[28] In his proving that Cathay was nothing other than China, Góis connected the two projects, if such they were, though at the end he could do so only through an intermediary. He did not meet Ricci but managed to get a letter to him despite having only the vaguest notion of an address. Ricci sent a Portuguese-speaking Chinese Jesuit brother to find Góis and bring him to Peking, but Góis died before they could make the last part of the journey.[29] The way in which the report of Góis's death is given makes it seem unlikely that he thought himself on a journey of inculturation based on respect for Muslims.

One wonders about Didier's desire to see a symmetry here between the Mughal mission and its extension in the journey to "Cathay" on the one hand and the Chinese mission of Ricci and his companions on the other. What seems to be lacking in the records of the former is the kind of admiration for the culture, beliefs, and philosophy of the Muslims that one sees in the mission's approach in China. It was precisely Akbar's distance from what his Jesuit guests perceived to be Islam that made him admirable. Even though before Jerome Xavier was sent to the Mughal court he is said to have worked on the translation of the first part of Valignano's *Historia*, yet still it is hard to imagine him being anywhere as positive toward Muslims as Valignano was toward the Japanese—notwithstanding the latter's disdain for Buddhism, a common thread that ran through the South Asian and East Asian missions.[30]

We certainly find in the figure of Bento de Góis the sense of connectedness that is part of the definition of globalization and a concern, as it were, to put the pieces of the world together in their proper relation. Of the figures we examine in this chapter, he certainly comes closest to the ideal of a globalized vision. What is still lacking, however, at least in the reports that we have, is any indication of affection or admiration for the Muslims he encountered—not even for their piety or devotion, much less for the details of their belief. In all the literature emerging from this supposed project of Irano-Islamizing Christianity, the only good Muslims to emerge are the powerful who sit lightly toward the dogma and ritualism of their religion, who can laugh at its authorities, and who give a generous hearing to the Jesuit preachers, taking their side against fellow believers.

It could be true, though we cannot document it clearly, that it was indeed Xavier who had given Góis what Didier refers to as his "unofficial mission"—to convert Islam from the inside as an "islamo-christian preacher"—and had trained him for it.[31] However, virtually nothing in the accounts of his journey indicates that his concern was conversion in the usual sense. Had he lived, of course, the unrivaled experience he had on the journey would have been invaluable for providing a sense of what it meant to be Muslim across that stretch of Central Asia and how one might speak of Christian faith in that situation.

Mission among the Muslims of Spain

A rather different dynamic was at work in the Jesuit engagement with Muslims in Europe. In 1687, the year in which Tirso González de Santalla's *Manuductio* (Manual for the conversion of Muhammadans) was first published in Madrid, he became the thirteenth superior general of the Society.[32] It is the period before his rather controversial generalate that interests us, however, because for almost twenty years he had been involved in preaching missions to Muslims in various parts of Spain. This work has a bearing on the second part of his *Manuductio*, which deals directly with the question of Islam, for it has a significant autobiographical strand, born of pastoral experience, woven throughout an otherwise fairly predictable apologetic and polemic. In approaching this work, one also has to take into account the particular history of Spain and its remaining Muslim population—many slaves and servants who were openly Muslim, and others from a converso background, who were descendants of Muslims who had been coerced into converting to Christianity and were still often suspected of dissimulation.[33] Ignatius gives us an indication in chapter 2 of the *Autobiography* of how vexed was the relationship he had with Muslims when he was still in his searching phase; and even later, as superior general, he found himself able to advocate military action against the Muslims.[34]

The centuries-long tension between Europe and the Ottoman Empire sharpened the animosity of Jesuits and others toward Islam. It was only in 1683 that the second siege of Vienna was lifted, and though Europe rejoiced at the victory, the Ottoman Empire remained strong. It took the Jesuit Nicolò Pallavicino close to three hundred pages to expound for the Christian princes who had formed the Sacra Lega against the Turks the divine plan behind the current prosperity of the Church against the Muslims, and he urged them to keep up the pressure.[35] One can see from the effusiveness of the dedicatory letter of the German edition of González's *Manuductio* something of the political climate in which it was written. Addressed to "the most august and unvanquished Roman Emperor Leopold I," it goes on to celebrate fulsomely his victory over the Ottomans and the reestablishment of Christian practice in the Hungarian Empire. The emperor has the strength of a Samson or a Hercules and the military prowess of a David! The emperor is assured that while he "was using fire and sword in Hungary to strike the Muhammadan Hydra, with its monstrous heads as numerous as its notorious errors, [the Society] was wielding stylus and quill to achieve the same end."[36]

Although Jerome Xavier's dedications to Akbar and Jahāngīr shared something of that same, sometimes fawning courtly style, he obviously could not draw attention to the conflict between the Christian powers of Europe and the Muslim empires not only around the Mediterranean but also in the colonies of the Mediterranean powers. The Ottoman Empire was in expansion mode in the sixteenth and seventeenth centuries, as were the other two "gunpowder empires" of the Mughals and the Safavids. If this was a period of globalization for the Society, it also witnessed the clash of global pretensions. None of the Jesuit missionaries who journeyed east needed to be reminded of the global reach of Islam, from the Iberian Peninsula to the Malay Archipelago and the northwestern provinces of China. The three successor empires to the "global" commonwealth of the Abbasid period were still in a territorial struggle with the emerging global vision of European expansion, and occasionally among themselves, and it may have been difficult for Jesuits, whether in Europe or abroad, not to take theological sides in this political struggle.[37]

Tirso González was far from being the only theologian or indeed the only Jesuit writing about Islam in those decades. His work is replete with lengthy citations from other authorities, and he acknowledges his reliance on two sixteenth-century authors in particular, one of whom, Juan Andrés, gave the impetus that launched him on his project.[38] González's *Manuductio* differs markedly from Xavier's *Fuente de Vida* in that González is more concerned with addressing actual Muslims rather than their philosophically cultured despisers as represented by Xavier's Philosopher.[39] Certainly in Xavier's context there were Muslims of the kind that González wished to convert, yet Xavier had his sights trained on the philosopher-king. On paper he succeeds whereas in the field he had failed. In the European context González, on the contrary, recounts many frustrations and failures along with a few successes.[40] In book 3 of the second part of his *Manuductio*, he recounts a dialogue (*colloquium*) with a promising Muslim he calls Amete Solymam—a Latinized approximation of an Arabic name, probably Hamid Suleiman—though to label it a "dialogue" is perhaps being too generous to González. After Amete declares his difficulty with the Trinity and the Incarnation, the Jesuit scarcely draws a breath for twenty-seven very dense pages of argumentation. In the end the speechless Amete admits he does not know how to answer what González has said, but he still cannot be persuaded to ask for baptism. González continues:

> The Jesuits in our College in Malaga had treated this man very kindly, and at the end, speaking to him in a very friendly and familiar way I said, "My friend, Amete, before the judgment seat of God you will not be able to plead ignorance. I have clearly preached the truth to you. If you still doubt that what I have said is true, pray to God to show you the truth, to illumine the darkness of your mind and to teach you the way of salvation. After having heard so many arguments, you should at least remain in some doubt as to whether it is necessary for your eternal salvation to adopt the Christian religion. This is a matter of the utmost importance. Therefore, pray earnestly to God to enlighten you. And in order that you may be worthy to be enlightened by God, flee vice, cultivate piety, love God above all things and your neighbor as yourself, and observe diligently the precepts of the Decalogue, for they are binding on all people."[41]

How different from that idealized ending in Xavier's dialogue in *Fuente de Vida*, where the Philosopher surrenders himself entirely to his newfound conviction!

We might surmise that González's preparedness to leave the matter between the Muslim and God reflects the conviction underlying the *Spiritual Exercises*, expressed in Annotation 15: God deals directly with each person, and that person does so with his or her creator.[42] The insistence and the strategies that González recommends, however, are far from the even-tempered reserve that Ignatius wishes to see in a retreat director. González probably feels himself absolved of that duty since the matter at hand is not at all a choice among varying goods (which is the presumption of the *Exercises* when a decision about the disposition of one's life is to be made); rather, it is a choice, González is convinced, between truth and falsehood.

After many signs of charity, González says, he embraced Amete warmly, sent him off with Robert Bellarmine's *Short Christian Doctrine*, and asked him to read it attentively in the hope that perhaps sometime he might come to acknowledge the truth of the Christian faith. Though González did not know for certain, he fervently hoped that what he heard was true: During a grave illness Amete eventually requested baptism and died a Christian.[43]

Though one might not expect it from González's title of the second part, "in which is demonstrated the falsity of the Muhamaddan religion," a strong sense of passion and urgency comes through his work. Indeed, there are repeated treatments of the errors of Islam, polemics against Muhammad and the Qur'an, and detailed expositions of Christian doctrine, but this book is the work of a committed missionary who had labored for years at his task. He oscillates between the warmth of individual interactions with Muslims and rather theatrical fire-and-brimstone preaching. The chapter headings reveal his practical concern:

> Book Six, in which is taught the method (*praxis*) for converting Muhammadans, drawn from the experience of the author, and in which are listed the themes for the sermons and points . . . with which they can be filled out: Chapter I—How useful it is to hold public exhortations for Muhammadans; Chapter II—How to gather Muhammadans to listen to these public exhortations; . . . Chapter VI—How to overcome the obstinacy of Muhammadans who recognize the truth of the Christian religion but who decline to accept baptism or who delay it; etc.[44]

The Muslims should not be forced to come but encouraged with reasons and signs of goodwill, the first of which is payment. González reminds his readers that the people they desire to reach are generally day laborers who cannot afford to lose a day's wages to attend the meeting. Therefore, the preacher and his benefactors need to make up that wage.[45]

González devotes the first part of the *Manuductio* to demonstrating with clear arguments the truth of the "Roman Catholic Christian Religion." He notes in a prefatory remark that the whole work takes its title only from the second part regarding "the falsity of the Muhamaddan religion," for that part represents his primary interest. The book's first part, he adds, is applicable to other situations. Although in its treatment of doctrine it is essential to the overall task of converting Muslims, it is also very useful for dealing with Jews, heretics (i.e., Protestants), and any sects that oppose the Christian religion.[46]

What González acknowledges, in effect, is that Muslims, Christians (of various stripes), and Jews belong to the same conversation about the nature of God, about how to interpret the history of God's dealings with the world, and, in particular, about how to understand the event of Jesus Christ. Those who disagree with the Roman Catholic position in this conversation are said to be heretics. Yet heresy is a charge one makes against those members of one's own community of faith who have gone beyond bounds in what they claim. For Christians to accuse Muslims of heresy—as theologians have done since the days of John of Damascus in the eighth century—is, perhaps ironically, to acknowledge that they belong to, or at least begin within, the same world of discourse. González as much as states this at the beginning of the second part of his work when he enumerates the errors of the Muslims. Moreover, each one of them is attributed also to certain early heretics of Christian history, among them Marcion, Cerdo, Sabellius, Cerinthus, Arius, Origen, the Manichaeans, the Donatists, and the Anthropomorphists.[47] Some of these errors González also ascribes to the Jews.

It could also be said that the Qur'an sees Christians and Jews, though particularly the former, as heretics. That is, they are people who have experienced the revelation of God's one truth but have exaggerated certain aspects of it to the point of error, one that could in theory be corrected, thus returning the errant sheep to the fold. See, for example, Qur'an 4:171: "People of the Scripture, do not exaggerate in your religion and do not say about God anything but the truth. The Messiah, Jesus son of Mary, was but the messenger of God, and His word which He conveyed to Mary, and a spirit from him. So put your faith in God and his messengers, and do not say 'Three.' Stop it—it will be better for you! God is but one god." The Qur'an is at best ambivalent with regard to the salvation of Christians. The most prominent positive statement is Qur'an 2:62, which states, "Those who believe, and the Jews, and the Christians, and the Sabaeans—whoever believes in God and in the Last Day, and who does good works—they shall have their reward with God. They shall have no fear, nor shall they grieve."[48] However, other verses are more trenchant in their criticism and state quite bluntly that exaggeration has tipped over into unbelief: "They have become unbelievers those who maintain that God is the Messiah, son of Mary. . . . They have become unbelievers those who maintain that God is the third of three" (Qur'an 5:72–73). Nonetheless, the Qur'an takes it for granted that this matter is something like a family dispute and that what is at issue is how to understand the relationships among the various elements of a common religious universe: God, Jesus, Mary, angels, scriptures, prophets, law, resurrection, judgment, forgiveness, salvation, and so on.

That this disagreement might seem to be a family matter does not mean it is less intense or conflictual. Muslims are to Christians (and vice versa) the "proximate other"—that is, the Other who is problematic for being too much like us or perhaps even claiming to be us.[49] We may inhabit the same world of discourse, but we also contest it.

Globalization and the Limits of Pluralism

This consideration of Christian-Muslim polemics in the early modern period opens up for us the question of the relationship between globalization and pluralism. It is often taken for granted that global experience and a globalized vision naturally lead to a pluralist attitude to religion. Exclusivism is presumed to be associated with a narrow, parochial view of the world, and inclusivism seems hegemonic in other ways.[50] However, the assumption that pluralism in religion logically follows from a healthy process of globalization needs to be critically examined. The experience of the *plurality* of religions—an undeniable phenomenon—is one thing; quite another is the adoption of a *pluralist* understanding of the relationships among religions. Indeed, while the meaning of plurality is clear enough, the precise attitude, policy, or ideology represented by the term "pluralism" is not at all clear. It might represent simply a resigned secularist shrug at the impossibility of judging among what seem equally preposterous claims about the divine. It might be a methodological commitment to evenhandedness and neutrality on the part of scholars who study religions, or it could be a governmental policy not to favor any one sect but to adopt a certain neutrality for the sake of political peace. In theological terms pluralism can be a relativizing attitude that postulates a fundamental unity to all religions and so sees no real significance in the differences among them of doctrine, worship, and experience. Alternatively, it can be a presumption that religions are simply incommensurable, with each having its own permanent, separate, and perhaps even divinely willed validity.

If we accept Roland Robertson's rough definition of *globalization* as the increased awareness of the unity of the world as a whole, taking the globe as a focus for human activities, then many understandings of pluralism begin to look more like isolation or balkanization than globalization.[51] They tend toward more or less sullen truces between irreducibly different entities rather than toward a complex and demanding engagement with difference. If the Jesuit missionaries we have been looking at might not qualify as pluralists these days, at least by some definitions, it may be because they brought to their task a conviction of the unity of the divine project with regard to humanity. The breadth of the world they were discovering did not change that belief; rather, it gave them an opportunity to search for the evident signs of that divine activity in the cultures and religions of the people they encountered. If globalization entails the increased awareness of the world as a single whole, then it should not be surprising that these men would have approached other believers as participants in a single conversation about the truth of the one God and about what God desires for humanity—what they often called the "law of God."

A central element of Christian faith has always been that there is only one "economy of salvation"; that is, God has one unified vision for humanity, not several, and one project for realizing that vision, not a variety.

From that premise, however, two different conclusions can be drawn. The first would be that since God's only project is the "Christian project," nothing outside the Christian dispensation has any value. This long-held position in Christian history still has its supporters. The alternative conclusion would be that everything recognizably positive even beyond the Christian community is in some way part of the same divine project to bring humanity to its fulfillment, and as such it has its own inherent value. This approach is adopted in the Second Vatican Council and was prepared, albeit remotely, in many respects by the work of people like Ricci.

In chapter 2 of this volume, Francis Clooney notes with regard to those Jesuits who were developing arguments against Hindu and Buddhist notions of rebirth that "they assume that there is not only intelligibility and room for conversation and debate across religious and cultural lines but also a real meaning to 'the human' that has value across cultural and religious divides and can be appealed to as an ideal." The approach may not have taken sufficient account of how that sense of the human and the rational had been shaped by a specifically Christian or Western vision that was not universally shared or easily transferable. Yet that does not seem justification enough for positing, as many pluralist approaches would, the incommensurability of culturally and geographically diverse worldviews or the irreducibility of metaphysical assumptions. The "Copernican revolution" in theology for which pluralists call would isolate each religion in a separate orbit, making the others ultimately untouchable.[52] As George Karuvelil observes, one's own tradition functions neither as the static center of a Ptolemaic system nor as just another planet in a Copernican view of the religious universe; rather, it is the horizon against which one views all of reality. The ultimacy that one's own tradition commands comes not from any empirically demonstrable uniqueness but from its existential character as an encompassing horizon.[53] As Clooney observes, the Jesuits who developed their pan-Asian critique against notions of rebirth were unable to see the essential role that belief played in constituting entire horizons of meaning. Given that they were newcomers to the cultures they were addressing, they had yet fully to understand what it meant to inhabit that religion as an encompassing horizon.

Those Jesuits encountering Muslims were in a somewhat different situation. The two religions were laying claim to the same horizon and from the beginning were in contestation with each other, with the Qur'an proposing itself as a sort of corrective to the misreading of previous messages. Jesuit polemicists and missionaries kept returning to the same few matters that they thought dealt a mortal blow to any Muslim's faith: the carnality of Muhammad, the mediocre pragmatism of Muslim law compared with the sublimity of the evangelical counsels, the impossibility that the law of Christ would be superseded, and defenses of the doctrines of the Incarnation and the Trinity. Yet we see repeatedly that although opponents might be reduced to silence, their conviction is rarely shaken, and they do not seek baptism. As the polemicists show little understanding of, and even less sympathy for, what it actually means to be Muslim, they can only be amazed at the "obstinacy" of their interlocutors in the face of evident truth. They think the keystones of Islam's arches have been convincingly removed, and yet it still stands. After long centuries of a scarcely unchanged apologetic strategy in the Church, these Jesuits seemed neither ready to take seriously the perplexities expressed by their Muslim interlocutors nor able to acknowledge that they themselves had not yet found the way to proclaim the Gospel convincingly to that large part of the human race who already believed in the God of Abraham and found Christian affirmations about God incomprehensible or even blasphemous.

The process of globalization, when it comes to religion, is not a fight to the death among the competing visions until only one is left standing, nor is it a process of gradual homogenization. It is rather an exploration of inevitably different yet encompassing horizons that are never static because the interaction inevitably and constantly reshapes them. Still coming to see the world as a unity does not necessarily reduce all perspectives on it to a single one.

Pluralism has often been conceived principally in soteriological terms—that is, with many separate paths leading to the top of the same mountain. What does it matter as long as we all reach either the same goal or, in any case, the goal we wanted to reach? It has been seen as the cure for the kind of hectoring and threats so vividly portrayed by Tirso González in his *Manuductio* and even for the cooler philosophical argumentation of Xavier's *Fuente de Vida*. All paths, all laws, in this view, lead to salvation. However, the inadequacy of this separate-paths-to-the-one-salvation approach is illuminated if we consider the analogy of climate change. In the first place, the separate paths approach negates any real link between actions and their consequences, between what we strive to make of ourselves and what we actually become.[54] Furthermore, it presumes that the paths we choose are all just variations on a theme and that they intersect only tangentially, if at all, with those of others. In the emerging global consensus about climate change, we realize the extent to which the earth and its atmosphere are an interconnected whole; thus, the actions, decisions, and policies of individuals or nations have a bearing on all. Claims to individual rights and national sovereignty with regard to carbon emissions, therefore, are seen as fundamentally flawed. In a similar way, the kind of pluralism that views religious traditions as isolated and sovereign is untenable. Religions do not propose simply a password or exam key that guarantees a final rescue or an escape to another dimension. Rather they offer a comprehensive vision of what it means to be in a healthy (drawing on the root meaning of "salvation") relationship with the divine and with the rest of creation—a relationship that begins now. Like a healthy climate, salvation in this sense is global, so it is inextricably bound up with the beliefs and actions of others and of all of us together. Thus the religious conversation about what constitutes a sound relationship with God and a healthy relationship with others is as urgent as the struggle to come to a common understanding about protecting the air and water that sustain our life together.

Conclusion

The three Jesuits we have considered in this chapter might be seen as posing a challenge to our presumptions about globalization. We cannot but be struck by the global geographical reach of their missions, particularly that of Góis in his journey from India, through Central Asia, to China. Even Tirso González conceived of his work as having universal applicability, as well he might have, for he would become superior general of the Society. The breadth of their experience, however, seems to have failed to break them out of a centuries-old and already rather stale and unproductive approach to Muslims and their faith. The global reach that the expanding European empires made materially possible for them opened up a firsthand encounter with another global vision that had already succeeded in establishing itself from the Balkans to Bengal and beyond into East and Southeast Asia and that saw itself as a competitor politically and economically as well as religiously. While Ricci, Valignano, and de Nobili had a sense of newness and discovery in the religions and cultures of China, Japan, and India, Xavier, Góis, and González seem to have found only the familiar enemy, presumed to have been vanquished in argument long ago yet unaccountably still resistant to the clear truth of the Gospel. Succeeding waves of globalization have been little different. Though the polemics and the contestation might now take advantage of vast technological advances offered by the digital age, the hatreds and the refusals track well-worn paths.

At the same time, it must be said, these men shared with their brother Jesuits a deep conviction that the world, however extensive it might eventually prove to be, was a unity; that humanity shared one origin and rationality; and that God had but one vision for humanity's end. This belief might seem to be (and undoubtedly often enough degenerates into) merely a desire for a religious hegemony that will mirror and underwrite the colonial project. However, a truly global vision cannot be satisfied with the balkanization of religions, or the *cuius regio, eius religio* solution of the Westphalian settlement. We see in all these exemplars of early Jesuit mission the shared conviction that a single global conversation can be had about God and humanity, and all have access to it through a shared rationality and human sensibility.

Notes

1. For a concise but nonetheless detailed account of the Jesuits on mission in northern India up to the suppression, see Henry Hosten, SJ, *Jesuit Missionaries in Northern India and Inscriptions on Their Tombs, Agra (1580–1803)* (Calcutta: Catholic Orphan Press, 1907).

2. Editors' introduction to Fr. Monserrate, SJ, *The Commentary of Father Monserrate, S.J., on His Journey to the Court of Akbar*, trans. John S. Hoyland, annotated S. N. Banerjee (London: Oxford University Press, 1922), xiv. The most Hoyland seems to have left out is the occasional gratuitously offensive adjective.

3. The word "Musalman" here might seem significant, for, as Didier observes, this term and its variants (Persianized forms of the Arabic *muslim*) did not appear in European languages until much later. It was already attested in English in the sixteenth century but, according to Didier's authorities, not in French until 1680 and not in Spanish before 1765. See Hugues Didier, *Fantômes d'Islam et de Chine: Le Voyage de Bento de Góis, S.J., 1603–1607* (Paris: Chandeigne, 2003), 202, n. 1. The *Oxford English Dictionary*, though without giving citations, also dates the first appearances of the word in Italian, French, and Portuguese to the sixteenth century. The original Latin, however, does not read *musulmanus* but rather *Mahammedis* (of Muhammad). For "Muslim" Monserrate always uses the term *Agarenus* (Hagarene, from the name of Ishmael's mother, Hagar). Antonio Monserrate, SJ, *Mongolicae legationis commentarius*, ed. H. Hosten, Jesuit Letters and Allied Papers on Mogor, Tibet, Bengal, and Burma (Calcutta: Asiatic Society of Bengal, 1914), 575.

4. Monserrate, *Commentary*, 63.

5. Ibid., xv–xix.

6. Frank Lechner, *Globalization: The Making of World Society* (Chichester, UK: Wiley-Blackwell, 2009), 16.

7. Camps lists sixteen works certainly attributed to him and others doubtfully so. Arnulf Camps, OFM, *Jerome Xavier S.J. and the Muslims of the Mogul Empire: Controversial Works and Missionary Activity* (Schöneck, Switzerland: Nouvelle revue de Science missionnaire suisse, 1957).

8. Jerónimo Javier, SJ, *Fuente de vida: Tratado apologético dirigido al rey mogol de la India en 1600* (San Sebastián: Universidad de Deusto, 2007), 71–72. "En este livro presentamos a V[uestra] A[lteza] la su[m]ma de la verdadera lej che Dios N[uestro] S[eñor] ha al mundo revellado, pera se salvarem los hombres, fuera de

la quoal pera ninguno aj salvaçión." Didier, who edited the text of 278 folios, refers to Xavier's style, not without good reason, as "un castellano aportuguesado." Hugues Didier, "Jerónimo Javier, un Navarro en la India," in *Actas del I Congreso Ibero-asiático de Hispanistas Siglo de Oro e Hispanismo general*, ed. Vibha Maurya and Mariela Insúa (Pamplona: Universidad de Navarra, 2011), 151.

9. Among the many witnesses to this, Rudolf Acquaviva, in a letter of September 27, 1582, to his provincial in Goa, writes concerning Akbar, "I am afraid that he and some of his people may make use of me to disprove the Muhammadan religion and then avail of some matter out of Holy Scripture, not for the benefit of our religion but for some other purpose, because there are those who feel that the King is bound to come out with something new one day." In John Correia-Afonso, SJ, ed., *Letters from the Mughal Court: The First Jesuit Mission to Akbar, 1580–1583* (St. Louis: Institute of Jesuit Sources, 1981), 116.

10. Javier, *Fuente de vida*, 548.

11. Hugues Didier, "Muslim Heterodoxy, Persian *Murtaddun* and Jesuit Missionaries at the Court of King Akbar (1580–1605)," *Heythrop Journal* 49 (2008): 902.

12. For example, see Xavier's life of Christ in Persian. Pedro de Moura Carvalho, *Mir'āt al-quds (Mirror of Holiness): A Life of Christ for Emperor Akbar: A Commentary on Father Jerome Xavier's Text and the Miniatures of Cleveland Museum of Art, Acc. No. 2005.145*, trans. Wheeler M. Thackston (Leiden: Brill, 2012). The work is basically a Gospel harmony with some materials from Josephus, from apocryphal gospels, and from medieval legend. It only shows subtly the signs of its Mughal context—for example, in its citation at length of the Song of the Suffering Servant from Isaiah and in other elements that underline the reality of Jesus's death. The Cleveland manuscript begins with a highly Islamized introduction (241) most unlikely to be from Xavier. A manuscript of the same work in London begins with an introduction, much more likely to be original, that invokes the Trinity rather than God and Muhammad (241n2). Exactly the same Trinitarian introduction appears in the version with facing Latin translation by Ludovico de Dieu, published in Leiden in 1639 (opening pages of this 1639 version appear in Carvalho, *Mir'āt al-quds*, 5, fig. 0.2).

13. See an extensive citation from 'Abdus Sattar's *Majālis-i Jahāngīrī* in Sanjay Subrahmanyam, "A Roomful of Mirrors: The Artful Embrace of Mughals and Franks, 1550–1700," in *Globalizing Cultures: Art and Mobility in the Eighteenth Century*, Ars Orientalis 39, ed. Nebahat Avcıoğlu and Finbarr Barry Flood (Washington, DC: Smithsonian, 2010), 39–83. The chronicler 'Abd al-Qādir Badā'ūnī, though no friend of the Jesuits or of Akbar's policies, was probably quite accurate when he wrote, "These accursed people brought in a description of Dajjal (Anti-Christ) and applied his attributes to our Prophet, on whom be peace, the very opposite of all Dajjals." Cited in M. Athar Ali, "Muslims' Perception of Judaism and Christianity in Medieval India," *Modern Asian Studies* 33, no. 1 (February 1999): 246.

14. Quoted in Jivanji Jamshedji Modi, "The Parsees at the Court of Akbar

and Dastur Meherji Rana," *Journal of the Bombay Branch of the Royal Asiatic Society* 21 (1904): 78.

15. See Henry Hosten, SJ, editor's introduction to Monserrate, *Commentarius*, v–vii. See also J. S. Grewal, "The Sikh Movement during the Reign of Akbar," in *Akbar and His India*, ed. Irfan Habib (Delhi: Oxford University Press, 1997), 243–55.

16. See Camps, *Jerome Xavier*, 51–73.

17. For one account of some notable conversions, see Pierre du Jarric, *Akbar and the Jesuits: An Account of the Jesuit Missions to the Court of Akbar*, trans. C. H. Payne (New York: Harper & Brothers, 1926), 127–36.

18. On Góis's journey, see Cornelius Wessels, SJ, *Early Jesuit Travellers in Central Asia: 1603–1721* (The Hague: Martinus Nijhoff, 1924), 1–41, particularly 3.

19. Fernão Guerreiro, SJ, *Jahangir and the Jesuits, with an Account of the Travels of Benedict Goes and the Mission to Pegu, from the Relations of Father Fernão Guerreiro, S.J.*, trans. C. H. Payne (New York: R. M. McBride, 1930).

20. See Góis's letter to Fr. Nuno Rodrigues in Didier, *Fantômes*, 57.

21. 'Isa is the Qur'anic version of the name of Jesus. '*Isawi* might possibly have been intended to mean "Jesuit." In any case the acknowledgment of Jesus would have been clear to any Muslim, and he seems to have adopted it later in the journey.

22. See du Jarric's account of the meeting with the merchant returning from Cathay in Guerreiro, *Jahangir and the Jesuits*, 119–23.

23. Didier, *Fantômes*, 55–56.

24. The matter is discussed throughout Jesuit letters to and from the Mughal court, and Akbar himself confirms it in a *firman* of February 1583 addressed to the Jesuit provincial at Goa. See Correia-Afonso, *Letters*, 121–22. One finds this tale of privilege borne out in the less enthusiastic observations of Thomas Kerridge, an English merchant-ambassador, during the reign of Jahāngīr: "Those Jesuits do so bewitch the king &c with daily presents, as glasses, china dishes, varieties of wine &c., that nothing is denied them, have way to the king at all times, confer and talk with him, live at his charge." Cited in Richmond Barbour, "Power and Distant Display: Early English 'Ambassadors' in Moghul India," *Huntington Library Quarterly* 61, no. 3/4 (1998): 358.

25. See Matteo Ricci, SJ, "Le voyage de Bento de Góis selon 'La description de la Chine' de Matteo Ricci," nos. 829–30, in Didier, *Fantômes*, 92–94.

26. Didier, *Fantômes*, 202.

27. Guerreiro, *Jahangir and the Jesuits*, 171.

28. Didier, *Fantômes*, 205–7.

29. Guerreiro, *Jahangir and the Jesuits*, 155–60.

30. Camps, *Jerome Xavier*, 3. On Valignano, see Vittorio Volpi, *The Visitor: Alessandro Valignano, a Great Italian Master in Asia*, Fonti e Studi 18 (Rome: Bulzoni, 2013); and J. F. Moran, *The Japanese and the Jesuits: Alessandro Valignano in Sixteenth-Century Japan* (London: Routledge, 1993).

31. Didier, *Fantômes*, 193ff. Góis writes effusively of the instructions and ad-

vice that Xavier had given him before his departure from Agra. However, we do not have textual evidence of their content.

32. Tirso González de Santalla, SJ, *Manuductio ad conversionem Mahumetanorum, in duas partes divisa: In prima, veritas religionis christianæ catholicæ romanæ manifestis argumentis demonstrator, in secunda, falsitas mahumetanæ sectæ convincitur* (1687; repr., Dillingen: Joannis Caspari Bencard, 1689). For an extensive presentation of the figure of Tirso González, with ample quotations from the *Manuductio*, see Emanuele Colombo, *Convertire i musulmani: L'esperienza di un gesuita spagnolo del seicento* (Milan: Bruno Mondadori, 2007); and the much shorter study in English by the same author, *"Even among Turks": Tirso González de Santalla (1624–1705) and Islam*, Studies in the Spirituality of the Jesuits, vol. 44, no. 3 (St. Louis: Seminar on Jesuit Spirituality, 2012). See also Bernard Vincent, "Musulmans et conversion en Espagne au XVIIe siècle," in *Conversions islamiques: Identités religieuses en Islam méditerranéen*, ed. Mercedes García-Arenal (Paris: Maisonneuve et Larose, 2001), 193–203; and the very admiring Elías Reyero, SJ, *Misiones del M.R.P. Tirso Gonzalez de Santalla, XIII prepósito general de la Compañia de Jesús, 1665–1686* (Santiago: Tipografía Editorial Compostelana, 1913).

33. For the secondary literature on this, see Colombo, *"Even among Turks,"* 12–13nn32–33.

34. Ibid., 36ff.

35. Nicolò Maria Pallavicino, *Le Moderne Prosperità della Chiesa Cattolica contro il Maccomettismo* (Rome: Komarek, 1688).

36. Written by the provincial of the Upper German Province after Gonzáles had already been elected superior general. González, *Manuductio*, 1:n.p.

37. During the first mission, Fr. Monserrate was to have been part of an embassy to Europe, bearing a letter from Akbar apparently to Philip II of Spain, a much-crowned monarch whose various dominions touched every continent. This diplomatic mission never eventuated, but the letter, for all its courtliness, shows that Akbar had a global vision of his role and of the importance of harmony among "the exalted tribe of princes" to establish peace in the world. The purpose of the embassy was, Banerjee speculates, to enlist Philip's help against the Ottomans. Monserrate, *Commentary*, ix–x. The full text of the letter, with a translation, is given in Edward Rehatsek, trans., "A Letter of the Emperor Akbar Asking for the Christian Scriptures," *The Indian Antiquary* 16 (1887): 135–39.

38. For other contemporary Jesuit writings on Islam, see Thomas Michel, SJ, "Jesuit Writings on Islam in the Seventeenth Century," in *A Christian View of Islam: Essays on Dialogue by Thomas F. Michel, S.J.*, ed. Irfan A. Omar (Maryknoll, NY: Orbis, 2010), 123–48. See also Emanuele Colombo, "Jesuits and Islam in Seventeenth-Century Europe: War, Preaching and Conversions," in *L'Islam visto da Occidente: Cultura e religione del Seicento europeo di fronte all'Islam*, ed. Bernard Heyberger et al. (Genoa: Marietti, 2009), 315–40. On González's indebtedness to earlier authors, see Colombo, *"Even among Turks,"* 16; and González, *Manuductio*, 2:3–4.

39. Didier speculates that the main reason Xavier's work, although indexed

and ready for the press, was not published was "the mere fact that it was not in fact a treatise on Islam . . . but a presentation of Christianity for King Akbar and his friends, that is to say, for an incredible new category: Islamic non-believers or post-Muslims." Didier, "Muslim Heterodoxy," 928–29.

40. One of the most celebrated conversions that González recounts is the story of Baldassare Loyola, a Moroccan prince who had been enslaved, converted, and later became a Jesuit. In fact, he reprints Baldassare's own published account, written at the command of his spiritual father (*Manuductio*, 2:53–58). The man died in Madrid while awaiting passage to the Mughal mission in 1667. This was a fascinating episode in the history of the Society's relationships with Muslims. See Emanuele Colombo, "Baldassare Loyola de Mandes (1631–1667), prince de Fez et jésuite," in *Les musulmans dans l'histoire de l'Europe*, ed. Jocelyne Dakhlia and Bernard Vincent, vol. 1, *Une integration invisible* (Paris: Albin Michel, 2011), 159–93; and more recently Emanuele Colombo, "A Muslim Turned Jesuit: Baldassare Loyola Mandes (1631–1667)," *Journal of Early Modern History* 17 (2013): 479–504.

41. González, *Manuductio*, 2:155, preceded by his full twenty-seven-page exposition on the Trinity for his Muslim questioner (128–55).

42. Annotation 15 states that a Jesuit leading others through the Spiritual Exercises should refrain from urging exercitants "to one state of life or way of living more than to another"; instead he "should permit the Creator to deal directly with the creature, and the creature directly with his Creator and Lord." Ignatius of Loyola, *The Spiritual Exercises of St. Ignatius*, trans. Louis J. Puhl, SJ (1951; repr., New York: Vintage Books, 2000), 8–9.

43. González, *Manuductio*, 2:155.

44. Ibid., 2:313–14.

45. Ibid., 2:291.

46. Ibid., 2:proemium. González helpfully suggests that those who are being sent to regions where there are heretics rather than Muslims could just take the first volume.

47. Ibid., 2:3. He attributes the list to Martin Vivaldo (1545–1605) in some annotations that the Dominican moralist made on another book.

48. This is repeated almost verbatim at Qur'an 5:69, except that the order in which the groups are named is different. For a discussion of these passages and their interpretation, see Jane Dammen McAuliffe, *Qur'anic Christians: An Analysis of Classical and Modern Exegesis* (Cambridge: Cambridge University Press, 1991), 98–105. On the question of the salvation of non-Muslims, see Mohammad Hassan Khalil, *Islam and the Fate of Others: The Salvation Question* (New York: Oxford University Press, 2012). González criticizes the Qur'an for taking the position that each group can be saved through its own law (*Manuductio*, 2:32–34).

49. See Jonathan Z. Smith's 1985 essay "What a Difference a Difference Makes," in his *Relating Religion: Essays in the Study of Religion* (Chicago: University of Chicago Press, 2004), 251–302.

50. For a more nuanced presentation of these traditional categories in the theology of religions, see Paul F. Knitter, *Introducing Theologies of Religions* (Maryknoll,

NY: Orbis, 2002). And in defense of the usually maligned exclusivism, see Mara Brecht, "What's the Use of Exclusivism?," *Theological Studies* 73, no. 1 (March 2012): 33–54.

51. Roland Robertson, *Globalization: Social Theory and Global Culture* (London: Sage, 1992).

52. See, for example, John Hick, *God and the Universe of Faiths*, rev. ed. (London: Fount Paperbacks, 1977), 120–32.

53. George V. Karuvelil, SJ, "Absolutism to Ultimacy: Rhetoric and Reality of Religious 'Pluralism,'" *Theological Studies* 73, no. 1 (March 2012): 55–81.

54. This has been one of the motivations for the development of a more particularist version, with separate paths proposing (and perhaps even being able to deliver) different religious ends, or different "salvations" in the plural. Even though one might be able to recognize the value of a particular religious end proposed by a tradition different from one's own, it will always seem penultimate. For example, a Buddhist might think of Christian notions of heaven as admirable enough; however, someone "in heaven" would still have a ways to go before reaching nirvana. See S. Mark Heim, *Salvations: Truth and Difference in Religion* (Maryknoll, NY: Orbis, 1995).

4

JESUITS IN IBERO-AMERICA
Missions and Colonial Societies

ALIOCHA MALDAVSKY

One can only really understand the missionary action of the Society of Jesus in Ibero-America from 1549 to 1767 within a larger context: the early modern Iberian expansion in which the Jesuits participated and that made them truly a "global religious order."[1] Though much recent scholarly work on the missionary action of the Jesuits in America has been able to move beyond apologetic historiography, it is still to some extent couched in terms of the Jesuits' "contribution" to modernity. This way of thinking occludes important questions about how the Jesuits themselves changed as a result of their missionary activity, but current research is nevertheless making some progress on such questions as the interaction between global and local Jesuit policy, the differences between Jesuit missionary theory and practice, and a closer analysis of the motivations of both the missionaries and the indigenous peoples.

Jesuit archival material has enabled historians and anthropologists to explore cultural and political transformations in native societies, the roles of the indigenous people in religious encounter, and how the Jesuits themselves reacted to social and political contexts on the American continent—contexts that shaped not only their missionary activity but also the ways in which they wrote about it. Thus we are beginning to understand how the Society of Jesus changed its way of proceeding in the different contexts of its missionary activity—not only how, as has often been said, it "accommodated" to the native cultures it encountered but also how it interacted with the new colonial societies emerging in America under Iberian political rule and was itself changed by this accommodation.

This process of interaction and adaptation to local conditions took place in what has begun to be called an "early globalization," which was led by the Iberian monarchies and peoples. It connected continents on a large scale from the fifteenth century onward. But this global early modern world did not arise just as a matter of people constantly moving from one place to another. It was, more important, a matter of new social experiences as people from different continents began living together and developing new kinds of hierarchic patterns and colonial forms of domination. Ibero-America comprised a quite unique set of new societies, with people coming—either freely or under coercion—from four continents. When we focus on the Jesuits' missionary action in Ibero-America, we are studying the interaction between a global religious order on the one hand and people dealing with the social and political processes resulting from an early modern globalization on the other hand.

This chapter surveys recent developments in the historiography of that interaction. In the first section I explore what a "mission" amounted to in the Ibero-American context that early modern Jesuits faced. In the second I stress the importance of understanding their interactions not only with the indigenous peoples but also with the emerging colonial societies. The final section considers the dynamics of the religious and colonial encounters between the missionaries and the native peoples.

The Many Definitions of Mission in Ibero-America

From its beginnings the Society of Jesus was associated with the religious aspect of Catholic Iberian expansion. An emblematic illustration of this connection between European expansion and the new congregation came just two years after Pope Paul III approved the order in 1540, when King John III of Portugal sent Francis Xavier to Asia. The Jesuits were primarily interested in missionary and conversion activities in conformity with their fourth vow to the pope and the desire of the first founders to travel to Jerusalem. As matters turned out they had to engage in more settled activities, such as education and preaching, not only in the European countries where they worked but also in the imperial provinces to ensure the Society's survival and ongoing recruitment.

The Jesuits were sent to Brazil in 1549. They had sole responsibility for missionary work to convert the indigenous peoples. They built colleges, residences, and *aldeias* (villages), or centers for conversion programs and for the social discipline of the Tupí population.[2] When the six Jesuits arrived in Brazil, they accompanied the first governor-general of the colony, Tomé de Sousa, a point that illustrates the royal approval and support they enjoyed. The Society of Jesus, following the pattern of Portuguese colonization, concentrated its efforts on the coastal zones. By the end of the sixteenth century, it had established Jesuit colleges in Olinda, Salvador de Bahia (the political capital of the colony and the center of the Jesuit Province), and Rio de Janeiro. The Jesuits also had a significant presence in other coastal zones such as São Paulo. In Brazil the fathers developed the *aldeamento* system, or the establishment of evangelization villages that brought together indigenous peoples of diverse origins, mostly Tupí, and with the Jesuits administrating the settlements. By 1585 the Jesuits were living in five Brazilian aldeias and making regular visits to six other places not under their direct control. As did the other Portuguese in Brazil, they looked toward the *sertão*, the inland space hitherto untouched by the European colonists. Thus Jesuits from Brazil soon arrived at the frontier with the areas under Spanish possession and approached the Guaraní in Paraguay, who would later be under the care of the Jesuits from Peru.

At the behest of King Philip II of Spain, the Jesuits also went to Peru (1568) and Mexico (1570) with a view to founding colleges and helping with the conversion of the indigenous population. This latter enterprise had already begun by the mendicant orders, which had been well established in indigenous parishes (called *doctrinas*) since the 1520s.

The development of the Society of Jesus on any continent depended on the cities. Hispano-American cities, with their Spanish residents, were a showcase for the Hispanic way of life and culture and served as a means of colonization. The foundation of colleges and Jesuit residences (equivalent to other orders' convents) depended on the good will of the king and of the local Spanish population who could finance them.

Because the Jesuits arrived late in the Spanish colonies and were reluctant to take charge of parishes, their missionary activity took place in four different contexts: cities, indigenous parishes, frontier missions, and rural missions.

Cities

The Jesuits' education policies for the local Spanish population, or criollos, were very similar to their programs for reinforcing the Catholic faith in the different European contexts where they operated, and for that reason their work can fairly be described as a missionary activity. This sort of education among the Spaniards nevertheless led to the creation of colleges exclusively dedicated to the sons of the native nobility.

Alongside Jesuit educational work in the cities, confraternities also developed that were devoted to the different populations, among them indigenous peoples, slaves, and people of African descent. Again their work was similar to that in European cities, where the Jesuits also encouraged the foundation of Marian congregations. Lay believers could learn and practice exercises of piety and examinations of conscience, take confession and frequent communion, and participate in the early modern "refashioning of Catholicism."[3] The confraternities reflected distinctions of gender and social status within the population. Ethnic distinctions were not a novelty of the Americas, for Spain and Portugal already had slaves of sub-Saharan and North African descent. In Ibero-America, however, the indigenous population in the cities grew during the latter third of the sixteenth century and concentrated in particular districts. There followed the creation of pious organizations dedicated specifically to the needs of indigenous peoples.

Indigenous Parishes

In Peru and Mexico Jesuits took responsibility for only a few indigenous parishes—Juli, Santiago del Cercado, Tepotzotlán—because typically such work was not allowed by their *Constitutions* (internal rules). These few parishes had many similarities with the later development of the reduction system in Paraguay, as well as with the Chiquito and Mojo missions that started in the second half of seventeenth century. They all suggest that models for developing native congregations on the American continent circulated between the different religious orders, because the basic pattern was first developed by the mendicant orders in New Spain and in the Andean region within the *encomiendas* (labor dependencies). The system of course evolved in various ways in the different colonial contexts of the Central Andes, coastal Brazil, and New Spain. Here Spaniards and Portuguese were concerned about a supply of indigenous labor, and they sought to maintain and keep it under control at all costs.

The Jesuit *Constitutions* had prohibited members of the Society to be parish priests, mostly as a way of safeguarding their mobility and financial disinterestedness. But the Jesuits in America were compelled to rethink their initial project of itinerancy and mobility.

The local model already developed by mendicant orders in Spanish America put the responsibility of indigenous rural parishes in the hands of religious orders from the beginning. Those parishes, called *doctrinas de indios*, generally existed within the encomienda system. In this system a Spaniard had the right to extract tribute and work from a specific group of natives, but he did not have any right over the land. In exchange the *encomenderos* (owners of the encomiendas) were responsible for their people's evangelization. Bartolomé de Las Casas, a Dominican friar and defender of indigenous populations against Spanish imperialism, criticized the system, and the claim that the encomenderos were lords over vassals met some royal resistance. Eventually Charles V's New Laws of 1542 and Philip II's subsequent policy dealt with the Indians in a different way: Either they were appointed to another encomendero after two generations, or else they were ruled directly by royal officers. In these latter cases the encomienda became royal, and the Indians paid tribute directly to the king. During the 1560s the encomenderos were banned from living among indigenous peoples. From that point the missionaries and parish priests were, in theory, the only Europeans to share daily native life; thus they became important agents of royal colonial policy.

The Jesuits were initially criticized in Peru because of their refusal to accept indigenous parishes. Eventually they were compelled to do so in the 1570s in at least two places—Santiago del Cercado, a district of Lima peopled mostly by immigrants and rootless Quechua-speaking Indians from other places, and Juli, an important village under royal rule located near Lake Titicaca and whose people spoke Aymara, a language the Jesuits were interested in learning. Tepozotlán, a village located north of Mexico City and also under royal rule, became another doctrina under Jesuit supervision in 1618. It was located on the road to the frontier territory occupied by the Chichimeca population, who opposed Spanish colonial rule. In all of these villages, as well as in the Brazilian aldeias, the Jesuits became parish priests, organizing daily religious life and putting into practice their methods of evangelization. Moreover, the Jesuits used the villages under their control as schools where their young students who needed immersion in indigenous languages could be sent.[4] Though these villages in Brazil and in the central regions of Spanish America were never free from the economy of colonialism, the Jesuits tried as far as possible not to be under the control of Iberian individuals.

Frontier Missions

In some places the Jesuits were able to negotiate a specific status. Typically these missions were located on the edge, where missionaries were recognized as guardians of the imperial frontiers: the northern new Spanish missions; missions in Chile, where the indigenous people resisted Spanish rule; and in the lowlands of the Andes, the Guaraní, Mojo, Maynas, and Chiquito missions. In these different contexts, Jesuit missionaries had to adapt to the colonial and geopolitical situations. They invented new strategies for conversion and evangelization while maintaining credibility and legitimacy with the Spanish colonial rulers and with other religious institutions. The idea of "defensive war," put forward by Luis de Valdivia in 1612 from the southern Chilean frontier, might be considered one example of such a strategy. Another was the negotiation of a particular status for the Guaraní reductions in Paraguay, freeing them from encomienda and forced labor (*servicio personal*), as a quid pro quo for their protecting, with the use of force, the imperial frontier with territory belonging to Portugal.[5]

Rural Missions

Although scarcely studied by historians, an important Jesuit missionary activity in Ibero-America, apart from the colleges and residences, took place in the rural missions. José de Acosta considered these itinerant and temporary missions, similar to those developed by the order in Europe, to be one of the most important means of developing contact with the indigenous peoples. The mobility involved in such work was closer to the Society's self-understanding than was the care of parishes. The rural missions were also an excellent means of supporting and controlling parish priests and of instilling the values of the Catholic Reformation.

In the Andean territories, some Jesuits at the end of the sixteenth century devoted themselves to this activity, making a kind of specialty of traveling along difficult mountain pathways. These missions brought together two or three Jesuits with different and complementary skills, whether priests (both professed fathers and spiritual coadjutors), brothers (technically, temporal coadjutors), or scholastics. Scholastics or brothers, for example, might be fluent in indigenous languages, but they would not be able to hear confessions or administer sacraments. Short-term missions of this kind were important in the training of young recruits. They needed to work in a very practical way, developing skills that could not really be learned in colleges that were inevitably centered on intellectual skills.

The contrast between the ordered discipline of the colleges and the improvised life of the missions indeed brought to the surface among the Andean Jesuits unresolved questions about the centrality of mobility to Jesuit obedience and spirituality. Occasionally superiors would take issue with the free and easy ways of the specialists in this sort of mission and curb their activity. Nevertheless, these generally brief missionary journeys into relatively close territory were greatly esteemed by the Roman authorities of the Society, because they showed how the American provinces were fulfilling the Society of Jesus's main aims.

One particular feature of such missions in the Andes was their role in campaigns for the "extirpation of idolatry" that the archbishops of Lima led in the 1610s, 1650s, and 1660s.[6] The discovery of "idolatrous worship" among Andean people in the region around Lima provoked vigorous campaigns of repression. Those Lima Jesuits engaged on rural missions, who had hitherto worked without conflict, took an active part in these campaigns, which historians have interpreted as a means of imposing new religious rules on the Andean Catholics and priests. At any rate, the extirpation of idolatry campaigns allowed the Jesuit college in Lima to give a new impetus to its missionary activity. The accounts of rural missions can be found in the annual official letters sent back to Rome, and historians and anthropologists have used them as primary sources for understanding how the Jesuits engaged native cultures.

In their pastoral work, the Jesuits built up an impressive corpus of material in indigenous languages, the significance of which extends beyond the narrowly apostolic. Some Jesuit linguists wrote dictionaries, textbooks for the study of native languages, catechisms, and collections of sermons and confession-related material. They were thus using their humanistic and theological skills for the education of the local clergy and for codifying, reformulating, and translating Christian doctrine in such a way that it could be taught to the newly converted population. This work became particularly significant after the Council of Trent. At that point linguistic and intellectual work became a tool for the Catholic Reformation in the Iberian colonial territories, whereas previously the tasks of converting and evangelizing had been principally carried out by the mendicant orders in very diverse ways. By helping establish common, standard languages (*lenguas generales*) for communication in the Americas and by giving a written form to many Amerindian oral languages, the Society of Jesus also influenced local linguistic choices that are still evident today. An illustrative case in point is the trilingual—Spanish, Quechua, and Aymara—catechism compiled by Jesuits of mestizo origin under the supervision of José de Acosta in the context of the Third Council of Lima and published in 1585.

This American context was very different from that of Asia, which was also a theater of Portuguese maritime expansion. In Asia, where there was no question of Portuguese conquest, many places in India, China, and Japan exhibited religious coexistence. Of course, the missions of Goa and Madurai were very different from the tolerated presence of the Jesuits in the Chinese court or in Japan.[7] Nevertheless, in America, colonial domination gave the apostolic activity of the Society of Jesus a distinctive coloring, for all its different kinds of missionary work developed without any strong predefined strategy.

Jesuits, Missions, and Colonial Societies

The different missionary activities in America always depended on political negotiations with both local and royal governments. They could also be jeopardized by internal tensions and divisions among the Jesuits, by their scarcity in number, and by the conflicting pull of teaching activities. Tensions arose in large part because the Society of Jesus was interacting with societies that were in the process of construction, societies that exhibited both colonial features and the characteristics of the ancien régime.

Inevitably clashes occurred at the local level with powerful interest groups in Iberian societies. The canonical issues that flared up with Archbishop of Lima Toribio de Mogrovejo in the 1580s or with Juan de Palafox y Mendoza in seventeenth-century Mexico reflected tensions that were present also in Europe. But other difficulties were more specific. In Peru the Jesuits clashed with Viceroy Francisco de Toledo in the 1570s because of their reluctance to take on indigenous parishes.

Problems also arose when some Jesuits spoke out on sensitive issues, such as the legitimacy of the Spanish conquest, of the Indian labor system, or of slavery. Thus in the 1570s Luis López, a Jesuit professor of theology educated in Salamanca, was arrested by the Inquisition and probably wrongly accused of solicitation, or the seduction of women, during confession. In the first years of the Jesuits' presence in the Andes, Luis López and other Jesuits criticized the Spaniards' greed or their bad example for the indigenous peoples. In the 1600s Diego de Torres Bollo, who would later found the Paraguayan province and reductions, wrote an important report to the president of the royal Council of the Indies, advocating royal protection for the indigenous population and denouncing the injustices and exploitation of labor caused by the Spaniards' greed.[8]

The Jesuits from Peru used such arguments when they sought to extend the Guaraní mission system in Paraguay that Franciscan missionaries started in the late sixteenth century. The Jesuits negotiated with the Spanish authorities in a specific frontier context for the foundation of thirty reductions during the seventeenth century along the Paraná, Uruguay, and Guaira Rivers. Portuguese *paulistas*, or "slave hunters," threatened the frontier between both Iberian empires by attacking the Guaraní population. In exchange for securing the frontier and controlling the indigenous population, the Jesuits of the newly founded Paraguayan province negotiated in 1608 with the Governor Hernando Arias de Saavedra and the president of the Audiencia de Charcas Francisco de Alfaro that the Guaraní would not be submitted to the encomienda and would escape the labor system. Instead, they would pay their tributes directly to the king. About seventy thousand Guaraní lived during the seventeenth and eighteenth centuries in this protective mission system built both by the Jesuits and by the indigenous peoples under the rule of their native authorities. War was never far off, but they lived in relative security.[9]

On the Brazilian side of the frontier, the Jesuits at the end of the sixteenth century were regularly in conflict with Portuguese colonists about exercising control over indigenous peoples coming from the sertão. Paulistas criticized the Jesuits who were willing to exert temporal and spiritual administration over the aldeias.[10] It is indeed true that the Jesuits condemned the colonists' illegitimate ways of reducing indigenous peoples into slavery, but recent research shows also the sharp debates within the Society of Jesus about slavery. To gain economic autonomy, the Jesuits in Brazil not only entered the transatlantic slave trade system to produce sugar in their plantations but also ended up justifying indigenous slavery with theological, scriptural, and legal arguments. For some Jesuit theologians, the slave status of Africans and indigenous peoples could be excused by virtue of their conversion to Catholicism.[11]

At the same time the local Iberian population had a genuine interest in the devotions promoted by the Jesuits and in their educational expertise for teaching the young local elites. This demand led to the rapid founding and financing of colleges in the main cities of Spanish America by local elites, especially the conquistador and encomendero families, and by indigenous authorities. The status of a founder of a college and the privileges it entailed (places of burial, places in the church, Masses), and the spiritual benefits of one's association with the rising religious order of the Catholic Reformation, explain this enthusiasm. Some encomenderos were also interested in the rural missions that the Jesuits managed with "their" Indians, helping them to strengthen those pseudo-feudal ties that the Crown was trying to undo in the last third of the sixteenth century, for instance, in the Andes. Legacies and endowments from members of colonial society provided the properties that supported the Society's activities financially and allowed it an economic independence.[12]

Though universities had already been founded in Lima and Mexico in the middle of the sixteenth century before their arrival, the Jesuits in the New World were expected to educate a new generation of American Europeans, the sons of the conquistadors. This initiation into the humanities needs to be read as part of a colonial project that served the interests both of the Crown and of local Spanish elites. Studying ancient authors was meant to help local Spaniards appropriate the European cultural heritage within the framework of a global Christian humanism.[13] The education of local indigenous elites, however, had a different aim. The Franciscans had started educating the sons of local authorities in New Spain and Quito by introducing them to European humanities.[14] Continuing this task in colleges in Tepotzotlán, Lima, and Cusco, the Jesuits' curriculum served to initiate the local elites into Spanish culture and to form local leaders well placed to mediate between the indigenous population and the colonial power.[15]

The Jesuits' engagement with colonial society extended to their recruitment of young men from the newly founded colleges, enabling the Society's demographic growth and geographical expansion in the American territories. Quite quickly by the seventeenth century, descendants of Spaniards known as creoles accounted for at least half of the members of the Hispano-American Jesuit provinces; by the beginning of the eighteenth century, they were a large majority.[16] This local recruitment embedded the Jesuits within colonial society and vice versa. At the same time missionaries never stopped arriving from Europe.

In Ibero-America this recruitment was limited to the colonists. Indians were never considered proper candidates for entering the Society, and mestizos were officially excluded at the end of the sixteenth century under the pressure of colonial ethno-social discrimination. By contrast the Jesuits in Japan were free from this kind of restrictive colonial ideology and promoted the recruitment of native members in a way that gained them credibility with leaders of the local population and enabled some members of the Society to learn and communicate in the indigenous languages.

In Ibero-America, however, the Jesuits could think only in terms of complementary skills: The locals had the linguistic expertise necessary for missionary work while the Europeans contributed their experience of the Society's way of proceeding.[17] But the theory was probably not matched by the practice. Though the Society's Roman authorities saw missionary work as a key activity, not all members of the provinces agreed.

A few native parishes and urban enterprises were directed at natives, but the rural missions in practice provided the unique opportunity to make limited contact with the native populations. Until the first decade of the seventeenth century, specialists conducted rural missions, but soon they became, at least in Peru, the main way of training young recruits to preaching and hearing confessions in native languages.[18] Internal Jesuit administrative records, however, show that not all of the creole recruits or young European missionaries were motivated to work on the missions with natives or to learn their languages. They wanted to work in the colleges, where they would be in contact with the Spaniards and Portuguese. Because of diverging views concerning the missionary activity, tensions between superiors could also arise over the relative freedom that missionaries enjoyed while working far from the colleges and from regular discipline.[19] In Brazil it was difficult to send young Jesuits to stay in the aldeias because of the contact with naked native women.[20] Spanish-American Jesuit provinces responsible for frontier missions addressed these problems by inviting recruits from Central Europe. In the main, they worked in the northern New Spanish missions and those of Paraguay from about 1650 onward.

These limits and tensions were part of the social framework within which Jesuit missionary activity took place in Ibero-America. Not surprising, young creoles coming from well-established families, with a social and juridical status defined by contrast with the natives, were unenthusiastic about having extended contacts with them. The harsh conditions of missionary life, the difficulty of the native tongues, and their intellectual and social motivations for entering the Society may also have played a part.

The Jesuits and the Religious-Colonial Encounter

Despite all this the Jesuits' missionary activity in the Americas left an important legacy. Their apostolic goals led Jesuits in America to produce a "multiplicity of writings": dictionaries, methods for learning indigenous languages, works of theoretical missiology, administrative correspondence, and accounts of local missionary practices.[21]

Because of their centralized governing organization and their global dispersion, the Jesuits developed a very sophisticated system of communication. The Jesuits everywhere aimed to maintain the original spirituality and way of proceeding articulated by the founders and to spread the news of the order's activities all over the world through official accounts that were published and circulated for this purpose in Europe.[22] The Jesuits' role in the circulation of knowledge about the different parts of the world has to be placed in its wider political, apostolic, and intellectual contexts.

First of all, conversions and missionary work involved an intellectual process, which was exemplified by Bernardino de Sahagún, a famous Franciscan who had spent his time collecting knowledge about indigenous peoples and societies of New Spain during the sixteenth century. Knowledge served as a strategic tool in the enterprise of converting people and extirpating their ancient beliefs and practices. The imperial and colonial framework within which that knowledge was produced should not be overlooked, not least because the missionaries themselves were very conscious of it.

Second, the global network the Jesuits managed to build made them key agents in the circulation of knowledge about Africa, Asia, and America until, and even after, the suppression of the Society. From the sixteenth century onward, the publication of compilations of *Litterae annuae* from all parts of the world was a deliberate Jesuit policy designed to publicize the Society's missionary activities, to gain European support, and to attract new members. In the eighteenth century the *Lettres édifiantes et curieuses* and the *Welt-Bott* continued this tradition but in a context of dispute and rivalry with other orders in Asia.[23] After the expulsion of the Jesuits from America in 1767, the Jesuits wrote books about Paraguay and the missions among the Guaraní people in defense of Jesuit achievements and in protest against their curtailment. Among these books, the works by José Manuel Peramás and José Cardiel, for example, influenced European representations of the reductions system into the twenty-first century.[24] This feedback of knowledge to Europe had some quite concrete effects: The Jesuit network, for example, did much to introduce quinine into the European practice of medicine and pharmacology.[25]

Historians, learning from anthropologists, are now conscious of possible differences between what missionaries actually did and what they thought they were doing. Jesuit sources reveal much about their cultural and political interaction and negotiation with the native population of the Americas (and, indeed, of any mission site). If we can be sensitive to the local contexts in which this documentation was produced, then it further enhances our understanding of contact situations, especially their processes of colonial domination and reciprocal interaction.

Juan Carlos Estenssoro Fuchs, working on Peru, has shown that the Jesuits helped establish a religious boundary between the Spaniards and native converts that, as such, strengthened and legitimated the colonial regime. José de Acosta defined natives in terms of their need for a long conversion process both to Christianity and to civility. Such a vision legitimated both the presence of the missionaries themselves and the colonial coercion.[26] The production of linguistic knowledge, conceived of as an instrument of learning and communication, and the naming and classification of the native populations, serving as a way of characterizing their aptitudes for Christian conversion, can be understood as further ways of imposing colonial order on an apparent chaos.

Jesuit anthropological discourse about indigenous peoples of the Americas had two complementary tendencies. Sometimes it labeled them as a kind of "barbarian," a term that includes all peoples from outside Europe. This approach, linked to Acosta, presented people living on the borders of the Iberian empires as wild, as lacking any social and urbane life.[27] But at other times, even if it seems contradictory, the Jesuits also tried to produce detailed classifications of the peoples they were seeking to convert and evangelize as they were becoming the most important Christian force in the frontier American territories.[28] Given that missionaries thought in terms of culturally and linguistically homogenous populations, an effective strategy required a classification of "nations," with languages, territories, political organizations, and cultural features. Their classifications did not always fit the complex reality, as Christophe Giudicelli shows with reference to the distinction between the Tarahumara and the Tepehuanes in northern New Spain.[29] Sometimes as the Jesuits assigned specific names and identities for peoples both within and beyond their missions, they ended up creating differences that might not originally have existed at all or at least not so clearly. Yet these classifications came to play a key role in circumscribing local indigenous nations and in creating a colonial geography.

Faced with differences of language among native peoples, the Jesuits effectively imposed a schematic order on the phenomenon by imagining common tongues, or lenguas generales. Writing about the Guaraní, Bartomeu Melià calls this "the major transformation imposed on language from a colonial perspective." But he also notes that the linguistic fragmentation sensitized the Jesuits to the apparent absence of strong sociopolitical unities.[30] At the same time the Jesuits created a specific culture around their missions, a culture in which they themselves were not the only, or even the major, actors.[31]

Jesuit writings and indigenous sources also show us the ambiguities in the transmission and appropriation of a Christian culture by the native converts, especially in frontier contexts.[32] Though the reductions transformed local indigenous societies, their native populations retained a higher degree of autonomy than those in the central regions of the Americas. Guillermo Wilde has shown that the geometrical order evoked by eighteenth-century documents on the Paraguay reductions did not fully correspond to a reality shaped by endemic war (both colonial and interethnic), by permanent ongoing contacts between convert natives and those who were still "pagan," by ecological and economic transformations, and by demographic and political changes. The Jesuits never fully ended the native practice of polygamy, given its absolute necessity for the maintenance both of family relationships and of broader alliances and bonds that were useful in a context of endemic war. Shamanic authorities might have lost their legitimacy, but native chiefs kept their political power in a newly defined form within the colonial municipal institutions that the Jesuits created. At the same time they never stopped using traditional means of legitimation, such as verbal eloquence. Missionary interaction generated a "mission culture," drawing both on native and colonial elements. This culture provided not only the natives but also the missionaries with a means of adapting to precarious situations.[33]

This mission culture gave rise to new forms of native political legitimation and ethnic coexistence, often based on cultural skills that the native elites had appropriated from the Jesuits. Extant texts in Guaraní and Spanish, especially from the eighteenth century, reveal that Jesuit missionaries in the reductions led a literacy campaign among the Guaraní.[34] Not all in the reductions had the chance to learn reading, writing, and musical skills, however; seemingly it was afforded only to caciques and chosen people already active in administrative and devotional life. Thus the indigenous peoples with these newly learned skills gained social and distinctive prestige within the reduction. Moreover, their social and cultural identities were transformed as a result of mastering reading and writing, and they experienced a new sense of identity and empowerment. Both before and after the expulsion of the Jesuits, they were enabled to practice a politically autonomous self-government. Writing letters to the king or to the governor; being able to communicate with fellow Guaraní or with the Jesuits, for example, in time of war; leaving historical records—all were among the new literate practices of the Guaraní that had been developed within the reduction system built by the Society of Jesus.[35] Those skills remained part of Guaraní culture after the expulsion of the Society of Jesus from the Hispanic domains in 1767 and the consequent demise of the missionary system.

Conclusion

The previous paragraphs fall short of a complete account of the Society of Jesus's missionary activity in the Iberian territories of America, but they do shed light on important issues. Much of the Society's activity depended on its interaction in local social contexts. From these contexts it took recruits from whom the Jesuits learned specific skills useful for the mission; however, the contexts also contributed to some of the Jesuits' internal tensions. This symbiosis with local societies exemplified the interdependence between social actors and religious institutions that was standard in the ancien régime's societies.

At the same time, the Society was also connected to global realities both through the ongoing permanent transfer of Europeans to America and through the circulation of people and information between Europe and the American provinces. Jesuit administrative documentation shows us the tensions of an institution in constant interaction with these circumstances, even if its fundamental principles remained stable. Until the eighteenth-century expulsions, this complex equilibrium could be maintained, mostly thanks to policies of the Iberian monarchies that allowed religious institutions to act with relative freedom as long as they fulfilled their tasks in colonial societies. In spite of a very early anti-Jesuitism, the Society of Jesus became well settled in local Ibero-American contexts and was able to gain relative economic autonomy. But the global project of the Society could not survive, at least not in the same way, amid the emerging secularized powers in Europe and their new relationships with religious institutions. Now a sharper distinction between the religious and the political spheres set in. "Church" came to designate an autonomous institution, which became national after the processes of Latin American independences. No longer could political powers tolerate bodies such as the Society of Jesus, with its special link to the papacy and its close social and economic interactions with local societies. These features did not fit within the new paradigm of the Church and state that became normative in nineteenth-century Latin America.[36] It was partly for such reasons that the Society of Jesus, after its restoration in 1814, encountered such great obstacles in returning to its former missions and colleges in the newly created nation-states of the continent.[37]

The interplay of local settlement and global mobility during the early modern period may well have produced, especially in the Ibero-American borderlands, some kind of distinctively Jesuit interaction with the indigenous peoples they converted and evangelized. But it must be stressed that these Jesuit interactions were part, and quite consciously so, of a larger reality of colonial coercion and political control. Moreover, the effects of Jesuit missionary action were never fully foreseeable. Indigenous peoples could in principle react in ways quite contrary to the missionaries' aims and expectations. The frontiers between Christians and non-Christians were fluid. What historians call "mission culture" was a constantly new context, with ever-new social interactions and hierarchies. The achievement of the Jesuits in early modern Ibero-America was in some ways lasting and durable. But at the time, it was also, and always, unpredictably fragile.

Notes

1. See Dauril Alden, *The Making of an Enterprise: The Society of Jesus in Portugal, Its Empire, and Beyond, 1540–1750* (Stanford: Stanford University Press, 1996); Michela Catto, Giulio Mongini, and Silvia Mostaccio, *Evangelizzazione e globalizzazione: Le missioni gesuitiche nell'età moderna tra storia e storiografia* (Rome: Società

Editrice Dante Alighieri, 2010); and Luke Clossey, *Salvation and Globalization in the Early Jesuit Missions* (Cambridge: Cambridge University Press, 2008).

2. See Charlotte de Castelnau-L'Estoile, *Les Ouvriers d'une vigne stérile: Les jésuites et la conversion des Indiens au Brésil, 1580–1620* (Paris: Centre culturel Calouste Gulbenkian, 2000).

3. See Louis Châtellier, *L'Europe des dévots* (Paris: Flammarion, 1987); and Robert Bireley, SJ, *The Refashioning of Catholicism, 1450–1700: A Reassessment of the Counter Reformation* (London: Macmillan, 1999).

4. See Castelnau-L'Estoile, *Les Ouvriers*; Aliocha Maldavsky, *Vocaciones inciertas: Misión y misioneros en la provincia jesuita del Perú en los siglos XVI y XVII* (Seville: Consejo Superior de Investigaciones Científicas, 2012); Pablo Abascal Sherwell Raull, "Tepotzotlán: La institucionalización de un colegio en la frontera chichimeca de la Nueva España (1580–1618)" (PhD diss., European University Institute, 2014); and Alexandre Coello de la Rosa, *El pregonero de Dios: Diego Martínez, SJ, misionero jesuita del Perú colonial (1543–1626)* (Valladolid: Universidad de Valladolid, 2010).

5. On "defensive war" in Chile, see Rolf Foerster, *Jesuitas y Mapuches, 1593–1767* (Santiago, Chile: Editorial Universitaria, 1996); Paolo Broggio, *Evangelizzare il mondo: Le missioni della Compagnia di Gesù tra Europa e America (secoli XVI–XVII)* (Rome: Carocci, 2004), 211–24; Guillaume Boccara, "El poder creador: Tipos de poder y estrategias de sujeción en la frontera sur de Chile en la época colonial," *Anuario de Estudios Americanos* 56 (2009): 65–94; Guillaume Boccara, "Antropología política en los márgenes del Nuevo Mundo: Categorías coloniales, tipologías antropológicas y producción de la diferencia," in *Fronteras movedizas: Clasificaciones coloniales y dinámicas socioculturales en las fronteras americanas*, ed. Christophe Giudicelli (Mexico City: Centro de Estudios Mexicanos y Centroamericanos, 2010), 103–35; and Jaime Valenzuela Márquez, "Misiones jesuitas entre indios 'rebeldes': Límites y transacciones en la cristianización mapuche de Chile meridional (siglo XVII)," in *Saberes de la conversión: Jesuitas, indígenas e imperios coloniales en las fronteras de la cristiandad*, ed. Guillermo Wilde (Buenos Aires: Editorial San Benito, 2011), 251–72. On Guaraní missions and war culture, see Barbara Anne Ganson, *The Guaraní under Spanish Rule in the Río de la Plata* (Stanford: Stanford University Press, 2003); Martín Morales, "Los comienzos de las Reducciones de la Provincia del Paraguay en relación con el Derecho Indiano y el Instituto de la Compañía de Jesús: Evoluciones y conflictos," *Archivum Historicum Societatis Iesu* (*AHSI*) 67, no. 133 (1998): 3–228; Martín Morales, "Violencia en el paraíso," in *Los jesuitas y la modernidad en Iberoamérica, 1549–1773*, ed. Manuel Marzal and Luis Bacigalupo (Lima: Fondo Editorial, Pontificia Universidad Católica del Perú, 2007), 387–420; and Guillermo Wilde, *Religión y poder en las misiones de Guaraníes* (Buenos Aires: Editorial San Benito, 2009).

6. On rural missions, see Broggio, *Evangelizzare*, 106–13; Maldavsky, *Vocaciones*, 125–206; and Macarena Cordero Fernández, "Rol de la Compañía de Jesús en las visitas de idolatrías: Lima, Siglo XVII," *Anuario de historia de la Iglesia* 12 (2012): 361–86. On "extirpation of idolatry," see also Kenneth Mills, *An Evil*

Lost to View? An Investigation of Post-Evangelisation Andean Religion in Mid-Colonial Peru (Liverpool: Institute of Latin American Studies, University of Liverpool, 1994); Pierre Duviols, *La lutte contre les religions autochtones dans le Pérou colonial: L'extirpation de l'idolâtrie entre 1532 et 1660* (1971; repr., Toulouse: Presses universitaires du Mirail, 2008); and Juan Carlos Estenssoro Fuchs, *Del paganismo a la santidad: La incorporación de los indios del Perú al catolicismo (1532–1750)* (Lima: Instituto Francés de Estudios Andinos, 2003).

7. See Ines Županov, *Missionary Tropics: The Catholic Frontier in India (16th–17th Centuries)* (Ann Arbor: University of Michigan Press, 2005); and Liam M. Brockey, *Journey to the East: The Jesuit Mission to China, 1579–1724* (Cambridge, MA: Harvard University Press, 2007). See also M. Antoni J. Ucerler's contribution to this volume.

8. See Paulina Numhauser Bar-Magen, "El silencio protagonista: Luis López y sus discípulos, antecedentes y misterios de una crónica jesuita," in *El silencio protagonista: El primer siglo jesuita en el virreinato del Perú, 1567–1667*, ed. Laura Laurencich and Paulina Numhauser Bar-Magen (Quito: Abya Yala, 2004), 95–113; and Giuseppe Piras, *Martín de Funes S.I. (1560–1611) e gli inizi delle riduzioni dei gesuiti nel Paraguay* (Rome: Edizioni di Storia e letteratura, 1998).

9. See Morales, "Los comienzos"; and Wilde, *Religión y poder*.

10. See Castelnau-L'Estoile, *Les Ouvriers*.

11. See Carlos Alberto de Moura Ribeiro Zeron, *Ligne de foi: La Compagnie de Jésus et l'esclavage dans le processus de formation de la société coloniale en Amérique portugaise (XVIe–XVIIe siècles)* (Paris: Honoré Champion, 2009).

12. See Aliocha Maldavsky, "Giving for the Mission: The Encomenderos and Christian Space in the Late Sixteenth-Century Andes," in *Space and Conversion in Global Perspective*, ed. Giuseppe Marcocci et al. (Boston: Brill, 2014), 260–84.

13. See Antonella Romano, "Classiques du Nouveau Monde: Mexico, les jésuites et les humanités à la fin du XVIe siècle," in *Missions d'évangélisation et circulation des savoirs, XVIe–XVIIIe siècles*, ed. Charlotte de Castelnau-L'Estoile et al. (Madrid: Casa de Velázquez, 2011), 59–85; and Pilar Gonzalbo Aizpuru, *La educación popular de los Jesuitas* (Mexico City: Universidad Iberoamericana, 1989).

14. See Pilar Gonzalbo Aizpuru, *Historia de la educación en la época colonial: El mundo indígena* (Mexico City: El Colegio de México, 1990); and Sonia Fernández Rueda, "Educación y evangelización: El colegio franciscano de caciques de San Andrés (Siglo XVI)," in *Passeurs, mediadores culturales y agentes de la primera globalización en el Mundo Ibérico, siglos XVI–XIX*, ed. Scarlett O'Phelan Godoy and Carmen Salazar-Soler (Lima: Pontificia Universidad Católica del Perú, Instituto Riva-Agüero, 2005), 129–45.

15. See Monique Alaperrine-Bouyer, *La educación de las elites indígenas en el Perú colonial* (Lima: Instituto Francés de Estudios Andinos, 2007).

16. Bernard Lavallé, "Españoles y criollos en la provincia peruana de la Compañía durante el siglo XVII," in Marzal and Bacigalupo, *Los Jesuitas*, 355.

17. Maldavsky, *Vocaciones*, 221–24.

18. Ibid., 61–69, 307–34.

19. See Aliocha Maldavsky, "The Problematic Acquisition of Indigenous Languages: Practices and Contentions in Missionary Specialization in the Jesuit Province of Peru (1568–1640)," in *The Jesuits II: Cultures, Sciences, and the Arts, 1540–1773*, ed. John O'Malley, SJ, et al. (Toronto: University of Toronto Press, 2006), 602–15; and Maldavsky, *Vocaciones*, 259–305.

20. See Castelnau-L'Estoile, *Les Ouvriers*.

21. Wilde, *Religión y poder*, 15.

22. See Markus Friedrich, "Circulating and Compiling the *Litterae Annuae*: Towards a History of the Jesuit System of Communication," *AHSI* 77 (2008): 3–39.

23. See Aliocha Maldavsky, "Pedir las Indias: Las cartas *indipetae* de los jesuitas europeos, siglos XVI–XVIII, ensayo historiográfico," *Relaciones* 132 (Fall 2012): 147–81; and Ronnie Po-chia Hsia, ed., *Noble Patronage and Jesuit Missions: Maria Theresia von Fugger-Wellenburg (1690–1762) and Jesuit Missionaries in China and Vietnam* (Rome: Institutum Historicum Societatis Iesu, 2006).

24. See José Manuel Peramás, *Platón y los Guaraníes* (1793; repr., Asunción: Centro Estudios Paraguayos "Antonio Gausch," 2004).

25. See Samir Boumedienne, "Avoir et savoir: L'appropriation des plantes médicinales de l'Amérique espagnole par les Européens (1570–1750)" (PhD diss., University of Lorraine, 2013).

26. See Estenssoro Fuchs, *Del paganismo*.

27. Much has been written about this anthropological discourse. See, for example, Alfred Métraux, "The Contribution of the Jesuits to the Exploration and Anthropology of South America," *Mid-America: An Historical Review* 26, no. 3 (1944): 183–91; Anthony Pagden, *The Fall of the Natural Man: The American Indian and the Origins of Comparative Ethnology* (Cambridge: Cambridge University Press, 1982); Joan-Pau Rubiés, "The Concept of Cultural Dialogue and the Jesuit Method of Accommodation: Between Idolatry and Civilization," *AHSI* 74, no. 147 (2005): 237–80; and Joan-Pau Rubiés, "Theology, Ethnography and the Historicization of Idolatry," *The Journal of the History of Ideas* 67, no. 4 (2006): 571–96.

28. For a more detailed approach to these naming strategies, see the suggestive work of Christophe Giudicelli, "Las tijeras de San Ignacio: Misión y clasificación en los confines coloniales," in Wilde, *Saberes de la conversión*, 347–71, which pertains to the next passage in the my text.

29. See Christophe Giudicelli, "Un cierre de fronteras . . . taxonómico: Tepehuanes y tarahumara después de la guerra de los tepehuanes (1616–1631)," *Anuario IEHS* 21 (2006): 59–78.

30. See Bartomeu Melià, *El Guaraní—conquistado y reducido: Ensayos de etnohistoria* (Asunción: Centro de Estudios Antropológicos, Universidad Católica, 1986); and Bartomeu Melià, "La lengua transformada: El Guaraní en las misiones jesuítica," in Wilde, *Saberes de la conversión*, 89.

31. About lenguas generales, see the dossier edited by Juan Carlos Estenssoro Fuchs and César Itier, "Langues indiennes et empire dans l'Amérique du Sud coloniale," *Mélanges de la Casa de Velázquez* 45, no. 1 (2015): 9–151.

32. For the case of Brazil, see Ronaldo Vainfas, *A heresia dos índios: Catolicismo e rebeldia no Brasil colonial* (São Paulo: Companhia das letras, 1995); Cristina Pompa, *Religião como tradução: Missionários, Tupi e "Tapuia" no Brasil colonial* (São Paulo: Bauru EDUSC, 2003); and Paula Montero, *Deus na aldeia: Missionários, índios e mediação cultural* (São Paulo: Editora Globo, 2006). See also Diego Bracco, *Charrúas, guenoas y guaraníes: Interacción y destrucción: Indígenas en el Río de la Plata* (Montevideo: Linardi y Risso, 2004); and María Cristina Bohn Martins, *Sobre festas e celebrações: As reduçõés do Paraguai (séculos XVII e XVIII)* (Passo Fundo, Brazil: Editora Universidade de Passo Fundo, 2006).

33. See Wilde, *Religión y poder*. See also Beatriz Vitar, *Guerra y misiones en la frontera chaqueña del Tucumán (1700–1767)* (Madrid: Consejo Superior de Investigaciones Científicas, 1997).

34. See Ganson, *Guaraní*, 183–84; and especially Eduardo Neumann, "Razón gráfica y escritura indígena en las reducciones Guaraníticas," in Wilde, *Saberes de la conversión*, 99–130.

35. Eduardo Neumann, *Letra de Índios: Cultura escrita, comunicação e memoria indígena nas Reduções di Paraguai* (São Bernardo do Campo, Brazil: Nhanduti Editora, 2015).

36. See Roberto Di Stefano, "¿De qué hablamos cuando decimos 'Iglesia'? Reflexiones sobre el uso historiográfico de un término polisémico," *Ariadna histórica: Lenguajes, conceptos, metáforas* 1 (2012): 197–222.

37. See Aliocha Maldavsky and Guillermo Wilde, "Paradojas de la ausencia: Las misiones jesuíticas sudamericanas y el imaginario posterior a la restauración," in *Las misiones antes y después de la restauración de la Compañía de Jesús: Continuidades y cambios*, ed. Leonor Correa Etchegaray, Emanuele Colombo, and Guillermo Wilde (Mexico City: Universidad Iberoamericana, 2014), 101–26.

5

THE HISTORY OF ANTI-JESUITISM
National and Global Dimensions

SABINA PAVONE

Anti-Jesuitism—defined as hostility directed toward the Society of Jesus in religious, cultural, and political circles—provides an important window on the reciprocal relationship between the Jesuits and globalization. Antagonism toward the Society between its founding in 1540 by Ignatius of Loyola and its suppression in 1773 demonstrates the close interplay of national and international forces in early modern European history. The "Jesuit system," constituted by a range of missionary and educational activities, was one of the first truly global networks and was closely connected with the European colonial enterprise.[1] The success of the Jesuits' global reach and their particular mode of proceeding—marked by central coordination and secrecy on the one hand and engagement in politics and society on the other hand—sparked hostile reactions from ruling elites in the Church and the state, both nationally and internationally.

The anti-Jesuitism that contributed to the suppression of the Society in the eighteenth century, first by monarchs and then by the papacy itself, did not disappear after the order's reestablishment in 1814. As the Jesuits gradually reforged a network in Europe and around the world, they confronted a new wave of antagonism linked to the rise of anticlericalism, particularly in France, parts of Southern Europe, and Latin America. The Jesuits' close identification with a more assertive papacy in the decades before and after the First Vatican Council (1869–70) generated enmity not only among Church progressives but also in the newly forged nation-states of Italy and Germany.

Since the Second Vatican Council (1962–65), by contrast, the Jesuits' embrace of a strong social justice agenda has provoked the ire of Church conservatives. Tracing the evolution of anti-Jesuitism over the centuries and into the era of Pope Francis, himself a Jesuit, provides a window into the national and transnational dynamics of the order through successive eras of globalization.

The Main Outlines of Anti-Jesuitism

Until recently anti-Jesuitism was a broad-brush term applied to running disputes between the apologists and defenders of the Society of Jesus. In recent years, however, a more nuanced historiographical debate has unfolded. Several studies have highlighted the semantic complexity of the idea of anti-Jesuitism and the consequent need to approach it from different perspectives, including the literary, rhetorical, and iconographic. They have distinguished between its political, cultural, and ecclesiastical forms. And they have emphasized its transnational dimension, reaffirming the necessity of studying the phenomenon not only from a European perspective but also from that of colonial contexts, particularly the Latin American.[2] Before developing a typology of different kinds of anti-Jesuitism and their evolution, it is worth sketching out how the phenomenon originated and developed.

From the outset the Jesuits had enemies. The establishment of the Society of Jesus, authorized by Paul III in 1540, provoked considerable dissension within the Roman Curia in part because of previous heresy trials against its founder. The innovations Loyola introduced in the practices of the new order, such as the abolition of singing the divine office in choir, gave rise to serious doubts in some quarters about its orthodoxy. Bishop Ascanio Cesarini's *Novi Advertimenti* (1564), one of the first anti-Jesuit pamphlets, cast particular suspicion on the rejection of the traditional occupations of the religious orders. In his *Catechisme des Jésuites* (1602), Étienne Pasquier went so far as to label the Jesuits a "hermaphrodite" order—neither secular nor religious.[3]

In these early decades the Jesuits' active engagement in the world began to elicit the suspicion and opposition of political authorities. From the time of Ignatius onward, the Society of Jesus chose a form of apostolate that involved living not on the margins of but in close contact with society and power, particularly through schools and universities but also as confessors to the elite. From early on this engagement provoked suspicion that the order sought to manipulate others for its own ends. Ignatius himself was fully aware of this dynamic. As early as 1546 in a letter to Simão Rodrigues at the Portuguese court, he noted that Jesuit involvement in temporal affairs, even when of little importance, was perceived as though "we wished to govern the world."[4] Even those well disposed to the Jesuits, such as Michel de Montaigne, had a high—and exaggerated—opinion of their influence. As Montaigne put it in his *Journal de voyage* (1580–81), "I believe that there has never been such a confraternity and order among us that has had such a rank or has produced such effects as those that they will achieve here, if their projects continue." He even suggested that "soon they will have all of Christendom in their power."[5]

As the Jesuit missionary and educational enterprise rapidly spread, the twin charges of religious heterodoxy and political machinations extended to its transnational activities as well. Through the experience of missions in Asia and the Americas, the Jesuits developed their particular vision of an empire that, within particular geographical and cultural contexts, inevitably came into tension with other imperial visions. Within the Catholic context, their openness to dialogue with other cultures as a means of conversion brought them into collision with the direct evangelizing strategy of the Roman Congregation de Propaganda Fide, for whom non-Christian cultures were an object of suspicion. Critics also invariably looked upon the Jesuit practice of *accomodarsi a tutti*, as Juan Alfonso de Polanco calls it, with mistrust. In many cases the adaptive spirit of the Jesuits was mistaken for a kind of deliberate camouflage that covered an unprincipled pursuit of self-advancement within the Church.[6]

Suspicion of Jesuit influence and methods in the international arena extended to political authorities as well. The Society's transnational organization, held together through networks of correspondence centered on Rome, proved increasingly at odds with the system of competing sovereign states that emerged after the Treaty of Westphalia (1648). The tension was reinforced by the Jesuit tendency to accommodate to new circumstances. In the international realm it often meant working pragmatically with colonial powers to set up missions and preach the Gospel, but it also could involve an openness to intercultural exchange with native peoples as a means to save their souls. Such accommodation not only ran afoul of Church conservatives, who worried about diluting the one true faith, but also contrasted with the repressive strategies preferred by colonial authorities, particularly in Spanish and Portuguese Latin America.

Against this broad backdrop, two different accusations, apparently contradictory but essentially intertwined, informed anti-Jesuitism as a cultural and political force—the perceived drives for universal empire on the one hand and for a "state within a state" at the national level on the other.[7] These claims were key components of what came to be known as the Black Legend—that is, the popular denigration of the Jesuits, particularly in Protestant Europe, as power hungry, unprincipled, bloodthirsty, and in league with the devil. As Peter Burke reminds us, it did not involve a uniform set of charges but more of a "repertoire of stereotypes, each of which was formed at a particular moment for particular reasons." For Burke the different strands of anti-Jesuitism can only be understood in interaction with particular events.⁸ From its beginnings anti-Jesuitism played out differently in different contexts—in Europe, the Americas, and Asia—as a response to the unique constellation of Jesuit missionary and educational enterprises in each location.⁹

Four Currents of Anti-Jesuitism

It is impossible to understand anti-Jesuitism without starting from the peculiar characteristics of the Society of Jesus itself and Ignatius's decision to engage with the world.¹⁰ The origins of anti-Jesuitism, nationally and internationally, are best explored through the founding documents of the order. A passage in one of the Declarations to the *Constitutions* echoes two of the major motifs of anti-Jesuitism.

> The more universal the good is, the more is it divine. Therefore preference ought to be given to those persons and places which, through their own improvement, become a cause which can spread the good accomplished to many others who are under their influence or take guidance from them. For that reason, the spiritual aid which is given to important and public persons ought to be regarded as more important, since it is a more universal good. . . . For the same reason, too, preference ought to be shown to the aid which is given to large nations such as the Indies, or to important cities, or to universities, which are generally attended by numerous persons who, if aided themselves, can become labourers for the help of others.¹¹

This passage contains the basic elements that led many to resent the Society of Jesus. To achieve a good that was as universal as possible, priority was to be given both to what we might anachronistically call "the ruling class" and to the mission to the Indies, a vast part of the globe with enormous potential for evangelization. The Declaration emphasized action on two fronts—the European and the colonial—that would increasingly come to characterize the Society of Jesus and make it the target of polemics. Interestingly the core elements of Jesuit identity and mission that made it attractive to the order's adherents and supporters—its openness to politics and society and its global horizon—also made it an object of suspicion and hostility.

Another source of anti-Jesuitism is the fourth vow of direct loyalty to the pope—"a special obedience to the sovereign pontiff in regard to the missions"—that Jesuit priests take.[12] The justification for the fourth vow provided in the *Constitutions* was more practical than theological: "For those who first united to form the Society were from different provinces and realms and did not know into which regions they were to go, whether among the faithful or the unbelievers; and therefore, to avoid erring in the path of the Lord, they subscribed to this vow in order that His Holiness might distribute them for the greater glory of God, in conformity with their intention to travel throughout the world."[13]

These founding documents, interpreted in a malicious light, provided fodder for the Jesuits' critics over the centuries. What from the Jesuit perspective was an organizational structure and way of proceeding designed to save souls and serve the common good for the greater glory of God appeared to their critics as a cynical and corrupt program of self-aggrandizement that threatened legitimate political and social order. During the period between the Society's founding and its suppression in 1773, one can identify four distinct but often mutually reinforcing currents of anti-Jesuitism that thrived on these allegations: the religious-political, the ecclesiastical, the Jesuit, and the Enlightenment currents.

Religious-Political Anti-Jesuitism

Religious-political anti-Jesuitism focused on the perceived political meddling of the order. Not surprising, it was most pronounced at the front lines of the Reformation, in Elizabethan England and in German lands divided along sectarian lines, but it also extended to nominally Catholic kingdoms—France, Spain, and Italy—where the Jesuits were denounced as defenders of papal power against temporal rulers. The criticism of the transnational character of the Society of Jesus was common to both Catholic and Protestant countries and, in the latter case, was reinforced by a deep, theologically grounded hostility toward the papacy.

In Elizabethan England the Jesuits were seen as the long arm of the Holy See, eager to return the Anglican Church established by Henry VIII to Rome.[14] The Society was persecuted under the Act of Supremacy (1558), which outlawed the recognition of the authority of foreign power, political or religious, within the realm and was directed primarily against Catholics aligned with the pope and the Spanish monarchy. Many Jesuits fled the country while some went underground, administering sacraments to the faithful. Anti-Jesuit pamphlets of the era accused the order of treason and of using "Jesuitical" techniques of concealment and "mental reservation"—essentially, deceiving for the cause—as part of a plot to overthrow the monarchy. Ferocious campaigns against leading Jesuits such as Robert Parsons and Edmund Campion—one of the order's first martyrs—made the survival of the Jesuits in the British Isles precarious.

Anti-Jesuit discourse was even more pronounced in those German territories that had followed Martin Luther in his break from Rome.[15] During the second half of the sixteenth century, attacks on the pope as the Antichrist and as a tool of Satan were increasingly directed at the Jesuits, who were popularly identified as the shock troops of the Counter-Reformation. German lands saw the first use of animal iconography to stigmatize the vices of the Jesuits. For example, Peter Canisius, the founder of the Society's first German province, was caricatured as "a dog of a monk, idolater, wolf, ass of the Pope, swindling trickster, shameless and miserable devil."[16] The purported link with the devil surfaced again and again in the German context. These charges often arose in tandem with accusations that the Jesuits had magical powers perhaps because—as Róisín Healy has suggested—"accepting the notion of Jesuit magic also helped Reformers to explain why the Jesuits had been so successful in conversion."[17]

While loyalty to the pope made the Jesuits the main target of Protestant polemicists, also bolstering religious-political anti-Jesuitism across Europe were those practices that they viewed as political and subversive: the running of colleges for young people, the use of the confessional to influence elites, and the exploitation of women. The accusation of political meddling was in part a response to the presence of Jesuit confessors close to many European sovereigns. The Society's founding of new colleges on European territory—and especially in border areas, such as the Habsburg Empire—was read as a project to dominate the state through the education of generations of young people with closer ties to the Society than to secular institutions. And while Ignatius did not set up a female branch of the order, the Jesuits did recruit wealthy and powerful women to its affiliated Marian congregations and offered them spiritual direction, sparking accusations that Jesuits were seducing members of the "weaker sex" to steal their inheritance.[18]

These themes are found in anti-Jesuit pamphlets published in Catholic countries including Italy, Spain, and Poland. Of the huge outpouring of pamphlets in Europe between the end of the sixteenth century and through the eighteenth century, among the most noteworthy were the *Monita Secreta Societatis Jesu*, a forged version of the Society's *Constitutions* published in 1614 in Krakow by a former Polish Jesuit, Jerome Zahorowski.[19] The force of the libel was due to its clear presentation and a certain plausibility regarding the sensitive issues outlined earlier: schools that gave access to youth, the confessional that gave access to elites, and the exploitation of women, an issue in the popular imagination that carried over from the economic and political to the sexual sphere. The Vatican denounced the *Monita Secreta* as a forgery and placed it on its Index of Prohibited Books in 1615. But it has remained in circulation and well known for centuries.[20]

The accusation that the Society constituted a "state within the state," without effective political or ecclesiastical oversight, went hand in hand with the idea of Jesuit aspirations to "universal monarchy" that was developed in the *Monita Secreta* and other publications. The Jesuits were seen as an impediment to establishing effective state political authority at home and abroad. One of the early, influential proponents of this view was the Venetian humanist Paolo Sarpi, who wrote in 1608:

> I have always marvelled at the politics of Jesuits and especially their manner of keeping secrets. It is a fine thing that they have their Constitutions printed, but then it is not possible to see a copy. I do not mean the rules that were printed at Lyons. Those are puerile. But I refer to the laws of their governance that they keep utterly secret. . . . There are not so many other persons in the world who all conspire to one end, who are handled with such precision, and who employ so much ardour and zeal in their work as the Jesuits.[21]

Sarpi saw the Society's network of confessors and schools in the service of the papacy and Habsburg Spain as a means to "raise up entire kingdoms against their natural rulers."[22]

In the seventeenth century majority-Catholic France emerged as the epicenter of anti-Jesuit polemics.[23] The country was home to the brilliant Blaise Pascal (1623–62), the most famous of the Jesuits' critics. While Pascal's attacks had a theological grounding in his Jansenism—a topic taken up in the next section—he also maligned the Jesuits as unprincipled political operatives who were willing to lie and steal to advance their aims. He joined others in accusing the Jesuits of putting the pope ahead of the French monarchy and even of endorsing regicide as a policy option. Along these lines the faculty of the Sorbonne publicly condemned the work by the Spanish Jesuit Juan de Mariana, *De rege et regis institutione* (1598), which held out the possibility of revolt against unjust kings. This line of anti-Jesuit critique culminated in 1760, four years before the Society's expulsion from France, in an influential volume by Louis-Adrien Le Paige, for whom the Society's *Constitutions* was a perverted blueprint of a "model of political society"—that is, a universal monarchy under Jesuit domination.[24]

Throughout the early modern period, accusations of Jesuit political meddling extended from the national to the international level. An increasingly global Jesuit network came into tension with the interests and priorities of new colonial empires in the process of formation. A considerable fraction of the European anti-Jesuit publications, taking a political reading of Ignatius's emphasis on the salvation of souls in the missionary enterprise, referred to the alleged ambition of the Jesuits to found a universal empire as a worldwide endeavor. The idea of a universal Jesuit empire was first fully articulated and critiqued by Louis de Montpersan in 1688 in his *La politique des Jésuites*. "The great pretension of the Jesuits and the height of their ambitious and insolent presumption," he wrote, was "to want to establish an absolute Empire—a tyranny over the spirits of all men so unbearable that they be forced to submit to their sentiments and blindly embrace all their maxims."[25]

Ecclesiastical Anti-Jesuitism

We have already seen how religious-political anti-Jesuitism, especially of a Protestant hue, very often linked attacks on the Jesuits with denunciations of the papacy as a transnational power under the sway of the order. In the Catholic context as well, the Jesuits were subjected to severe criticism over the centuries. The charge that the Jesuits were too willing to compromise with the world was at the heart of the anti-Jesuitism of Jansenism, a current of Catholicism in France that was closer to Protestantism in many respects. This conflict gave rise to the most significant and influential of all anti-Jesuit texts, Pascal's *Lettres provinciales*, which attacked the Jesuits for their casuistry, moral laxity with penitents, and hypocrisy in preaching the Gospel while engaging the world.[26] Outside of France, Bishop of Puebla Juan de Palafox y Mendoza, the influential Franciscan Valeriano Magni, and the Carmelite Enrico di Sant'Ignazio articulated the idea that a Jesuit world conspiracy threatened the Church.

In the international context rival missionary orders including the Franciscans and the Dominicans, who had preceded the Jesuits by several centuries, emerged as their most influential intra-Church critics. Their criticism of the Jesuit practice of accommodating Confucian rites in China and Malabar rites in India eventually won the day during the Rites Controversy that erupted around the middle of the seventeenth century.[27] It was a key transitional moment in the history of the Society of Jesus and in anti-Jesuitism, for the order was increasingly at odds not only with the

Westphalian system of sovereign states and its colonial enterprise but also with the homogeneous universalist vision of the Church as promoted by the Congregation de Propaganda Fide. After 1622, however, attention to what happened far from the Eternal City grew to the point that the Congregation de Propaganda Fide sent the dossier on the Rites Controversy to the Holy Inquisition. It condemned as incompatible with Catholic doctrine an alleged syncretism promoted by the Jesuits in China (between Catholicism and Confucianism) and in India (between Catholicism and Hinduism) through their policy of cultural accommodation. The controversy simmered over time, producing a succession of critical papal pronouncements that had little direct impact until Benedict XIV's definitive condemnation of certain Jesuit missionary practices in the 1740s.[28]

To some extent the Jesuits brought this scrutiny on themselves by publishing the correspondence from the missions to Europe, under the title *Lettres édifiantes et curieuses*, in some thirty-four volumes between 1702 and 1776. Over the entire period charges of alleged heterodoxy shaped by a suspicious and hostile reading of that correspondence informed a series of influential anti-Jesuit pamphlets, some circulating widely in multiple languages. Among those who launched polemical attacks on the Chinese rites were the Dominican Domingo de Navarrete and Juan de Palafox y Mendoza, and the memoirs of François-Marie de Tours stoked the disputes over the Malabar rites in India. The Jesuits' most famous critic in the Rites Controversy was the Capuchin Pierre Parisot, known as Père Norbert, for whom "the Jesuits were the Jansenists of China" and worse. While the Jansenists could at most be accused of misinterpreting the sacred texts, in his view the Jesuits were guilty of paganism and devil worship, accusations that were much more familiar in Protestant literature.[29]

Jesuit Anti-Jesuitism

Interestingly much of the most vehement anti-Jesuit literature emerged out of the order itself from ex-Jesuits alienated from the Society or from those within the Society who were unable to advance.[30] One example is the pamphlet *Monarchia solipsorum*, a vehement indictment of the Society of Jesus and its purported ambitions to establish a universal empire. It was a collaboration between two fascinating figures—the former Jesuit Giulio Clemente Scotti, the author of a number of pamphlets against the order, and Melchior Inchofer, a Hungarian Jesuit who was active in Italy and never left the Society. Inchofer collaborated with Scotti by providing contemporary materials that could make his attacks more plausible.[31] Inchofer was not an isolated case. Over the centuries a number of Jesuits reacted against what John O'Malley has called "elitism within the brotherhood" that "caused confusion and took a psychological toll."³² In certain cases those who produced hostile memoirs and treatises critical of the Society, its ambitions, and its methods had not progressed beyond ordination to their final vows, including the fourth vow of obedience to the pope.

The history of anti-Jesuitism among Jesuits themselves is one marker of internal tensions and even dissension within the Society over time. A common theme in critical Jesuit writings, echoed even in some by the influential Superior General Claudio Acquaviva (1581–1615), was that the order was in danger of breaking with the ideals of Ignatius and of descending into factions and political maneuvering.³³ These texts—which, unlike those of Scotti, generally remained in manuscript form and were only intended for internal circulation—very often refer to an erroneous interpretation of the concept of obedience on the part of the hierarchies of the Society.³⁴ Their aim seems to have been to initiate a debate on the future of the order, criticizing the behavior of the superiors who, the texts alleged, were driving a substantial number of adherents to abandon the Society.³⁵ A manuscript circulating in the late seventeenth century decried the tendency of superiors to alienate their subjects and asserted that "those who left the Society of Jesus are much more numerous than those who have left all the other orders put together."³⁶ This negative interpretation of departures from the Society has been a staple of anti-Jesuitism through the centuries.³⁷

Enlightenment Anti-Jesuitism

A fourth current, Enlightenment anti-Jesuitism, took hold with the rise of rationalist thought in the eighteenth century and the spread of anticlericalism and secularism in the wake of the French Revolution. Even before France and Spain expelled the Jesuits in the mid-eighteenth century, critics pointed to the Paraguay reductions, which include parts of contemporary Brazil, Paraguay, and Uruguay, as notorious examples of corrupt priestly rule. Here was a case of alternative political, religious, and even economic institutions—a self-contained and unaccountable departure from the European norm. While the reductions had some admirers, including Ludovico Antonio Muratori and Montesquieu, many others roundly criticized them as a dangerous accretion of clerical power.³⁸ One of the many eighteenth-century anti-Jesuit polemics decried their "ambition of sovereign control and their insatiable desire to accumulate immense riches" and lamented that "the Jesuits have become the Owners and Sovereigns of all the Indians, of the Lands that they occupy, of their Harvest, and their Work, and every day they expand without title and without permission."[39] Such charges, in this case focused on an alleged accumulation of economic power through colonial enterprises, were often joined to an Enlightenment critique of the Jesuits as the vanguard of a benighted, autocratic papacy still devoted to the theocratic ideal.

Most Jesuits certainly did subscribe to a Counter-Reformation political theology that envisioned secular power as ultimately subordinate to divine (and therefore also ecclesiastical) authority. They were not unique among Church orders in holding such views, but they were among the most visible, given their more public method of engagement with the world. For that reason as the eighteenth century progressed, the Jesuits were frequent targets of proponents of popular sovereignty and political absolutism, as well as of philosophes who championed reason against tradition and revelation. Voltaire, whose *Candide* critiques the Jesuits on multiple levels, was a prominent example of the latter.

By the middle of the eighteenth century, the Enlightenment strand of anti-Jesuitism had combined with earlier religious-political, ecclesiastical, and Jesuit currents to powerful effect. The idea of a Jesuit plot for world domination, one that echoed across all four variants, was rearticulated in widely read various works such as *Dictamen fiscal de expulsión de los jesuitas de España* by Pedro Rodríguez de Campomanes. Versions of the *Monita Secreta* circulating around this time painted the Jesuits as a secret, subversive, and dangerous sect. In the years prior to their final suppression in 1773, some Jesuits fought back by conjuring up the specter of a Jansenist plot, an interesting effort to turn the motifs of anti-Jesuitism against their opponents.[40] In the end Pope Clement XIV, under the illusion that sacrificing the Jesuits would protect the papacy from further attacks, yielded to the demands of the French and Spanish monarchies.

Anti-Jesuitism after the Restoration of the Society

The suppression of the Society of Jesus was not total. Catherine II of Russia refused to allow the publication of Clement's bull *Dominus ac redemptor* in her domains, thus allowing the Jesuits in the Polish provinces to survive. In 1801 Pope Pius VII granted the "Russian Jesuits" permission to reconstitute formally as the Society of Jesus within the confines of the Russian Empire. A number of refugees traveled there from around the world. The survival of the Jesuits kept anti-Jesuitism alive, however; pamphlets as well as a new generation of wider-circulation newspapers and journals continued to pillory the Society, which was deemed weakened but very much a threat. Some of the critiques extended to Russia proper. It is worth recalling that some of the masterpieces of nineteenth-century Russian literature, including Fyodor Dostoevsky's *The Idiot*, savage the figure of the duplicitous and conniving Jesuit. The term *Jezuitnikat'* ("Jesuitized") entered the Russian lexicon to denote hypocritical behavior.[41]

Once the papacy had recovered from the humiliation of the French Revolution and the Napoleonic Wars, Pius VII reestablished the Society of Jesus in 1814. Over the subsequent decades, the order made a slow recovery. Not only had it been stripped of its schools, missions, and other ministries, now also it had to rebuild in a hostile context marked by the rise of secularism and nationalism. As John McGreevy points out in chapter 6 of this volume, the United States, with its openness to immigrants and greater religious pluralism and tolerance, was unusual in providing the Society propitious conditions for renewal. In most of Europe and Latin America, by contrast, nationalism, anticlericalism, and anti-Jesuitism went hand in hand as the century progressed. Old charges of secrecy and conspiracy were given new life in a context of renewed hostility to a more assertive papacy. Ironically the first major Jesuit expulsion in this new era, in 1820, was from an erstwhile place of refuge, Russia, amid a wave of nationalist xenophobia.

There was a connection between the Russian experience of the order during the suppression decades and its subsequent political conservatism and ultramontanism through the nineteenth century and into the twentieth. Although the Jesuits who had found refuge in the Russian Empire belonged to different national communities, their common exile contributed to their overcoming the rise of ethnic and national particularism that had characterized the Society during the second half of the eighteenth century. A stronger common identity facilitated the growth of the order under the leadership of Superior General Jan Roothaan (1829–53), a dominant figure during the mid-nineteenth century. It also contributed to the close alignment between the Jesuits and a resurgent papacy under Pope Pius IX (1846–78) and his successors. A powerful institutional expression of this alliance was the Jesuit journal *La Civiltà Cattolica*. First published in Rome in 1851, it served as an official mouthpiece of the Vatican and a reliable defender of its doctrines, including the papal infallibility asserted at the First Vatican Council and the social teaching promulgated by Pope Leo XIII in *Rerum novarum* in 1891.

This strong Vatican-Jesuit connection contributed to a new wave of anti-Jesuitism in Europe and the Americas. In Italy and Germany, for example, the Jesuits were attacked as opponents of national unification. In *Il Gesuita moderno*, a scathing, influential book published in 1847, Vincenzo Gioberti coined the term "Jesuitism" to denigrate the Jesuits' opposition to modernity in general and Italy's national aspirations in particular. Opposition to Italian unity expressed "the fault that has always run through the history of this great religious order: the pursuit of its own unfettered power, and of dominance over all Catholic souls."[42] In the German context the Jesuits were critical of Otto von Bismarck's German unification drive in 1870–71 under Prussian, and therefore Protestant, leadership. Bismarck expelled the Jesuits from Germany in 1872, and the *Kulturkampf* against Catholic influence in the 1880s featured a propaganda campaign against the Society of Jesus that painted it as a subversive, alien force determined to weaken the German nation.

In France and the newly independent states of Latin America, a strong combination of nationalism and secularism fed an anti-Jesuit animus at different points during the nineteenth century. Jesuits were expelled from France in 1828, in 1880, and again in 1901; from Colombia in 1850; and from Brazil in 1889. Freemasonry emerged as one of the Jesuits' most influential rivals and critics. In Argentina in 1850, for example, the Jesuits were seen as instigators of the bishop of Buenos Aires's condemnation of Freemason influence in politics and society.[43] Bartolomé Mitre, who served as president of Argentina (1862–68) and was himself a Mason with close links to Italian anticlerical circles, coupled his insistence on Church-state separation with the slogan "Down with the Jesuits!" The identification of Catholicism with Jesuitism also played an important role in the politics of Uruguay during the latter part of the nineteenth century.[44]

The revival of Jesuit missionary activity in the nineteenth century was also a driver of some anti-Jesuitism. The new missions promoted by Pope Gregory XVI (1831–46), in the context of a second great wave of European colonial expansion, raised anew problems in the relationship between Catholic missionaries and colonial powers. The case of Madurai in British colonial India provides an example. A new Jesuit mission there was formed in 1838 and entrusted to French Jesuits from the Lyon Province. This provoked problems not only with the British governor, who favored English Catholic missionaries, but also with other missionary orders, such as the Missions Étrangères de Paris (Paris Foreign Missions), which took issue, as in the past, with the Society's greater openness to intercultural encounter.[45] But nowhere did tensions reach the stage they had during the Rites Controversy of the seventeenth and eighteenth centuries. During this second wave of globalization, which continued until decolonization in the post–World War II era, Jesuit missions tended to participate in imperial projects premised on the superiority of European cultures over that of others.

The Eclipse of Anti-Jesuitism: From Vatican II to Pope Francis

The emergence of anti-Jesuitism in the centuries after the founding of the Society of Jesus in 1540 had several related causes. One was the nature of the Society itself, with its combination of secrecy and centralization on the one hand and engagement with society and politics on the other hand. The Jesuits' two most prominent ministries, education and missions, had high visibility. Ignatius's desire to transform the world "for the greater glory of God" could be construed as an effort to accumulate and exercise power. And his principle of accommodation to time and circumstances for the salvation of souls could be read as unprincipled pragmatism that put convenience ahead of truth. Attacks on Jesuits for being power hungry and corrupt reverberated through the centuries and drew on all four of the currents of anti-Jesuitism outlined in this chapter: the religious-political, the ecclesiastical, the Jesuit, and the Enlightenment variants.

This survey suggests a close connection between the Jesuits, anti-Jesuitism, and globalization through the centuries. The coincidence of the founding of the order with the first great phase of European expansion created a global frame for the unfolding of the Society's missionary energy. In this first phase of globalization, criticism of the Jesuits' political involvement often referred to what they were doing outside Europe. With Jesuit missionaries in the Americas, India, and the Far East, charges of "Jesuit empire-building" had a certain plausibility. And the Jesuit way of proceeding, with its greater emphasis on cultural openness and dialogue as part of the missionary enterprise, fueled suspicions that the Jesuits were pursuing their own agenda, which was at odds with both the colonial powers and the Catholic Church. The complex politics that led to the suppression of the order in 1773 cannot be understood without reference to the Rites Controversy in Asia or to the reductions in the Americas. The order's global reach multiplied its enemies and fed irrational fears of a drive for world domination. The historical record includes a voluminous Jesuit conspiracy literature that served as one of the models for the infamous and influential anti-Semitic forgery *The Protocols of the Elders of Zion*.[46]

Anti-Jesuitism persisted in the century after the reestablishment of the order in 1814 and was reinforced by the rise of nationalism and secularism in Europe and Latin America. But its virulence and tenor changed. The order and its missionary and educational enterprises recovered only slowly and unevenly from the blow of the suppression; they were no longer a force to be reckoned with in European politics. Closely aligned with the papacy, they were subject to less ecclesiastical scrutiny. And persuaded as they were of European cultural superiority, the Jesuits were seldom at odds with the Western imperialist enterprise. Through the turn of the twentieth century, the Jesuits were criticized both by nationalists in Europe and Latin America as agents of papal power and by Church progressives as defenders of papal supremacy. But the savage and paranoid attacks of earlier centuries, with their imagined threat of a Jesuit world empire of ambition and deceit, had faded.

As Maria Clara Lucchetti Bingemer discusses in chapter 9 of this volume, anti-Jesuitism has further receded in globalization's contemporary phase, which can be dated to decolonization and the Church's opening to the modern world at the Second Vatican Council. Under Superior General Pedro Arrupe (1965–83), the Jesuits embraced a global social justice agenda. His emphasis on the "preferential option for the poor" was echoed by the Medellín Conference of Latin American Bishops in 1968, and in 1975 the Thirty-Second General Congregation of the Society famously articulated its mission as "the service of faith and the promotion of justice." This progressive turn, evident in the embrace of interreligious dialogue and an openness to liberation theology, earned the ire of conservatives in the Church and the order itself. Not all Jesuits within the order (particularly those in Italy) took a favorable view of Vatican II or of the emerging theologies of Latin America and India. During the special administration that the Holy See imposed on the Society following Superior General Pedro Arrupe's illness, the Society of Jesus had to endure the hostility of Pope John Paul II. Far from Europe the Jesuits continued to work for the promotion of justice, but ideologically speaking, after the passing of the Vatican II generation—Henri de Lubac, Jean Daniélou, Karl Rahner—European public opinion was largely unaware of their efforts. But nothing similar to the anti-Jesuitism of earlier eras emerged then or at any time since. The idea that the Society poses a political threat, nationally or internationally, has lost any plausibility and not least given its dwindling size, from around thirty-six thousand members at the close of Vatican II to about half that number today.

In this context it is not surprising that Pope Francis, the first Jesuit pope in history, has not provoked any upsurge in anti-Jesuitism. Francis has made no secret of his identity as a Jesuit, and his emphasis on social justice and intercultural dialogue exemplifies currents of Jesuit thought and practice from Ignatius through Arrupe. The first non-European pope, his path is inseparable from the legacy of the Jesuits in Latin America and around the globe. But his role as shepherd of the Catholic Church and of pastor to the world is anchored not in his Jesuit identity but in the institution of the papacy, which has emerged as a powerful global platform since the 1980s. To be sure, Francis's election saw an upsurge in Jesuit conspiracy theories on the margins of the Internet, most of them innocent of any awareness of their centuries-old pedigree. But in contrast to earlier ages, their impact on the public imagination is all but nonexistent. The strong connection between the Jesuit experience and anti-Jesuitism, which has unfolded nationally and internationally for more than four and a half centuries, appears to have come to an end in our global era.

Notes

1. On the Jesuit system in the American context, see Aliocha Maldavsky's chapter 4 in this volume. On globalization in the early modern period, see Serge Grusinski, *Les quatre parties du monde: Histoire d'une mondialisation* (Paris: La Martinière, 2004).

2. Key works in this growing literature include Pierre-Antoine Fabre and Catherine Maire, *Les Antijésuites: Discours, figures et lieux de l'antijésuitisme à l'époque moderne* (Rennes, France: Presses universitaires de Rennes, 2010); Michael Niemetz, *Antijesuitische Bildpublizistik in der Frühen Neuzeit: Geschichte, Ikonographie und Ikonologie* (Regensburg, Germany: Schnell & Steiner, 2008); and Susana Monreal, Sabina Pavone, and Guillermo Zermeño, eds., *Antijesuitismo y Filiojesuitismo: Dos identidades ante la restauración* (Mexico City: Universidad Iberoamericana, 2014).

3. Étienne Pasquier, *Le catéchisme des jésuites ou examen de leur doctrine*, ed. Claude Sutto (Québec: Université de Sherbrooke, 1982). See also Luce Giard, "Le 'Catéchisme des Jésuites' d'Étienne Pasquier, une attaque en règle," in Fabre and Maire, *Les Antijésuites*, 73–90; and Myriam Yardeni, "La pensée politique des 'Politiques': Étienne Pasquier et Jacques-Auguste de Thou," in *De Michel de l'Hospital à l'Édit de Nantes: Politique et religion face aux Églises*, ed. Thierry Wanegffelen (Clermont-Ferrand, France: Presses Universitaires Blaise Pascal, 2002), 495–510.

4. Ignatius, October 1546, in Ignatius of Loyola, *Epistolæ et Instructiones* (Rome: Monumenta Historica Societatis Iesu, 1964), 1:432. In a similar vein, he observed in another letter two years later that "many in this Roman court are of the opinion that we want to rule the world." Ignatius, November 3, 1548, *Epistolæ et Instructiones*, 2:251.

5. Michel de Montaigne, *Journal de voyage* (Paris: Gallimard, 1983), 223.

6. Sabina Pavone, "Between History and Myth: The *Monita secreta Societatis Jesu*," in *The Jesuits II: Cultures, Sciences, and the Arts, 1540–1773*, ed. John W. O'Malley, SJ, et al. (Toronto: University of Toronto Press, 2006), 57–58.

7. This was a standard accusation made not only against the Jesuits but also

against the Jews or the Freemasons. See Jacob Katz, *Jews and Freemasons in Europe, 1723–1939* (Cambridge, MA: Harvard University Press, 1970).

8. Peter Burke, "The Black Legend of the Jesuits: An Essay in the History of Social Stereotypes," in *Christianity and Community in the West: Essays for John Bossy*, ed. Simon Ditchfield (Aldershot, UK: Ashgate, 2001), 172. See also by the same author "Publicizing the Private: The Rise of 'Secret History,'" in *Changing Perceptions of the Public Sphere*, ed. Christian J. Emden and David R. Midgley (New York: Berghahn Books, 2012), 57–72.

9. The global dimension of anti-Jesuitism has been addressed in a project hosted by the University Iberoamericana in Mexico City. Within the ambit of a large project coordinated by Perla Chinchilla, see the volume edited by Monreal, Pavone, and Zermeño, *Antijesuitismo y Filojesuitismo*. On the variety of global Jesuit projects in the early centuries, see Paul Shore, *Jesuits and the Politics of Religious Pluralism in Eighteenth-Century Transylvania: Culture, Politics and Religion, 1693–1773* (Aldershot, UK: Ashgate, 2007); Sabina Pavone, *Una strana alleanza: La Compagnia di Gesù in Russia dal 1772 al 1820* (Naples: Bibliopolis, 2008); and Paolo Bianchini, ed., *Morte e resurrezione di un Ordine religioso: Le strategie culturali ed educative della Compagnia di Gesù durante la soppressione (1759–1814)* (Milan: Vita e Pensiero, 2006).

10. Sabina Pavone, *The Wily Jesuits and the* Monita Secreta*: The Forged Secret Instructions of the Jesuits; Myth and Reality* (St. Louis: Institute of Jesuit Sources, 2005).

11. Ignatius of Loyola and the Society of Jesus, *The Constitutions of the Society of Jesus and Their Complementary Norms: A Complete English Translation of the Official Latin Texts*, trans. Carl J. Moell, SJ (Saint Louis: Institute of Jesuit Sources, 1996), 286. I am indebted to Dominique Bertrand, *La politique de Saint Ignace de Loyola: L'analyse sociale* (Paris: Les Éditions du Cerf, 1985), 588, for the reminder of the importance of Declaration D of the *Constitutions*, chap. 2, pt. 7.

12. Ignatius and Society, *Constitutions*, 202.

13. Ibid., 373.

14. Thomas M. McCoog, SJ, *The Society of Jesus in Ireland, Scotland, and England, 1589–1597: Building the Faith of Saint Peter upon the King of Spain's Monarchy* (Aldershot, UK: Ashgate, 2012).

15. Róisín Healy, *The Jesuit Specter in Imperial Germany* (Boston: Brill, 2003); and Róisín Healy, "Anti-Jesuitism in Imperial Germany: The Jesuit as Androgyne," in *Protestants, Catholics, and Jews in Germany, 1800–1914*, ed. Helmut Walser Smith (Oxford: Berg, 2001), 153–81. See also for early modern Germany, Dean P. Bell, "Polemics of Confessionalization: Depictions of Jews and Jesuits in Early Modern Germany," in *"The Tragic Couple": Encounters between Jews and Jesuits*, ed. James William Bernauer and Robert A. Maryks (Leiden: Brill, 2013), 67–78.

16. Johann Wigand, *Scriptural Refutation of the Jesuit Catechism*, quoted in David Mitchell, *The Jesuits: A History* (London: Macdonald, 1980), 70.

17. Healy, *The Jesuit Specter*, 29. The idea that the Jesuits had magical powers also figures in Friedrich Schiller's novella *The Ghost Seer,* published in the late

1780s. In the novella a Jesuit first appears as an Armenian and then as a Russian in an example of another classic anti-Jesuit topos, the use of a disguise to deceive. See Ronnie Po-chia Hsia, "From Buddhist Garb to Literati Silk: Costume and Identity of the Jesuit Missionary," in *Religious Ceremonials and Images: Power and Social Meaning (1450–1750)*, ed. José Pedro Paiva (Coimbra, Portugal: Palimage Editores, 2002), 143–54; and Sabina Pavone, "Spie, mandarini, bramini: I gesuiti e i loro travestimenti," *Il Capitale Culturale: Studies on the Value of Cultural Heritage* 7 (2013): 227–47.

18. Gemma Simmonds, "Women Jesuits?," in *The Cambridge Companion to the Jesuits*, ed. Thomas Worcester, SJ (Cambridge: Cambridge University Press, 2008), 120–35. See also Silvia Mostaccio et al., eds., *Echelles de pouvoir, rapports de genre: Femmes, jésuites et modèle ignatien dans le long XIX siècle* (Louvain, Belgium: Presses Universitaires de Louvain, 2015).

19. Pavone, *Wily Jesuits*.

20. This claim also featured in another libel, more or less contemporaneous with the *Monita, Protocatastasis seu prima Societatis Iesu Institutio restauranda Summo Pontifici* by Guillaume Pasquelin (1575–1632), again a former Jesuit, published in Paris in 1614 and also included in the index in 1615.

21. Paolo Sarpi to Monsieur de l'Isle, Venice, September 2, 1608, in Bibliothèque Nationale de France, Cod. Italiani 508, 5r–6r.

22. Paolo Sarpi, *Opere*, ed. Gaetano Cozzi and Luisa Cozzi (Milan: R. Ricciardi, 1969), 308.

23. For France, see Eric Nelson, *The Jesuits and the Monarchy: Catholic Reform and Political Authority in France (1590–1615)* (Aldershot, UK: Ashgate, 2005).

24. Catherine Maire, "Des comptes-rendus des constitutions jésuites à la Constitution civile du clergé," in Fabre and Maire, *Les Antijésuites*, 401–28.

25. Louis de Montpersan, *La politique des Jésuites* (London, 1688), 61.

26. Girolamo Imbruglia, "Pascal tra propaganda e opinione pubblica: Le 'Lettere provinciali' e la critica dell'idolatria gesuita," in *Per Adriano Prosperi*, ed. Massimo Donattini, Giuseppe Marcocci, and Stefania Pastore, vol. 2, *L'Europa divisa e i nuovi mondi* (Pisa: Edizioni della Normale, 2011), 217–27. Moliere's *Tartuffe* was a biting and influential satire of these alleged Jesuit faults.

27. Joan-Pau Rubiés, "The Concept of Cultural Dialogue and the Jesuit Method of Accommodation: Between Idolatry and Civilisation," *Archivum Historicum Societatis Iesu* 74, no. 147 (2005): 237–80.

28. In addition to M. Antoni J. Ucerler's and Francis X. Clooney's chapters in this volume, see D. E. Mungello, ed., *The Chinese Rites Controversy: Its History and Meaning* (Nettetal, Germany: Steyler Verlag, 1994); and Ines Županov, *Disputed Mission: Jesuit Experiments and Brahmanical Knowledge in Seventeenth-Century India* (New Delhi: Oxford University Press, 1999).

29. Père Norbert, *Mémoires historiques sur les missions des Indes Orientales*, vol. 1 (Besançon, France, 1747), 510.

30. Sabina Pavone, "Antijésuitisme politique et antijésuitisme jésuite: Une comparaison de quelques textes," in Fabre and Maire, *Les Antijésuites*, 139–64.

31. One of Scotti's better-known pamphlets, *Denudata veritas*, charged that the order really was governed by the *Monita Secreta*.

32. John W. O'Malley, SJ, *The First Jesuits* (Cambridge, MA: Harvard University Press, 1993), 347.

33. Michela Catto, *La Compagnia divisa: Il dissenso nell'ordine gesuitico tra '500 e '600* (Brescia, Italy: Morcelliana, 2009); and Guido Mongini,*"Ad Christi similitudinem"*: *Ignazio di Loyola e i primi gesuiti tra eresia e ortodossia; Studi sulle origini della Compagnia di Jèsu* (Alessandria, Italy: Edizioni dell'Orso, 2011). On the general theme of dissent in the Society of Jesus, see the essays collected in Fernanda Alfieri and Claudio Ferlan, eds., *Avventure dell'obbedienza nella Compagnia di Gèsu: Teorie e prassi tra XVI e XIX secolo* (Bologna: Il Mulino, 2012).

34. On the theme of obedience, see Silvia Mostaccio, "'Perinde ac si cadaver essent': Les jésuites dans une persective comparative: La tension constitutive entre obéissance et le 'representar' dans les sources normatives des réguliers au premier âge moderne," *Revue d'histoire ecclésiastique* 105, no. 1 (2010): 44–73; Mostaccio, "Les enjeux de l'obéissance dans la Compagnie de Jésus: Les congrégations provinciales: pratiques et réflexions d'un espace intermédiaire (XVe–XVIIe siècles)," in *Mutations des religions et identités religieuses*, ed. Jean-Pierre Delville (Paris: Mame-Desclée, 2012), 179–90; and Mostaccio, *Early Modern Jesuits between Obedience and Conscience during the Generalate of Claudio Acquaviva (1581–1615)* (Farnham, UK: Ashgate, 2014).

35. On the theme of departures, see Sabina Pavone, "I dimessi della Compagnia negli anni del generalato di Francesco Borgia: Una nuova questione storiografica," in *Francisco de Borja y su tiempo: Política, Religión y Cultura en la Edad Moderna*, ed. Enrique García Hernán and María del Pilar Ryan (Valencia: Albatros Ediciones, 2011), 465–80.

36. *Discorso sopra la religione de' padri Jesuiti e loro modo de governare*, chap. 6, § 16, in *Scritture politiche, morali e satiriche sopra le Massime, Istituto e Governo della Compagnia di Gesù*, ca. late 1600s, in Archivum Romanum Societatis Iesu, F. G. 697, Rome.

37. A prominent example around the turn of the twentieth century is *Historia interna documentada de la Compañía de Jesús* (Madrid: Imprenta de Jaime Ratés Martín, 1913) by Miguel Mir, a former Jesuit. See Emilio La Parra López, "L'antijésuitisme des jésuites: *Historia interna de la Compañía de Jesús* du P. Miguel Mir," in Fabre and Maire, *Les Antijésuites*, 221–40.

38. See Girolamo Imbruglia, *The Jesuit Missions of Paraguay and the Cultural History of Utopia (1540–1789)* (Leiden: Brill, forthcoming); or Girolamo Imbruglia, *L'invenzione del Paraguay: Studio sull'idea di comunità tra Seicento e Settecento* (Naples: Bibliopolis, 1987). Ludovico Antonio Muratori wrote the *Cristianesimo felice nelle missioni de' padri della Compagnia di Gesù in Paraguai* (Venice: Presso Giambattista Pasquali, 1743).

39. Sebastião José de Carvalho e Melo, *Relazione breve della Repubblica, che i religiosi Gesuiti delle Provincie di Portogallo, e di Spagna hanno stabilita ne' Dominj Oltramarini delle due Monarchie, e della Guerra, che in esse hanno mossa, e sostenuta contro gli Eserciti Spagnuoli e Portoghesi* (Lisbon, 1757), art. 11, 79–80.

40. On this point, see Marina Caffiero, "La rhétorique symétrique: Discours et stratégies d'autolégitimation des jésuites," in Fabre and Maire, *Les Antijésuites*, 197–220.

41. Pavone, *Una strana alleanza*.

42. Luciano Malusa, "Gioberti, Vincenzo," in *Dizionario storico dell'Inquisizione*, ed. Adriano Prosperi (Pisa: Edizioni della Normale, 2010), 2:692. Interestingly, the fiercest critic in Italy promoted the idea of a federation of Italian states with the pope at its head. For once the Society and the papacy were not being tarred with the same brush.

43. Roberto Di Stefano, "El antijesuitismo porteño del siglo XIX," in Monreal, Pavone, and Zermeño, *Antijesuitismo y Filojesuitismo*, 178.

44. Susana Monreal, "'Catolicismo y jesuitismo son una misma cosa': Campañas antijesuíticas en Montevideo: 1893–1913," in Monreal, Pavone, and Zermeño, *Antijesuitismo y Filojesuitismo*, 193–216.

45. On the new mission of Madurai, see Sabina Pavone, "The Province of Madurai between the Old and New Society of Jesus," in *Jesuit Survival and Restoration: A Global History, 1773–1900*, ed. Robert A. Maryks and Jonathan Wright (Boston: Brill, 2014), 333–52.

46. See Norman Cohn, *Warrant for Genocide: The Myth of the Jewish World Conspiracy and* The Protocols of the Elders of Zion (New York: Harper & Row, 1967); Léon Poliakov, *La causalité diabolique*, 2 vols. (Paris: Calmann-Lévy, 1980–85); Pierre-André Taguieff, *Les Protocoles des Sages de Sion* (Paris: Berg International, 1992); and Cesare G. De Michelis, *The Non-Existent Manuscript: A Study of the Protocols of the Sages of Zion* (Lincoln: University of Nebraska Press, 2004).

6

RESTORED JESUITS
Notes toward a Global History

JOHN T. MCGREEVY

How might the Jesuits help us understand globalization? And how might globalization help us understand the Jesuits? The answers for the "old" Society of Jesus, before the 1773 suppression, are familiar. A rich historical literature now details the rapid expansion of the Jesuits into almost every corner of the globe in the first generations after Ignatius of Loyola, with Francis Xavier in Japan, Pedro Martínez in Havana, and José de Acosta in Peru before 1600. If Catholicism is the world's first global institution, then the Jesuits were indispensable to its geographical spread away from Europe. These Jesuits link the Age of Discovery to the Catholic variant on the Republic of Letters.

Our understanding of the Jesuits after the 1814 restoration, which coincided with a new phase of European global expansion, is less sophisticated in part because the Jesuits themselves focused more on institution building and internal affairs than their more self-confident predecessors did. In part, too, those opposed to the Jesuits successfully portrayed the Society as an obstacle to progress. François Guizot, a professor of modern history at the Sorbonne and later the prime minister of France, lamented persistent Jesuit opposition to "the development of modern civilization" and the "freedom of the human mind."[1]

Subsequent historians, even historians of Catholicism, have not rushed to prove Guizot wrong. And they have not done so partly because the Jesuits themselves did react against—even reject—some of the most powerful intellectual currents of the nineteenth century. Most Jesuits saw the century as more about persecution than progress and more about exile than creative energy. They kept an ironic distance from politicians and intellectuals who were applauding the march of "liberty and civilization" but were willing to expel troublesome religious orders. They urged their confreres to "stand up in the face of this infidel generation and in the face of this heathenish progress."[2]

The goal of this chapter is to better integrate the history of the Jesuits into global history, where the nineteenth century, in particular, has become the center of an effort to see international connections concealed behind a long-standing disciplinary focus on the nation-state. Some of the most global citizens of the nineteenth century were not cotton exporters developing global markets or physicians tracking the spread of disease. Instead, they were Jesuits. And these Jesuits are an entry point into a better understanding of global Catholicism, then and now the world's largest, most multilingual, and most multicultural institution.[3]

Nineteenth-Century Jesuit Globalization

The history of the Jesuits does not substitute for a history of the nineteenth-century Catholic whole. But it comes close. Growing from six hundred aged members in 1814 to almost seventeen thousand men a century later, the Society of Jesus moved from the margins of Catholic life to its center.[4] Across the globe the Jesuits orchestrated parish missions, built Catholic universities and schools, promoted devotions such as the Sacred Heart, and authenticated miracles. They became loyal allies and admirers of Pope Pius IX (1846–78). They became even more influential during the papacy of Leo XIII (1878–1903), whose closest advisers included a Jesuit who also was one of his brothers. More than any single group, they propelled the nineteenth-century Catholic revival. This movement of people, institutions, and ideas began in the aftermath of the French Revolution as memories of persecution and exile formed a Catholic subculture that is indispensable to an understanding of modern history.[5]

Other men's and women's religious orders, laypeople, priests, and bishops also led this nineteenth-century Catholic revival, of course, but the Jesuit reach, from the Roman Curia to far-flung mission stations, was unique. In the 1830s and 1840s alone, the Society established new missions in Syria (1831), Calcutta (1834), Argentina (1836), Madurai (1837), Nankin (1841), Canada (1842), Madagascar (1844), Algeria (1848), and Australia (1848).[6] Tiny Luxembourg sent Jesuit missionaries to Africa, South Asia, China, and North and South America.[7]

These Jesuits did not share our current sensitivity toward inculturation, and their architectural drawings and Latin textbooks conceded little to local context. In fact, the Jesuit orientation toward Rome as the focal point of a global Catholic community, and its focus on independent Catholic institutions (especially schools), Catholic devotional practices, admonitions against religious intermarriage, and insistence on the Church as the guarantor of salvation made Catholic practice more uniform in 1914 than it had been in 1814.[8] While eighteenth-century Catholics, especially in majority-Protestant or non-Catholic societies, worshipped discreetly and quietly catechized their young, nineteenth-century Catholics, often inspired or led by Jesuits, cultivated Catholic distinctiveness and a combative sense of the Church as a haven in a hostile world.

The presence of this communal Catholic subculture also ensured that Catholics and Protestants (in majority-Protestant countries such as the United States, Germany, and the Netherlands), Catholics and anticlericals (in France, Italy, and much of Latin America), Catholics and Muslims (the Philippines and parts of Africa), and Catholics and Buddhists (China) became more segregated from each other, not less, over the course of the nineteenth century. This segregation did not distinguish Catholicism. All of the world's great religious traditions—including parts of Protestant and Orthodox Christianity, Judaism, Islam, Hinduism, Buddhism, and Roman Catholicism—became more self-conscious about doctrine and uniformity of practice during the nineteenth century as new modes of travel and communications brought people into unprecedented proximity. Religious polemics did not lead to religious slaughter, a welcome restraint when compared to the Reformation era. But religious divisions, or what one historian terms a "new confessional age," fundamentally structured politics and culture.[9]

The first and most basic impetus behind Jesuit globalization was one of the great migrations of modern history, the decision of sixty million Europeans to leave the continent over the course of the nineteenth century. The Catholic contingent of this migration was immense, probably amounting to more than half of the total, led in sequence by immigrants from Ireland, Germany, Italy, and Poland. In this context Jesuits simply followed the Catholic tide.[10]

A second reason for Jesuit globalization was less predictable. Nothing marked Jesuit life in the nineteenth century more than instability, with Jesuits expelled from more than two dozen European and Latin American countries. The expulsions began in Russia and the Netherlands in the second decade of the nineteenth century, and by 1840, Jesuits had been expelled from Spain, Naples, France, and Portugal. These initial expulsions were lingering aftershocks of eighteenth-century controversies with monarchs, often Catholic monarchs, using the Jesuits as pawns in a contest with the Vatican over control of episcopal appointments and schools. The duration was often brief, with negotiations for the return of the Jesuits commencing soon after their expulsion.

In a second wave of expulsions between 1840 and 1901, the Jesuits were driven out, often multiple times, from Switzerland, various parts of modern-day Italy (including Rome, Piedmont, and Naples), New Granada (modern-day Colombia), Uruguay, Ecuador, El Salvador, Costa Rica, Peru, Austria, Spain, Germany, Guatemala, France, and Nicaragua. In Mexico a liberal government expelled "foreign-born" Jesuits.[11]

This second set of expulsions had different origins. Instead of quarrels between monarchs and bishops with the Jesuits as collateral damage, attacks on the Jesuits in the latter half of the nineteenth century came from leading intellectuals and politicians and represented a reawakening in a new context of the anti-Jesuitism documented by Sabina Pavone in chapter 5 of this volume. The emergence of the modern nation-state in the nineteenth century is a familiar textbook story, with Italy, Germany, Colombia, Mexico, the United States (after the Civil War), and many other countries developing stronger national governments, publicly funded education systems, and a novel focus on identifying with a nation's history and culture as opposed to the history and culture of a particular region.[12] A Catholicism headquartered in Rome, and especially the Jesuits as an international religious order, became understood as the most prominent threat and competitor to nationalist claims. Politicians, editors, novelists, and ministers all made the point: The Jesuits, with their schools, their cultivation of common religious devotions, and their loyalty to the papacy, might thwart the most important vehicle for progress—namely, the unified nation-state. To support the Jesuits, as one Mexico City editor explained, was to "detain the course of the century."[13]

The pivotal moment occurred in the 1840s. Jules Michelet and Edgar Quinet, two leading French intellectuals, offered a course on the Jesuits at the Collège de France, and their lectures were immediately printed to great acclaim. Their conclusion—that Jesuitism and ultramontanism menaced new nation-states and the rights of the individual—became commonplace in anti-Jesuit and anti-Catholic rhetoric. Either "Jesuitism must abolish the spirit of France," Quinet explained, "or France must abolish the spirit of Jesuitism."[14] Julio Arboleda, a Colombian statesman, drew upon his reading of Michelet and Quinet to express his fear that a Jesuit's *patria* must always be the Society of Jesus, not Colombia or any country.[15]

Leaders of almost all of the European revolutions of 1847–48 (and their Latin American admirers) expressed animosity toward the Jesuits. Most anti-Jesuit rhetoric came from Protestants, liberal Jews, and anticlericals, but some Catholics also criticized the Jesuits for thwarting the possible union of Catholicism and modern nationalism and for facilitating the antimodern stances of many Church leaders.[16] Some leading Catholics, not just Protestants, advocated banning the Jesuits from Prussia during the heady days of the Frankfurt Parliament.[17] Similarly Vincenzo Gioberti, an Italian priest who was influenced by Michelet and Quinet and who was one of the key figures of Italian nationalism, published a widely read attack on the Jesuits titled *Il Gesuito moderno*. In this and other writings, Gioberti pleaded with the pope to abandon political control of the Papal States and foster Italian unity, even as he bitterly castigated the Jesuits for inhibiting this vision. He defined the Jesuits as the "enemies of nationalities" and the "allies of despots."[18]

Nineteenth-century Jesuits could dismiss "ignominious stories" about the Society as a regrettable consequence of the "unbridled license of writing and reading in our times."[19] They could wryly contrast European mobs chanting against the Jesuits in the name of "progress" with the "good manners and cordiality" of putatively uncivilized Blackfeet and Flathead Indians meeting Jesuits in modern-day Montana and Idaho.[20] And they could note the incongruity of anti-Jesuit fervor given the small number of Jesuits—only 634 Jesuits lived in Germany when Otto von Bismarck and his allies expelled them in 1872—in any given country at any given time.[21]

Still all Jesuits recognized that they stood in an uneasy relationship with new emphases on individual freedom and national identity. "The Jesuits," Superior General Jan Roothaan explained to a colleague, "are [viewed] as an expression of Catholicism," and those who wish to "modernize" society must "destroy" them.[22]

The Society's New Foundations

The Jesuits disparaged the modern world with enough frequency to confirm liberal nationalist stereotypes. But distance from the heat of nineteenth-century polemics permits a cooler assessment of the multiple routes to modernity traveled by religious and secular communities, sometimes in spite of themselves.[23]

The Jesuit route began with an act of retrieval, an effort to reestablish the Society on foundations laid in the sixteenth and seventeenth centuries while skipping the more complicated history of the eighteenth century and the suppression.[24] The process began with a reassessment of Jesuit spiritual life. Roothaan, the most important superior general of the nineteenth-century Jesuits, insisted on an almost literal reading of the *Spiritual Exercises* of Saint Ignatius, the key document for spiritual formation within the order, and personally translated a new edition from the original Spanish text.[25]

Exactly how nineteenth-century Jesuits understood the Exercises—in daily meditations, annual retreats of eight days, a thirty-day retreat at some point during their training—is not easy to recapture. But the focus seems less on mystical experience and more on the Lord's passion and suffering, notably the regret that Jesus desired to "suffer more, while I am occupied only in trying to suffer less." Equally pervasive was a constant focus on humility, "mortification and abnegation." The "terrible enemy" of authentic Jesuit work, explained one pastor in New York, was "selfishness." Its remedy: "obedience."[26] That Roothaan's notes on the Exercises stress "the obedience of the Child Jesus" as a central spiritual model highlighted the difference between Jesuit piety and the simultaneous effort by figures such as Ralph Waldo Emerson to promote the virtue of self-reliance.[27]

Alongside a set of reenergized spiritual practices came a revitalized missionary ethos. Roothaan viewed evangelization as the Society's highest priority, and he worked carefully with like-minded bishops to send Jesuits to the far-flung corners of the world.

Roothaan specifically noted in an 1831 plea for missionaries that the "burden of every letter" from Jesuits already serving in the United States was a request for more missionaries to combat "ministers of error" (i.e., Protestant clergy) also "sent from Europe."[28] He worried that European Catholic immigrants, moving to "faraway countries, their numbers rising," might "go into Protestant churches to hear the *word* of God, and to even celebrate Easter."[29]

Many Jesuits responded to Roothaan's call, and the combination of expulsions and missionary fervor produced a remarkably cosmopolitan lived experience. This palpable sense that the entire world lay before them became evident when the Jesuits from particular European houses saw themselves and their friends sent to utterly distant locales—Madagascar or the Canadian Great Lakes, Maine or Bombay—based on global needs at a particular moment.

The appropriation of the distant past shaped Jesuit educational practice as well. Roothaan made a detailed study of the original sixteenth-century *Ratio studiorum* (*Plan of Studies*) for Jesuit schools and insisted that it again become operative as the restored Society began taking over new educational establishments.[30] Much secular education in nineteenth-century Europe and North America was also based on a classical foundation, but the Jesuit insistence on a specific curriculum almost entirely composed of Latin and Greek texts seemed to nationalist reformers yet another sign of the Society's distance from the modern world.

The effort to recast Jesuit intellectual life extended beyond the classroom. Even the most determined opponents of the Jesuits in the eighteenth century recognized the centrality of the Society to the era's scientific investigations, theatrical productions, and publishing ventures.[31] Nineteenth-century Jesuits sustained a fascination with science, particularly astronomy, but the dominant impulse again was to return to the sixteenth and seventeenth centuries, when a scholasticism derived from Thomas Aquinas dominated the intellectual life of the Society. An Irish Jesuit, looking around the room at the Twenty-First General Congregation of the world's Jesuits in 1829, admitted that "the Society can no longer boast of so many brilliant men as she had in the age when Scholasticism flourished." He nonetheless insisted that only scholasticism "has always been the Theology of the Society and the weapon with which our forefathers conquered the enemies of the Catholic Truth."[32]

Over the course of the nineteenth century, this scholastic revival, led by German and Italian Jesuits, triumphed over its intellectual foes within the Catholic world through a combination of intellectual firepower and papal patronage. In 1879 Pope Leo XIII mandated primacy of place for scholastic philosophy and theology in Catholic seminaries and universities.

Within the Church, the Jesuits worked to prevent any repeat of conflicts with the papacy. In contrast to the sixteenth and seventeenth centuries when Jesuits occasionally aligned themselves with local bishops and monarchs in disputes with the Vatican, nineteenth-century Jesuits understood themselves as papal loyalists. Roothaan even defended the memory of Clement XIV, the pope who suppressed the order in 1773, by insisting that the suppression had been forced upon the papacy.[33] After initial tension between Pope Pius IX and the Jesuits during the tumultuous events of the late 1840s, when Pius IX was mistakenly hailed as a "liberal," he became more tightly tied to the Society. During his two-year exile after the revolution in Rome, the pope urged the Jesuits to publish a journal of opinion, and immediately upon its founding in 1850, *La Civiltà Cattolica* became the most influential publication in the Catholic world. (Meeting with *Civiltà* editors every two weeks, the pope also took an active hand in editorial decisions.)[34]

In turn the Jesuits played pivotal roles in support of the controversial declaration of the Immaculate Conception of Mary in 1854, a signal event in the consolidation of papal authority and a decision setting Catholicism against other Christian churches. The Jesuits helped draft and defend Pope Pius IX's notorious 1864 *Syllabus of Errors*, with its denial that the papacy should reconcile itself with "progress, liberalism and modern civilization."[35] They supported (and again helped draft) the even more controversial declaration of papal infallibility in 1870 and defended the declaration against both those Catholics who judged it imprudent and non-Catholics for whom it confirmed stereotypes of Catholics being opposed to intellectual autonomy. When Leo XIII met in 1896 with Jesuit leaders from around the world, he emphasized that the Society's mission was to "defend the Church and the Roman Pontificate." That "we are living in evil times" where our "enemies are many," he asserted, heightened the need for "greater devotedness."[36]

Attempts by Catholics to reconcile faith with contemporary intellectual currents provoked a harsh Jesuit response. *La Civiltà Cattolica* bluntly described the very idea of a liberal Catholicism as "bizarre and monstrous," and in 1883 the Jesuits formally resolved as a body to "repudiate by name" the "doctrine known as Catholic liberalism."[37]

Outside the Church the Jesuits similarly disparaged liberalism, or the focus on individual autonomy that was so powerful in the aftermath of the revolutions in the United States, France, and Latin America. Instead, Jesuits helped sustain a more communal ethos in Europe and the Americas. Jesuits across the world, for example, promoted the work of the Catalan priest Jaime Balmes, whose *Protestantism and Catholicity Compared* was translated into all of the major European languages and became one of the era's most influential texts. (It was first published in Spanish as *El Protestantismo Comparado con el Catolicismo en sus Relaciones con la Civilización Europea* [Barcelona, 1842–44].) Balmes's fundamental claims—that Protestant liberty inevitably turned into anarchy and that Catholicism better fostered the mix of freedom and order necessary for an advanced civilization—proved useful to Catholics in countries where intellectuals assumed a tight link between Protestantism and progress. (Even in the most remote North American villages, the Jesuits routinely met ministers and even traders who accused them of impeding the "progress of civilization."[38]) Other Jesuits joined Balmes in developing a Catholic counternarrative to liberal accounts of progress, with the Reformation, in the Catholic view, as the precursor to absolutist monarchies—not constitutional democracy—and a fatal blow to what they understood as a more harmonious balance between authority and liberty.[39]

To most Jesuits the liberal focus on the rights of the individual threatened the foundations of society. Freedom of the press—permitting the publication of an "obscene" book as easily as a religious book—seemed a worrisome novelty. Freedom of religion had its benefits, as those Jesuits scarred by persecution appreciated. But freedom of religion as a principle, with any and all religious groups able to worship in public, educate their young, and proselytize, meant condoning religious error. Or as a French Jesuit based in Rome wrote, religious liberty could not be supported "in general and without distinction. It is evident that this liberty is an evil against which Christianity has struggled since its origin."[40]

The willingness of nominally freedom-loving European and Latin American politicians to expel the Jesuits in the 1840s clinched the case for liberal intolerance and demonstrated the need for "another kind of language of liberty."[41] Roothaan himself visited many European Jesuit houses during his exile from Rome between 1848 and 1850, and he recounted the dramatic tale of the public attacks on the Jesuits, the mobs of "red republicans" chanting outside Jesuit residences, and his flight from Rome in disguise.[42] Writing from Marseilles, occasionally in code to deceive government censors, he noted to one American Jesuit the "violent aggression" in Rome that made his exile inevitable.[43]

Memories of exiles, and the suffering and persecution preceding them, suffused official Jesuit documents. Each of the nineteenth-century superiors general composed dolorous letters—cumulatively a Jesuit jeremiad—that were read out loud in Jesuit residences around the world during mealtimes. Roothaan's successor as superior general, Belgian Peter Jan Beckx, thought it "most true [that] we are despised, persecuted, condemned to exile, deprived of the common rights of citizens and men."[44] Beckx's successor as Jesuit superior general, Anton Anderledy, had been expelled from Switzerland as a young man and sent initially to Green Bay, Wisconsin. Writing from Fiesole, Italy, because an anticlerical Italian government had again ejected the Jesuits from their headquarters in Rome, Anderledy complained of the "injustice of the times, and the bitter harassing of evil-minded men whom we see raging against the Church of God, and raging against the Society of Jesus."[45] Anderledy's successor, the Spaniard Luis Martín, bemoaned the "pitiless persecution" of the Jesuits by leaders "tainted and captivated with those principles which are absurdly called 'liberal.'"[46]

Jesuit Nationalism and the Reemergence of a Global Ethos

In 1914 the Jesuits inaugurated a centenary celebration. Having begun with a handful of beleaguered institutions, the Jesuits now ran 234 colleges in forty-three countries; sponsored dozens of scholarly, devotional, and missionary journals; served as advisers to the pope and in various high ecclesiastical positions; and, as a collective, constituted the most significant Catholic intellectual resource.

The celebration was ill timed, for it coincided almost exactly with the assassination of Archduke Franz Ferdinand and his wife, Sophie, in Sarajevo (with an Austrian Jesuit providing last rites) and the onset of global war. In this sense, though, the centenary also marked a transition as the war revealed a weakening of the determinedly cosmopolitan ethos of the mid-nineteenth-century Jesuits. During both the American Civil War (1861–65) and the Franco-Prussian War (1870–71), the Jesuits had served as chaplains but only after making a point of their neutrality and determinedly resisting any claim that nationalist states could draft Jesuits into military service.

Now the Jesuits understood themselves differently. To preserve their independence, the superior general and his staff moved from Rome to Switzerland when Italy entered the war in 1915, and journals such as *La Civiltà Cattolica* continued to bemoan militarist nationalism.[47] But Jesuits rushed to volunteer as chaplains for Germany, Italy, the United States, Austria-Hungary, Britain, Belgium, and France. In Italy 300 Jesuits labored in the army of a government that was still in a standoff with the pope over the independence of the Vatican. Twenty-six German Jesuits died in service, and 535 German Jesuits served as chaplains and stretcher bearers for Kaiser Wilhelm's reich despite extant anti-Jesuit laws. (The laws were repealed in 1917 because of the Jesuits' willingness to sacrifice for the German war effort and because government officials sought to placate Catholics.)[48] In France less than fifteen years after their final expulsion, Jesuits worked with French armies in the trenches of the Western Front, in North Africa, and in the Middle East, losing 163 French Jesuits in battle or from illnesses contracted during the war. Their surviving Jesuit colleagues repeatedly invoked the notion of France as the eldest "daughter" of the Church and asserted the "right" and "need" to serve one's country and even to sacrifice one's life for the nation.[49]

The origins of this Jesuit nationalism are complex. A waning anticlericalism in European intellectual culture was important, along with the broad appeal of nationalist sentiments to Jesuits, now more likely to have been raised as patriotic citizens or subjects. Imperial projects also played a role. In contrast to the endemic tension between the Jesuits and nationalist governments in the mid-nineteenth century, Spanish and American Jesuits in the Philippines, Belgian Jesuits in the Congo, and French Jesuits in Vietnam, Algeria, and Polynesia found themselves allied with imperial authorities, teaching their sons, hearing their confessions, and leaning on them for assistance in missionary ventures.

Jesuit globalization, then, like globalization generally, has its own history. Peaking in the nineteenth century as expelled European Jesuits brought an international Catholic style to the most distant corners of the globe, it faded during the more nationalist 1920s and 1930s. Jesuits still wrote each other in a common lingua franca, Latin, but now they were more likely to spend their careers either within the orbit of one nation-state or allied to an imperial venture that reinforced national loyalties.

A more global ethos only reasserted itself in the wake of the Second World War and decolonization. An official turning point occurred at the Second Vatican Council, where, for the first time, bishops born in Africa, Asia, and Latin America participated as equals with their European colleagues. (At the First Vatican Council in 1869–70, only a handful of missionary bishops, all born in Europe, represented the world east of Russia, south of Naples, and west of Galway.) After the Council, Jesuits from Latin America, India, and the Philippines began reflecting on what it might mean to enrich, not simply receive, North American or European Catholic traditions.[50]

Karl Rahner, a German Jesuit and one of the Second Vatican Council's most notable figures, emphasized these themes in an influential essay on the Council that began, interestingly, as a talk delivered partially in German and simultaneously translated into English to faculty and students at a Jesuit seminary in Cambridge, Massachusetts. To Rahner the Council signified the emergence of a "world Church in a fully official way." In the nineteenth century the Church "exported a European religion as a commodity it did not really want to change . . . together with the rest of the culture and civilization it considered superior."[51]

No longer, Rahner argued, could Catholicism be understood as simply "a European export." And indeed, the loyalty of nineteenth-century Jesuits to the papacy, their enthusiasm for Catholic devotions such as the Sacred Heart, their condemnations of modernity, their suspicions of the nation-state, and their fascination with the miraculous now seemed an unwelcome detour from the theological road leading to the Second Vatican Council.

One son of this global Catholic community is Jorge Bergoglio, or Pope Francis, an Argentine Jesuit and the first modern pope from outside Europe. He is alert to the history sketched in this chapter and, in one of his initial interviews, encouraged secular intellectuals to abandon old tropes equating Catholicism with the "darkness of superstition" and the "modern culture of the Enlightenment" with "the light of reason."[52] He repeatedly invokes as models those Jesuits who were willing to immerse themselves in the life of people on the margins of society, including a Spanish Jesuit who spent his career with native peoples in Alaska. When he speaks of a "globalization of indifference" marking the current divide between rich and poor, he injects Catholic social thought into ebullient discussions of the "flat" global economy.[53]

The Jesuit superior general at the moment of this book's composition, Adolfo Nicolás, also understands this global Church firsthand. Born and educated in Spain, he studied in Tokyo and Rome and then returned to Asia, serving a six-year stint as a director of an institute at Ateneo de Manila University, for the bulk of his ministerial career. Following his election, he urged the world's Jesuits to develop a more self-consciously global orientation. "Can we not go beyond the loose family relationships we now have as institutions," he asked, "and re-imagine and re-organize ourselves so that, in this globalized world, we can more effectively realize the universality which has always been part of Ignatius's vision of the Society?"[54]

The answers are not yet in. Certainly the character of twenty-first-century globalization—marked by decreasing inequality among nations but increased inequality within them and by a reassertion of nationalist sentiment in countries such as China and Russia even as international organizations plant deeper roots—provides a new context for Jesuit work. And the changing demographics of the Jesuits—declining in numbers in Europe and the Americas while growing in Africa and Asia—must shape strategic decisions made within the Society. The modest point of this chapter is that contemporary Jesuit global connections, forged in the era of text messages and Skype, necessarily follow paths winding back to the expulsions and missionary efforts of the reestablished Society of Jesus in the nineteenth century.

Notes

The material in this chapter is adapted from McGreevy's forthcoming book, *American Jesuits and the World*, scheduled for publication by Princeton University Press in the spring of 2016.

1. François Guizot, *The History of Civilization in Europe*, ed. Larry Siedentop, trans. William Hazlitt (1828; repr., New York: Penguin Classics, 1997), 209.

2. Peter Jan Beckx, SJ, "Letter to the Fathers and Brothers of the Society of Jesus on the fruit to be gathered from the examples of blessed Peter Canisius and John Berchmans," 1865, in *Renovation Reading*, by Woodstock College (Woodstock, MD: Woodstock College, 1886), 353; and Joseph E. Keller, SJ, "Exhortation at the Opening of the Scholasticate at Woodstock," September 23, 1869, Maryland Province Archives (MPA) 1010-X-2, Georgetown University Library, Washington, DC.

3. On Catholicism as part of global history, see Vincent Viaene, "International History, Religious History, Catholic History: Perspectives for Cross-Fertilization (1830–1914)," *European History Quarterly* 38 (2008): 578–607. On the nineteenth century, C. A. Bayly, *The Birth of the Modern World, 1780–1914: Global Connections and Comparisons* (Malden, MA: Blackwell, 2004) is exemplary on religion.

4. Hilario Azzolini, "Prospectus Numericus Societatis Iesu Ab anno 1814 ad 1932," *Archivum Historicum Societatis Ieus* 2 (1933): 90–92.

5. Margaret Lavinia Anderson, "The Limits of Secularization: On the Problem of the Catholic Revival in Nineteenth-Century Germany," *Historical Journal* 38 (1995): 647–70; and Austin Iverveigh, ed., *The Politics of Religion in an Age of Revival* (London: Institute of Latin American Studies, 2000).

6. Alexandre Brou, *Cent ans de missions, 1815–1934: Les Jésuites missionaires au XIXe et au XXe siècle* (Paris: Éditions Spes, 1935), 297–98.

7. Jean-Marie Kreins and Josy Brisens, SJ, "Les Jésuites Luxembourgeois et l'Expérience Missionnaire dans le Monde aux XIX et XX Siècles," in *Le face-à-face des Dieux: Missionaires luxembourgeois en outre-mer*, ed. Andre Neuberg (Bastogne: Musée en Piconrue, 2007), 127–31.

8. For an elegant demonstration, Henrietta Harrison, *The Missionary's Curse and Other Tales from a Chinese Catholic Village* (Berkeley: University of California Press, 2013), 65–91.

9. Olaf Blaschke, "Das 19: Jahrhundert. Ein Zweites Konfessionelles Zeitalter?," *Geschichte und Gesellschaft* 26 (2000): 38–75.

10. For sixty million—a gross figure that does not count returns—between 1820 and 1920, see Kevin O'Rourke and Jeffrey Williamson, *Globalization and History: The Evolution of a Nineteenth-Century Atlantic Economy* (Cambridge, MA: MIT Press, 1999), 119. For comparisons with global migrations in Asia, Africa, and the Indian Ocean, see Adam McKeown, "Global Migration, 1846–1940," *Journal of World History* 15, no. 2 (2004): 155–89.

11. Anti-Jesuitism has attracted considerable attention from historians, although the absence of a synthetic work touching on Europe and North and South America has submerged the topic's importance. For anti-Jesuitism in France, see Geoffrey Cubitt, *The Jesuit Myth: Conspiracy Theory and Politics in Nineteenth-Century France* (Oxford: Clarendon Press, 1993), and Michel Leroy, *Le Mythe Jésuite: De Béranger à Michelet* (Paris: Presses universitaires de France, 1992); in Italy, Giacomo Martina, SJ, "Motivi e Radici dell'Opposizione Piemontese alla Compagnia di Gesù," in *La Compagnia di Gesù nella Provincia di Torino: Dagli Anni di Emanuele Filiberto a quelli di Carlo Alberto*, ed. Bruno Signorelli and Pietro Uscello (Turin: Società piemontese di archeologia e belle arti, 1998), 411–27; in the Czech lands, Marie-Élizabeth Ducreux, "L'antijésuitisme Tchèque au XIXe Siècle," in *Les Antijésuites: Discours, figures et lieux de l'antijésuitisme à l'époque moderne*, ed. Pierre-Antoine Fabre and Catherine Maire (Rennes: Presses universitaires de Rennes, 2010), 518–36; in Germany, Michael B. Gross, *The War against Catholicism: Liberalism and the Anti-Catholic Imagination in Nineteenth-Century Germany* (Ann Arbor: University of Michigan Press, 2004), 259–91, and Róisín Healy,

The Jesuit Specter in Imperial Germany (Boston: Brill, 2003); in Mexico, Paolo Chenillo Alazraki, "Liberalismo a prueba: La expulsión de 'extranjeros perniciosos' en México durante la República Restaurada (1867–1876)," *Revista de Indias* 72, no. 255 (2012): 377–408; and in Latin America more widely, Susana Monreal, Sabina Pavone, and Guillermo Zermeño, eds., *Antijesuitismo y filojesuitismo: Dos identidades ante la restauración* (Mexico City: Universidad Iberoamericana, 2014).

12. John Breuilly, "On the Principle of Nationality," in *The Cambridge History of Nineteenth-Century Political Thought*, ed. Gareth Stedman Jones and Gregory Claeys (Cambridge: Cambridge University Press, 2011), 77–109.

13. James E. Sanders, *The Vanguard of the Atlantic World: Creating Modernity, Nation and Democracy in Nineteenth-Century Latin America* (Durham: Duke University Press, 2014), 142.

14. Jules Michelet and Edgar Quinet, *Des Jèsuites* (Paris: Hachette, 1843), 196; and Cubitt, *Jesuit Myth*, 137.

15. Jorge Enrique Salcedo Martínez, SJ, "The History of the Society of Jesus in Colombia, 1844–1861" (PhD diss., Oxford University, 2011), 159–60.

16. For example, Ari Joskowicz, *The Modernity of Others: Jewish Anti-Catholicism in Germany and France* (Stanford: Stanford University Press, 2014), 53, 55.

17. Klaus Schatz, SJ, *Geschichte der Deutschen Jesuiten*, vol. 1, *1814–1872* (Münster: Aschendorff, 2013), 131.

18. Vincenzo Gioberti, *La Suisse, Pie IX et les Jésuites: Extraits Traduits du Gesuita Moderno de Vincenzo Gioberti* (Lausanne, Switzerland: Imp. Bonamici et comp., 1847), 2.

19. Jan Philipp Roothaan, SJ, "On Present Calamities and on Zeal for Perfection," 1847, in *Select Letters of Our Very Reverend Fathers General to the Fathers and Brothers of the Society of Jesus*, by Jesuits (Woodstock, MD: Woodstock College, 1900), 270.

20. John Baptist Miege to Urban Miege, 1847, in *Bishop East of the Rockies: The Life and Letters of John Baptist Miege, S.J.*, ed. Herman J. Muller, SJ (Chicago: Loyola University Press, 1994), 10.

21. Healy, *Jesuit Specter*, 1.

22. Roothaan to Joseph Anthony De Pilat, September 4, 1847, in *Epistolae Joannis Phil. Roothaan Societatis Iesu praepositi generalis XXI*, ed. Ludovicus de Jonge, SJ, and Petrus Pirri, SJ (Rome: Apud Postulatorem Generalem S.I., 1940), 5:940.

23. For a canonical statement, S. N. Eisenstadt, "Multiple Modernities," *Daedalus* 129 (Winter 2009): 1–26. In a more theoretical key, Charles Taylor, *A Catholic Modernity?*, ed. James L. Heft, SM (New York: Oxford University Press, 1999), remains indispensable.

24. John W. Padberg, SJ, "A Body Brought to Life Again: Organization, Spiritual Vitality and Missionary Dynamism in the Restored Society of Jesus in the Nineteenth Century," *Center for Ignatian Spirituality* 24 (1993): 30–56.

25. Marcel Chappin, "John Philipp Roothaan: 'The General of the Spiritual Exercises?,'" *Center for Ignatian Spirituality* 24 (1993): 46–56.

26. Philip Cardella, Fourth Exhortation to the Community in New York,

November 10, 1889, in Philip Cardella, SJ, Papers 1–9, Georgetown University Library, Washington, DC.

27. Ignatius of Loyola, *The Spiritual Exercises of St. Ignatius of Loyola*, ed. Jan Philipp Roothaan, trans. Charles Seager (Baltimore: J. Murphy, 1850), 143–44.

28. Jan Philipp Roothaan, SJ, "On Desire for the Missions," 1831, in *Renovation Reading*, by Woodstock College, rev. and enlarged ed. (Woodstock, MD: Woodstock College, 1931), 58.

29. Roothaan to Joseph Anthony de Pilat, April 12, 1844, in Roothaan, *Epistolae*, 4:298.

30. Miguel Anselmo Bernad, "The Faculty of Arts in the Jesuit Colleges in the Eastern Part of the United States: Theory and Practice (1782–1923)" (PhD diss., Yale University, 1951), 129; and Society of Jesus, *The Jesuit Ratio Studiorum of 1599*, trans. Allan P. Farrell (Washington, DC: Conference of Major Superiors of Jesuits, 1970).

31. Mordechai Feingold, "Jesuits: Savants," in *Jesuit Science and the Republic of Letters*, ed. Mordechai Feingold (Cambridge, MA: MIT Press, 2003), 1–45; and John O'Malley, ed., *The Jesuits: Cultures, Sciences, and the Arts, 1540–1773* (Toronto: University of Toronto Press, 1999).

32. Fr. Peter Kenny, "Father Kenny on Scholasticism," Peter Kenny file IIC 127a, box 82, Woodstock College Archives (WCA), Georgetown University Library, Washington, DC.

33. Pierre Blet, "Jésuites Gallicans au XVIIème Siècle?," *Archivum Historicum Societatis Iesu* 29 (1960): 55–84; and Roothaan to Fr. Xavier de Ravignan, December 31, 1852, in Roothaan, *Epistolae*, 2:82.

34. Francesco Dante, *Storia della 'Civiltà Cattolica' (1850–1891): Il Laboratorio del Papa* (Rome: Edizioni Studium, 1990), 57–78.

35. Burkhart Schneider, "Der Syllabus Pius' IX und die Deutschen Jesuiten," *Archivum Historiae Pontificiae* 6 (1968): 317–69.

36. Fr. Chandlery, "An Account of the Audience Granted to the Holy Father Leo XIII to Our Rev. Procurators on October 5, 1896, compiled from the notes of Rev. Frs. Chandlery and others of the Fathers Present," MPA 5-I, Georgetown University Library, Washington, DC.

37. "Ripugnanza del Concetto di Cattolico Liberale," *Civiltà Cattolica* 8 (1869): 5; Twenty-Third General Congregation of the Society of Jesus, Decree 12, 1883, in *For Matters of Greater Moment: The First Thirty Jesuit General Congregations: A Brief History and a Translation of the Decrees*, ed. John W. Padberg, SJ, Martin D. O'Keefe, SJ, and John L. McCarthy, SJ (St. Louis: Institute of Jesuit Sources, 1994), 465.

38. Nicholas Point, SJ, to Fr. Frémiot, SJ, March 18, 1850, in Maryland Letters box, New York Province of the Society of Jesus, New York City. Into the twentieth century, *Protestantism and Catholicity Compared* was read out loud in Jesuit residences in the United States at mealtimes. See "Prefect of Reading List," October 4, 1904, in WCA file Ia 3.3a, box 1, Georgetown University Library, Washington, DC.

39. Michael Printy, "Protestantism and Progress in the Year XII: Charles

Villers's *Essay on the Spirit and Influence of Luther's Reformation* (1804)," *Modern Intellectual History* 9, no. 2 (August 2012): 303–29; and Giovanni Perrone, *Il Protestantesimo e la Regola di Fede* (Milan: Presso Carlo Turati, 1854), 401–71.

40. R. P. Rozaven, SJ, Votum, 1831, in *La Condamnation de Lamennais: Dossier*, ed. M. J. Le Guillou and Louis Le Guillou (Paris: Beauchesne, 1982), 121, 125.

41. Larkin to unknown recipient, March 20, 1848, John Larkin Papers, New York Province of the Society of Jesus, New York City.

42. "Father Roothaan's Visit to Maynooth College, 1848," *Letters and Notices* 20 (1890): 353.

43. Schatz, *Geschichte der Deutschen Jesuiten*, 1:46; and Roothaan to Brocard, April 6, 1848, MPA 93-XIII, Georgetown University Library, Washington, DC.

44. Beckx, "Letter," 351.

45. Anton Anderledy, SJ, to Society of Jesus, May 16, 1884, Roman file, Saint Joseph's University Archives, Philadelphia, PA.

46. Luis Martín, "On Some Dangers of Our Times" (1896), in Jesuits, *Select Letters*, 503.

47. Giacomo Martina, SJ, *Storia della Compagnia di Gesù in Italia (1814–1983)* (Brescia, Italy: Morcelliana, 2003), 178–79, 255–57.

48. Schatz, *Geschichte der Deutschen Jesuiten*, vol. 2, *1872–1917* (Münster: Aschendorff, 2013), 316; and Healy, *Jesuit Specter*, 215–26.

49. Marie-Claude Flageat, *Les Jésuites Français dans la Grande Guerre: Témoins, Victimes, Héros, Apôtres* (Paris: Editions du Cerf, 2008).

50. Horacio de la Costa, SJ, "The Missionary Apostolate in East and Southeast Asia," 1972, in *Selected Homilies and Religious Reflections*, ed. Robert M. Paterno (Manila: Philippine Province of the Society of Jesus and Ateneo de Manila University, 2002), 252–71.

51. Karl Rahner, SJ, "Towards a Fundamental Theological Interpretation of Vatican II," *Theological Studies* 40, no. 4 (1979): 717.

52. Pope Francis, interview by Eugenio Scalfari, *La Repubblica*, October 9, 2013, http://www.repubblica.it/cultura/2013/10/01/news/papa_francesco_a_scalfari_cos_cambier_la_chiesa-67630792/.

53. Pope Francis, "Homily of Holy Father Francis," Lampedusa, Sicily, July 8, 2013, http://w2.vatican.va/content/francesco/en/homilies/2013/documents/papa-francesco_20130708_omelia-lampedusa.html; and Antonio Spadaro, SJ, "'Wake up the World!'—Conversation with Pope Francis about the Religious Life," trans. Donald Maldari, SJ, *La Civiltà Cattolica* (2014): 3–17, http://www.laciviltacattolica.it/articoli_download/extra/Wake_up_the_world.pdf.

54. Adolfo Nicolás, SJ, "Depth, Universality, and Learned Ministry: Challenges to Jesuit Higher Education Today," remarks presented at conference on Networking Jesuit Higher Education: Shaping the Future for a Humane, Just, Sustainable Globe, Mexico City, April 23, 2010, http://www.sjweb.info/documents/ansj/100423_Mexico%20City_Higher%20Education%20Today_ENG.pdf.

7

HISTORICAL PERSPECTIVES ON JESUIT EDUCATION AND GLOBALIZATION

JOHN W. O'MALLEY, SJ

In this volume we are dealing with two basic questions: How does globalization help us understand the Jesuits, and how do the Jesuits help us understand globalization? Although answers to those questions must inevitably overlap, I concentrate on the latter. In so doing I modify it a bit to ask also how their example might act as a corrective to the way globalization is generally perceived and pursued today.

More specifically I ask whether there is something in the Jesuit tradition of education (formal schooling) that makes it particularly relevant in today's global, multicultural world. I, in fact, believe there is, but if we answer the question affirmatively, then we need to be precise and at the same time large minded because the Jesuit tradition of schooling seems at first glance to be so essentially and characteristically Western as to preclude a positive answer.

The Jesuit tradition of education emerged from a melding of three earlier traditions developed in the Mediterranean Basin more than two millennia ago. The first was a philosophical-scientific tradition based on Greek texts, principally Aristotle's metaphysics, natural philosophy, and works on logic and dialectics. By Aristotle's analysis and codification of the process of reasoning itself and of every aspect of the physical world as it was known at the time, he took a giant step in the professionalization of learning. But it was only in the thirteenth century that such professionalization achieved stable and enduring form in the institution known then and now as the university, perhaps the greatest achievement of the Middle Ages.[1]

The second tradition was not philosophical-scientific but literary, based on the prose and poetry of ancient Greece and Rome. This tradition of learning was less formal than the philosophical-scientific tradition and embodied different principles and values.[2] It was soon formalized into a program of education, later known as "humanistic," that became standard for elites in the ancient world. Like the other tradition, however, the institution did not receive a stable form relative to the modern era until the Renaissance of the fifteenth century when it became known by different names but most often simply by the term "college."[3] Although from their beginning and through their subsequent history these two traditions of learning and schooling were rivals, they were also partners. They borrowed from each other and were reciprocally influential.

By the second or third century CE, and especially by the fourth, they helped shape—and yet were shaped by—the third tradition, Christianity, which had earlier entered the Hellenistic world from Palestine. One of the most salient and differentiating features of this Christian tradition as it interacted with the late-antique culture of the Mediterranean world was "spiritual conquest" through conversion of the Other, a feature that had become especially prominent in the West by the time of the Portuguese and Spanish voyages of discovery in the early modern era.

When the Jesuit order was founded in the mid-sixteenth century, both the university and the humanistic college were established and highly respected institutions in the cultural life of the era. The Jesuits were therefore formed by both of these traditions, but they did not receive them passively. As they made them their own, they modified them and shaped them according to a developing fourth tradition—namely, the Society of Jesus itself. The story of Jesuit education is largely the story of how the Jesuits interacted with these two institutions and how they imbued them with characteristics distinctive of themselves. Among those characteristics was the essentially global orientation of the Society of Jesus.

Founded in 1540 the Jesuits defined themselves as a missionary order. They were a group of men preparing to go anywhere in the world and preach the Gospel to the Other. Within ten years of their order's founding, the Jesuits were already in places as distant from Europe as Brazil, India, and Japan. Once they began to undertake formal schooling as their primary ministry, they carried that ministry with them wherever they went, and they instinctively saw that it had to be adapted to different circumstances and cultures. In this way and others, the Jesuits' way of proceeding created a pastoral, cultural, and intellectual style that to a greater or lesser extent, depending on circumstances, gave the Jesuit schools a distinctive profile.

The Two Basic Institutions of Schooling: Their Character, Values, and Goals

The great turning point in the history of Western education occurred in the thirteenth century with the founding of the first universities. What is most striking about that institution in its medieval origins is how rapidly, within just a few generations, it attained mature form and established the basic structures and procedures that, in their fundamental functions, purpose, and organizational strategies, have changed so little in the intervening nine hundred years. I am referring to set curricula, textbooks, examinations, differentiated schools or departments, deans, presidents (rectors), faculty privileges and duties, and most especially public certification of professional competence through the awarding of degrees—for instance, master of arts, doctor of medicine, and doctor of laws. The world had never known anything quite like the medieval university.

Even more startling and fundamental is how, at its inception in the thirteenth century, the university already embodied and promoted a set of values that still undergirds universities today, such as the supreme importance of dispassionately analyzing and critically thinking about subjects, of restlessly questioning received wisdom, and of exploring every aspect of the physical world. These values led universities to pursue two goals, which universities today continue to pursue: First is intellectual problem solving, or, in more contemporary terms, the production of knowledge. Closely related is the second goal of career advancement through the acquisition of professional/technical skills. Students attended the university to become prepared to make a career. As it does now, a university degree then spelled upward socioeconomic mobility. The university qua university did not concern itself with anybody's eternal salvation, with playing a constructive role in the Church or society, or with the students' personal development.

By the sixteenth century Europe was dotted with universities, great and small. The University of Paris was one of the oldest and is still the most prestigious in Western Europe. From 1528 until 1535, Ignatius of Loyola studied there. In Paris he gathered nine companions who, a few years later in Rome, helped him found the Society of Jesus. By that time they all had obtained master of arts degrees, an achievement of which they were proud. Their formal education at Paris was among the best and the most professional that the times provided. These "friends in the Lord," as Ignatius and the others described themselves, not surprisingly determined that recruits to the Society they founded must have a university-style education of comparable quality to their own.

Not until two centuries after the founding of the first universities did the literary tradition develop its own institution, the college, largely in reaction to the university and as an alternative to it. An erstwhile rival to the university, it borrowed from the university certain structures—especially in the Jesuit system—such as set curricula and advancement through examinations. While the college therefore shared some traits with the university, it diverged in notable ways. The college did use set textbooks, but they were by authors and of genres and subjects that found no place in the philosophical-scientific university curriculum. In time the subjects came to be called "the humanities," but more revealing is the original Renaissance term *studia humanitatis*, which is perhaps best translated as "humane letters"—that is, subjects that treat human strivings, failings, passions, and ideals as expressed especially in poetry, drama, oratory, and history.[4]

It was no accident that the person most responsible for reasserting this tradition was a literary figure, the poet Petrarch (1304–74). By the middle of the fourteenth century, he had already articulated three grievances against the university that became standard among critics of the universities. First, the universities did not teach the "literary" subjects, which, in the view of these educators, were the subjects that illuminated the great questions of human life as it is really lived and that thus helped students deal with them. Second, and related to the first, the university was indifferent to the ethical, spiritual, religious, emotional, and physical development of its students. "Getting ahead" seemed to be the university's core value. The third complaint, related to the other two, was that the university did not seem concerned with the body social and politic, or with the obligation all human beings have to contribute to the well-being of society at large.

Thus, the principal aim that undergirded the humanistic tradition was different from the university's; the humanists wanted to produce a certain kind of *person*. The tradition was thus radically student centered or, to use the Jesuit expression, imbued with *cura personalis* (care for the student's entire well-being). The humanistic core of the curriculum raised questions pertinent to human life—questions of virtue and vice, of greed and redemption, of the ambivalence of human decision making, and, yes, of salvation and damnation. It treated them not through abstract principles—as found, for instance, in Aristotle's *Nicomachean Ethics*—but through stories, poetry, plays, and historical narratives that dramatized moral alternatives and the consequences of one's choices for oneself and for others. As Petrarch said, "It is one thing to know, another to love; one thing to understand, another to will. [Aristotle] teaches what virtue is, I do not deny that;

but his lesson lacks the words that sting and set afire and urge toward love of virtue and hatred of vice."[5]

The ideal graduates, in other words, were responsible participants in the community in which they lived, concerned for the common good, and ready to make sacrifices for it. They were prepared to assume a leadership role as circumstances required. Thus, rhetoric—here understood as the art of the speech act, the art of persuasion, the art of winning consensus—was the culminating discipline in the curriculum, for it taught students how to communicate effectively with ordinary people and win their backing for worthy causes. As the Roman author Quintilian (c. 35–c. 97 CE) put it, this style of education sought to produce *vir bonus dicendi peritus*, or a "good human being with the oratorical skills" to lead others to make good choices.[6]

Because an effective speaker had to grasp the temper of his audience and adapt his message to it, accommodating persons, times, places, and circumstances was at the very heart of the lesson of classical rhetoric. This aspect of the humanistic tradition would make a big impact on the Jesuits' way of proceeding, especially as they moved into cultures strange to them in their global outreach.

Renaissance humanists did not think their education was impractical. In fact, they thought it was more practical than what universities offered because, by its emphasis on precise and persuasive speech, it taught the most important art, the art of the word, which not only provided tools for influencing others but also was identical with the art of *thinking* itself. The theorists of this tradition realized, at least implicitly, that having a thought and finding the right word to express it were not two acts but one. Until persons had the right word they did not have the eureka, or the experience of insight. Until that moment, they had only a musing, a rumination, a groping. Training in this tradition thus resulted in acquiring the most important skill one needed to make one's way in the world and have an impact.

The humanistic school became a pan-European phenomenon that cut across confessional divides, growing as popular in Protestant settings as in Catholic ones, even if with slightly different emphases and ethos. The sheer number of Jesuit schools makes them stand out in this panorama. But more important, with their emphasis on active learning, on public performances of various kinds, on the adaptability of the tradition to contexts outside Europe, and especially on the spiritual development of the student based on principles of Saint Ignatius's *Spiritual Exercises*, they modified the tradition in important ways and made it their own.

The Jesuits

Within months of gaining papal approval of the order in 1540, Francis Xavier was on his way to Lisbon, whence he departed for India. Thereafter, the Jesuits never flagged in their missionary zeal. Nonetheless, in 1548, just eight years after their founding, they opened their first school in Messina in Sicily. It was the initial step in a momentous process that would lead them to combine the ideal of missionaries on the move with that of resident schoolmasters.

The school at Messina was a humanistic school, engaging the same curriculum the humanists had laid out and doing so with the same goals in mind. The Jesuits had to see a compelling compatibility between their Christian mission and what these schools, whose ancient inspiration was pagan, professed to do. Not until much later did the Jesuits ever attempt to explain the compatibility, but we can easily infer some of its essential elements. The quintessence of the *Spiritual Exercises* is, to use an old-fashioned expression, the development of the inner-directed person, or a human being who acts not from rote conformity to ethical standards but out of sincere, heartfelt, and discerning appropriation of them. In other words, like the humanist educational program, the *Exercises* also seek to produce a certain kind of *person*.

Although the *Exercises* have proved themselves helpful to people in all walks of life, they are geared more directly toward persons engaged in an active life in the Church or society, as suggested by the meditations on "The Kingdom of Christ" and "The Two Standards." The *Exercises* hoped to help the person who, in the first instance, participated in the affairs of the day. With its base in the *Exercises*, the spirituality of the Jesuit order itself has traditionally and correctly been described as an active spirituality.[7]

Good judgment ("prudence") was the virtue the humanists wanted especially to cultivate in students, and it correlates with the process of spiritual discernment central to the *Exercises*. By means of spiritual discernment through attention to one's inner journey, the *Exercises* hope to help the person toward good decision making. Of course, the humanist ideal and that of the *Exercises* are far from being the same thing, but, as I have suggested, there is a correlation between them.

Moreover, the accommodation of persons, places, and circumstances as a guiding principle in rhetoric finds a congenial partner in the spiritual traditions of the Jesuits. Saint Ignatius built accommodation into the *Exercises* themselves. They can be given as a form of catechesis, as an ongoing process over many months while the person is still engaged in the usual daily tasks, or, ideally, as the person's only occupation over the course of a full month in a sequestered situation. The individual Exercises within the *Spiritual Exercises* are to be tailored to times, places, and especially the circumstances of the individual making the spiritual journey. Moreover, in his correspondence as superior general, Ignatius was careful to allow Jesuits who were on the scene to make decisions appropriate to the situations in which they found themselves.[8]

In the early pages of the *Spiritual Exercises*, Saint Ignatius sets forth a fundamental attitude, or a presupposition (*praesupponendum*), to guide the person during the retreat. As he puts it, "It is necessary to suppose that every good Christian is more ready to put a good interpretation on another's statement than to condemn it as false" (no. 22). Even amid the bitter religious and political polemics the Jesuits sometimes engaged in, they wanted to mark their dealings with the Other with this ideal. In the Christian context of the Renaissance, the student in Jesuit schools studied the pagan classics of Greece and Rome not only as models of literary style but also as moral examples for emulation and inspiration. If noble Romans could be so admirable, how much more should the Christian be! Erasmus, the most widely read author of the era, dramatically expressed the idea through a speaker in his sublime dialogue "The Godly Feast" ("Convivium religiosum"): "Saint Socrates, pray for us!"[9] In the same vein, the Jesuit exegete Cornelius à Lapide (1567–1637), a professor at the Jesuits' Roman College, said of a passage from Epictetus, "O wonder! These words ring of the Gospel, not just moral philosophy."[10] The benign hermeneutic of other cultures and their moral strivings exemplified in such statements marked the approach of many (though certainly not all) Jesuits to the non-Western cultures they encountered in their missions overseas.

As expressed by the best theorists of this style of education, the moral imperative at the heart of the humanistic tradition of schooling implied self-sacrifice for the good of others. It obviously correlated with the Christian message of loving one's neighbors, even to the point of laying down one's life for them, as Jesus taught by word and example.

In Roman antiquity the best theorist of humanist education along with Quintilian was Cicero (106–43 BCE), who was undoubtedly the Jesuits' favorite author. Most Jesuits knew well Cicero's *De Officiis* (*On Responsibility for Others*), a text they taught in classrooms year after year. In it Cicero eloquently expressed the ideal of sacrifice for the good of others, especially in the pursuit of justice. Here are two pertinent passages:

> We are not born for ourselves alone . . . we as human beings are born for the sake of other human beings, that we might be able to help one another. We ought therefore to contribute to the common good

of humankind by reciprocal acts of kindness, by giving and receiving from one another, and thus by our skill, our industry, and our talents work to bind human society together in peace and harmony. (1.7.22, my translation)

The duties prescribed by justice must be given precedence over everything else, including the pursuit of knowledge, for such duties concern the welfare of other human beings, and nothing ought to be more sacred in our eyes than that. There are some people who either through absorption with their own self-advancement or through some other more basic coldness toward others, claim that all they need to do is tend to their own business, and thus they seem to themselves not to be doing any harm. But this means that while they avoid active injustice, they fall into another: they become traitors to the life we must all live together in human society, for they contribute to it none of their interest, none of their effort, none of their means. (1.9.29)

In 1550 the Jesuits received approval from Pope Julius III of a refinement and elaboration they had drawn up of the original charter that, in 1540, had won them papal approval as a religious order in the Catholic Church. In the new document, they had somewhat expanded the list of ministries in which the Jesuits would engage. It concludes with the provision that the Jesuits are "to perform any other works of charity according to what will seem expedient for the glory of God and the *common good*" (my emphasis).[11] Up to that point the ministries on the list had been derived directly or indirectly from the Bible or traditional Christian usage. However, the common good derives not from those sources but from philosophy, a secular discipline. It suggests a concern for this world and thus an enlargement of the Society's scope beyond evangelical and ecclesiastical goals. The older religious orders doubtless in some measure had this concern, as their histories clearly show, but the up-front and official commitment to it in this Jesuit document is the first in the history of such institutions.

Renaissance theorists of humanistic education made clear the benefits to the common good that their schools conferred by producing upright citizens dedicated to that end. The Jesuits enthusiastically picked up this theme. When in 1550 they opened a school in Tivoli near Rome, they promoted it as contributing to the well-being of the city (*ad civitatis utilitatem*). When in 1550 they urged the bishop of Murcia in Spain to establish a Jesuit school there, they told him it would be a great benefit to "the republic" by producing good priests, good civic officials, and good citizens of every status.[12] That the Jesuits used this standard humanist talk indicates the breadth that began to mark their desire "to help souls," as they characteristically described their goals and purpose.

In 1551 Ignatius's executive secretary, Juan Alfonso de Polanco, wrote in Ignatius's name an extremely important and revealing letter to Antonio de Araoz, provincial of Spain. Polanco listed fifteen goals the Society hoped to accomplish through its schools. The goals fall into three categories: benefits for the Society of Jesus itself, benefits for the students, and benefits for the locality. Except for the goals regarding the Society, almost any Renaissance humanist could have composed the list. The letter is remarkable, moreover, for not mentioning confessional or apologetic concerns. The fifteenth and final goal Polanco offers is comprehensive and directed exclusively to the common good: "Those who are now only students will grow up to be pastors, civic officials, administrators of justice, and will fill other important posts to everybody's profit and advantage."[13]

Despite many trials and tribulations, the school at Messina turned out to be a roaring success. The Jesuits, including Saint Ignatius, thus undertook the enterprise of formal schools in such an enthusiastic and comprehensive way that it became the primary and premier ministry of the order. By the time Ignatius died in 1556, the Jesuits operated thirty-five or more schools, nineteen of which were in Italy. In 1552 they opened their first school north of the Alps in Vienna. By 1565 they had thirty in Italy alone and had just opened two in Poland at Braniewo and Pułtusk. Within a generation, therefore, the Jesuit commitment to schooling can only be described as massive, and by the seventeenth century it was almost overwhelmingly so. To list a few typical examples: by 1640, a century after the Society's founding, the Jesuits operated forty schools in the small area of present-day Belgium, some sixty in France, some ninety on the Italian mainland along with twenty-two on the island of Sicily, and thirty in the Polish-Lithuanian Commonwealth.

This engagement was not confined to Europe. At the same time the Jesuits had some fifteen schools in the province of Mexico, eleven in the Viceroy of Peru, nine in Goa in India, and more in other far-flung locales. A few decades later they had close to forty schools and other major institutions in Mexico, Guatemala, and Cuba alone. By the time the Society was suppressed worldwide in 1773, it operated some seven hundred schools of various kinds around the globe. No such network of schools under a single aegis had ever been known before.

Most of these schools followed a curriculum only modestly adapted from the European template. However, as Antoni Ucerler points out in chapter 1 of this volume, the situation was notably different in Japan. At the insistence of Alessandro Valignano (1539–1606), the superior who enjoyed from the superior general almost plenipotentiary authority, the Jesuits established two schools at which students were taught to read and write in both Latin and Japanese. This curriculum also included training in Japanese etiquette. Instead of classical Greek, the students studied classical Japanese and Chinese texts, based on the assumption that, like the pagan classics of Roman and Greek literature, they contained a wisdom worth learning. As in Europe and elsewhere, training in "virtuous conduct" was the first aim. The school at Funai was one of the world's first international and even intercultural colleges, where both Japanese and European students studied in the same classroom.

The Japanese mission reminds us, moreover, that we should not confine the Jesuits' educational ministry to the conventional classroom. In 1583 the Italian Jesuit Giovanni Niccolò founded an art school and studio that had an extraordinary impact on Japanese art outside the mission community. The school (or "seminary," as the sources call it) grew over the years and by the end of the century may have employed as many as forty artists. Students painted in oil on copper, on wood, and, occasionally, on canvas. They also executed paintings in Japanese watercolors.[14]

Jesuit Universities

If it was the humanist philosophy of education that initially drew the Jesuits into education, we must never forget that the founders were graduates of the University of Paris and cherished the training they received there in that tradition of education. Moreover, they were among the educators of the era who believed the university tradition and the humanistic tradition were compatible. Thus they also believed the values those traditions respectively embodied and promoted were compatible as well. In the Jesuits' first decade, before they began to establish their own schools, they sent recruits to the order to study at well-established universities such as Paris, Louvain, and Padua. Once their own schools were established, they prescribed for recruits a rigorous program in academic philosophy and theology, as well as a foundational program in the studia humanitatis.[15]

It is not surprising, therefore, that the larger Jesuit schools began to teach some of the university disciplines. Principal among them was natural philosophy, the seedbed for the development of modern science and a subject that was especially attractive to the young laymen for whom the schools were intended. Soon the Jesuits began to operate a relatively small number of universities and, unlike many other universities of the era, always included a program in the humanities. The first of these schools was the Roman College, which opened its doors in 1552 as a humanistic school but rapidly developed into a prestigious university with an international faculty that was much more highly regarded than its local counterpart, the University of Rome (La Sapienza).

Within twenty years of the founding of the Roman College, the philosophical faculty had achieved wide recognition for its program in mathematics, which included subjects such as optics, acoustics, and astronomy, all under the leadership of Father Christoph Clavius (1538–1612). Under Clavius's influence, the Jesuit schools began to establish for themselves a lively mathematical tradition that recent scholarship has shown to be much more systemic than previously thought.[16] Confirmation of the high regard in which Clavius was held is his membership in the papal commission that, under Pope Gregory XIII, produced the Gregorian calendar, which we still use today. Clavius and Christoph Grienberger, his important but lesser-known contemporary, trained the first generation of those remarkable Jesuits whom Matteo Ricci (1552–1610) led and who made their way to Beijing in the late sixteenth century. They won entrance into the imperial court principally by virtue of their skill in mathematics and astronomy. In the early eighteenth century, the French Jesuits there persuaded Emperor Kangxi to allow them to undertake the mapping of his empire. The project turned out to be the largest and most successful cartographic enterprise in the history of the world up to that time.[17]

The Jesuits' vocation as missionaries provided them with extraordinary opportunities for creating knowledge in geography, cartography, anthropology, and botany. The reports the missionaries shared with their confreres teaching in the schools became available to the larger academic community for two reasons special to the Jesuits. First, members of the Society were encouraged to keep up a steady correspondence among themselves.[18] Second, what they wrote, especially about "curious" phenomena, was produced by men who were or had been teachers, and it was fed into a network of Jesuit teachers who knew how to exploit this information and release it into the public domain. Meanwhile, dozens upon dozens of botanizing Jesuits described and gathered plant specimens from as far away as China, Ceylon (Sri Lanka), Paraguay, and Canada and sent them back home to various schools. This phenomenon enabled Jesuit teachers in Europe and elsewhere to assemble cabinets, create botanical gardens, and publish multivolume compendiums of natural history. Often closely associated with their schools was a Jesuit pharmacy in which were distributed natural remedies such as quinine ("Jesuit bark") that missionaries also sent back. All across Europe, Jesuits also taught the geography they learned from the missionaries' maps.

José de Acosta's (1539–1600) firsthand description of the lands and peoples of "the Indies" and his reflections upon it in his *Historia natural y moral de las Indias* (*Natural and Moral History of the Indies*) are among the most important and famous Jesuit publications in this vein. First appearing in 1590, within two decades it went through four editions in Spanish, two in Dutch, two in French, three in Latin, two in German, and one in English. His work was anthropology before the discipline of anthropology was established. Its basic message for Europeans entering cultures as diverse as that of the Incans, Chinese, and Guaraní was that they must understand how profoundly different these cultures were from those of Europe and adapt their behavior accordingly. Accommodation is a leitmotif of the *Historia*.

Intensive study of languages—Greek, Latin, and the local vernacular—became part of every Jesuit's education. While Jesuits were thoroughly trained in "the art of the word," members of the older religious orders had no such training in their official plan of study. Thus not surprising, it was especially the Jesuits who, while on European missions to foreign lands, produced in great number the grammars and dictionaries of the respective indigenous languages. Their achievement implies they entered into the very mind-set of the indigenous peoples speaking those languages. In so doing, the Jesuits were also obeying a mandate to learn the language in the country in which they resided, as laid down by Ignatius in the *Constitutions* of the Society (1.8.3).

The best-known instance of Jesuit adaptation and even identification with non-European culture is the mission to China that Ricci inaugurated but his superior and mentor, Valignano, masterminded. Having insisted in Japan that the Jesuits adopt the Japanese diet, architecture, and customs, including the traditional tea ceremony, Valignano then handpicked Ricci and Michele Ruggieri to follow the same pattern upon entering China. Ricci's mastery of the language and of Chinese literary classics surely helped win his acceptance in Beijing as much as his mathematical skills did. Of his own writings in Chinese, perhaps the most telling is his "Treatise on Friendship" (*Jiaoyoulun*), a translation of Western maxims on friendship.

Roberto De Nobili (1577–1656) and Saint John de Brito (1647–93) pioneered similar paths in India. Although the Jesuits never officially ratified the policy of making such radical adaptation, no other religious order had members who were allowed, and even encouraged, to pursue such sweeping inculturation, which was surely in part a result of the humanistic education the Jesuits had received. In that education they had come to respect and learn from the pagan cultures of Greece and Rome, and through their study of rhetoric, they had learned the key importance of accommodation to times, places, cultures, and circumstances if they wanted their message to be heard.

The most famous monument of the Jesuit educational tradition is the *Ratio studiorum* (*Plan of Studies*), which was issued in 1599. The result, typical for the Jesuits, of widespread consultation and discussion within the Society, its purpose was to ensure high standards and uniform practices in Jesuit schools in different parts of the world. The *Ratio* consists essentially of a series of job descriptions for officials and teachers. It lays down the goals for each stage of the students' development and the pedagogical exercises to ensure those goals are met. While it reflects and codifies assumptions about education that were common in the era, it does not articulate what those assumptions are; however, the assumptions and the values on which such assumptions are based are derived from a combination of the university and humanistic traditions.

The *Ratio* had many merits, but in time the almost sacrosanct stature it achieved in the Society made it difficult for Jesuit schools to adapt to changing circumstances. At least some of the schools were able to overcome this limitation. For instance, the College of Nobles, founded in Milan in 1682, had an outstanding reputation. The curriculum was up to date and taught by celebrated teachers, including Roger Boscovich (1711–87), the most widely esteemed Jesuit scientist of the era. Besides Latin, the three hundred or so students learned French and German, and they studied astronomy, mathematics, physics, history, geography, and hydrography. The repertoire of the college theater included a few comedies inspired by Molière and a tragedy derived from Corneille. Jean Racine's *Athalie* served as a model for tragedies about biblical figures written by the Jesuits and performed by the students. The experience in Milan was not unique.[19] In Paris the Collège Louis-le-Grand had an outstanding faculty of Jesuit teachers and writers that drew a correspondingly brilliant body of students, including Voltaire. The college became especially noted for its elaborate ballets.[20]

From the Restoration of the Society until Today

As a result of a convergence of forces inimical to the Society of Jesus, Pope Clement XIV suppressed the order worldwide in 1773. The suppression was an unmitigated catastrophe for the Jesuits and for their educational enterprises. It was often enforced brutally. The Jesuits' libraries, sometimes by far the best in a town or city, were destroyed and their schools closed or otherwise lost to the Church. If individual Jesuits were lucky enough to escape exile and imprisonment, they were still scattered, dispossessed of their houses, and forced to fend for themselves. Although some fared reasonably well by entering the diocesan clergy or otherwise finding means of support, many never recovered from the disorientation, the mental anguish, and the sense of loss the situation caused them.

By an unexpected and ironic turn of fate, Pope Pius VII was able in 1814 to bring the order back to life and restore it throughout the world. The relatively few Jesuits who survived opened their doors to novices and, as best they could, began once again to pursue their ministries as before. They now did so, however, in a Western world that had radically changed in the wake of the Enlightenment and the French Revolution. Although in a few nations they recovered some of their buildings and other assets, they more generally had to begin from scratch in almost all of their overseas ventures. This situation made their attempts to reestablish their schools especially difficult. Whence, for instance, were the funds to come that were required for buildings, equipment, personnel, and operating expenses?

In Europe and Latin America in the nineteenth century, the Jesuits often suffered exile due to their conservative and sometimes ultraconservative political stance, a problem that hit their educational institutions especially hard. France, for instance, banished them three times: in 1828, in 1880, and again in 1901. At their banishment in 1901, they had to leave behind twenty-four schools as well as churches and other institutions.

By and large the Jesuit schools tried to follow modestly updated versions of the *Ratio studiorum*, a program that appealed particularly to politically conservative parents, but they inevitably had to make adjustments.[21] Gradually the classics of modern vernacular literatures began to fill the space once filled by the Latin and Greek classics. Meanwhile, in society at large, that quintessentially Western institution, the university, continued to be adopted, adapted, and developed virtually everywhere in the world; thus it became such a global institution that its Western origins were forgotten. The Jesuit universities, of course, shared in this phenomenon.

A certainly unintended consequence of the expulsions from their homelands was the manpower that the banished Jesuits supplied for the Society's installations in Asia, Africa, and North America. Despite problems, the order continued to grow. Throughout the nineteenth century, virtually all the Jesuit-run schools were based on the model of the humanistic college, although, as in the past, some of them had programs that could qualify them as being at least a quasi-university. By the first decades of the twentieth century, however, a number of these schools divided themselves into two distinct academic institutions—one of which qualified as secondary, the other as tertiary.

The tertiary institutions gradually became more complex and sophisticated to keep pace with the increasingly more complex and sophisticated developments in the world at large. Besides the traditional schools of law and medicine, they now began to add other professional schools such as business, nursing, education, architecture, and others as well. Adjustments were made. By the 1960s a major change set in as many of them belatedly adopted the model of the university as primarily a locus for research and the creation of knowledge.[22] Whereas before the suppression the universities in the Society rarely had more than a thousand students, Jesuit universities now might have ten times that number or more. Even with these momentous changes, Jesuit universities still clung to the humanistic ideal of helping the students develop into ethical and publicly aware persons. Some thus came to describe themselves as "student-centered research universities," an ideal that gave them a distinctive profile in contrast with that of large state-sponsored institutions.

That profile became more specific in the latter half of the twentieth century, an indication that the Jesuits were entering a new phase of their history. They lost their nostalgia for the ancien régime and embraced modern political realities. Like other ethically sensitive persons, they became increasingly aware of the injustice of the wide and growing disparity between rich and poor that inflicted great hardships on large populations. This consciousness and their efforts to help led them to sometimes run up against brutal military regimes, which insulated the system from reform.

In their Thirty-Second General Congregation, which met for three and a half months in 1974–75, the Jesuits issued an important decree titled "Our Mission Today: Service of Faith and Promotion of Justice."[23] In a more compelling and explicit way than ever before in the Society's history, the decree committed the Society of Jesus to struggle against oppression of the poor and the politically powerless. It updated, specified, and notably intensified the mandate to work for the common good that is found in the Jesuits' foundational documents. The Congregation envisaged that the promotion of justice would be a hallmark of all Jesuit ministries, including the schools. Superior General Pedro Arrupe assigned the schools the specific goal of producing "men and women for others" who would be intent on working for a more just society. Most likely unwittingly, he echoed the ideal that Cicero proposed long ago when he admonished that "we are not born for ourselves alone." More fundamentally, the mandate to promote justice echoed, amplified, and updated the anguished cries of the prophets of ancient Israel in favor of the widow, the orphan, and the alien.

The decree "Our Mission Today" served as a powerful and much-needed reminder to Jesuits of the social and moral dimension that marked their educational ventures from the beginning of the order. As a result of the decree, Jesuit schools around the world undertook a thorough examination of conscience as they sought the ways they might make the decree operative while the schools still maintained their academic integrity. The secondary schools, smaller and less complex, tended to move ahead effectively and relatively speedily. The process in the universities was slower and more difficult, but as Thomas Banchoff outlines in chapter 12 of this volume, the Society developed effective measures bit by bit.

Today by far the largest percentage of Jesuits is still engaged in education. In 2013 there were 189 Jesuit universities or other postsecondary institutions around the world. India has 54, followed by the United States with 28, Brazil with 8, and Mexico with 7. The Jesuits established a meaningful presence in South Korea only in 1960, making the founding of a university their highest priority. In Seoul they almost immediately broke ground for Sogang University, which has since achieved a distinguished reputation. Japan is unique in that, besides the well-regarded Sophia University in Tokyo, the Jesuits operate Elizabeth University for Music in Hiroshima. In Africa both the francophone and anglophone Jesuits conduct schools on the tertiary level.

Jesuits sponsor an incomparably larger number of secondary schools. In South Asia alone (primarily India), the Jesuits are responsible for 229 secondary schools plus another 164 primary and middle schools. In Canada and the United States, there are 79 Jesuit secondary schools. This number includes both traditional high schools and nontraditional schools such as the network of Cristo Rey schools, which enroll disadvantaged boys and girls to prepare them for university.

Older than Cristo Rey and incomparably more extensive is the Fe y Alegría system in Central and South America. In 1955 the Jesuit José María Vélaz set out to create an effective program for the education of Venezuela's most deprived children. In pursuit of this goal, he launched the spectacularly successful Fe y Alegría, whose purpose is to promote through education a more just society in which all members are capable of participating constructively. Today in almost every country of Latin America, as well as Spain, Chad, and elsewhere, the system enrolls almost a million students across its many programs. The network consists of more than two thousand centers in which some twenty-five hundred service units function. It makes use of a thousand school plants and sixty-seven radio stations. A Jesuit acts as the coordinator for the International Federation of Fe y Alegría, and some hundred Jesuits are involved in its operation worldwide.

Meanwhile, an internal transformation of the membership in the Society has been taking place. The geographic distribution of entrants to the Society has reversed from what it was several decades ago when by far the greatest number of new Jesuits came from the developed world. In recent decades, seventy-five percent of new recruits have come from outside Europe and North America. The Society of Jesus, a global institution from its first moments, is becoming a global institution in an altogether different way. Whereas Europeans once staffed the order's schools around the world, their staffs now principally feature Jesuits hailing from the local culture.

Conclusion

I suggest that elements in the Jesuit tradition of education fit into today's globalized, multicultural world. The first such element is simply the extensive international network of schools already in place. Second, the staffs and sponsors of these schools are personnel drawn from the local scene who are thus sensitive to indigenous cultural traditions while still being conscious participants in a global network and global Church. Third, this global network of schools is much more than a static map on a page. At the urging of the superior general, these schools are beginning to cooperate more effectively with one another, and the fruitful exchanges of ideas, of resources, and even of personnel are an increasing reality.

Fourth, the schools in this network, according to the tradition of the Society, train students in skills that will enable them to sustain or improve not only the socioeconomic situation in which they and their families find themselves but also that of the city, state, and country in which they live. In the global context of today, the schools can draw on the Jesuit tradition of adaptation and of respect for the Other that has marked many Jesuit enterprises through the centuries. In today's multicultural Society of Jesus, such respect is simply a given.

Fifth, the tradition also insists that the schools help students develop into ethically responsible adults. Underlying that insistence is the conviction that an ethically responsible life is a truly satisfying human life. Such a life is the fulfillment of the Creator's purpose and the fulfillment of the dignity every person has as a child of God, called to a life lived in the self-giving we call "love." In that regard, the Jesuit schools draw on the tradition of spirituality expressed especially in the *Spiritual Exercises* and the Jesuit *Constitutions*.

Sixth, the roots of the ethical tradition in Jesuit schools are found in the works of pagan authors such as Aristotle and Cicero. Like many others, the early Jesuits believed these texts, though pagan, were compatible with the Christian tradition and a helpmate to it. Today this ethical impulse in the Jesuit tradition finds resonance in both Catholic and non-Catholic faculty and students.

Finally, in their ideals and in their actual practice, the schools are symptomatic of how the Jesuits help us understand and even correct globalization as it is now generally perceived and pursued. They stand as a corrective to the predominantly economic model. They stand as exemplars of a more humane model in which working together for the common good is basic. Moreover, they show that such a model is possible because it is happening. They implicitly proclaim that only if such a model prevails will the globe survive.

Notes

1. John W. O'Malley, SJ, *Four Cultures of the West* (Cambridge, MA: Harvard University Press, 2004), 78–125; Hilde de Ridder-Symoens, ed., *A History of the University in Europe*, vol. 1, *Universities in the Middle Ages* (Cambridge: Cambridge University Press, 1992); Hilde de Ridder-Symoens, ed., *A History of the University in Europe*, vol. 2, *Universities in Early Modern Europe (1500–1800)* (Cambridge: Cambridge University Press, 1996); Filippo Iappelli and Ulderico Parente, eds., *Alle origini dell' Università dell'Aquila: Cultura, università, collegi gesuitici all'inizio dell'età moderna in Italia meridionale* (Rome: IHSI, 2000); Paul F. Grendler, *The Universities of the Italian Renaissance* (Baltimore: Johns Hopkins University Press, 2002); and Paul F. Grendler, *The University of Mantua, the Gonzaga and the Jesuits, 1584–1630* (Baltimore: Johns Hopkins University Press, 2009).

2. O'Malley, *Four Cultures*, 127–77; Henri-Irénée Marrou, *A History of Education in Antiquity*, trans. George Lamb (New York: New American Library of World Literature, 1964); Henri-Irénée Marrou, *Saint Augustin et la fin de la culture antique* (Paris: E. de Boccard, 1938); Takis Poulakos and David Depew, eds., *Isocrates and Civic Education* (Austin: University of Texas Press, 2004); Ekaterina Haskins, *Logos and Power in Isocrates and Aristotle* (Columbia, SC: University of South Carolina Press, 2004); and Craig W. Kallendorf, ed. and trans., *Humanist Educational Treatises* (Cambridge, MA: Harvard University Press, 1999).

3. Paul F. Grendler, *Schooling in Renaissance Italy: Literacy and Learning, 1300–1600* (Baltimore: Johns Hopkins University Press, 1989).

4. Anthony Grafton and Lisa Jardine, *From Humanism to the Humanities* (Cambridge, MA: Harvard University Press, 1986).

5. Petrarch, "On His Own Ignorance and That of Many Others," trans. Hans Nachod, in *The Renaissance Philosophy of Man*, ed. Ernst Cassirer, Paul Oskar Kristeller, and John Herman Randall, Jr. (Chicago: University of Chicago Press, 1971), 103–4.

6. Vincenzo Scarano Ussani, "*Romanus sapiens* and *civilis vir*: Quintilian's Theory of the Orator Acting for the Benefit of the Imperial Power," in *Quintilian and the Law: The Art of Persuasion in Law and Politics*, ed. Olga Eveline Tellegen-Couperus (Leuven, Belgium: Leuven University Press, 2003), 288.

7. See the still-classic study by H. Outram Evennett, *The Spirit of the Counter-*

Reformation, ed. John Bossy (Cambridge: Cambridge University Press, 1968), especially 43–66.

8. John W. O'Malley, SJ, *The First Jesuits* (Cambridge, MA: Harvard University Press, 1993), 354.

9. See, for example, the seven volumes titled *Literary and Educational Writings* in *Collected Works of Erasmus*, vols. 23–29, various editors (Toronto: University of Toronto Press, 1978–89).

10. Quoted in François de Dainville, *La naissance de l'humanisme moderne* (Paris: Beauchesne, 1940), 223.

11. Antonio M. de Aldama, *The Formula of the Institute: Notes for a Commentary*, trans. Ignacio Echániz (St. Louis: Institute of Jesuit Sources, 1990), 7.

12. O'Malley, *First Jesuits*, 210. Also see John W. O'Malley, SJ, *Five Missions of the Jesuit Charism: Content and Method* (St. Louis: Seminar on Jesuit Spirituality, 2006).

13. O'Malley, *First Jesuits*, 212–13.

14. Gauvin Alexander Bailey, *Art on the Jesuit Missions in Asia and Latin America, 1542–1773* (Toronto: University of Toronto Press, 1999), especially 66–74.

15. Cristiano Casalini, *Aristotele a Coimbra: Il Cursus Conimbricensis e l'educazione nel Collegium Artium* (Rome: Anicia, 2012).

16. Antonella Romano, *La Contre-Réforme mathématique: Constitution et diffusion d'une culture mathématique jésuite à la Renaissance* (Rome: École française de Rome, 1999). See also Marcus Hellyer, *Catholic Physics: Jesuit Natural Philosophy in Early Modern Germany* (Notre Dame, IN: University of Notre Dame Press, 2005); Mordechai Feingold, ed., *Jesuit Science and the Republic of Letters* (Cambridge, MA: MIT Press, 2003); Mordechai Feingold, ed., *The New Science and Jesuit Science: Seventeenth-Century Perspectives* (Dordrecht, the Netherlands: Kluwer Academic Publishers, 2003); and Luís Miguel Carolino and Carlos Ziller Camenietzki, eds., *Jesuítas, ensino e ciências: Séculos XVI–XVIII* (Casal de Cambra, Portugal: Caleidoscópio, 2005).

17. Roberto Ribeiro, SJ, with John W. O'Malley, SJ, eds., *Jesuit Mapmaking in China: D'Anville's Nouvelle Atlas de la Chine (1737)* (Philadelphia: Saint Joseph's University Press, 2014).

18. Steven J. Harris, "Mapping Jesuit Science: The Role of Travel in the Geography of Knowledge," in *The Jesuits: Cultures, Sciences, and the Arts, 1540–1773*, ed. John W. O'Malley, SJ, et al. (Toronto: University of Toronto Press, 1999), 212–40.

19. Giovanna Zanlonghi, *Teatri di formazione: Actio, parola e immagine nella scena gesuitica del Sei-Settecento a Milano* (Milan: Vita e Pensiero, 2000).

20. Judith Rock, *Terpsichore at Louis-le-Grand: Baroque Dance on the Jesuit Stage in Paris* (Saint Louis: Institute of Jesuit Sources, 1996); and Alessandro Arcangeli, "The Ballroom and the Stage: The Dance Repertoire of the Society of Jesus," in *I Gesuiti e la Ratio Studiorum*, ed. Manfred Hinz, Roberto Righi, and Danilo Zardin (Rome: Bulzoni, 2004), 67–73.

21. See John W. Padberg, SJ, *Colleges in Controversy: The Jesuit Schools in France*

from Revival to Suppression, 1815–1880 (Cambridge, MA: Harvard University Press, 1969).

22. See William Clark, *Academic Charisma and the Origins of the Research University* (Chicago: University of Chicago Press, 2006).

23. John W. Padberg, SJ, ed., *Jesuit Life and Mission Today: The Decrees and Accompanying Documents of the 31st–35th General Congregations of the Society of Jesus* (Saint Louis: Institute of Jesuit Sources, 2009), 298–316.

PART II

CONTEMPORARY CHALLENGES

8

THE JESUITS AND THE "MORE UNIVERSAL GOOD"
At Vatican II and Today

DAVID HOLLENBACH, SJ

This chapter explores several ways in which Saint Ignatius of Loyola's vision of the "more universal good" has helped shape Jesuit ministries in recent decades. First, it highlights several Jesuit contributions at the Second Vatican Council (1962–65) that are especially relevant to the global context of today. Second, it argues that these contributions at Vatican II are rooted in Jesuit spirituality and traditions. Third, it sketches several ways in which Ignatius's vision of the universal good is setting the agenda for the contemporary Society of Jesus in the context of contemporary global society. Finally, it makes some suggestions about possible future Jesuit contributions to the global common good.

Jesuits at Vatican II: A "World Church" and Respect for the Other

Two Jesuits were among the theological advisers who helped the Second Vatican Council address the issues arising from globalization in creative new ways: Karl Rahner helped the Council come to a deepened theological vision of the Church's identity as a truly global community, and John Courtney Murray enabled the Council to move the Catholic community from its previous opposition to religious liberty to strongly supporting it and opening the Church to newfound respect for people of other religious traditions. Their contributions have led the Catholic community to significant engagement with issues of human rights, global justice, and interreligious understanding in the years since the Council.

During the Council, Pope John XXIII's 1963 encyclical *Pacem in terris* set the stage for the new global role of the Church that emerged with Jesuit help at the Council. The encyclical highlighted a "phenomenal growth" in human interdependence being stimulated by technological progress and increased mobility, leading to a truly world economy and deepened political interaction among peoples.[1] Pope John saw the well-being of people in one country as increasingly interlinked with the well-being of other countries' populations in what he called the "universal common good." The pursuit of this global common good, particularly regarding the goods of security and peace, is becoming more important than in earlier eras.

In a more negative vein, Pope John argued that the international institutions needed to advance the global common good were insufficiently developed. In his words, "both the structure and form of governments, as well as the power which public authority wields in all the nations of the world, must be considered inadequate to promote the universal common good." John XXIII therefore called for institutions of global governance "with power, organization and means co-extensive with these problems, and with a world-wide sphere of activity."[2]

The Second Vatican Council took the pope's call to attend to the universal common good very seriously. It saw the global reach of the Church itself as giving it both a capacity and a mission to contribute to the universal common good. Growing interdependence was an emerging sign of the times that made the Church's global mission to support the growth of the unity of the human family particularly urgent. The Council approached this aspect of the Church's mission in explicitly theological terms. Two of the most important conciliar documents—the Dogmatic Constitution on the Church, *Lumen gentium*, and the Pastoral Constitution on the Church in the Modern World, *Gaudium et spes*—used almost identical language. These documents proclaimed that the promotion of the unity of the human family "belongs to the innermost nature of the Church, for the Church is, 'thanks to her relationship with Christ, a sacramental sign and an instrument of intimate union with God, and of the unity of the whole human race.'"[3]

The theology behind this teaching that the Church should be both a sacramental sign and an instrument of unity, both with God and among all members of the human family, had been developed earlier by several theologians, including the German Jesuit Karl Rahner, arguably the greatest Catholic theologian of the twentieth century. Before the Council, Rahner had argued that the manifestation of God's grace in the sacramental life of the Church should not be seen as restricted to the seven individual sacraments, such as baptism and the Eucharist. Sacramental grace should join believers together in the living unity and love to which God calls all of humanity.[4] The Christian community should thus be a sign or sacrament of God's intent for the human race. It should help the larger society discover that its deepest destiny is a life of solidarity, and the Church should work to help society attain this solidarity. The Church, therefore, has a mission to promote the common good. Because aspects of the common good are becoming more global in scope, the Church's mission includes working for the universal common good, which John XXIII had seen as increasingly important. Rahner's theology thus contributed to forming the Council's reflection on how the Church should respond to the challenge of building up the global common good.

More than a decade after Vatican II, Rahner provided an insightful analysis of what took place at the Council and its implications for the global mission of the Church. He suggested that perhaps the Council's most significant long-term influence was the way it had transformed the Church's self-understanding from that of a primarily European community to that of a genuinely global body. In Rahner's interpretation, Vatican II was "in a rudimentary form still groping for identity, the Church's first official self-actualization as a world Church."[5] No longer was it a European institution, with missionary outposts in the non-European world; now it was a global body with members from all the cultures of the world. A transformation of this magnitude, Rahner argued, had occurred only once before—that is, during the Church's first centuries, when Christianity shifted from being a movement within Palestinian Judaism to the genuinely new religious community that became European Christendom. The dramatic shift at the Council was due, at least in part, to the fact that the bishops who assembled in the Council came from around the world. Given the experiences the bishops brought to the Council, the Church needed to take very seriously global religious and cultural diversity, political divergence, and economic differences.

Until his death in 1984 Rahner continued to reflect on the globalization of the Church's identity. In an essay titled "Aspects of European Theology" published a year before he died, Rahner affirmed that Church thinking can no longer be based solely in a theology that grew up in the soil of Greco-Roman civilization. Today the Church has already inculturated itself in the various civilizations of the globe or is in the process of doing so.[6] Catholicism must thus come to grips with understandings of what it is to be human that are grounded in beliefs such as the transmigration of souls. It must learn how to approach the Islamic *ummah* (people) theologically and not just politically, and it must thereby stand ready to critique and perhaps change some elements of the Western Christian tradition that "a false ecclesiastical conservatism passes off in an all too facile way as genuine Christian achievements."[7] Moreover, Christian thinkers in the West will be called to assist those in other parts of the global Church to relate the Gospel to their non-Western cultures. Westerners possess important resources, such as the historical and scientific methods pioneered in the West, that can be of real help in this task. However, if Western Church leaders and theologians are to provide such help to the Church of the rest of the world, then they will have to do so with great humility and be open to learning from the non-Western Church.

These suggestions that the Church should play an increasingly global role hold considerable promise in the face of the deep divisions and often bloody conflicts in the world today. But they can also raise fears that such an enhanced role for the Church could lead to an oppressive restriction of freedom or to the suppression of religious and cultural diversity. Through much of its history, the Catholic Church did not hesitate to rely on the coercive power of the state to help promote its mission. Another Jesuit, the American John Courtney Murray, made a key contribution that helped the Catholic community rethink this position, thus assisting it to address global realities in a way that respects human freedom and the human rights of those with other beliefs.

Murray's great contribution at Vatican II was the role he played in shaping the Council's full support for the right to religious freedom. The Declaration on Religious Freedom (*Dignitatis humanae*) explicitly acknowledges that the Council "intends to develop the doctrine of recent popes" on the rights of the human person, on the constitutional order of society, and, more specifically, on religious freedom.[8] This explicit statement of the Council's intent to develop or change Christian doctrine is extraordinary, for the Church has often seen changeless commitment to past tradition as a sign of its fidelity to the Gospel. Murray identified the development of doctrine as the key issue the Council had to address to deal effectively with the challenges that religious and cultural pluralism raise.[9] He had become convinced that the Catholic community needed to affirm the right to religious freedom as a result of his work with Protestants, Jews, and secular thinkers on how to build a peaceful international order in the context of the Cold War. Murray knew from his experience that the Church's contribution to peace and justice required respect for religious freedom. Moreover, after having ecclesiastical authorities restrict his own ability to write and speak about religious freedom in the late 1950s, he had a personal stake in advancing the Church's commitment to freedom and rights.

Murray's argument for the development of Church teaching had several levels.¹⁰ First, it was explicitly theological, asserting that the human person is a spiritual being whose spirit reaches beyond all earthly realities in its quest for meaning. Ultimately this quest can only be satisfied by one's union with God, and it can be attained only through a freely made act of faith. Second, this theological stance had direct political consequences in that it implied a limit to the power of the state. Citizens should be free from state control in their religious belief; thus, we can speak of a civil right to religious freedom. Moreover, since citizens should also be free in other, broader ranges of their social lives, religious freedom also was linked with the full range of civil and political rights. In turn, then, religious freedom and the requirements of constitutional democracy were closely connected in Murray's view. Finally, he distinguished a broad vision of ethics from the more narrow scope of civil law. Because the state is limited, the reach of its power and civil law does not extend to promoting the full common good in a given society but only to the basic moral requirements of social life that the Council called "public order." Public order includes certain moral values: public peace, justice, and those standards of public morality on which consensus exists in society.¹¹ The state should promote these basic requirements of social life, and the Church can legitimately call upon the state to do so; however, the Church ought not ask the government to use coercive law to promote moral or religious values that go beyond the requirements of public peace and justice. Instead, the Church itself, the family, and the many other groups that form civil society should build up these fuller values.

Murray's thought clearly affirmed the central importance of freedom, especially religious freedom, in the life of every individual person and in the life of a good society. In Murray's view, a good society must be a free society. This vision is enshrined in the words of *Dignitatis humanae* that Murray himself surely wrote: "[T]he usages of society are to be the usages of freedom in their full range. These require that the freedom of the human person be respected as far as possible, and curtailed only when and insofar as necessary."¹²

This advancement in the Church's commitment to freedom through Murray's influence has been crucial to the Church's role in global society in the decades following the Council. Since Vatican II the Roman Catholic Church has made important contributions to the global advancement of democracy in Portugal and Spain in the late 1960s, in numerous countries in Latin America as well as the Philippines and South Korea in the 1970s and '80s, and in Poland in the 1980s, with this latter intervention contributing to the collapse of the Soviet Union in the early 1990s.¹³ Murray's work clearly helped set the Church on a path toward its significant global role in the promotion of human rights, democracy, and respect for religious and cultural differences today.

In the work of both Rahner and Murray, therefore, the Jesuits helped contribute to a fresh definition of the global mission of the Church. These two theologians, of course, were certainly not the only thinkers who helped the Council move in this new direction. But their work shows that the Jesuit spirit can make important contributions in an increasingly globalized context and that the realities of globalization engage with Saint Ignatius's insight that the Jesuit mission should serve the more universal good in creative ways.

Echoes of Early Jesuit Universalism

In the contributions of Rahner and Murray to the Council, we can hear clear echoes of Ignatius's expansive vision of the goals that the Jesuit order he founded should pursue. Rahner and Murray were deeply rooted in Ignatian spirituality and in the tradition of Jesuit thought and practice. So it is useful to note several ways the Jesuit tradition influenced their contributions to the global role of the Church.

The "Formula of the Institute of the Society of Jesus," the official papal document that established the Society in 1540 and was revised in 1550, noted that the order's activities should be directed "according to what will seem expedient to the glory of God and the common good."[14] This single phrase evokes central features of Ignatius's religious vision. It combines a commitment to God—the glory of God—and a commitment to human well-being, or the common good. Ignatius's vision of the common good extended well beyond the common good of the city-state that Aristotle had in mind when he said the common good of the polis should be the aim of human morality, beyond the good of the medieval kingdoms envisioned in Thomas Aquinas's understanding of the common good, and beyond the public good sought by Renaissance republics closer to Ignatius's own time. Ignatius saw the good that should define Jesuit ministries as "universal," as the good of the whole of humanity extending to the ends of the earth. Ignatius wrote that "the more universal the good is, the more it is divine." Thus he believed Jesuits should choose ministries that give preference "to persons and places which, once benefited themselves, are a cause of extending the good to many others."[15]

At their best, Jesuits have envisioned "the more universal good" not as the unidirectional transfer of a European vision of the good life to non-European societies but as an exchange between different understandings of what truly good lives could look like. The phrase "the more universal good" appears many times in the Jesuit *Constitutions* as the criterion for decisions about what is required for the fuller service of God, humanity, and the Church.[16] As discussed earlier in this volume, the commitment to the more universal good led some of Ignatius's early followers to be among the first Westerners to travel beyond Europe's boundaries and have encounters with the cultures of India, China, and the Americas. Ignatius's closest early companion, Francis Xavier, voyaged from Europe, around Africa, and on to India and Japan in his ministry and died off the coast of China in 1552. Alessandro Valignano, a key successor to Xavier, was dispatched in 1573 to oversee Jesuit works in East Asia. As Antoni Ucerler details in chapter 1 of this volume, Valignano developed "adaptation" to local cultures and other religious traditions as a key element in the style of Jesuit ministry in Asia. Other Jesuits followed the adaptationist approach in their missions: Matteo Ricci in China, Roberto de Nobili in India, and Alexandre de Rhodes in Vietnam. In their ministries they learned the local languages, often becoming the first Westerners to do so.

It has been argued that the development of authentic freedom is one of the principal fruits of the *Spiritual Exercises* of Saint Ignatius. The *Exercises* presuppose that responding to God and following Christ can occur only through a deep engagement of human freedom.[17] The early Jesuits certainly needed considerable inner freedom to travel to unfamiliar lands and to risk challenging the ecclesiastical and cultural institutions of Europe by becoming more appreciative of the new worlds they encountered. While they manifested many of the same prejudices as their European contemporaries, in some notable instances, they had the freedom to rise above these biases and appreciate the achievements of these cultures, seeking to learn as well as to teach. This was evident in their sometimes controversial adaptations of Christian doctrine and worship in light of indigenous religions, such as the so-called Chinese rites.

One could argue, therefore, that some significant elements in the tradition of Jesuit spirituality are particularly suited to responding to the challenges of globalization today. One could also argue that Rahner and Murray drew on these strands of Jesuit tradition in their contributions to Vatican II. The development of Jesuit ministries after the Council provides some further evidence that such an argument is on the right path.

Jesuits and the Universal Common Good Today

Ignatius's commitment to the more universal good and the Jesuit contributions to Vatican II's vision of a truly global Church have both had an important influence on Jesuit ministries during the fifty years since the close of the Council. Vatican II's emphasis that the Church's mission includes working to secure the global common good through the advancement of human rights, justice, and peace has surely been one reason the Society of Jesus has been committed to these goals since the Council. The Jesuits' Thirty-Second General Congregation (GC 32) convened in 1974–75 to consider the implications of Vatican II for the development of Jesuit ministries. The Congregation's most important conclusion was that working for justice in society is an essential dimension of Jesuit efforts to advance people's faith in God and in the Gospel of Christ. The Congregation described the identity of the Jesuits this way: "What is it to be a companion of Jesus today? It is to engage, under the standard of the Cross, in the crucial struggle of our time: the struggle for faith and that struggle for justice which it includes."[18] It defined the corporate mission of the Society in similar terms: "The mission of the Society of Jesus today is the service of faith, of which the promotion of justice is an absolute requirement."[19]

This commitment to the promotion of justice as an essential dimension of the service of faith has had a dramatic influence on the ministries of Jesuits, leading some to increase their work directly with the poor. Several years after the conclusion of GC 32, Jesuit superior general Fr. Pedro Arrupe gave an interview with the press about the growth in the Jesuits' commitment to working for justice and serving the poor. Arrupe noted that implementing the Congregation had just begun and still had a long way to go. But he noted, as a sign that change had been launched, that some provinces of the Society had freed Jesuits from their existing ministries to work more directly with the poor. Such initiatives, he said, had been numerous in Asia, Africa, and Latin America, and they were also occurring in the industrialized countries. Arrupe cited the seventeenth-century Paraguay reductions—settlements for indigenous people that were overseen by the Jesuits—as a precedent for Latin American Jesuits' contemporary efforts to help educate the poor through programs such as Fe y Alegría, a network of Jesuit schools that serves the poor across the region. He noted a distinguished Jesuit secondary school in India as an example of how some Jesuit educational institutions had shifted from educating children of the elite to recruiting students from among the very poor.[20]

Fr. Arrupe could also have noted developments under way in Jesuit secondary education in the United States. A few years before GC 32, the founding document of the Jesuit Secondary Education Association (JSEA) of the United States had stated that Jesuit high schools must "go beyond the criteria of academic excellence" to honestly evaluate their effectiveness in bringing students to grasp the importance of "both the Christian reform of social structures and renewal of the Church."²¹ Following GC 32, JSEA initiated workshops throughout the Jesuit school system in the United States on integrating the promotion of justice into the school's mission.²² Today the ideal Jesuit high school graduate is seen as "committed to doing justice" and as a person who "has been inspired to develop the awareness and skills necessary to live in a global society as a person for and with others." Though this commitment will only come to fruition in adulthood, the graduate will have begun to move toward it as a result of his or her Jesuit education.²³

GC 32 also had significant influence on the intellectual work of Jesuits in diverse parts of the world. The Woodstock Theological Center at Georgetown University followed up the Congregation's proclamation that a commitment to justice is a requirement of Christian faith with an influential collection of theological essays on the relationship of faith and justice.²⁴ A few years later the Woodstock Center expanded its work on the social implications of Christian faith with a set of studies on the relationship between Christian thought and the promotion of human rights in the Americas. Among the several Latin American Jesuits who contributed to these studies produced by Woodstock was Ignacio Ellacuría, the president of the University of Central America in San Salvador, whose life and legacy Maria Clara Bingemer addresses in chapter 9 of this volume.²⁵ Ellacuría, as well as others who contributed to the Woodstock volumes on human rights, stressed the close linkage between human rights and the alleviation of poverty. Jesuit transnational collaboration thus led to some serious theological and social analyses of the relationship between promoting justice, overcoming poverty, and changing oppressive patterns of global economic interaction. Similar themes could be found in the work of Jesuit intellectuals in Africa. For example, the Cameroonian Jesuit Engelbert Mveng wrote passionately about the need to overcome the consequences in Africa of the slave trade and colonization by European nations. Mveng called these consequences "anthropological poverty," the deprivation not only of material well-being but also of people's history, language, culture, faith—indeed, their very humanity.²⁶

The international impact of Jesuit intellectual exploration of globalization has also been evident in a series of conferences on exploring "Catholic Theological Ethics in the World Church," organized primarily by the American Jesuit James Keenan. In 2006 in Padua, Italy, this initiative gathered four hundred moral theologians from more than fifty countries, and in 2010 more than six hundred theologians from seventy-five countries convened in Trent, Italy, all to examine the ethical challenges of a globalizing world. Subsequently a series of regional international meetings have been held, and many writings have resulted. This initiative is the most truly global intellectual undertaking in the history of the Catholic Church. Its impact will likely be significant and lasting.[27]

These global commitments have not been without cost. Most dramatic has been the loss of Jesuits' lives during their work for justice. Ignacio Ellacuría was murdered along with five other Jesuits and two women at the Jesuit residence in San Salvador on November 16, 1989. The Salvadoran military, which was closely allied with the country's economic elite, organized the assassinations. Engelbert Mveng was assassinated on April 22, 1995, in Yaoundé, Cameroon. His assassins have still not been publicly identified or held accountable, though there is little doubt of their links to the political and economic elites of Cameroon. When GC 32 approved its decree linking the service of faith and the promotion of justice, a Brazilian Jesuit reportedly declared, "There will be many martyrs that come from this." In fact, there have been many. More than fifty Jesuits have died violently since 1975 because of their work with and on behalf of poor, marginalized persons.[28]

Less dramatically the commitment to justice has led some critics to conclude that the Jesuits have become excessively engaged in secular social and political action and have abandoned their time-honored ministries. It is true that traditional Jesuit ministries emphasized preaching, administering the sacraments, guiding people in the Spiritual Exercises, and undertaking other clearly religious activities. It is also true that Jesuits have traditionally been known for their educational work among the social elite. Familiarity with the originating Jesuit charism, however, indicates that engaging with the poor has been a key aspect of Jesuit ministry from the time of Saint Ignatius. John O'Malley, SJ, in his definitive study *The First Jesuits*, stresses that the ministries of the early Jesuits included not only preaching the Word and administering the sacraments but also performing works of mercy such as assisting the poor. The early Jesuits helped the poor both through directly assisting individual persons and by founding new institutions when adequate institutional response was lacking.[29] There can also be little doubt that efforts to understand and influence political life, for good and occasionally for ill, have been notable in Jesuit ministries through much of the order's history.[30] Recent developments, therefore, are in harmony with the founding charism of the Jesuits.

The experience of Jesuits who see their work for justice as an expression of their commitment to the Gospel has also led them to discover similar links between Christian faith and the work for greater understanding across cultures and dialogue with the world's religions. The Jesuits' Thirty-Fourth General Congregation (GC 34), held in 1995, issued a decree reaffirming that the promotion of justice is an essential element of the order's ministry in the service of Christian faith. At the same time, GC 34 issued decrees promoting cross-cultural understanding (Decree 4) and interreligious dialogue (Decree 5). In doing so the Congregation also affirmed the Jesuit efforts to advance interreligious and cross-cultural understanding that were already under way. To note a few examples, the Jesuit Aloysius Pieris is deeply engaged in dialogue with Sri Lankan Buddhism, and Michael Amaladoss pursues similar engagement with Indian Hinduism. Francis X. Clooney, a Jesuit based in the United States and a contributor to this volume, has helped develop the intellectual basis for an emerging field that has become known as comparative theology.[31]

GC 34, like these thinkers, sees the pursuit of interreligious and cross-cultural understanding as an essential expression of Christian love for one's neighbor and universal respect for the dignity and rights of all people. Such efforts are also increasingly important preconditions for peace and justice among diverse communities in a globalizing world. GC 34 thus stressed that Jesuit ministry has four dimensions: service of faith, promotion of justice, adaptation to other cultures, and commitment to interreligious dialogue. In today's interdependent globe, these four aspects of ministry are closely interconnected in the overall work of the Church and of the Society of Jesus.[32]

The early Jesuit experience of seeking the more universal good has therefore been developing over the half century since Vatican II into efforts to create ministries suited to the religious and social needs of an increasingly globalized world. The ministries being developed seek to advance the union of men and women with God and with each other through proclaiming the Gospel in ways that advance justice and enhance understanding among diverse cultures and among religions through dialogue. It is not surprising, therefore, that the Thirty-Fifth General Congregation (2008) stressed that Jesuit ministries should be at the "frontiers" where injustice prevails and where cultures and religious traditions are encountering each other in new and more vigorous ways.[33]

Possible Directions for the Future

In recent years Jesuits and Jesuit institutions have surely been pursuing this vision of ministry at the frontiers, making notable contributions to the enhancement of justice, cultural dialogue, and interreligious understanding. But they have a considerable way to go before the normative aspirations of the recent Jesuit General Congregations are adequately expressed in action. In 2010 Superior General of the Society Adolfo Nicolás stated that Jesuit ministries should be reconsidered in light of the challenges of global interdependence. He noted that the institutions through which Jesuits carry out their ministries have an extraordinary potential to serve the universal good stressed by Ignatius. But Nicolás also observed that "until now, we have not fully made use of this 'extraordinary potential' for 'universal' service."[34]

In light of Nicolás's concern, we can conclude with several observations about how the Jesuits' contributions and their ministries to the universal common good might be enhanced in the years ahead. The first observation is drawn from what might seem a rather unexpected source, the recent work of the Jesuit Refugee Service (JRS), which Peter Balleis addresses in more detail in chapter 11 of this volume. The organization deals with crisis situations that are often quite far removed from the more "mainstream" Jesuit ministries such as education, the Spiritual Exercises, and pastoral work among people living much more routine lives than those of refugees. An outstanding thesis written by Daniel Villanueva, SJ, however, suggests that reflection on the JRS approach can contribute to other Jesuit undertakings. Villanueva's work, titled "The Jesuit Way of Going Global," draws specifically on the example of JRS to provide some lessons for enhancing the Jesuits' broader ministry in the global age.[35]

An aspect of JRS's work that is particularly relevant for other Jesuit ministries in our global age can be drawn from the definition of its mission. JRS sees its ministry as having three dimensions: accompaniment, service, and advocacy. Accompaniment means being with the people being served. For JRS it involves being with the refugees on the ground, listening to their stories, and showing them through one's genuine personal presence that their human dignity is important and that they are not forgotten. Many refugees say this personal support is the most important help they have received from JRS. It also has a deep impact on those providing the ministry, stimulating their further commitment to action; therefore, when JRS staff accompany the refugees, it leads to further service. By directly interacting with them, the workers gain firsthand knowledge of the refugees' needs, which in turns shapes the workers' service. For example, engaging with refugees and migrants has led JRS to establish education programs for refugee children and for refugees living in very poor urban areas. Most recently it has prompted the development of the program Jesuit Commons: Higher Education at the Margins. This initiative electronically links Jesuit educational universities in several parts of the world with people in great need and gives them access to higher education. The initial programs of Jesuit Commons offer online higher education courses to refugees in camps in Malawi, Kenya, Syria and Jordan.[36] This new initiative, still quite modest in scope, arose from accompanying refugees and listening to them speak of their needs, hopes, and dreams. Creative service arises from accompaniment.

Accompaniment and the service that develops from it in turn lead to seeing the need to advocate change in policies and institutions. For example, from accompanying and serving refugees, JRS workers learned that many displaced people had been wounded by land mines. This knowledge led JRS to research why military forces continue to use these mines so widely and ultimately to JRS's participation in the global campaign to abolish them. Not only did this advocacy emerge from the practical engagement of accompaniment and service, it was also shaped by intellectually careful analysis and by dialogue between practitioners and analysts. It helped generate a campaign that eventually succeeded in having most of the countries of the world—sadly not including the United States—ratify the global treaty abolishing land mines, a campaign that received the Nobel Peace Prize.[37] Thus, accompaniment, service, and advocacy support each other and can have an impact on public opinion and a real influence on public policy and social institutions.

The service's making electronic higher education available online to refugees and advocating land mine abolition do not provide a template for what all Jesuit ministries should be doing, but these examples do suggest that accompaniment could play an analogous role in other ministries in a world increasingly aware of its cultural, religious, and social diversity. There is no escaping encounters with such diversity in our global age. Efforts to serve people and to advocate policies on their behalf must avoid presuming that one already knows what needs to be done, even if one has expertise in the area at issue. Rather, service and advocacy need to arise both from listening to people's understanding of their own needs and hopes and from being receptive to how people see the realities they face. JRS calls this listening and receptivity "accompaniment." It might also be described as a kind of contemplative openness to the depth of the beauty and misery that mark the lives of the people one seeks to serve. Such contemplative accompaniment can be essential to genuine understanding across the social and cultural rifts that divide our world.

Pope Francis, who is himself a Jesuit, stresses the importance of accompaniment in shaping the overall ministries of the Church in his apostolic exhortation *The Joy of the Gospel* (*Evangelii gaudium*). He calls for the Church and all its ministers to develop in the "art of accompaniment." This art, the pope says, "teaches us to remove our sandals before the sacred ground of the other (cf. Ex 3:5)." Recognizing the sacredness in persons in turn leads to "prudence, understanding, patience" in responding to their needs and a reluctance to stand in judgment of them. Accompaniment, Francis says, is rooted in a genuinely contemplative stance toward others. When the Other is poor or living in degraded situations, it "permits us to serve the other not out of necessity or vanity, but rather because he or she is beautiful above and beyond mere appearances." Accompaniment can thus engender a loving service of the poor and advocacy on their behalf. It inspires an "option for the poor" that goes beyond ideology. By responding to those in need with "loving attentiveness" and "true concern for their person," it helps avoid forms of service that turn out to be veiled ways of advancing "one's own personal or political interest."[38]

Thus, Pope Francis proposes a style of ministry marked by a humility and an openness to the Other that is analogous to the qualities JRS sees at the heart of accompaniment. Those being served should be approached with a readiness to listen to them. The willingness to listen to others can lead to the discovery of both who they are and who one is oneself. Such listening is not a marginal aspect of the life of a Christian believer; rather, it is "a profound and indispensable expression" of Christian faith.[39] The pope affirms that this dialogic or relational approach to understanding flows from the belief that the deepest truth is God's embrace and possession of us, not our possession of God. In the human apprehension of truth, the full or absolute truth of God transcends our full grasp. We always remain on the way to full understanding. Traveling this path can only be done with integrity if we accompany one another in humility. Thus we need to listen with care as well as speaking, to receive from one another as well as seeking to serve each other, to contemplate the reality of the world's achievements and miseries as well as taking action. Thus we are on a journey or "pilgrimage" with believers and non-believers, Christians and non-Christians. Indeed, Pope Francis uses the term "pilgrim" thirteen times in *The Joy of the Gospel*. As Francis is a follower of St. Ignatius, his word choice should not be surprising, for in the *Autobiography*, Ignatius refers to himself simply as the pilgrim.

The spirit of accompaniment, therefore, holds promise for being able to shape the ministries of the Church and the Jesuits in ways that reach well beyond the work of JRS. Indeed, if Pope Francis is right, accompanying one another by listening as well as speaking, in dialogue and relationship, should be seen as essential to the human condition itself. The pope's dialogic understanding of the human condition reflects what John O'Malley has called the "style" of dialogue adopted by the Second Vatican Council. In O'Malley's words, at the Council "for the first time in history, official ecclesiastical documents promoted respectful listening as the preferred mode of proceeding, as a new ecclesiastical 'way,' a new ecclesiastical style."[40]

This dialogic style also has notable Ignatian roots. Ignatius states that the "presupposition" of the *Spiritual Exercises* is that every good Christian should be "more ready to put a good interpretation on another's statement than to condemn it as false." If this good interpretation does not hold up, the one who has made the statement should "be asked how he understands it. If he is in error, he should be corrected with all kindness. If this does not suffice, all appropriate means should be used to bring him to a correct interpretation, and so defend the proposition from error."[41] A spirit of dialogue is thus the presupposition of the dynamics of the *Spiritual Exercises*. It can and should be the presupposition of all Ignatian and ecclesial ministries. Indeed, the Jesuit vision, based on the *Spiritual Exercises*, could suggest that all people, whatever their vocation or faith, are called to accompany one another in pursuit of the universal common good that all share in by listening as well as speaking and by seeking to discern where the community is being led.

This presupposition has great relevance in our global age. Cultures and religious traditions are interacting in newly intensive ways with a potential for conflict that has too often led to actual violence. The Ignatian tradition of working for the universal good of the whole human community through accompaniment and efforts at mutual understanding has the potential to address this new interaction and interdependence creatively. Learning from those in need as we seek justice, and from other cultures and religious traditions as we seek peace, is a requirement both of the Gospel and of our human condition as pilgrims in history. The dialogic style of Vatican II, the spirit of accompaniment of JRS, the presupposition of the *Spiritual Exercises*, and the emphasis Pope Francis puts on the "art of accompaniment" as a mark of the Church on pilgrimage all highlight ways toward more just and peaceful—or at least less oppressive and violent—forms of globalization. The early Jesuits were among the first participants in the globalizing developments of the early modern era. As we reflect on the challenges we face now, perhaps some aspects of the Jesuit tradition as it continues on its pilgrimage can help us find better paths to the global common good of our day.

Notes

1. John XXIII, *Pacem in terris*, Encyclical on Establishing Universal Peace in Truth, Justice, Charity, and Liberty, April 11, 1963, sec. 130, http://w2.vatican.va/content/john-xxiii/en/encyclicals/documents/hf_j-xxiii_enc_11041963_pacem.html.

2. Ibid., sec. 134–37.

3. Vatican Council II, *Gaudium et spes*, Pastoral Constitution on the Church in the Modern World, December 7, 1965, sec. 42, in *The Documents of Vatican II,*

ed. Walter M. Abbott, SJ, trans. Joseph Gallagher (New York: Guild Press, 1966). The internal quote is from Vatican II's Dogmatic Constitution on the Church, *Lumen gentium*, sec. 1.

4. Karl Rahner, SJ, *The Church and the Sacraments*, trans. W. J. O'Hara (1961; repr., New York: Herder and Herder, 1963). The French Jesuit Henri de Lubac had earlier contributed to this development in his *Catholicism: Christ and the Common Destiny of Man*, trans. Lancelot C. Sheppard and Elizabeth Englund (1938; repr., San Francisco: Ignatius Press, 1988).

5. Karl Rahner, SJ, "Towards a Fundamental Theological Interpretation of Vatican II," *Theological Studies* 40, no. 4 (December 1979): 716–27.

6. Karl Rahner, SJ, "Aspects of European Theology," in *Theological Investigations*, trans. Hugh M. Riley (New York: Crossroad, 1988), 21:82–83. This essay originally appeared in 1983.

7. Ibid., 93.

8. Vatican Council II, *Dignitatis humanae*, Declaration on Religious Freedom, December 7, 1965, sec. 1, in Abbott, *Documents of Vatican II*. Emphasis added.

9. See John Courtney Murray, SJ, "Vers une intelligence du développement de la doctrine de l'Église sur la liberté religieuse," in *Vatican II: La liberté religieuse: Déclaration "Dignitatis humanae personae,"* ed. Jérôme Hamer and Yves Congar (Paris: Cerf, 1967), 111–47.

10. Murray's mature argument for religious freedom is expressed in an economical way in an essay he wrote primarily for the bishops at the Council, "The Problem of Religious Freedom," which is in John Courtney Murray, *Religious Liberty: Catholic Struggles with Pluralism*, ed. J. Leon Hooper, SJ (Louisville, KY: Westminster/John Knox, 1993), 127–97. Originally published as *The Problem of Religious Freedom* (Westminster, MD: Newman Press, 1965).

11. Murray incorporated these arguments into Vatican II's Declaration on Religious Freedom, esp. sec. 1–7. See Murray's comments in footnotes to the English translation of the Declaration in Abbott, *Documents of Vatican II*.

12. *Dignitatis humanae*, sec. 7, as translated in Abbott, *Documents of Vatican II*. See also John Courtney Murray, SJ, "Arguments for the Human Right to Religious Freedom," in Murray, *Religious Liberty*, 229–44.

13. For evidence of the strong alliance of Catholicism and democracy that has developed since the Second Vatican Council, see José Casanova, "Civil Society and Religion: Retrospective Reflections on Catholicism and Prospective Reflections on Islam," *Social Research* 68, no. 4 (Winter 2001): 1041–81. See also Samuel Huntington, "Religion and the Third Wave," *The National Interest* 24 (Summer 1991): 29–42.

14. This goal is stated in the apostolic letter of Pope Julius III *Exposcit debitum* (July 21, 1550), which gave papal approval to the Formula of the Institute of the Society of Jesus. The relevant passage in English translation is in *The Constitutions of the Society of Jesus and Their Complementary Norms: A Complete English Translation of the Official Latin Texts*, trans. Carl J. Moell, SJ (St. Louis: Institute of Jesuit Sources, 1996), 4.

15. Ignatius of Loyola, *Constitutions of the Society of Jesus*, no. 622, in *Constitutions of the Society of Jesus and Their Complementary Norms*, 286.

16. See, for example, *Constitutions of the Society of Jesus*, nos. 618 and 623, in ibid. See also John W. O'Malley, SJ, "To Travel to Any Part of the World: Jerónimo Nadal and the Jesuit Vocation," *Studies in the Spirituality of Jesuits* 16, no. 2 (1984).

17. See Michael J. Buckley, SJ, "Freedom, Election, and Self-Transcendence: Some Reflections upon the Ignatian Development of a Life of Ministry," in *Ignatian Spirituality in a Secular Age*, ed. George P. Schner (Waterloo, Ontario: Wilfrid Laurier University Press, 1984), 65–90.

18. Thirty-Second General Congregation of the Society of Jesus (GC 32), Decree 2, no. 2, in *Jesuit Life and Mission Today: The Decrees and Accompanying Documents of the 31st–35th General Congregations of the Society of Jesus*, ed. John W. Padberg, SJ (St. Louis: Institute of Jesuit Sources, 2009), 291, para. 12 in this edition.

19. GC 32, Decree 4, no. 2, in Padberg, *Jesuit Life*, 298, para. 47 in this edition.

20. Pedro Arrupe, SJ, "The Impact of GC 32 on the Society: The Jesuits Moving toward the Year 2000. Interview with Father Arrupe to the Roman Daily *Avvenire*," in *Justice with Faith Today: Selected Letters and Addresses*, ed. Jerome Aixala, SJ (St. Louis: Institute of Jesuit Sources, 1980), 2:263–65.

21. Jesuit Secondary Education Association (JSEA), "The Preamble (1970)," in JSEA, *Foundations: A Compendium of Documents on Jesuit Secondary Education* (1994), section 1 of the PDF, http://www.jsea.org/sites/default/files/resources/attachments/Foundations.pdf.

22. See the report by Edwin J. McDermott, SJ, "Faith and Justice (1976)," in JSEA, *Foundations*, section 6.

23. JSEA, "Profile of the Graduate at Graduation" (2010), http://www.jsea.org/pedagogy/graduate.

24. John C. Haughey, ed., *The Faith That Does Justice: Examining Christian Sources for Social Change* (New York: Paulist Press, 1977).

25. See Ignacio Ellacuría, SJ, "Human Rights in a Divided Society," in *Human Rights in the Americas: The Struggle for Consensus*, ed. Alfred Hennelly and John Langan (Washington, DC: Georgetown University Press), 52–65. The second volume from the Woodstock Center's project on human rights in the Americas that stressed the link between human rights and poverty alleviation is Margaret E. Crahan, ed., *Human Rights and Basic Needs in the Americas* (Washington, DC: Georgetown University Press, 1982).

26. Engelbert Mveng, SJ, "Impoverishment and Liberation: A Theological Approach for Africa and the Third World," in *Paths of African Theology*, ed. Rosino Gibellini (London: SCM Press, 1994), 156.

27. For an overview of the Catholic Theological Ethics in the World Church initiative, see its website, at http://www.catholicethics.com/.

28. Those who have been killed because of their engagement in the struggle for justice are named in the publication of the Jesuits' Social Justice and Ecology Secretariat, *Promotio Justitiae* 117, no. 1 (2015): 30–34. See also Patrick Howell, SJ, "The New Jesuits: The Response of the Society of Jesus to Vatican II, 1962–2012:

Some Alacrity, Some Resistance," *Conversations in Jesuit Higher Education* 42 (September 1, 2012): 10.

29. John W. O'Malley, SJ, "Works of Mercy," in *The First Jesuits* (Cambridge, MA: Harvard University Press, 1993), esp. 165–67. Also see O'Malley's chapter 7 in this volume.

30. For a discussion of the early Jesuits' engagement with political thought, see Harro Höpfl, *Jesuit Political Thought: The Society of Jesus and the State, c. 1540–1630* (Cambridge: Cambridge University Press, 2008).

31. For a useful brief description from a theological standpoint of the work of Pieris, Amaladoss, and Clooney, as well as that of some other Jesuits working on matters of interreligious, intercultural, and social justice concerns since Vatican II, see Mary Ann Hinsdale, "Jesuit Theological Discourse since Vatican II," in *The Cambridge Companion to the Jesuits*, ed. Thomas Worcester, SJ (Cambridge: Cambridge University Press, 2008), 298–318. Also see Clooney's chapter 2 in this volume.

32. See GC 34, Decree 2, no. 19, in Padberg, *Jesuit Life*, 529, para. 47 in this edition.

33. See GC 35, Decree 2, no. 20, in ibid., 741, and Decree 3, whose title is "Challenges of Our Mission Today: Sent to the Frontiers," in ibid., 744–54.

34. Adolfo Nicolás, SJ, "Depth, Universality, and Learned Ministry: Challenges to Jesuit Higher Education Today," remarks presented at the conference on Networking Jesuit Higher Education: Shaping the Future for a Humane, Just, Sustainable Globe, Mexico City, April 23, 2010, 7, http://www.sjweb.info/documents/ansj/100423_Mexico%20City_Higher%20Education%20Today_ENG.pdf. The internal quotes are from GC 35, Decree 3, no. 43, and Decree 2, no. 20.

35. Daniel Villanueva, SJ, "The Jesuit Way of Going Global: Outlines for a Public Presence of the Society of Jesus in a Globalized World in the Light of Lessons Learned from the Jesuit Refugee Service" (STL thesis, Weston Jesuit School of Theology, 2008).

36. See Peter Balleis's chapter 11 in this volume and the website of the Jesuit Commons, http://www.jc-hem.org.

37. For descriptions of some of the work of the Jesuit Refugee Service related to the abolition of land mines, see material at the "Ban Landmines" link on JRS's Asia Pacific region website, http://www.jrsap.org/campaigns_focus.cfm?TN=PROMO-20150608050650.

38. The quotes in this paragraph are from Pope Francis, *Evangelii gaudium*, Apostolic Exhortation on the Proclamation of the Gospel in Today's World, November 24, 2013, nos. 169, 171, 172, and 199, http://w2.vatican.va/content/francesco/en/apost_exhortations/documents/papa-francesco_esortazione-ap_20131124_evangelii-gaudium.html.

39. Pope Francis, "Letter to a Non-believer," a response to Dr. Eugenio Scalfari of the Italian newspaper *La Repubblica*, September 4, 2013, http://w2.vatican.va/content/francesco/en/letters/2013/documents/papa-francesco_20130911_eugenio-scalfari.html.

40. John W. O'Malley, SJ, "The Style of Vatican II," *America* 188, no. 6 (February 24, 2003): 12–15; and John W. O'Malley, SJ, *What Happened at Vatican II?* (Cambridge, MA: Belknap Press of Harvard University Press, 2008), 11–12, 43–52, 305–8.

41. Ignatius of Loyola, *Spiritual Exercises*, no. 22, trans. Louis J. Puhl, SJ (Westminster, MD: Newman Press, 1957), 11.

9

THE JESUITS AND SOCIAL JUSTICE IN LATIN AMERICA

MARIA CLARA LUCCHETTI BINGEMER

In our globalized world, even a small event in one part of the earth can have effects on other continents. Gradually globalization has grown from an economic phenomenon into something much broader. Economics is now just one element of the spread of Western political and cultural influence across the planet in a trend one can trace from the early modern phase of globalization up through today. Fueled by technological and military superiority, European civilization has spread gradually over the world in different, mutually reinforcing ways, including political domination, economic exploitation, and the imposition of culture. What began as a matter of trade and colonization has become a much wider and deeper form of expansionism encompassing not only material domination but also a particular Western worldview.[1]

From its inception in the mid-sixteenth century, the Society of Jesus was part of this wider movement. In founding the Catholic Church's first avowedly missionary religious order, Saint Ignatius of Loyola (1491–1556) was clear from the selection of his first nine companions that the men of his order would have to be prepared to venture to the farthest and least familiar corners of the earth. From the earliest decades, the Jesuit mission and identity were anchored not only in Catholic orthodoxy and Renaissance humanist ideals but also in a global perspective and a spirit of universality.[2]

This chapter explores how this universality took shape in Latin America, a poor continent marked by colonization, oppression, and marginalization through the early modern and modern phases of globalization. It then turns to the contemporary phase of globalization, which coincides with Vatican II (1962–65) and the Latin American Church's growing self-confidence and influence, evident in the development of social doctrine ("the preferential option for the poor") and the theology of liberation. A final section takes up the life and legacy of Ignacio Ellacuría, SJ (1930–89), the rector of the University of Central America (UCA), who was martyred in 1989. Ellacuría's life and work exemplify the efforts of the Jesuits, and of others in the Church, to imagine and practice a globalization that is not dehumanizing but instead attentive to the spirit of the Gospel and the pursuit of justice.

The Global Outlook of the Society of Jesus

From the beginning, the Society of Jesus was distinguished by its international membership as well as by the worldwide scope of its objectives and apostolic influence. These factors contributed directly to the Jesuits' role in the globalization of Western culture through their educational institutions; their contributions to science, literature, and the arts; and the intercultural dialogue arising from their missionary enterprises.[3] The Jesuits' ingrained globalism arose from Ignatius's reading of the Gospel itself as universal and transcultural. Like Christian evangelizers throughout history, Ignatius read in Christianity an offer of salvation and fullness of life that could answer the fundamental yearnings of humanity everywhere regardless of its particular revelation in the life of Jesus.[4]

This specific opening to the universal was rooted in Ignatian spirituality. Saint Ignatius was always a man of great desire, ambitions, and dreams; however, he was also convinced that the greater and the lesser had to complement each other in mutual dependence. The great desires, unless they take flesh in what is small and limited—that is, in particular social and ecclesial settings—remain illusory and unreal. Thus, the experiences of the Spiritual Exercises are attuned to universal aims and how to achieve them through the offering of one's life and the following of Jesus Christ in poverty, in humiliation, in insults, and in being rejected by the world.[5] So it was that Ignatius suggested to those making the Exercises that they should go out in poverty, spiritual and actual, to preach and be received under the standard of Jesus Christ in a life of humiliations and humility.[6]

What Ignatius had in mind was an apostolic community of religious men sent on missions to preach the Gospel to every creature and nation. This universal vision was reinforced by the contemplation on the Incarnation in the Exercises, in which the three divine persons—the Father, the Son, and the Holy Spirit—look down lovingly on the surface of the earth and see all humanity divided by differences, violence, and sin.[7] The

Trinity's "decision" to send the Son to redeem humanity is taken in view of this whole world with all these divisions, reflecting as they do injustice, violence, and the nonacceptance of difference. But the practical import of this Trinitarian decision can be contemplated in the poor house of a young woman, nameless and socially insignificant, at the margins of time and space—Mary of Nazareth. It was Ignatius's desire that his followers should live near the poor in order to experience and share their situation and offer their help.

This determination to have his men approach their missions in a spirit of poverty and of eagerness to encounter the poor set the Jesuits' way of proceeding apart from that of the other missionary orders of the colonial period. They were the only religious order that understood evangelization to be inseparable from inculturation. Many of the earliest evangelizers had sought to preach the Good News in dialogue with other cultures, with Saint Paul's mission to the gentiles serving as the paradigmatic example.[8] However, Christianity had become increasingly bound to emerging western European culture throughout the Middle Ages. In this historically conditioned form Europeans carried the Christian faith with them on their colonial enterprises beginning in the sixteenth century. Thus, conversion to Christianity came to entail not only a purely religious confession but also an assimilation with the invading culture and a corresponding rejection of indigenous values.[9] The Jesuit tradition, by contrast, was marked by a significant effort to move into the reality and culture of others.[10]

Although much of the colonial legacy in South America fits the pattern of forced cultural assimilation as well as religious conversion, some Jesuit missionaries in Latin America took more culturally tolerant approaches. At the start of the seventeenth century, the Jesuits, who followed the Franciscans and Dominicans as colonial latecomers, were entrusted with the organization of frontier outposts, known as reductions, in a region centered on modern-day Paraguay. The most famous example was the Guaraní Republic, where the Jesuits not only Christianized the indigenous people but also affirmed those features of native culture that they felt were compatible with human dignity and a Christian life. Many made genuine efforts to learn native languages (often as a means of catechesis) and resisted encroachments by slave traders. The Jesuits' affirmation of the humanity of the natives, and a degree of autonomy from colonial rule, earned the enmity of Spanish and Portuguese rulers and contributed to their expulsion from Latin America in the mid-eighteenth century and to their eventual worldwide suppression in 1773.

Had the Jesuits not been forced to leave these areas, their experience might have led to a more open engagement with indigenous peoples generally that, in turn, could have begun a constructive dialogue with the scientific and technological developments of modern civilization.[11] The failure here brings home to us the fragility of their original achievement (an issue Aliocha Maldavsky addresses at length in chapter 4 of this volume). At the same time, the early experience of the Jesuits in Latin America also points to the possibility that, even in the colonial era, the order possessed a global outlook and engaged in activities that respected cultural particularity.

The expulsion of the Jesuits from Portuguese Brazil in 1759 and from Spanish America in 1767 meant that the Society of Jesus was absent throughout the process of Latin American independence and the formation of the new Latin American nations around the turn of the nineteenth century. With the abolition of royal patronage, Church-state relations went through a tumultuous period after independence. In fact, for several decades, the Vatican preferred to leave episcopal sees vacant rather than concede to the new republican governments the privileges of the old *patronato real* (royal patronage) to nominate bishops. After its restoration in 1814, the Society of Jesus encountered great difficulties in returning to its former missions and colleges in Latin America. Moreover, even after their slow return to some countries, they frequently faced renewed expulsions by liberal regimes throughout the nineteenth and early twentieth centuries.[12] Only during the first half of the twentieth century were the Jesuits able to consolidate their renewed presence in Latin America and to begin to establish new educational institutions—colleges and universities, which would soon gain their traditional prestige as elite institutions.

Vatican II, the Society of Jesus, and a New Departure in Latin America

With the end of World War II and decolonization, a new phase of globalization began under US leadership. Latin American nations joined the new United Nations system created after 1945 but remained bound within the US sphere of economic, political, and military influence—a condition that was reinforced during the early decades of the Cold War. The Cuban Revolution of 1953–59 was a political turning point. Much of Latin America and the rest of the world viewed it as the beginning of an anti-imperialist struggle to break the bonds of dependence on those first world countries that were perpetuating unequal North-South relations reminiscent of colonialism.[13]

The presence and role of the Church in this new context became a matter of controversy. Since the end of the nineteenth century, the Church had been conscious of having lost the working classes. The publication of

Pope Leo XIII's encyclical *Rerum novarum* in 1891 was an attempt to repair the breach that had opened between the Church and the poor during the Industrial Revolution. It would be another seventy years before the Church in Rome turned seriously to the world outside Europe and North America, attuned to the experience of the poor and their fears and aspirations.[14] On September 11, 1962, a month before the beginning of Vatican II, Pope John XXIII made a broadcast that surprised both the Church and the wider world. He affirmed, "Where the underdeveloped countries are concerned, the Church presents herself as she is. She wishes to be the Church of all, and especially the Church of the poor."[15]

As confirmed in the Council's documents, the idea of a "Church of the poor" set a new direction for the whole Church and especially in Latin America, where it led to a structural critique of an evangelization conducted for elites and in the service of vested interests.[16] In the 1960s the Jesuits in Latin America underwent a profound transformation in tandem with the process of aggiornamento connected with the Second Vatican Council, with the deep renewal of the entire Society of Jesus under Superior General Pedro Arrupe (1965–83), and with the general transformation of the Latin American Church following the Medellín Conference of Latin American Bishops in 1968. Out of this movement grew a new method of theology—the theology of liberation—that took as its starting point what it means to be a Christian in a continent of poor and oppressed people.

But the seeds of this transformation had been planted earlier by some individual Jesuits who played a pioneering role in the development of social Catholicism in Latin America. Fr. Alberto Hurtado (1901–52), canonized as a saint by Pope Benedict XVI in 2004, was one of the most prominent examples, being an influential author and a founder of the Hogar de Cristo shelters and of the important journal *Mensaje*. Hurtado had been a student of Jean-Baptiste Janssens's at Louvain University before the latter became the general of the Society. In 1949 Hurtado helped draft Superior General Janssens's letter to Jesuit provincials on the social apostolate, the Society's first important official document on how to approach issues of social justice.[17] Although addressed to the entire Society, the instruction was particularly directed to Latin American Jesuits. In the letter Janssens exhorts the masters of novices to inculcate in them a social consciousness from the beginning of their novitiate.

The Twenty-Ninth General Congregation of the Society of Jesus in 1946 had already made a parallel appeal to establish centers of social research and social action. In 1955 Janssens appointed the Cuban Jesuit Manuel Foyaca, a sociologist and editor of the journal *Justicia Social Cris-*

tiana, as the special visitor to Latin America to promote the foundation of Jesuit Centers of Social Investigation and Action (Centros de Investigación y Acción Social [CIAS]) throughout Latin America. Until 1962 Focaya visited all nineteen Jesuit provinces, vice provinces, and missions in Latin America. Out of this initiative would eventually emerge some of the most important Jesuit social centers in Latin America: Instituto Latinoamericano de Doctrina y Estudios Sociales in Chile, Centro Gumilla in Venezuela, Instituto de Estudios para el Desarrollo in Colombia (now Centro de Investigación y Educación Popular), and Instituto Brasileiro de Desenvolvimento in Brazil.

At the time, there were already twenty-three such centers around the world, eleven of them in Latin America. In July 1966 the directors of all the Latin American centers convened for the first time in Lima to draft their common statutes. Arrupe announced that December the formation of the Latin American Council of CIAS. He referred to the centers as instruments in "the transformation of minds and social structures towards a greater awareness of social justice."[18]

The Medellín Conference of Latin American bishops in August 1968 adopted a new, three-point agenda for the Church: approach faith and justice together, inseparably united, as priorities; put an emphasis on the theological method of "see, judge, and act"; and orient a new, Bible-centered model of the Church toward local conditions rather than ecclesial structures.[19] These points were confirmed again at the Puebla Conference of 1979, when the bishops officially endorsed a preferential option for the poor, a theology of liberation, and the foundation of basic ecclesial communities.

All of these changes in the Church had a great impact on the Jesuits and their understanding of their global mission. In May 1968 Arrupe held a meeting with the Jesuit major superiors of Latin America in Rio de Janeiro. In light of Vatican II, the superiors produced a policy statement for the Society, reconfiguring and rethinking its apostolate in every field:

> We intend to orient our whole apostolate . . . to participate, as best we can, in the common quest of all peoples (whatever their ideology may be) for a freer, more just, and more peaceful society. We want the Society to be actively present in the temporal life of humankind today: having as its sole criterion the Gospel message as interpreted by the church, exercising no power in civil society and seeking no political goals, seeking solely to shape the consciences of individuals and communities.[20]

The provincials ended their document with provocative questions for the Jesuits of Latin America: "Are we capable of responding to the world's expectations? Are our faith and charity equal to the anxiety-ridden appeals of the world around us? Do we practice self-denial sufficiently, so that God is able to flood us with light and energy? Does personal prayer have its proper place in our life, so that we are united with God in this great human task that cannot succeed without God?"[21]

Here we can see the ideal of Saint Ignatius as described by his colleague Jerónimo Nadal in his exhortation to be "at once a contemplative and in action."[22] Such too was the personality of Arrupe, both a visionary and a mystic, in his leadership as general of the Society of Jesus. Thus inspired by the Council, Latin American Jesuits made deep changes to dedicate all their apostolic enterprises to the liberation and development of the continent's poor people. One could see in this post-conciliar period the Society's growing commitment in favor of the poor and oppressed. The mystical life generated by this commitment was ardent and impressive.[23] Also many wanted, at least in some measure, to share in the effects of injustice and oppression with the poor.[24]

After this meeting in Rio de Janeiro, the Jesuits had another gathering that would have a major impact on the future of the order—the Thirty-Second General Congregation in 1974–75. Its pivotal declaration was the response expressed in its Decree 2: "What is it to be a Jesuit? . . . It is to engage, under the standard of the cross, in the crucial struggle of our time: the struggle for faith and that struggle for justice which it includes."[25]

While Decree 4 defined "the Service of Faith and the Promotion of Justice" as the core of the Jesuit mission, Decree 5 on "the work of inculturation" insisted that faith and Christian life need to be expressed in the language and the cultural categories of the peoples who are the subject of evangelization.[26] This point was particularly relevant in Latin America, Africa, and Asia. With this new emphasis on inculturation, the Jesuit mission recovered one of the central dimensions of the Jesuit way of proceeding from the early Jesuits' fruitful encounters with non-Western cultures.

Theology of Liberation

According to Gustavo Gutiérrez in his seminal 1971 book, *Teología de la liberación*, liberation theology is best understood as "a critical reflection on praxis."[27] Gutiérrez himself also says, however, that the theology of liberation does not begin simply from a critical analysis of reality; rather, it begins with a mystical experience, a deep encounter with the Lord in the face of someone who is poor. In practice it encompasses the threefold method of see, judge, act. In an unjust and oppressive system, theology cannot exist without a social analysis of reality (seeing) that, in turn, can then be measured against scriptural revelation (judging). The process of judging helps the Christian to discern the wrongs inherent in a particular society and to formulate and undertake political and ecclesial strategies to mediate them (acting). In this lens, the theology of liberation is not a theoretical program; it is conceived of as an instrument for the poor in their own process of liberation. The ultimate objective is to support the struggles of poor people in building a new society by working alongside them so that they can become the real agents of their own history.

Many of the Jesuits had anticipated the main lines of liberation theology. At the 1968 meeting in Rio de Janeiro, Latin American Jesuits had promised "to work for bold reforms that will radically transform existing structures" and "promote social peace." They continued: "The integration of social life within the Christian way of life calls for theological and philosophical reflection that will take in the whole world and its pressing problems."[28] In conversation with leading thinkers such as Gutiérrez and Leonardo Boff, then a Franciscan, some Jesuits developed the ideas at the level of theology, contributing to a growing literature. Others implemented an approach of "inserting" Jesuit communities among the poor.[29] There was a natural affinity with Arrupe's agenda, with its insistence on "the service of faith and the promotion of justice," as it was proclaimed at the 1975 General Congregation. His successor, Father Peter-Hans Kolvenbach, had no hesitation in stating that Latin America had "opened the eyes of Jesuits to the preferential love for the poor and to true and integral liberation as the priority perspective for the present-day mission of the Society." It was rightly said to be "the beginning of a new phase in social Catholicism."[30]

One of the key areas for reflection and practice related to these ideas was the sphere of education. "As far as our universities are concerned," the 1968 meeting had stated, "the recentness of their establishment and the difficult task of maintaining them make them truly difficult apostolic enterprises. Their academic and economic difficulties are aggravated even more by the fact that they must now provide a broader-based opportunity for education to all."[31] In fact, since the 1950s, Jesuit educational institutions in Latin America had been undergoing a dramatic change from an almost exclusive dedication to the formation of middle- and upper-class youth to an increasing dedication to the popular education of underprivileged youth and adults. The foundation of the first Fe y Alegría school in 1955 in Venezuela by Fr. José María Vélaz, SJ, represented a turning point. Sixty years later Fe y Alegría is an international nonprofit organization that administers around three thousand primary and secondary educational centers for more than half a million students from impoverished and excluded communities in eighteen Latin American countries, as well as others in Europe and Africa.

This profound transformation did not happen without contentious and, at times, acrimonious debates, both within the Society of Jesus and between the Society and other groups, in many Latin American countries. One need only recall three of the most acrimonious episodes: the decision in 1971 to close the Instituto Patria, the most prestigious and elitist Jesuit school in Mexico; the conflicts at the Catholic Universidad Andrés Bello in Venezuela between 1968 and 1972 that showed the deep cleavages not only between the Jesuit rector and the students but also between polarized sections of the Jesuit community on campus and in the city; and the contentious debates about the future of the upper-class branch of the Colegio San Ignacio "El Bosque" in Santiago, Chile. The last conflict led to the consensual decision reached in many places throughout Latin America that Jesuit upper-class schools and elite institutions could be maintained as long as they reoriented themselves in line with the Jesuit mission in the service of faith and the promotion of justice and thus contributed to the education of "men and women for others."[32]

The transformation of the Latin American Jesuits became most difficult and dangerous in those contexts in which social and political conflicts led to violent confrontations between highly repressive military dictatorships and revolutionary guerrilla movements. Such was the case in the Southern Cone, particularly in Argentina and Chile, and in Central America, particularly in El Salvador. Jesuit communities were often caught in the crossfires between the warring factions in their countries and within the global Society of Jesus. They also found themselves involved in the theological and ecclesiological disputes between sectors of the Latin American Church and the attempt of the Roman Curia under Pope John Paul II and Joseph Cardinal Ratzinger, prefect of the Congregation for the Doctrine of the Faith, to curb and discipline the excesses of liberation theology.

In his opening address to the delegates of the Thirty-Second Jesuit General Congregation on December 3, 1974, Pope Paul VI captured the essence of the Jesuit mission and charism in difficult times: "Wherever in the Church—even in the most difficult and extreme fields, in the crossroads of ideologies, in the social trenches—there has been and is now conversation between the deepest desires of human beings and the perennial message of the Gospel, Jesuits have been and are there."[33] Listening among the delegates was Jorge Bergoglio, the young Jesuit provincial from Argentina. He had the difficult task of maintaining the unity and the apostolic obedience of a Jesuit province that reflected internally the deep divisions and conflicts of an Argentinian society that would soon be caught in the violence of a civil and military "dirty" war. Bergoglio found himself having to pursue simultaneously the seemingly opposite objectives of protecting the Jesuits and of assisting the victims of the repression. The life of this Argentinian Jesuit—from his service as a young provincial, to his internal exile, to his becoming episcopal pastor of Buenos Aires, to his elevation to Pope Francis—provides a window on the turbulent times and the deep transformation of the Society, the Latin American Church, and the continent as a whole.[34]

The Social Mission of Jesuit Higher Education and the Legacy of Ignacio Ellacuría

The legacy of the Jesuit educator Ignacio Ellacuría provides another equally revealing window on these transformative decades—in the history of the Society, the Latin American Church, and the continent as a whole—with lessons for our contemporary understanding of globalization. In his life and even more so in his death, Ellacuría came to embody the renewed educational mission of the Society of Jesus in Latin America. As a professor and rector of the Jesuit University of Central America (UCA) in San Salvador, Ellacuría took this mission in radically new directions. His original thought, his sustained practice, and his martyrdom at the hands of the Salvadoran Army in 1989 serve as a test case, enabling us to better understand the relationship between the Society of Jesus and contemporary globalization.[35]

UCA in El Salvador was established in 1965 shortly after the founding of two Jesuit sister institutions—UCA of Nicaragua (1960) and the Rafael Landívar University in Guatemala (1961). From the outset the mission of UCA went beyond the quality of instruction or even the personal attention given to students to encompass a reflection on and a response to the dramatic questions of poverty and oppression in the country. The new direction was not a complete departure from the prevalent conceptions of the Catholic and Jesuit universities to that time, but certainly it had a different emphasis that was quite decisive for the public face of the university. The task of the university was being defined more by the urgencies of social justice than by theological orthodoxy or explicit evangelization. In pursuit of its mission, UCA was always concerned with maintaining its independence not only from the civil and political authorities of the time but also from the religious and ecclesiastical ones.[36] UCA faculty and leaders, Ellacuría among them, were openly critical of other Jesuit universities that appeared more preoccupied with religious questions than with the pressing needs of the vast majority of the population, the poor.[37]

But such a stand brought obvious risks and, eventually, persecution. Solidarity with the poor and the struggle for justice were perceived as a serious attack on national security and stability. In many countries in Central America and in the Southern Cone, established oligarchies and the political right felt threatened by the critical and prophetic positions being taken by the Catholic Church after Vatican II and by the Jesuits in particular, who were often indiscriminately associated with the armed opposition to the regime. Against this background of violence and the threat of violence, Ellacuría's committed option for the poor, in defense of their dignity and liberation, was not simply an intellectual choice. He also was following the example of the life of his friend Archbishop Óscar Romero, who was martyred in 1980 as he was celebrating Mass. Romero's own radical prophetic commitment had grown after the assassination of Fr. Rutilio Grande, another Jesuit, in 1977 on his way to evening Mass. Despite the explicit death threats, Ellacuría and other Jesuits pressed ahead, secure in the confidence that they had the support of Father Arrupe.[38]

The most powerful statement of Ellacuría's progressive vision for the Church and the world, and its roots in the Jesuit experience, was his commencement address at the University of Santa Clara in 1982. He began with the local context of UCA's work, "oriented, obviously, on behalf of our Salvadoran culture, but above all, on behalf of a people who, oppressed by structural injustices, struggle for their self-determination—people often without liberty or human rights." From there he moved to a deeper reflection on the role of the university, one that "must be concerned with the social reality—precisely because a university is inescapably a social force: it must transform and enlighten the society in which it lives." And he connected his appeal with a wider reference to a theological frame in which the poor the world over remain the focus of Christian reflection and action. "Liberation theology has emphasized what the preferential option for the poor means in authentic Christianity," he told his listeners. "Such an option constitutes an essential part of Christian life—but it is also an historic obligation. For the poor embody Christ in a special way; they mirror for us his message of revelation, salvation and conversion. And they are also a universal social reality."[39]

This deep commitment to the poor was not an ideological precept or a theoretical offshoot of liberation theology. It was rooted in his personal experience of Christian faith and his lifelong cultivation of Ignatian spirituality, with an emphasis on the sacrifice of the Cross, which calls us to lives of service. Ellacuría's colleague Fr. Jon Sobrino has drawn attention to this Christian mysticism, with its identification of the poor with the "crucified people," in his important essay "The Forgotten Ellacuría: What

Must Not Be Allowed to Decay." In stark terms Sobrino confronts the reader with the reason why it may be more convenient to overlook such a deeper reality, because "to enter seriously into the reality of the 'crucified people' calls us into question, and may even lead to self-accusation: do we, as intellectuals and human beings, have something to do with the crucifixion of the poor, and if so, what?"[40]

According to Sobrino, Ellacuría's mysticism was grounded in three interrelated dimensions. First, he dwelled on the marginalized, "crucified people" who have to be brought down from the Cross, even though the act of doing so—of living lives of compassionate service to the poor—might lead to oneself ending up on a cross. Second, there was the challenge of working for what Ellacuría proposed as a "civilization of poverty," something to be envisioned as contrary and superior to the civilization of wealth that is responsible for the grave sickness of the prevailing civilization. Such a civilization of poverty and its power of salvation destabilize us because rationally it seems close to madness and scandal.[41] Finally, in the Mass following Romero's death, Ellacuría's reflection that "with Monsignor Romero, God passed through El Salvador" points to the ultimate, beneficent reality of the divine saving grace, of the God whose presence is manifest in martyrs and other victims of injustice.[42]

For Sobrino, in these three matters, the principle of God's partiality becomes manifest. All of them point to the dialectical tension between the universal and the particular so present in the *Spiritual Exercises* of Saint Ignatius and so dear to Ellacuría. God's revelation appears as something partial. It forces us to go beyond an abstract universalism and to begin concretely with what is considered "below" in history—that is, the perspective from the reality of the poor and the victims. This reality, according to Sobrino, is freighted with truth and salvation. Further, it demands a "praxis"—another of Ellacuría's key terms—that liberates the oppressed.[43]

Only by taking into account such aspects of Ellacuría's "mystical thought" do we recognize what is most important in his contribution and understand what Sobrino calls "the total Ellacuría."[44] In this totality are not only his experience of El Salvador, its structures of injustice, and a range of influences—from the Spanish philosopher Xavier Zubiri, to the German theologian Karl Rahner, SJ, to socialist thinkers—but also his calling as a Jesuit, his mysticism, and his spirituality. All are sources of meaning and consistency to his life.[45] One cannot know Ellacuría, the intellectual, completely without understanding his experience with the life and witness of Archbishop Romero, the *Spiritual Exercises* of Saint Ignatius, and, of course, the example of Jesus of Nazareth.[46] As with Jesus of Nazareth, Ellacuría's death casts light on his life and his thought. Conversely, his death cannot be read and interpreted independently of his life and his thoughts.

Superior General of the Society Peter-Hans Kolvenbach had reaffirmed this evangelical and pastoral option for the poor at the opening of the UCA academic year in March 1988, the year before the massacre of the Jesuit community. "You know that as Jesuits we are challenged and questioned by the Lord's Gospel, by the social teaching of the Church, and by the cries of the poor of this land that rise up to heaven," he told his listeners. "We see too that we must do this within the preferential option for the poor, looking at God and the world from their point of view, letting ourselves be inspired by them and placing ourselves at their service in a common effort among us all and with divine grace. I think that this university has made a serious effort to take up this Christian and human ideal here in El Salvador."[47]

The true legacy of this pioneering, visionary community of UCA El Salvador lies in the distinctive model of the university that it aimed to build. UCA let go of the rhetoric of development that marked its foundation in 1965 and, through a creative and critical awareness of reality, came to understand its mission was to serve the oppressed nation in which it was situated.[48] In the words of Charles J. Beirne, one of the Jesuits who joined UCA to fill the void left by the martyred Jesuits and to continue their mission, "The UCA placed itself by the side of the poor, and sought to be their voice until the day when they could speak for themselves. It took sides, but in the way on which Ignacio Ellacuría constantly insisted: *universitariamente*—in the way proper to a university."[49]

Conclusion

Jesuits were latecomers to the military and spiritual conquest of the Americas by the Iberian colonial powers, for the mendicant orders had started the process almost half a century before the foundation of the Society of Jesus.[50] But very soon the Jesuits found their particular niche, based on the two ministries that have defined them through the ages—educational institutions in the urban centers of the colonial empire and missions to the religious Other, or the indigenous peoples at the peripheries of the empire. The Jesuits' role in protecting the Guaraní and other indigenous peoples from the most rapacious forms of colonial exploitation, and their status as a transnational order that was careful to protect its relative autonomy from the Catholic monarchs, eventually contributed to the Jesuits' expulsion from Ibero-America before their global suppression in 1773.

Absent from the process of independence and from the formative period of the postcolonial Latin American nations, the Jesuits were not welcomed by the politically dominant, liberal anticlerical elites and only began to reestablish their educational institutions in the first half of the twentieth century. Since the 1960s the educational ministries and evangelical mission of the Society of Jesus have been radically transformed as they have increasingly shifted the focus of their service to the margins of society, assuming a critical role with respect to neoliberal ideologies and projects of globalization. The life and work of Ignacio Ellacuría, SJ, beautifully exemplifies this transformation. As a scholar and university administrator, he developed and applied Ignatian spirituality in the service of the poor and marginalized. In the process he added a rich layer of meaning to the idea of a "preferential option for the poor" that Superior General Pedro Arrupe and his successors so powerfully articulated. In the quarter century since his martyr's death in 1989, Ellacuria's example has proven an inspiration not just for the Church in Latin America but also for the world.

To struggle for social justice "from below" continues to be a central challenge for the Society of Jesus, for the Church as a whole, and for global humanity. The experience of Latin America since the Second Vatican Council has shaped the Jesuits' approach to globalization that today is marked by a strong identification with the poor and an engagement with the theology of liberation—not as a monolithic system of thought and action but as a structured reflection on the contemporary demands of the Gospel. At the same time the Jesuits, for their part, have had a modest impact on the wider dynamics of globalization. Their lived emphasis on a preferential option for the poor and on the active accompaniment of the marginalized provides witness to an understanding of globalization and global solidarity at odds with the reigning neoliberal conceptions. Today a Jesuit pope who hails from Latin America continues to challenge society, the Church, and the world to make service to the poor an ethical and practical imperative. As Pope Francis put it before an international audience in 2013, "A way has to be found to enable everyone to benefit from the fruits of the earth . . . and to satisfy the demands of justice, fairness and respect for every human being."[51]

Notes

1. João A. Mac Dowell, SJ, "Os jesuítas e a globalização: Uma alternativa?," in *A globalização e os jesuítas: Origens, história e impactos*, ed. Maria Clara Lucchetti Bingemer, Inácio Neutzling, SJ, and João A. Mac Dowell, SJ (São Paulo: Edições Loyola, 2007), 1:13.

2. Maria Clara Lucchetti Bingemer, "Globalização: O que tem isso a ver

com os jesuítas?," in Bingemer, Neutzling, and Mac Dowell, *Globalização e os jesuítas*, 1:9.

3. Ibid., 1:10.

4. Mac Dowell, "Os jesuítas," in Bingemer, Neutzling, and Mac Dowell, *Globalização e os jesuítas*, 1:16–17.

5. Ignatius's *Spiritual Exercises*, no. 98, reads: "Eternal Lord of all things, I make my oblation with your favor and help, in presence of your infinite Goodness and in presence of your glorious Mother and of all the Saints of the heavenly Court; that I want and desire, and it is my deliberate determination, if only it be your greater service and praise, to imitate you in bearing all injuries and all abuse and all poverty of spirit, and actual poverty, too, if your most Holy Majesty wants to choose and receive me to such life and state."

6. See the "Meditation on Two Standards," *Spiritual Exercises*, nos. 136–47.

7. *Spiritual Exercises*, nos. 101–9, especially no. 106.

8. The standard example is Paul on the Athenian Areopagus in Acts 17, as discussed by M. Antoni J. Ucerler, SJ, in chapter 1 of this volume.

9. Mac Dowell, "Os jesuítas," in Bingemer, Neutzling, and Mac Dowell, *Globalização e os jesuítas*, 1:17.

10. In addition to the Guaraní reductions in South America, key examples include the experiences of Matteo Ricci, the Malabar rites in the East, and the efforts of Roberto de Nobili in India.

11. Mac Dowell, "Os jesuítas," in Bingemer, Neutzling, and Mac Dowell, *Globalização e os jesuítas*, 1:19. On this point, see the critical remarks in Luiz Felipe Baêta Neves, *O combate dos soldados de Cristo na terra dos papagaios: Colonialismo e regressão cultural* (Rio de Janeiro: Forense-Universitária, 1978). More positive accounts can be found, for example, in Clovis Lugon, *A república comunista cristã dos guaranis* (Rio de Janeiro: Paz e Terra, 1968); and Bartolomeu Melià, SJ, "As missões jesuítas nos Sete Povos das Missões," in Bingemer, Neutzling, and Mac Dowell, *Globalização e os jesuítas*, 2:255–58.

12. For a general overview, see Jeffrey L. Klaiber, SJ, *The Jesuits in Latin America, 1549–2000: 450 Years of Inculturation, Defense of Human Rights, and Prophetic Witness* (St. Louis: Institute of Jesuit Sources, 2009). For a particular case, see José del Rey Fajardo, SJ, "La restauración de los jesuitas expulsados de Venezuela (1767–1916)," *Archivum Historicum Societatis Iesu* 83, no. 165 (2014): 61–109.

13. Rodolfo Gil Benumeya, "Tradición y actualidad en la evolución internacional del socialismo árabe," *Revista de Política Internacional* 89 (1967): 37–54; and Érica Reis de Almeida, "O Pan-Africanismo e a formação da OUA," *Revista geopaisagem* 6, no. 12 (July/December 2007), http://www.feth.ggf.br/África.htm. For Latin America, see Enzo Faletto, "Los años 60 y el tema de la dependência," *Estudos Avançados* 12, no. 33 (May/August 1998): 109–17.

14. Walbert Buhlmann, *The Coming of the Third Church* (Maryknoll, NY: Orbis, 1977).

15. John XXIII, "Radio Address Concerning the Second Vatican Council," September 11, 1962, http://www.ewtn.com/library/PAPALDOC/johnxxiiiradio.htm.

16. Henrique C. de Lima Vaz, SJ, "Igreja Reflexo vs. Igreja Fonte," *Cadernos Brasileiros* 46 (1968): 17–22.

17. Jean-Baptiste Janssens, SJ, to all Jesuit provincials, "Instruction on the Social Apostolate," October 10, 1949, http://www.sjweb.info/sjs/documents/Janssens_eng.pdf.

18. Quoted in Fernando F. Franco, SJ, ed., *Jesuit Social Centres: Structuring the Social Apostolate* (Rome: Social Justice Secretariat, 2005), 5, http://www.sjweb.info/sjs/documents/Studio_ENG.pdf.

19. See the final documents of the Medellín Conference: Latin American Episcopal Council (CELAM), *The Church in the Present-day Transformation of Latin America in Light of the Council*, ed. Louis M. Colonnese (Bogotá: General Secretariat of CELAM, 1970), vol. 2.

20. Latin American Provincials of the Society of Jesus, "The Jesuits in Latin America," in *Liberation Theology: A Documentary History*, ed. and trans. Alfred T. Hennelly, SJ (Maryknoll, NY: Orbis Books, 1990), 77–83, quotation from no. 3. The original Spanish version can be found at http://www.cpalsj.org/wp-content/uploads/2013/06/Reunion-de-los-Provinciales-Jesuitas-de-AL-con-Arrupe.pdf.

21. Ibid., no. 10.

22. For the spirituality associated with this phrase, see Joseph F. Conwell, SJ, *Walking in the Spirit: A Reflection on Jerónimo Nadal's Phrase "Contemplative Likewise in Action"* (St. Louis: Institute of Jesuit Sources, 2003). See also Philip Endean, SJ, "The Concept of Ignatian Mysticism," *The Way Supplement* 103 (May 2002): 77–86.

23. For the final documents of the Third CELAM Conference (Puebla, Mexico, 1979) in their original Spanish, see http://www.celam.org/conferencia_puebla.php.

24. Pedro Arrupe, SJ, "Discours d'ouverture à la Congrégation des Procureurs," in *Foi et justice: La dimension sociale de l'évangélisation*, by Jean-Yves Calvez (Paris: Desclée de Brouwer, 1985), 56.

25. Thirty-Second General Congregation of the Society of Jesus, Decree 2, nos. 1–2, in *Jesuit Life and Mission Today: The Decrees and Accompanying Documents of the 31st–35th General Congregations of the Society of Jesus*, ed. John W. Padberg, SJ (St. Louis: Institute of Jesuit Sources, 2009), 291.

26. Decrees 4 and 5, along with the rest of the documents of the Thirty-Second General Congregation, can also be found in Padberg, *Jesuit Life*.

27. See, about this, Gustavo Gutiérrez, OP, *A Theology of Liberation: History, Politics, and Salvation* (Maryknoll, NY: Orbis, 1973); and the original, *Teología de la liberación: Perspectivas* (Lima: Centro de Estudios y Publicaciones, 1971).

28. Latin American Provincials, "Jesuits in Latin America," in Hennelly, *Liberation Theology*, no. 5.

29. I am referring here to Jesuit communities that moved out of institutional settings or comfortable houses to live as or with the poor. See Benjamin González Buelta, SJ, *Bajar al encuentro de Dios: Vida de oración entre los pobres* (Santander, Spain: Sal Terrae, 1988).

30. Charles Antoine, *Le sang des justes: Mgr Romero, les jésuites et l'Amérique Latine* (Paris: Desclée de Brouwer, 2000), 12.

31. Latin American Provincials, "Jesuits in Latin America," in Hennelly, *Liberation Theology*, 77–83, quoted by Charles J. Beirne, SJ, *Jesuit Education and Social Change in El Salvador* (New York: Routledge, 2013), 69.

32. Klaiber, *Jesuits in Latin America*, 273–79.

33. Address to the Thirty-Second General Congregation of the Jesuits, December 3, 1974, in *L'Osservatore Romano* (English edition), December 12, 1974, no. 2, p. 4.

34. For a compelling narrative, see Austen Ivereigh, *The Great Reformer: Francis and the Making of a Radical Pope* (New York: Henry Holt, 2014).

35. Five other members of the UCA Jesuit community were also murdered. Fr. Jon Sobrino, the other prominent liberation theologian, was spared because he was in Thailand at the time. Two women were also killed—Julia Elba Ramos, the house's cook, and her teenage daughter Celina.

36. Beirne, *Jesuit Education*, 40.

37. From the 1970s onward, UCA carried out its mission through a Center for Theological Reflection, a pastoral center named after Archbishop Romero, a library, and two journals—*Carta a las Iglesias* and the *Revista Latinoamericana de Teología*. They offered various academic programs ranging from pastoral courses to masters degrees, all of which contributed to the religious life of the country.

38. Arrupe made this support quite explicit at the Puebla Conference in 1979, when he came to take part in the Latin American bishops' assembly. In an interview, he was asked about the death threats against the Jesuits in El Salvador. He replied that he himself had asked them to stay "because the Society of Jesus doesn't let itself be distracted by threats." See Calvez, *Foi et justice*, 69.

39. Ignacio Ellacuría, SJ, Commencement Address at Santa Clara University, June 1982, http://www.scu.edu/Jesuits/ellacuria.html.

40. Jon Sobrino, SJ, "El Ellacuría olvidado: Lo que no se puede dilapidar," *Revista Latinoamericana de Teología* 27, no. 79 (January–April 2010): 70.

41. In Ellacuría's own words: "The civilization of poverty is so called in contrast to the civilization of wealth—not because it seeks universal impoverishment as an ideal. . . . What I want to underline here is the intrinsically dialectical relationship between wealth and poverty. In a world configured sinfully by the dynamisms of capital and wealth, we need to put on the table a different dynamism, one that overcomes the first in a salvific way." Ignacio Ellacuría, SJ, "Utopía y profetismo desde América Latina: Un ensayo concreto de soteriología histórica," *Revista Latinoamericana de Teología* 17 (1989): 170–71.

42. As quoted in Teresa Whitfield, *Paying the Price: Ignacio Ellacuría and the Murdered Jesuits of El Salvador* (Philadelphia: Temple University Press, 1994), 109.

43. Sobrino, "Ellacuría olvidado," 70.

44. Ibid., 69.

45. See also Ignacio Ellacuría, SJ, "A Latin American Reading of the *Spiritual Exercises* of Saint Ignatius," *Spiritus: A Journal of Christian Spirituality* 10, no. 2 (Fall

2010): 205–42; and J. Matthew Ashley, "Ignacio Ellacuría and the *Spiritual Exercises* of Ignatius Loyola," *Theological Studies* 61 (2000): 16–39.

46. Sobrino, "Ellacuría olvidado," 70–71.

47. Jim McDermott, "Let Us Look Together to Christ: An Interview with Jesuit General Peter-Hans Kolvenbach," *America*, November 26, 2007, http://americamagazine.org/issue/635/article/let-us-look-together-christ.

48. See Ignacio Ellacuría, SJ, "Is a Different Kind of University Possible?," in *Towards a Society That Serves Its People: The Intellectual Contribution of El Salvador's Murdered Jesuits*, ed. John J. Hassett and Hugh Lacey (Washington DC: Georgetown University Press, 1991), 177–207. See also UCA, *Las Funciones Fundamentales de la Universidad y su Operativización* (San Salvador: Talleres Gráficos UCA, 1979).

49. Beirne, *Jesuit Education*, 227.

50. Robert Ricard, *The Spiritual Conquest of Mexico: An Essay on the Apostolate and the Evangelizing Methods of the Mendicant Orders* (Berkeley: University of California Press, 1982).

51. Pope Francis, "Address of His Holiness Pope Francis to Participants in the 38th Conference of the Food and Agricultural Organization of the United Nations (FAO)," June 20, 2013, http://w2.vatican.va/content/francesco/en/speeches/2013/june/documents/papa-francesco_20130620_38-sessione-fao.html.

10

GLOBAL HUMAN DEVELOPMENT AND THE JESUITS IN ASIA

JOHN JOSEPH PUTHENKALAM, SJ, AND DREW RAU

Over any discussion of globalization hangs a looming sense that the phenomenon is an unstoppable force transcending the control of individual and national actors and even lying beyond the scope of moral criticism. Since the 1960s and the acceleration of globalization through revolutions in communications and transportation technology, the Society of Jesus has avoided such paralyzing fatalism and addressed the injustices that have kept vulnerable communities sidelined even as globalization has made the world smaller. In his 2014 World Day of Peace message, Pope Francis—the first Jesuit pope—called on the nations of the world to recognize the moral dimensions of globalization:

> Fraternity is an essential human quality, for we are relational beings. . . . The ever-increasing number of interconnections and communications in today's world makes us powerfully aware of the unity and common destiny of the nations. In the dynamics of history, and in the diversity of ethnic groups, societies and cultures, we see the seeds of a vocation to form a community composed of brothers and sisters who accept and care for one another. But this vocation is still frequently denied and ignored in a world marked by a "globalization of indifference" which makes us slowly inured to the suffering of others and closed in on ourselves.[1]

As the pope's remarks suggest, globalization is a matter of perspective. The ethical stance that we adopt and the philosophical and religious resources that we draw on shape a particular position. The Jesuit perspective since the Second Vatican Council has been to insist on the moral as well as the economic dimension of globalization and to emphasize the challenge it poses for principles of solidarity, social justice, and the common good.

The concept of "global human development," developed through the resources of Catholic social thought, has proved a powerful tool for the Society of Jesus in its efforts not only to diagnose but also to address the ethical dimension of globalization. After a historical overview of earlier phases of globalization, this chapter examines the idea of global human development—its development and practice in society—with a particular focus on the contemporary experience of India. Much of the last quarter century's globalization-driven economic growth has taken place in Asia, where many social problems of extreme poverty and crippling social inequality persist. India, where the first generation of Jesuit missionaries ventured some 450 years ago and where many Jesuits in the world now live and work, is a fitting place to explore the ethical and political challenges of globalization and how best to address them today.

The Historical Setting of Globalization

Globalization is not a new phenomenon. The millennium from 500 to 1500 CE witnessed a transcontinental flow of economies, cultures, and religions as soldiers, traders, and missionaries interacted over much of Asia, Africa, and Europe. Aided by advances in maritime and military technology, Spain and Portugal launched the early modern phase of globalization, creating far-flung empires as far away as the Western hemisphere.

After a second wave of globalization driven by the technological advances of the Second Industrial Revolution, we have found ourselves for several decades in the midst of a third wave of a far-reaching economic globalization premised on neoliberal capitalism that links local and national markets around the world into a truly global financial system. Like the earlier eras, the contemporary one has seen both great triumphs in fostering an awareness of our common humanity and terrible tragedies perpetrated by the powerful against the weak.[2]

Officially established in 1540, the Society of Jesus was part of the early modern wave of globalization that saw the Jesuits preaching their faith around the world, often in collaboration with the forces of European colonialism. While the Jesuits' religious and social work often had the added effect of smoothing the conditions for local acceptance of foreign rule, there are notable examples of Jesuit resistance to the unjust repercussions of European expansionism and competition for global domination. For example, the Jesuit-led communities in South America, the reductions, were sometimes the only barrier keeping slave traders from exploiting the Guaraní people. The Jesuits opposed the 1750 Treaty of Madrid, which set a boundary between the Spanish and Portuguese territories, in part out of concern that both empires had a proven record of cruelty toward native peoples.[3]

In Asia in the sixteenth and seventeenth centuries, early Jesuit missions were not part of a territorial expansionist enterprise. Western power ran up against ruling dynasties in Japan, China, and India that were able to set limits on Western incursions. In these contexts, prominent Jesuits including Francis Xavier (1506–52) and Matteo Ricci (1552–1610) adopted a pragmatic, flexible approach, engaging with local cultures in a spirit of dialogue while pursuing their missionary goals. After the European monarchs and the papacy in the eighteenth century suppressed the Jesuit order—in part as a response to their relative independence from political and ecclesiastical authority and their accommodationist approach to non-Europeans—the nineteenth century saw a revived Jesuit order participate in the more far-reaching colonial enterprise of the modern phase of globalization. In an era of nationalism and imperialist expansionism, Jesuits were not counted among the vocal critics of a new wave of exploitation that, in contrast to the earlier period, extended deep into Africa and Asia.

In our current era, Jesuits are not only riding the wave of globalization but also working to correct its injustices. Our present situation—characterized by impressive but inequitable economic growth—has its roots in the conflicts of the twentieth century. The Second World War left much of Europe decimated, compelling the continent's imperial powers to relinquish sovereignty over their colonies abroad to native authorities who were frequently ill prepared to administer what were often artificially united territories. Competition between two superpowers, the United States and the Soviet Union, with two conflicting politico-economic ideologies—democratic capitalism and state socialism—dominated world politics until the Soviet Union unexpectedly collapsed in 1991. The subsequent decades have seen the full emergence and dominance of neoliberal, market-led approaches to economic, social, and political development on a global scale.[4]

The current phase of globalization, the most intensive to date, has generated aggregate economic growth and contributed to the rise of a middle class in China, India, and elsewhere. But extreme poverty remains a pressing problem, as a billion human beings still survive on only $1.25 per day. As the UN Department of Economic and Social Affairs explained in its 2010 report, "As poverty levels remained stagnant or increased despite economic growth, it became clear that growth by itself does not reduce poverty, and macroeconomic recovery does not necessarily translate into significant social improvement."[5] Furthermore, improvements in living standards have sometimes been achieved in ways that may be detrimental to the environment and the global community in the long term.[6] Increasing rates of industrial production and the spread of consumer cultures are taxing the world's ecosystems more and more. It is against this backdrop that the idea of *human* development, embraced and developed by the Society of Jesus, has been forcefully articulated.

The Concept of Human Development

Rejecting a tunnel-visioned quest to boost GDP, a growing number of scholars and development professionals have been turning to a more holistic, human-centered approach designed to contribute to social progress through individual empowerment in areas such as education and health. A systemic focus on macroeconomic goals and indicators tends to leave many behind while efforts to maximize human potential can advance both social justice and long-term development strategies. Amartya Sen and Martha Nussbaum have been among the most articulate and influential proponents of a human capabilities approach that highlights the dignity, rights, and capacities of all citizens as contributors to national and international economic development.[7]

The first annual *Human Development Report* by the United Nations Development Programme (UNDP) in 1990 marked a critical turning point for development professionals who were eager to move away from the existing neoliberal paradigm. That first report concisely laid out the guiding principle behind human development work—"People are the real wealth of a nation"—and established the fundamentals of this socially conscious approach. Human development, it argued, "is about more than GNP growth . . . it is a process of enlarging people's choices. The most critical of these wide-ranging choices are to live a long and healthy life, to be educated and to have access to resources needed for a decent standard of living. Additional choices include political freedom, guaranteed human rights and personal self-respect."[8] Current UNDP administrator Helen Clark points out that, through the influence of the *Human Development Report*, "the human development approach has profoundly affected an entire generation of policy-makers and development specialists around the world—including thousands within UNDP itself and elsewhere in the UN system."[9]

Since UNDP began publishing the *Human Development Report*, developing countries—often with the financial assistance of developed countries, nongovernmental organization (NGOs), and intergovernmental organizations (IGOs)—have made great strides in providing their citizens with higher levels of education and allowing them to live longer, healthier lives. Some developing countries are even emerging as economic powerhouses: India, Brazil, Turkey, Mexico, Thailand, and South Africa have grown their economies while expanding their citizens' opportunities through new social policies, antipoverty programs, and international agreements.[10] China has also become the world's second-largest economy after the United States and raised hundreds of millions of its citizens out of poverty in the most voluminous economic uplift in history.[11] Still the financial and social benefits of these economic advances have not always been equitably distributed. Significant levels of poverty remain a major issue in these countries and even more so in the far greater number of countries that have not experienced economic growth on the same scale.

In September 2000 the UN convened the largest gathering of world leaders in history at the Millennium Summit, where the governments of the world collectively adopted the United Nations Millennium Declaration in an unprecedented commitment to expand human development in underserved populations across the globe.[12] The Millennium Declaration set out eight goals—known as the Millennium Development Goals (MDGs)—with specific targets for governmental and nongovernmental actors alike to achieve by the 2015 end date: the eradication of extreme poverty; universal primary education; gender equality; reductions in child mortality; improvements in maternal health; progress against HIV/AIDS, malaria, and other diseases; environmental sustainability; and global partnership for development.[13] The Millennium Summit, the declaration, and the MDGs were a testament to the growing influence of the human development paradigm. At the dawn of a new century, world leaders embraced development targets focused on human welfare rather than on aggregate economic performance.

Although most MDGs were not met by 2015, their pursuit has brought enormous improvements to an untold number of people's lives around the world and has shifted the trajectory of development work toward a wider human lens on development in all its dimensions. The world community now envisions an ambitious post-2015 agenda around "sustainable development goals" that will build on fifteen years of progress to date.[14] Those goals and their pursuit will target an increasingly visible and problematic aspect of development that a 2013 UNDP report called "a paradox of our time"—that is, the increasing social inequality accompanying overall increases in wealth. The report noted that "the richest eight percent of the world's population earn half of the world's total income" and that "within many countries, wealth and income inequalities have reached new heights, handicapping efforts to realize development outcomes and expand the opportunities and abilities of people."[15]

The problem of growing inequality, alongside persistently significant levels of absolute poverty, is exacerbated by what the editors of this volume call the "subjective dimension of globalization." As the individual's awareness of his or her participation in global humanity grows, driven by improvements in communications technology and the growth of the Internet, so too does an awareness of the widely disparate life chances afforded others due to their varying national, economic, and social circumstances. Meeting the hopes of billions for better lives for themselves and their children is a political as well as a practical challenge for any successful human development agenda going forward.

The Jesuits Engage Globalization

The Society of Jesus has accompanied—and shaped—the gradual development of the global human development perspective during the contemporary phase of globalization. Under Fr. Pedro Arrupe (1907–91), who served as the superior general of the Society of Jesus from 1965 to 1983, the Jesuits were early critics of the dominant market-driven understanding of economic development. In a May 1968 letter to Jesuit bishops in Latin America, Arrupe coined the phrase "preferential option for the poor," echoing Ignatius himself, who wrote to his fellow Jesuits at Padua, "Our commitment to follow a poor Lord quite naturally makes us friends of the poor."[16] In this spirit the Thirty-Second General Congregation of the Society of Jesus, meeting in 1974–75, took up the challenge of Vatican II and of Paul VI's 1967 encyclical *Populorum progressio* in advancing the vision of a world of greater justice and solidarity. In its famous Decree 4, the Congregation defined the Jesuit mission as "the service of faith and the promotion of justice." In terms that anticipated the rise of the human development paradigm, it noted that "there are millions of men and women in our world, specific people with names and faces, who are suffering from poverty and hunger, from the unjust distribution of wealth and resources and from the consequences of racial, social, and political discrimination."[17]

Social service has always been a fundamental component of the Jesuit mission and identity, and its many manifestations are known collectively as the order's social apostolate. In keeping with the pragmatic orientation of Ignatius of Loyola and his successors, the Jesuits have taken up positive aspects of globalization—the ease of communication and travel, the technological innovations, the sense of global citizenship—to serve those affected by its more negative aspects. Some of the better-known initiatives of the past several decades include the Jesuit Refugee Service, created at Arrupe's initiative, and Fe y Alegría, the Latin America–based network of schools serving the underserved. But the social apostolate includes a much wider range of activities, from research centers studying social issues, to direct social action, to official Jesuit publications and the writings of members of the order.

To better codify these activities and the teachings that guide them, the Jesuits convened the International Congress of the Social Apostolate in Naples in 1997, and the group produced a document to inform Jesuit social work known as the *Characteristics of the Social Apostolate of the Society of Jesus*. The document lays out the purpose of the Jesuits' social action: "to build a fuller expression of justice and charity into the structures of human life in common, to bring the justice of the Gospel to society and culture."[18] The *Characteristics* takes a multidimensional approach to economic and social activity, emphasizing its cultural, religious, and political sources and significance. The document is oriented around three overarching economic forces: the market, poverty, and globalization.

The market, according to this authoritative document, is a "historical expression of the need for human beings to support each other and to fulfill their present and future potentialities."[19] It is neither an inherently positive nor an inherently negative force, though it can be brandished to inflict damage on individuals and communities. "The challenge is not to destroy the relationship of trade, but to place it at the service of human fulfillment in harmony with creation; to situate it in a context of equality of basic opportunity for all people; and to dignify it by liberating it from the forces of domination and exploitation that distorted it into the mode of production that proliferated in the western world."[20] While the Jesuit approach to the market does not condemn it as such, it is deeply critical of the way the market operates—especially on the global level—in today's world.

The sections on poverty are notable not just for their content but also for their choice of authoritative source material. Citing the UN's 1997 *Human Development Report*, the *Characteristics* notes that poverty "is much more than low income" and "reflects poor health and education, deprivation in knowledge and communication, inability to exercise human and political rights and the absence of dignity, confidence and self-respect."[21] At the Social Apostolate Congress, Superior General of the Society Peter-Hans Kolvenbach made a strong connection between the struggle against poverty, understood in a wider human development lens, and the promotion of justice. He called poverty and misery "non-values which simply should not exist and which in no way express the will of the Creator," sharing a perspective that has historically informed Jesuit ministries that serve the poor.[22]

The Social Apostolate Congress's handling of the topic of globalization was the most difficult to navigate as delegates from around the world approached it out of their very different national and regional experiences. The *Characteristics* notes three dominant perspectives on globalization at the gathering: a condemnation of economic globalization as a driver of inequality, a critique of cultural globalization as a destroyer of local cultures, and a more moderate critical position recognizing the positive aspects of globalization, "which have to be humanized."[23] While the delegates were not in a position to determine whether the economic and social realities of each of the world's countries and regions aligned with a single understanding of globalization, they did agree that neoliberal global capitalism ought to be resisted to the extent that it prioritized "macro-economic growth over and above the welfare and life of the poor."[24] The critique of globalization set out in the *Characteristics* draws both on Catholic social thought, with its emphasis on the dignity of the human person, and on the idea of global human development as articulated in the seminal 1990 UN *Human Development Report*.

Importantly the Congress did not remain at the level of theory and critique. One of its greatest contributions was the elucidation of a distinctively Jesuit approach to social *action*. Building on Ignatius's emphasis on service and Arrupe's articulation of an "option for the poor," the *Characteristics* elaborates the idea of "insertion among the poor":

> To be inserted means to have continuous prolonged contact with the poor—those who suffer misery, injustices, violent conflict, exclusion—and to enter into real relationship with those whom we accompany and serve and whose concerns we research. . . . Insertion means entering with the poor into a personal and cultural relationship so real that trust can develop. Seeing things their way and taking on their viewpoint shapes how we see, understand and interpret many things, from details of daily life to large issues and transcendent values. Insertion marks our reading both of the Gospel and of social reality.[25]

With poverty remaining one of the greatest social challenges of today's global age, the Jesuits' commitment to remain intimately involved in ministering to the poor is more important than ever, if somewhat less visible than their work in the educational sector. The plight of the poor in India, and the Jesuit response to it, provides an instructive example of the Society's pursuit of social justice in the context of globalization.

The Jesuits and Human Development in India

Given the long history of Jesuits of Asia—as old as the order itself—it is not surprising that Indian Jesuits were at the center of the globalization debate at the Social Apostolate Congress. Within two years of the official founding of the Society of Jesus, Francis Xavier had set sail for India and traveled from there to Japan. Chapter 1 by Antoni Ucerler and chapter 2 by Francis Clooney in this volume relate the story of the Jesuits' intercultural and interreligious encounters with the powerful empires in China, Japan, and Mughal India through the early modern period of globalization. In the 131 years between the reestablishment of the Jesuit order in 1814 and the end of World War II, the Jesuits reengaged in Asia as part of the wave of European expansionism and often in close cooperation with colonial powers. In our contemporary global era, in line with the social justice ethos articulated forcefully by Fr. Arrupe and his successors, the Jesuits maintain an active presence across this diverse region, empowered by the technological and socially connective aspects of globalization even as they work to address its socially, culturally, and economically destructive elements.

In the 1980s and 1990s as the contemporary phase of globalization picked up steam, Asian Jesuits were among its most prominent critics. At the 1997 Social Apostolate Congress, Jesuits from South Asia in particular "urged that the Society should take a clear position condemning the system." The report of the Jesuits of India sheds some light on the roots of their principled position in the country's social realities: "India today is a country of class and caste inequalities." It notes that almost half its population suffered from "malnutrition, illiteracy, and ill health and are victims of the same urban-rural, class-, caste-, and sex-based differences."[26] The Congress, with its call for "insertion" among the poor, gave an impetus to the work of the India-based social apostolate, which has deep historical roots.

New Patterns of Social and Political Activism

Established in 1973 to fulfill the Jesuit mandate to translate faith into action, Jesuits in Social Action (JESA) is the umbrella organization overseeing all social justice activities across the Society of Jesus's South Asian Assistancy, and its activities span the countries of India, Sri Lanka, Nepal, Bhutan, Bangladesh, Pakistan, and Afghanistan. During the Jesuit formation process, every scholastic from all nineteen of the assistancy's provinces participates in JESA programs to better understand and experience the social reality of the region and its peoples. JESA is active on a variety of levels, doing everything from coordinating social action campaigns, to researching national issues and policies affecting marginalized communities, to advocating with and on behalf of those communities, and more.[27] Since 2004 JESA is also the guiding force behind the South Asian People's Initiative (SAPI), a coalition of faith-based and secular organizations in India, Sri Lanka, and Nepal united in a commitment to human dignity and human rights.[28] A priority for both JESA and SAPI is serving the marginalized and includes social, cultural, and political interventions.

Ahead of the 2014 Indian general election, some sixty-five SAPI members across India held discussions on eight overarching national issues: the economy, health, education, environmental management, social concerns, political reform, cultural issues, and concerns over security and governance. Many of these issues, particularly the economic and cultural ones, were affected by the influence of globalization and the question of how the country should respond to it. The result of the SAPI discussions was the People's Manifesto, which the organization publicized in January 2014 to educate citizens on their rights and on the standards they must demand from unsuccessful candidates who wish to contest election results.[29] Fostering political awareness is a critical component of JESA's efforts, which often intersects with aspects of the globalizing forces at work in the region.

Another area of Jesuit activism is the disparity between urban and rural life—a widespread symptom of globalization as markets streamline international commerce through big cities. The financial growth of cities has drawn wealthier and better-educated people from the countryside into these commercial hubs, leaving rural villages impoverished, economically isolated, and politically ignored.[30] Maharashtra Prabodhan Seva Mandal (MPSM), a nonprofit group managed by the Bombay Province of the Society of Jesus, works for rural and tribal awakening (*prabodhan*) through community organization, economic growth, educational initiatives, and natural resource development without prejudice to caste or creed. In October 2011, for example, the Central Board for Worker's Education of the Indian government's Labour Ministry asked MPSM to host two-day training camps in villages across the province to foster greater awareness of the benefits villagers are eligible to receive under the popular Mahatma Gandhi National Rural Employment Guarantee Act. Because of the stark urban-rural economic divide in India, this law enjoys widespread support, not least of all from JESA, which has seen how the law has assisted local communities in improving their infrastructure to achieve their development needs. By undertaking collaborative action with local political units, MPSM was able to mobilize people to obtain the benefits of progressive national legislation.[31]

Support for Disadvantaged Tribal Groups

JESA is also actively involved on the topic of environmental management and sustainability and how these issues relate to the lives of members of disadvantaged tribal groups (*adivasi*), which tend to comprise the poorest and least powerful sections of Indian society. The sacredness of the natural world to the indigenous worldview and tribal social structures, as well as the critical role it plays as a source of food and medicine, makes environmental degradation a concern of the highest order for this population. Such degradation often occurs at the hands of development projects financed by international firms. Ironically conservation efforts such as the creation of national parks and biosphere reserves are destructive to adivasi life in other ways: They force large-scale indigenous population displacements that rob entire communities of their way of life as well as their ancestral home. The effects of climate change and incursions by Maoist rebels in some areas have further threatened the stability of these sacred ecosystems and the people who inhabit them.

In service to the unique circumstances of adivasi culture, JESA researches, publishes on, and advocates for ecological protection and environmental and legal policies that benefit adivasi groups, such as instituting native titles to land and giving tribes the right to veto development projects.[32] One example is the Attappadi Adivasi Development Initiatives (AADI), which operate in the Palakkad District of Kerala and particularly the Attappadi Forest Reserve area. AADI addresses the human development needs of the local adivasi by facilitating programs that the adivasi plan and execute themselves.[33] Though Kerala is the Indian state with the highest human development index, the adivasi typically remain at the bottom rung of the socioeconomic ladder.[34] As such, the adivasi's situation in Kerala is reflective both of the growing inequalities that are increasingly characteristic of our contemporary era of globalization and of Jesuit efforts to counter such effects in practice.

One of the problems faced across Kerala that impacts the adivasi is rampant alcohol abuse. The state leads the rest of the country in consumption, creating a host of social issues—rises in alcohol-related divorces, abuse, diseases, and deaths—that have made life in Kerala even more difficult.[35] In response to the rise of alcohol abuse among the Palakkad adivasi and the resultant social ills, in 2013 AADI helped coordinate a program of street theater performances designed to spread awareness of the ruinous effects that alcoholism has had on adivasi villages, tearing families apart and thwarting individual and communal development efforts. Street plays in twenty-nine villages presented tragic stories of alcohol's destructive force on families that educated viewers on the negative health and social consequences of heavy drinking. Many villagers who attended the performances reported gaining a clearer sense of their own issues with alcohol and pledged to stop drinking and to put the money saved toward their children's education and food for their families.[36]

Along with economic dislocations, globalization also spreads a hegemonic Western culture that can challenge, and potentially destroy, local cultures as people lose sight of their heritage in their rush to embrace a homogenizing global consumer culture.[37] As a means of protecting and celebrating adivasi cultures, AADI put together multiple *gramostsavam* (village-festivals) in May 2013, in which seven hundred adivasi participated in a variety of indigenous cultural practices to help keep their sense of tribal identity strong. Adivasi cultural groups performed for and addressed the crowd in their native tribal tongues amid gatherings of local tribal leaders and dignitaries. During the gramostsavam, the provincial superior of the local Jesuit province laid the foundation stone for a new AADI cultural center. The festivals continued with a four-day cultural campaign in which the AADI *Kalasangam* (cultural troupe) visited twenty-nine adivasi villages to gain and spread awareness of the issues impacting their way of life. That most adivasi in Kerala are not Christian is evidence of the Jesuits' commitment both to intercultural dialogue and to serving the disadvantaged, no matter what their religious affiliation.

Transnational Initiatives in Asia

Although the focus here has been on the work of the Jesuit social apostolate in Asia as it responds to injustices related to the processes of globalization, the Jesuits have also found ways to utilize the strengths of globalization to serve people as well. Ease of travel, instant communication, and the ability to seamlessly move money across borders have allowed concerned citizens in one country to efficiently collect and deliver aid to marginalized citizens in other countries. Many well-known international nonprofits are involved in such work, but the Jesuits have a special capacity to engage the younger generation in global social action through their far-flung network of schools. Whereas high-profile nonprofits such as Amnesty International and Médicins Sans Frontières are able to rally huge international audiences to specific causes, student groups are a way for genuine local-to-local relationships to flourish. The lack of such personal transnational relationships is often what leaves our global age feeling soulless and disconnected, as Pope Francis described with his phrase "globalization of indifference." Micro-level organizations such as student groups at individual high schools and universities represent an opportunity not only to restore the human connections that ought to underlie our economically integrated world but also to inculcate an appreciation for universal human dignity and the global common good in the minds of youth today who will go on to become tomorrow's leaders.

One example of such an organization that is active in India is MEGUKO (an acronym from the Japanese for Action for the Self-reliance of Children in Asia). An NGO based at Sophia University in Tokyo, MEGUKO dates to 1975, when the Jesuit Anselmo Mataix and a group of students formed the organization to extend economic support to poor children in developing countries. Today this student-run NGO consists of about fifty young men and women who organize various activities—charity concerts, campus bazaars, and street donation drives in which students stand in front of railway stations and university buildings appealing for small contributions—to support the educational needs of economically underprivileged children in India and the Philippines. MEGUKO currently sponsors about a thousand children in both countries.

Not content to provide support from a distance, MEGUKO also sponsors an exposure-insertion program during summer holidays for about three weeks, allowing Sophia students to better connect with and understand the lives and needs of their organization's beneficiaries. In India most of MEGUKO's partner institutions are in the state of Gujarat, where they serve mostly tribal students, and in the Philippines the program's beneficiary students, who call themselves "Sophia-MEGUKO Scholars," are mostly from households in city slums and rural areas. Japanese participants alternate their visits between India and the Philippines each year, allowing them to assess the conditions of the schools they are assisting and to ensure that MEGUKO aid is helping and being used properly. Oftentimes Sophia students returning from these trips will be so affected by their experiences that they change their lifestyles and further devote themselves to international issues of social justice.[38]

All of the examples of Jesuit-led and inspired social engagement recounted here recall the Society's commitment to "the service of faith and the promotion of justice," powerfully articulated at the Thirty-Second General Congregation in 1974–75. They further exemplify the idea of "insertion among the poor" that was so powerfully articulated by the Social Apostolate Congress of 1997, with its call for "entering with the poor into a personal and cultural relationship so real that trust can develop." It is often forgotten that the first ministry of the Society, under Saint Ignatius, was to spread the Gospel and serve the poor, for it was soon overshadowed by the order's impressive entry into the field of education. In India—now home to almost half of the world's Jesuits, more than any other country in the world—the social apostolate is more relevant than ever. Whatever aggregate economic gains that globalization delivers in India and elsewhere, the Gospel imperative to minister to the poor and to defend their dignity as children of a loving God will be with us into the future.

Conclusion

This book analyzes how the Jesuits have influenced historical processes of globalization from the early modern period onward and how those processes influenced the Society of Jesus in turn. In Asia during the sixteenth century, the arrival of Saint Francis Xavier and his Jesuit companions to the shores of India unfolded under the patronage of the Portuguese Empire and its political and commercial ambitions. The Jesuits' openness to intercultural encounter in South and East Asia, while noteworthy, was constrained by that colonial context. Since Vatican II in the 1960s, in our contemporary global era, the Society of Jesus has played a more independent and activist role and has been critical of the excesses of economic globalization and the materialism and inequality it generates. In this new context, the socio-pastoral involvement of the Jesuits in India and other Asian provinces aims to discern, analyze, critique, and take action so that the Society can serve as a true messenger of the joy of the Gospel. With the Church now determinedly independent from the interests of empires and nation-states, the social mission of the Jesuits in Asia is no longer primarily one of converting others. Instead, it is more akin to an ongoing effort at self-conversion, a recommitment to living out the teachings of Jesus to love and to serve the poor.

With a global network rooted in this service to others, in the disciplined study of social issues, and in a special concern for the poor, the Society of Jesus entered this age of globalization well positioned to address its concomitant injustices: persistent poverty, growing inequality, environmental degradation, and cultural destruction. The Jesuits have risen to meet the challenges of a new world with their old strength—namely, a focus on *cura personalis*, or "care for the whole person." While the idea of global human development, resonant with Catholic social teaching, is increasingly recognized among development professionals and at the level of the United Nations, the pursuit of economic growth at all costs continues to exacerbate globalization's negative side. Looking forward, therefore, the Jesuit social apostolate must be proactive in understanding how globalization affects marginalized communities. And the Society must continue to leverage the positive side of globalization—the deeper solidarity and greater collaboration that revolutions in communications and transportation technologies have enabled—to preach and advance social justice as a Gospel imperative.

The papacy of Francis is an example of this positive potential. Through his global travels, his communications outreach, and his personal example, Francis has challenged Catholics and non-Catholics alike to overcome a "globalization of indifference" and to work toward a more just world. As it was for Arrupe and for Ignatius before him, service to the poor remains the touchstone. In one of the most memorable passages of his 2013 apostolic exhortation *Evangelii gaudium*, Francis reminds us that for such service to be effective and fulfilling, it must be anchored in interpersonal, human encounter. "No one must say that they cannot be close to the poor because their own lifestyle demands more attention to other areas," he writes. At the same time, Francis impels us, personal encounter is no substitute for social and political action, for "as long as the problems of the poor are not radically resolved by rejecting the absolute autonomy of markets and financial speculation and by attacking the structural causes of inequality, no solution will be found for the world's problems."[39] The dual emphasis on the human and the global dimensions of development will be critical if the Jesuits, the Catholic Church, and the world are to master the challenges that lie ahead.

Notes

1. Pope Francis, "Message of His Holiness Francis for the Celebration of the World Day of Peace," December 8, 2013, sec. 1, https://w2.vatican.va/content/francesco/en/messages/peace/documents/papa-francesco_20131208_messaggio-xlvii-giornata-mondiale-pace-2014.html.

2. John Joseph Puthenkalam, SJ, "World Economic Order and Norms for Capitalistic Globalization," *Sophia Economic Review* 57 (2012): 1–15, http://econ-web.cc.sophia.ac.jp/research/journal/data/57-01.pdf.

3. Barbara Anne Ganson, *The Guaraní under Spanish Rule in the Río de la Plata* (Stanford: Stanford University Press, 2003), 93.

4. Richard Pomfret, *Diverse Paths of Economic Development* (New York: Harvester Wheatsheaf, 1992).

5. United Nations Department of Economic and Social Affairs, *Rethinking Poverty: Report on the World Social Situation 2010*, ST/ESA/324 (New York: United Nations, 2009), 135, http://www.un.org/esa/socdev/rwss/docs/2010/fullreport.pdf.

6. World Commission on Environment and Development, *Our Common Future* (Oxford: Oxford University Press, 1987), 32.

7. See, among other examples from these authors, Amartya Sen, *Commodities*

and Capabilities (Amsterdam: North-Holland, 1985); Amartya Sen, *Development as Freedom* (New York: Alfred Knopf, 1999); Martha Nussbaum, *Frontiers of Justice: Disability, Nationality, Species Membership* (Cambridge MA: Belknap Press, 2006); and Martha Nussbaum and Amartya Sen, eds., *The Quality of Life* (Oxford: Clarendon Press, 1993).

8. United Nations Development Programme (UNDP), *Human Development Report, 1990* (New York: Oxford University Press for UNDP, 1990), 1, http://hdr.undp.org/sites/default/files/reports/219/hdr_1990_en_complete_nostats.pdf.

9. Helen Clark, foreword to *Human Development Report, 2010—the Real Wealth of Nations: Pathways to Human Development*, by UNDP (New York: Palgrave Macmillan for UNDP, 2010), iv, http://hdr.undp.org/sites/default/files/reports/270/hdr_2010_en_complete_reprint.pdf.

10. UNDP, *Human Development Report, 2013—the Rise of the South: Human Progress in a Diverse World* (Canada: Gilmore Printing Services, 2013), http://hdr.undp.org/sites/default/files/reports/14/hdr2013_en_complete.pdf.

11. Hu Angang, Hu Linlin, and Chang Zhixiao, "China's Economic Growth and Poverty Reduction (1978–2002)," paper presented at the joint conference of the International Monetary Fund and the National Council of Applied Economic Research, New Delhi, India, November 15, 2003, https://www.imf.org/external/np/apd/seminars/2003/newdelhi/angang.pdf.

12. United Nations, "World Leaders Adopt 'United Nations Millennium Declaration' at Conclusion of Extraordinary Three-Day Summit," press release, September 8, 2000, http://www.un.org/press/en/2000/20000908.ga9758.doc.html.

13. UNDP, "The Millennium Development Goals: Eight Goals for 2015," UNDP, 2015, http://www.undp.org/content/undp/en/home/mdgoverview/mdg_goals.html.

14. UNDP, "A Global Partnership for Development: Where Do We Stand?," UNDP, 2015, http://www.undp.org/content/undp/en/home/mdgoverview/mdg_goals/mdg8/.

15. UNDP, *Humanity Divided: Confronting Inequality in Developing Countries* (New York: UNDP, November 2013), xi, http://www.undp.org/content/dam/undp/library/Poverty%20Reduction/Inclusive%20development/Humanity%20Divided/HumanityDivided_Full-Report.pdf.

16. Christopher Rowland, ed., *The Cambridge Companion to Liberation Theology* (Cambridge: Cambridge University Press, 1999), 179; and Society of Jesus, *Characteristics of the Social Apostolate of the Society of Jesus* (Rome: Social Apostolate Secretariat at the General Curia of the Society of Jesus, 1998), vii, http://www.sjweb.info/sjs/documents/PJ_069_ENG.pdf.

17. Thirty-Second General Congregation of the Society of Jesus, Decree 4, "Our Mission Today: The Service of Faith and the Promotion of Justice," 1975, no. 20, http://www.sjweb.info/documents/sjs/docs/D4%20Eng.pdf.

18. Society of Jesus, *Characteristics*, iii.

19. Latin American Provincials of the Society of Jesus, "A Letter on Neo-Liberalism in Latin America," Mexico City, November 14, 1996, http://www.sjweb.info/documents/sjs/docs/Neolib_96ENG.pdf, as quoted in Society of Jesus, *Characteristics*, xxxi.

20. Ibid.

21. UNDP, *Human Development Report, 1997* (New York: Oxford University Press for UNDP, 1997), http://hdr.undp.org/sites/default/files/reports/258/hdr_1997_en_complete_nostats.pdf, as quoted in Society of Jesus, *Characteristics*, xxxi.

22. Society of Jesus, *Characteristics*, xxxii.

23. Ibid.

24. Ibid.

25. Ibid., xvi–xvii.

26. Ibid., xxxi.

27. Jesuits in Social Action (JESA), "JESA," New Delhi, http://www.jesaonline.org/index.php?option=com_content&view=section&id=1&layout=blog&Itemid=16.

28. JESA, "SAPI," http://www.jesaonline.org/index.php?option=com_content&view=section&layout=blog&id=4&Itemid=14.

29. JESA Secretary, "SAPI Brings out People's Manifesto in View of the General Election in India," 2014, http://www.jesaonline.org/index.php?option=com_content&view=article&id=685:sapi-brings-out-peoples-manifesto-in-view-of-the-general-election-in-india.

30. Amitabh Kundu and Debolina Kundu, "Globalization and Exclusionary Urban Growth in Asian Countries," working paper 2010/70 (Helsinki: World Institute for Development Economics Research, United Nations University, June 2010), http://www.wider.unu.edu/publications/working-papers/2010/en_GB/wp2010-70/_files/83696427046666267/default/wp2010-70.pdf.

31. JESA, "Promoting Development through MGNREGA (October 2011 to June 2012)," http://www.jesaonline.org/index.php?option=com_content&view=article&id=612:promoting-development-through-mgnrega-october-2011-to-june-2012.

32. Anthony Dias, SJ, "Environmentalism of the Poor," Report for the Xavier Institute of Social Research, St. Xavier's College, Mumbai, April 29, 2012, http://www.jesaonline.org/images/stories/files/environmentalism%20of%20the%20poor.doc.

33. Attappadi Adivasi Development Initiatives (AADI), "Attappadi Adivasi Development Initiatives," http://www.aadiattapadi.com.

34. Filippo Osella and Caroline Osella, *Social Mobility in Kerala: Modernity and Identity in Conflict* (London: Pluto Press, 2000).

35. "Kerala's Love Affair with Alcohol," BBC News, March 12, 2010, http://news.bbc.co.uk/2/hi/south_asia/8557215.stm.

36. AADI, "Attappadi Adivasi Development Initiatives."

37. Gowher Rizvi, "Emergent India: Globalization, Democracy, and Social Justice," *International Journal* 62, no. 4 (Autumn 2007): 753–68.

38. For more information on MEGUKO, see http://meguko.net.

39. Pope Francis, *Evangelii gaudium*, Apostolic Exhortation on the Proclamation of the Gospel in Today's World, November 24, 2013, sec. 201–2, http://w2.vatican.va/content/francesco/en/apost_exhortations/documents/papa-francesco_esortazione-ap_20131124_evangelii-gaudium.html.

11

GLOBAL HUMAN MOBILITY, REFUGEES, AND JESUIT EDUCATION AT THE MARGINS

PETER BALLEIS, SJ

In his remarks to a gathering of the world's Jesuit universities in 2010, Superior General of the Society of Jesus Fr. Adolfo Nicolás, SJ, drew a direct link between pressing global issues and the aims of Jesuit higher education: "What are the challenges of the Society? The only answer is: the challenges of the world. There are no other challenges."[1] This socially driven approach is what has kept Jesuits on the front lines of issues of justice in an increasingly globalized world for the past 475 years. As it has in centuries past, the Society of Jesus continues to follow patterns of human mobility in its outreach to marginalized populations. Today this is nowhere more evident than in the Society's work with a particular population of international dimensions—refugees and migrants. Through the Jesuit Refugee Service (JRS), the Society seeks to apply the Jesuits' traditional strength in education, and their nearly half a millennium of experience on the forefront of globalizing developments, to assist in the human development and formation of this vulnerable group.

Human Mobility and Communication: The Thriving Dynamics of Globalization

The global response of the Society of Jesus to today's refugee crisis needs to be understood within the history and tradition of the Jesuits and the expanding depth and breadth of globalization. The process and phenomenon of globalization are not new, although the term itself has only been formed in the last three decades. The various aspects of this process reach from economics and free markets, imperial politics and colonization, to technology and communications and, most important, human mobility. Mobility and communications are strong features of the Society of Jesus too.

Human history is a history of mobility. Homo sapiens spread from East Africa to all other continents over a time span of several hundred thousand years. Recent history is also marked by the movement of ethnic groups and whole populations. Human mobility is the key factor of any process of globalization throughout history and through the present day. What differs today from the past is the increasing speed of this mobility due to technological progress. From walking on foot, riding on horseback, and sailing on ships to traveling by train, car, and aircraft, human mobility has increased in terms of the number of people on the move, the speed of their movements, and the consequent virtual shrinking of large distances.

Likewise, communication—the mobility of knowledge—has accelerated from sending a message by carrier, by post, by use of the telegraph, and now by phone and the Internet. Technological inventions have changed the methods by which knowledge can be transmitted. The Gutenberg printing press revolutionized everything in its day as mass-produced books became the carriers of knowledge to all ends of the earth. Today the Internet makes any and all information accessible in even the remotest places, at the margins of this world. Like the printing press more than five hundred years ago, the Internet is now a watershed for the overall process of globalization. The swiftness of mobility and communications today gives us a clear sense of the exponential growth of globalizing forces as the world and its people become increasingly interconnected across borders and cultures. The process of globalization, although as old as humanity, has accelerated significantly over the last five hundred years, the historic period in which the Society of Jesus has been in existence.

At the height of European nationalism and the First World War, Fr. Pierre Teilhard de Chardin, a French Jesuit and paleontologist, used deep insights drawing on evolutionary theory and his scientific knowledge of the genesis of Homo sapiens to develop his vision of a human world that moves naturally toward greater knowledge and interconnectedness. The totality of this increasingly interconnected knowledge around the globe can be seen as a reality that Teilhard termed the "noosphere," or the sphere of human knowledge that is every bit as real, even if not as immediately tangible, as the atmosphere itself. This idea envisions a continuous process of globalization that transcends human mobility and learning to constantly achieve an ever-greater interconnectedness of knowledge. Today's technologies, especially the Internet and all that it enables, have made this vision more real and tangible than ever before. Teilhard's conception of the noosphere in many ways predicted and explained the rapid acceleration of globalization that we are witnessing today.

Some crosscutting aspects of globalization are relevant to the Society of Jesus: mobility and communications, global and local structures, the common good and values, faith and justice, encounters with other cultures and religions, conflicts with national borders, international collaboration, and, of greatest significance to the Jesuits, education and knowledge. These aspects of globalization have shaped the Society of Jesus over its history since its foundation in 1540, and the Jesuits themselves have equally contributed to the process of globalization. We can divide this history into roughly three parts: the first phase from the sixteenth through the eighteenth century until the suppression of the Society of Jesus in 1773, the second phase after the restoration of the Society in 1814 through the nineteenth and early twentieth centuries, and the third and contemporary phase after the end of the Second Vatican Council in 1965.

"The World Is Our Home": The Jesuits from the Sixteenth to the Eighteenth Century

The sixteenth century experienced a major leap in this steady process of globalization. The discoveries in navigation and ship technology gave the kingdoms of Spain and Portugal the means to reach the shores of other continents and to discover lands, peoples, and cultures unknown to Europe. In 1492 Christopher Columbus was the first Spaniard to reach the coast of the Americas. Within a single century, Spanish and Portuguese ships, soldiers, salesmen, migrants, and missionaries had reached the shores of all the Americas, Africa, and Asia. Both countries had built their global empires and divided the world in two parts. The use of superior military power and technology, the slave trade, and the exploitation of the resources of the conquered indigenous peoples are the dark sides of this process. Spanish and Portuguese encounters with new peoples and their cultures and religions opened up completely new worlds. The new knowledge of the world as a half-unexplored globe exploded into the minds of Europeans. Art, paintings, reports, and books spoke about these new worlds.

Ignatius of Loyola was born in 1491, only one year before the Spanish kingdom in which he lived would uncover the existence of the Americas for the Old World. He served as a young man at the court in Arévalo. Globalization was the context of his life, and the horizon of the New World most certainly had some impact on his own worldview. The first Jesuits were all born into this time of great changes and developments. A global perspective, mentality, and mobility profoundly shaped the friends of Ignatius who became the first Jesuits in 1540. Jerónimo Nadal, one of the most influential Jesuits of the first generation, formulated the phrase, "The world is our home."[2] This global thinking encouraged the early Jesuits to spread to South and North America, Africa, South Asia, and East Asia within a decade of their existence as a recognized order of the Catholic Church. The looser requirements of the Society relative to other Catholic religious orders left these Jesuits uniquely capable of spreading themselves to the far reaches of the earth, for they were permitted to live and recite the Divine Office alone rather than only within a structured community of peers fixed in one location. The mission Jesus gave to the apostles—"Go into the whole world"—gained a new and global dimension through the structure of the Society. An important lesson on globalization is drawn from the Jesuit experience here: The more autonomous its members, the more global the organization. The Jesuits sailed together on ships with conquistadors, soldiers, and traders. Their intention, however, was not to conquer but to save souls. They saw the human dignity in the newly encountered peoples and believed in their right to salvation and to hear the Word of God.

Having undergone professional training in civil administration at the court in Arévalo and with the help of his secretary Juan de Polanco, Ignatius of Loyola set up the standards and rules of communication among the Jesuits in all parts of the world so that they could be in touch with one another and the superior general in Rome. Letters communicated invaluable information about the new worlds and their inhabitants. The Jesuits used the most modern means of communication, the printing press, which was invented in the same historical period. Letters and reports were printed and widely distributed. It took only two years for information about events in Japan to be printed and communicated to the Jesuits in Mexico. The letters became a way of learning about the new worlds.

In 1599 the *Ratio studiorum*—the collection of rules standardizing Jesuit education—was established. Although it gave primacy to theology and philosophy, which were not considered humanistic disciplines at the time, most Jesuits schools either did not in fact teach them or taught them only in a very truncated form. Most Jesuit schools were humanistic, for the *Ratio* saw the humanities as foundational disciplines that ought to be taught in all schools. As John O'Malley details in chapter 7 of this volume, this humanistic curriculum standardized the pedagogical method, the humanistic content of Jesuit education, and the structure to be replicated in all Jesuit schools across Europe, the Indies, and the Americas. Jesuit education became a global standard and spread with the Jesuits to all parts of the world through the global proliferation of their humanistic schools. The latest scientific innovations in astronomy, geography, and many other disciplines were shared with students in all regions. For example, the Guaraní natives in the Jesuit reductions in South America learned musical theory and mastered European musical instruments to the point where they were able to produce new compositions. The curriculum was the same everywhere. Jesuit novices could begin their studies in Europe and be transferred to the New World, where they could seamlessly continue their studies.

Colonialism was the historical framework within which the Jesuits were incorporated and into which their early development was intertwined. They were part of the colonial process, founding colleges for colonists, but at the same time they also tried to integrate the local peoples. They sought to be inclusive, integrating and educating the mestizos in Latin America. The Jesuits even made attempts to integrate other cultures into their curriculum, as was the case in Japan. Jesuit education used all the modern means available at the time: books, art, theater, and music. Their education aimed toward the ideal of *humanitas*, the study of the humanities as framed by Ignatian pedagogy. Jesuit education was also meant to be free and accessible to everybody. However, in their commitment to a free education, some Jesuit colleges had plantations with slave labor to make their model economically sustainable. Thus they let the justice of their ends blind them to the injustice of their means in a way that was standard for the time but that we now recognize as a basic violation of human dignity.

Two distinct characteristics marked this period in the history of the Jesuits—mission and education. The dynamics of both could be seen in the tension between the mobility required by missionary activity and the stability of the colleges.

The global project of the Jesuits violently ended with their political expulsion from nearly all of their missions in the Portuguese and Spanish domains—especially Brazil and the Philippines—by 1767 and the ecclesiastic suspension of the Society of Jesus by Pope Clement XIV in 1773. The suppression of the Society of Jesus demonstrated just how far the Jesuits had ridden the wave of globalization ahead of the politics of their time. In an age of growing nationalist sentiments and state centralization, their spiritual and intellectual convictions drove them to take an internationalist outlook and remain independent of national authorities. After these tensions reached a boiling point and Europe's political elites successfully pushed the Vatican to disenfranchise the Society, some Jesuits managed to continue their work in Orthodox Russia and Protestant Prussia, whose non-Catholic rulers had no interest in enforcing the will of the Roman pontiff and thus helped the Society survive. This experience holds a lesson that the Jesuits can teach us about globalization: Being global may put you in danger, but it also keeps you safe as you will always have somewhere to go. The period of the suppression of the Society of Jesus (1767–1814) also happened to coincide with a slowdown of the contemporary globalization process that was due in large part to the Napoleonic Wars.

Moving with the Migrants: The Jesuits in the Nineteenth and Twentieth Centuries

The European population had already begun to move in large numbers to the Americas in the eighteenth century. This migration reached its peak in the nineteenth and twentieth centuries. Within a few decades millions of settlers had migrated from Europe to South America and North America to find a new life in the New World. This massive migration reaccelerated the stalled globalization of the early nineteenth century. Human migration happened from Europe to the Americas, Australia, and South Africa, as well as from China within Asia and from India to Africa.

The restoration of the Society of Jesus in 1814 coincided with this movement of people toward the New World, and the Jesuits moved along with the settlers. The Jesuits regained the missionary drive they had once had in the "old Society." In North America they established schools and the first universities in the new settlements. Education was central to the work of the Jesuits moving and working with migrants. The humanities—liberal arts and Ignatian pedagogy—was the norm for Jesuit colleges and universities. Having a global norm and standards of education made it easy for the Jesuits to move flexibly with the migrants, to be mobile and global. As a common standard, a transferable and scalable model, was key to their global mobility, Jesuit educators used the same textbooks everywhere and served Catholic migrant populations. Colleges were still places of evangelization but differed from the old mission approach of conversion. Jesuit education now aimed at the formation of people.

For example, German and Swiss Jesuits moved with the German migrants in the late nineteenth century to southern Brazil. The parishes and schools were crucial to the new colonies. Likewise, the Jesuits moved with the Pioneer Column of Cecil Rhodes to establish the Zambesi mission in 1889. The mission schools started by the Jesuits are still of great importance in Zimbabwe.

This period also saw the formation of the modern nation-state. Nationalism was on the rise. As a cosmopolitan and international body, the Jesuits were opposed to the idea of the nation-state and to all the premises of nineteenth-century liberalism: freedom of religion, freedom of the press, and separation of Church and state. These problems led to the forcible expulsion of Jesuits from several European countries in the late nineteenth century. They were expelled again and again from Spain, France, and several Latin American countries because they were such a conservative force in those countries' politics at the time. They were expelled from Germany and in exile from 1872 until 1917, after which they could stay and work again legally. Nationalism, particularly in its violent manifestations in the First and Second World Wars, again slowed down the process of globalization and integration. In the late 1950s and 1960s the process picked up once more and has continuously accelerated over the last three decades.

JRS and "All People of Good Will": The Jesuits after Vatican II

The end of the Second Vatican Council in 1965 and the promulgation of its resulting declarations, constitutions, and decrees marked the beginning of a new era for the Roman Catholic Church. Taken as a whole, Vatican II can be seen as a renewal of the Church's mission in the face of a world that had become more diverse and interconnected than ever before. For the first time the pope addressed his thoughts not only to the Catholic faithful but to "all people of good will." Among the documents of Vatican II, *Nostra aetate*, the Declaration on the Relation of the Church to Non-Christian Religions, represents with distinct clarity the reorientation of traditional Catholic thought and social work to the context of a globalizing world: "The Church, therefore, exhorts her sons, that through dialogue and collaboration with the followers of other religions, carried out with prudence and love and in witness to the Christian faith and life, they recognize, preserve and promote the good things, spiritual and moral, as well as the socio-cultural values found among these men."[3] For the Jesuits this spirit of openness to other religions and cultures paved the way for the Society to bear witness to its faith through more multicultural engagements, allowing it to serve all students of good will without conversion being an explicit aim of such interactions. Instead of traveling across the world in order to convert non-Christians to the faith, the Jesuits would now live their faith by traveling across the world to help people simply because they needed the help.

The Jesuits soon faced a challenge that allowed them to put this new framework into practice on a global level. In 1979 and 1980 the whole world watched the dramatic news unfold of the boat people fleeing in large numbers from the repressive regime in Vietnam and the genocide in Cambodia. Many risked and lost their lives on the high seas. Moved to take action in the face of the crisis, Fr. Pedro Arrupe, SJ, superior general of the Society of Jesus, wrote to the whole Society on November 14, 1980:

> Around Christmas time, last year, struck and shocked by the plight of thousands of boat people and refugees, I felt it my duty to send cable messages to some 20 Major Superiors around the world. Sharing my distress with them, I asked what they in their own countries and the universal Society could do to bring at least some relief to such a tragic situation.
>
> Their response was magnificent. Immediate offers of help were made in personnel, know-how and material; supplies of food and medicine as well as money were sent; direct action was taken through the mass media to influence government and private agencies; services were volunteered in pastoral as well as organizational capacities; and so on.
>
> As a follow up to this first wave of action, I called a Consultation in the Curia to consider what response the Society might make to the increasingly serious refugee problem throughout the world. . . .
>
> . . . Furthermore, the help needed is not only material: in a special way the Society is being called to render a service that is human, pedagogical and spiritual. It is a difficult and complex challenge; the needs are dramatically urgent. I have no hesitation in repeating what I said at our Consultation: "I consider this as a new modern apostolate for the Society as a whole, of great importance for today and the future, and of much spiritual benefit also to the Society."
>
> . . . In the light of our consultation and after further discussion with my General Counsellors, I have decided to set up within the Curia a service to co-ordinate Jesuit refugee work, which will henceforth be referred to as the "Jesuit Refugee Service" (JRS).[4]

In view of this tremendous refugee crisis, the Society of Jesus responded as a global body on a human, spiritual, and pedagogical level. Fr. Arrupe created an entirely new apostolate and global organizational structure, a modern international nongovernmental organization (INGO) that followed the criteria of the Society's long tradition of nearly five hundred years. Combining a humanistic approach to education and a dedication to providing spiritual help for people—serving their souls—Ignatian pedagogy found a new, modern, and global expression in the Jesuit Refugee Service. Through its multifaceted activities across the globe, JRS pursues its stated mission to accompany, serve, and advocate for the rights of refugees.

Caring for Forcibly Displaced People: The JRS Today

Since its founding, JRS has developed into an INGO that offers direct services to assist, protect, and advocate for the rights of a million refugees and internally displaced people in forty-five countries around the world. JRS is working in particular in the crisis zones of today: Syria in the Middle East; the Sahel zone, Sudan and South Sudan, the Central African Republic, and especially eastern Congo in Africa; Colombia and border regions in Latin America; and Afghanistan, Sri Lanka, and Myanmar in Asia. JRS has seventeen hundred contracted workers and close to five thousand refugees working with stipends in camps across the globe. About fifty religious sisters and more than sixty Jesuits work full time in JRS. Beyond these ordained Catholic leaders, the staff of JRS boasts tremendous cultural and religious diversity, with Christians, Muslims, Hindus, Buddhists, adherents of traditional African beliefs, atheists, and secular practitioners all working together through the organization. The annual budget reached $50 million in 2013. The three key areas of direct services are humanitarian aid, mostly in the forms of food and shelter; education from kindergarten to university; and psychosocial and pastoral services.

Unfortunately the number of refugees and forcibly displaced people rose to a new peak in 2014, with more than fifty million people—the highest number since World War II—having been forcibly displaced. In addition to this already harrowing number, more than 150 million people are migrating not because of force but out of necessity for a host of different reasons. They have been pushed out of their country of birth due to the government's unsound political and economic policies or to environmental and climatic changes. In addition to its work with refugees, the Society of Jesus has made working with migrants an apostolic priority for the whole Society.

With the exponential growth of the global population, human mobility increased in absolute numbers and was accelerated further by air travel in the twentieth century. Today of the estimated 200 million migrants or forcibly displaced people, most are migrant workers with regular visas and permits, but millions do not have documents and are very vulnerable to exploitation and expulsion. This latter group includes refugees, internally displaced people, and several million trafficked people whose plight is similar to that of victims of the slave trade in the seventeenth and eighteenth centuries. Instead of millions of Europeans moving to the New World, millions of migrant workers from Latin America, the Caribbean, and Central America are moving today toward the United States and Europe. The flow of migrants and refugees from Africa and the Middle East to Europe takes on tragic dimensions, with people frequently drowning in the Mediterranean Sea. The present drama of migrants and refugees perishing in the Mediterranean Sea replicates the drama of the boat people from Vietnam and Cambodia in the late 1970s.

JRS is a *novum* (new thing) in the Society of Jesus because as an international organization—an apostolic workforce—directly linked to the superior general, it does not fall under the normal structure of the Society of Jesus. This unique structure is not always easily understood by the normal levels of governance of the Society of Jesus. Despite some difficulties, it presents a new model of organizing the Society's response to major issues at a global level. A great deal can be learned from this experience.

By its very nature, JRS is driven by the Jesuits' compassion for the plight of refugees. It is a service for poor and marginalized people often living at the frontiers and on the conflict lines of our world. Based on Gospel values and humanitarian principles, JRS reaches out to people of different cultures and faith traditions. Intercultural and interreligious dialogue and working together pervade the praxis of JRS in a global world where cultures and religions live ever more closely together.

The strength of JRS is its ability to be at the same time local and global, horizontal and hierarchical, and flexible on its mission and stable in its educational commitment. Mobility and dynamism are essential to the work of JRS. Thanks to the inherent versatility and resourcefulness of its enterprise and to its robust global communications system, JRS is recognized as a valuable educational organization in the world of refugees.

Global Jesuit Online Education at the Margins

JRS works in the conflict zones of the world, where people, cultures, and interests meet and clash. Most conflicts today occur in areas with low levels of human development, education, income, and life expectancy. One can conclude in a simple formula that low education and high poverty make for high conflict. Education is thus a vital necessity to transform such societies into peaceful places in which diverse peoples can live together.

Education is a largely unmet need of refugees, and less than 1 percent of refugees have access to higher education. JRS thus far has been very much engaged in primary and secondary education and various skills formation courses. But Jesuits have recognized the need for greater higher education resources for refugees and have begun to take action. Jesuit universities in 2007 formed Jesuit Commons, a digital entity, as a global platform to share resources and connect institutions via the Internet. In 2010 Superior General Fr. Nicolás explained well the need for such an initiative:

First, an important challenge to the learned ministry of our universities today comes from the fact that globalization has created "knowledge societies," in which development of persons, cultures and societies is tremendously dependent on access to knowledge in order to grow. Globalization has created new inequalities between those who enjoy the power given to them by knowledge, and those who are excluded from its benefits because they have no access to that knowledge. Thus, we need to ask: who benefits from the knowledge produced in our institutions and who does not? Who needs the knowledge we can share, and how can we share it more effectively with those for whom that knowledge can truly make a difference, especially the poor and excluded? We also need to ask some specific questions of faculty and students: How have they become voices for the voiceless, sources of human rights for those denied such rights, resources for protection of the environment, persons of solidarity for the poor?

In this connection, the work-in-progress of the "Jesuit Commons" . . . is extremely important, and it will require a more serious support and commitment from our universities if it is to succeed in its ambitious dream of promoting greater equality in access to knowledge for the sake of the development of persons and communities.[5]

Fortunately the superior general's words have been heeded by a growing number of universities, which have teamed up to foster this dream of expanding equal access to knowledge. Jesuit Commons led to the concrete education project Jesuit Commons: Higher Education at the Margins (JC:HEM), which is being implemented in close collaboration with JRS as a global partner. The key aim of JC:HEM is to deliver higher education through online means to refugees living in camps and other areas. Jesuit universities work together in this effort, sharing their resources: content, courses, and faculty time. The composition of participating universities has grown beyond the original group of US Jesuit universities, and the number and origins of faculties helping as online teachers in this project are expanding too. Their students are living in the Kakuma refugee camp in northern Kenya, in the Dzaleka refugee camp in Malawi, on the Thai-Burmese boarder, in Afghanistan, and in Amman, Jordan. International in origin, culture, and religion, the students are forming a global community of learners along with their teachers. The inter-university collaboration at work here—a network of Jesuit higher education institutions—is precisely what Fr. Nicolás had envisioned when he spoke of his desire for "the establishment of operational consortia among our universities focused on responding together to some of the 'frontier challenges' of our world which have a supra-national or supra-continental character."[6]

The cornerstones of the JC:HEM program are a diploma in liberal arts and an educational experience framed by Ignatian pedagogy. All students study the same global curriculum together. So far the curriculum has comprised courses donated by universities, adjusted to the reality of refugees, and awarded as credits by Regis University in Denver, Colorado. The first fifty-two students graduated and received their diploma in September 2013. Asked which courses they appreciated most, they mentioned philosophy, logic, and Eastern religions. These unexpected favorites encouraged JC:HEM to solicit more feedback so, just as at traditional universities, it could tailor the educational experience to student needs and interests. This is a manifestation of the very essence of Ignatian pedagogy at work in teaching the Jesuit curriculum of liberal arts.

Since the pilot phase, as a partner of JRS, JC:HEM has further developed its global curriculum of liberal arts, taking into account the great cultural and religious diversity of JRS students across the globe. Updates to the curriculum will continue to be based on Ignatian pedagogy and use the latest insights in online learning and technology to deliver content via the Internet to computers, tablets, and smartphones. In addition to the learning centers in Kenya, Malawi, Thailand, Myanmar, Afghanistan, and Jordan, JRS and JC:HEM have started to expand the program to the Philippines, Sri Lanka, and Chad and hope to do so in the Democratic Republic of the Congo.

In many ways the global online initiative of JC:HEM reflects elements found in the early educational approach of the Jesuits. Using the latest technology for communication has always been a part of the Jesuit model, from the printing press four hundred years ago to the Internet and information technology today. Jesuit schools continue to thrive through their one standardized yet adjustable curriculum of humanities, an educational model that can be transferred, scaled up, and sustained. Education was free and accessible to the poor in the early days, and making it so again is the goal of JC:HEM. Just as the early Jesuits went to the ends of the world to establish their missions, JC:HEM and JRS are trying to reach refugees and the poor at the margins and respond to their needs through a collaborative, global network of Jesuit universities. The dream is big because the challenge of providing higher education for the poor is so big. It is as if JC:HEM is a small board surfing on top of the big wave of technological changes in online higher education and riding its movement forward.

Leading Jesuit universities now perceive JC:HEM as a very valuable experiment from which important lessons can be drawn. The campus-based universities of the Society of Jesus—the classic model of universities—are seriously challenged by globalization, the technological shifts in communications technology that have helped accelerate that globalization, and the difficulties of delivering education on more economic terms in today's world. Private education has become inaccessible to most people. JC:HEM tries to respond directly to these three challenges by developing a new model that is global, through which people from all margins of this world can study together in one virtual classroom and form a real global community of learners. The program blends the traditional model of Ignatian formation of people through a learning community with the most modern means of online learning. Using the latest technologies and breakthroughs in online services, JC:HEM is able to fulfill its mission in deeper and broader ways every year. JC:HEM tries to make knowledge and education accessible to poor people, integrating them into the global community and bringing their knowledge and wisdom into the global process. A world is only truly global when all are integrated into it and not left neglected on the margins, and our world is growing together more every day through rapid and increased communication and knowledge. JC:HEM is an experiment and a model of what Jesuit higher education at the margins can look like: truly global, at the cutting edge of technology, and more economic in delivering education. Although JC:HEM is still small, it is at the spearhead of a profound global process moving toward ever-greater interconnectedness, communication, and knowledge.

The online-tertiary project of JC:HEM together with JRS is a moderate beginning and humble attempt at what could become a great network of knowledge and learning that reaches across the globe to marginalized peoples. People will feel less of a burden to leave their homes and go elsewhere to acquire knowledge now that knowledge and global connectedness can come to them. Globalization has entered a new phase.

JC:HEM is the beginning of a global network of people at the margins learning together in the same virtual classroom, across cultures and religions. The curriculum is a global one that brings global and local together. This pilot model demonstrates how very stable Jesuit institutions of education can suddenly become mobile and move to the margins through online interfaces, working together as a global education network rooted in the humanities and representing the best of the Jesuit educational tradition.

The Internet and online learning are as revolutionary as the Gutenberg printing press was in its day. At that time Jesuits brought knowledge with them in the form of books to new countries and peoples, and in these new settings Jesuits gathered further knowledge into more books that spread across the world. The same process of knowledge transmission is at work today with the Internet, only operating more rapidly and at a far more voluminous level. The model of JC:HEM follows in the footsteps of the Society's finest educational traditions, forming people as leaders and human persons through a distinct pedagogy based on the spiritual worldview of the Jesuits. The human being is seen in a community and not as an isolated individual. JC:HEM helps people form learning communities that study together locally in the computer lab and globally through the virtual classroom. By transforming their thinking, these students will transform the world.

Refugees who are under international protection, displaced people, and stateless people are all very specific groups with a global character. The nation-state has failed to protect them. They have become international and global citizens who, in the midst of their great struggles, further enhance the process of globalization. The work of the Society of Jesus with these groups of people is deeply in line with the Jesuits' long tradition of serving migrants and displaced people in a mobile way through education, as well as their tradition of being embedded in the globalization process and the deeper phenomenon of the emerging global noosphere, to borrow the Jesuit trailblazer Teilhard's term.

Jesuits Sailing on the Wave of Globalization

The Jesuits never determined, nor do they today, the grand global processes driven by human mobility and communications and transportation technology, and perhaps they even have less influence now than in centuries past. But Jesuits have shown their ability to sail with the wind and on the wave of global transformations and processes in the sixteenth and seventeenth centuries of exploration of new worlds, in the eighteenth and nineteenth centuries of European migration, and with the present-day movements of migrants and refugees that have arisen since the Second Vatican Council. The mobility of the Society of Jesus is one of its primary characteristics and enables it to move with people who are on the move. Jesuits sailed in the boats of the conquistadors, soldiers, and traders of the Spanish and Portuguese empires, but they had their own agenda of working for the salvation for all human beings, spreading the Word of God, and advancing human dignity. Education became their main tool to promote human dignity and development. After traveling on the boats of European migrants to the New World, Jesuits set up Catholic schools and universities in line with their tradition. Today they fly in airplanes along with businesspeople, migrant workers, maybe at times weapons dealers and fighters—people who have their own global agendas—and harness the Internet as they pursue their educational mission. While the Society of Jesus does not always catch the wave of opportunity—sometimes missing it, other times being rolled over by it—today it is surfing on the big wave of profound technological revolutions in education through enhanced communications and information technology.

Notes

1. Adolfo Nicolás, SJ, "Depth, Universality, and Learned Ministry: Challenges to Jesuit Higher Education Today," address to conference on Networking Jesuit Higher Education: Shaping the Future for a Humane, Just, Sustainable Globe, Mexico City, April 23, 2010, http://www.sjweb.info/documents/ansj/100423_Mexico%20City_Higher%20Education%20Today_ENG.pdf.

2. John W. O'Malley, SJ, *The First Jesuits* (Cambridge MA: Harvard University Press, 1993), 12.

3. Paul VI, *Nostra aetate*, Declaration on the Relation of the Church to Non-Christian Religions, October 28, 1965, sec. 2, http://www.vatican.va/archive/hist_councils/ii_vatican_council/documents/vat-ii_decl_19651028_nostra-aetate_en.html.

4. Pedro Arrupe, SJ, "The Society of Jesus and the Refugee Problem," letter to all Jesuit Major Superiors, November 14, 1980, http://jrsusa.org/Assets/Sections/Downloads/ArrupeLetter.pdf.

5. Nicolás, "Depth, Universality."

6. Ibid.

12

JESUIT HIGHER EDUCATION AND THE GLOBAL COMMON GOOD

THOMAS BANCHOFF

The dual global and civic character of Jesuit higher education has historically set it apart. Within fifty years of its founding in 1540, the Society of Jesus managed an international network of colleges and universities dedicated to humanistic education for the common good. The network disappeared with the suppression of the Society in 1773 and was reforged during the century after its reestablishment in 1814. Over the last fifty years, with the opening of the Second Vatican Council (1962–65) and the acceleration of globalization, the global and civic dimensions of Jesuit higher education have grown more tightly interconnected. Today most of the more than 150 Jesuit institutions of higher learning around the world aspire not just to academic excellence, *cura personalis* (care for the whole person), and service of faith but also to the promotion of justice on the international as well as the local and national levels. The Jesuit higher education network is increasingly oriented to the *global* common good.

Jesuit institutions are not alone in the contemporary higher education landscape in seeking to combine the global and the civic. Educating global citizens and leaders has become a mantra for many colleges and universities worldwide, whatever their founding mission and ethos. If Jesuit institutions are to remain at the frontier of global education, they will have to find creative new ways to build on a unique 475-year legacy of global and civic engagement.

This chapter tracks the evolution of the global and civic dimensions of Jesuit higher education through the three successive phases of globalization: the early modern, modern, and contemporary. It shows how both dimensions, present at the outset, have grown more intertwined as successive waves of globalization have made the world—and its economic, social, and political problems—more interdependent. It concludes that deeper collaboration across the Jesuit network to promote the global common good, through teaching, research, and outreach, will succeed best when it is grounded in a distinctive educational philosophy and advances specific institutional interests.

The Emergence of the Jesuit Higher Education Network

The worldwide growth of Jesuit colleges and universities in the decades following the founding of the Society of Jesus in 1540 was rapid and unforeseen.[1] Ignatius and his first companions had met at the University of Paris, and they placed a high value on broad humanistic studies. But as John O'Malley notes in chapter 7 of this volume, education did not figure in the initial concept of the order; rather, the original impetus was a missionary one. Jesuit colleges began mainly as training institutions for unexpectedly large numbers of young recruits and as residences at existing universities. But soon the Society was accepting invitations to run schools to meet a wider social demand for education. First at Messina in Italy in 1548 and then gradually across Europe and in overseas colonial empires in Asia and Latin America, an international educational network took shape. By the time of Ignatius's death in 1556, the number of Jesuit colleges had reached more than thirty. By the mid-eighteenth century, it would reach more than seven hundred.

The word "college" in the early modern era was not at all synonymous with our contemporary concept of a college or university. Before the suppression of the Society a typical Jesuit school was organized around a rigorous seven-year program centered on the liberal arts and accepted students as young as ten years of age.[2] Smaller numbers of students might go on to study law, medicine, or theology at one of the Society's universities, defined as an institution with the authority to confer master's and doctoral degrees. Some Jesuit institutions, such as the Roman College, founded in 1551, began as colleges and soon offered advanced degrees, gaining university status. Mixed models emerged when the Society accepted invitations from the patrons of existing universities to set up faculties of theology or philosophy, or to assume overall academic administration, as was the case of the University of Vienna in 1623. Outside of Europe, universities such as St. Paul's in Macau, founded in 1594, and St. Francis Xavier in modern-day Bolivia, founded in 1624, depended on the patronage of the Portuguese and Spanish colonial empires. Efforts to distinguish

Jesuit colleges and universities, and to track their numbers through time, are complicated by this institutional heterogeneity and range of different ownership and management models.[3]

The global spread of Jesuit institutions was not simply a response to social demand and imperial expansion. It was also animated by the global cast of Ignatius's vision of the order, itself inspired by the missionary horizon that opened during the Age of Discovery. His *Spiritual Exercises*, originally composed in the 1520s, posited the geographic and cultural expanse of the world as the arena for God's plan of salvation. In a remarkable passage, he challenged the believer to imagine God gazing with compassion on people across "the face of the earth, in such great diversity in dress and manner of acting. Some are white, some are black; some at peace, some at war."[4] In this vein the original 1540 "Formula of the Institute" posited the world as a frame of reference. Jesuits are to follow the pope, "whether he shall send us to the Turks or any other infidels, even those who live in the region called the Indies, or among any heretics whatever, or schismatics, or any of the faithful."[5] This global orientation, more pronounced than that of either the Franciscans or the Dominicans, shaped the Jesuits' international higher education enterprise from the start.

While global expansion was enabled by social and geopolitical changes and promoted by a global orientation, it was sustained in practice by strong organization. The growth and maintenance of the network grew out of a creative combination of standardization and flexibility. Standardization arrived early with the course of study, or *Ratio studiorum*, that was finalized and approved by the General Congregation of the Society in 1599. The *Ratio* provided detailed and binding instructions for administrators and teachers across multiple years and subjects. In practice it was enforced through a detailed system of reporting and accountability within particular Jesuit provinces and all the way to Rome. Centralization did not breed uniformity, however, as the *Ratio* provided for some flexibility in the selection and presentation of course material. Education, like other Jesuit ministries, was often marked by pragmatic adaptation to local circumstances around the world. In the powerful indigenous empires of China, India, and Japan, Jesuit missionaries learned the local languages and customs and, where they were permitted to set up schools, sometimes educated Christians and non-Christians side by side. In the Americas, where the Society's schools and universities operated under the authority of colonial empires, less accommodation took place. But here too the Ignatian emphasis on the unity of all humankind and on Renaissance humanism often fostered an appreciation of native culture and traditions in ways that other educational institutions did not.

This combination of global reach and sensitivity to local circumstances in the Jesuit educational enterprise should not be confused with liberal cosmopolitanism. Ignatius and his followers saw the breadth and diversity of the world, made imaginable in an age of exploration, not as an opportunity to encounter other civilizations as equals but as an invitation to expand the scope of Jesuit missionary and educational activity. The great missionaries of the early decades, including Francis Xavier, Matteo Ricci, and Roberto de Nobili, were of course persuaded that Catholicism was the one true faith. The encounter with non-Christians in their particular circumstances, an occasion to appreciate and adopt certain elements of their cultures, was embedded within the missionary enterprise. As Francis Clooney and Daniel Madigan argue (in chapters 2 and 3, respectively, of this volume) on the Jesuit approach to Hinduism and Islam, the Jesuits' appreciation of other traditions had clear limits. Even in Funai, Japan, where as Antoni Ucerler points out in chapter 1, some students read European and Japanese classics side by side, the curriculum was built on a Western model.

Education for Civic Life and the Common Good

An important distinguishing strand of Jesuit higher education in its early centuries was its public or civic dimension. The Society's overriding goal was, of course, religious. The 1540 "Formula of the Institute" presents the Jesuits as "founded chiefly for this purpose: to strive especially for the progress of souls in Christian life and doctrine and the propagation of the faith." When they adjusted the formula in 1550, they made a strong social component explicit: Jesuits should also be ready "to reconcile the estranged, compassionately assist and serve those who are in prisons or hospitals, and indeed to perform any other works of charity, according to what will seem expedient for the glory of God and the common good."[6] As the *Constitutions*, a subsequent founding document, made clear, the Christian call to service was the founding rationale for the educational apostolate. "Through a motive of charity," it noted, "colleges are accepted and schools open to the public are maintained in them for the improvement in learning and in living, not only of our own members but more especially of those from outside the Society."[7]

The openness of Jesuit schools to the wider society, including to students of lesser means, embodied a particular Christian understanding of the common good, a concept borrowed from the Stoics. And the invocation in the *Constitutions* of *living* as well as learning underscored the humanist ideal that a classical education should have a moral as well as an intellectual rationale. The rigor of the *Ratio* was designed to build character as a means of furthering both the salvation of the soul and the improvement of society. Thus, Jesuit education incorporated what today would be called the "co-curriculum," which encompassed student organizations and activities such as theater and ministry to the local poor. Ignatius highlighted the power of education to transform society. "From among who are at present merely students," he wrote in a 1551 letter, "in time some will depart to play diverse roles—one to preach and carry on the care of souls, another to the government of the land and the administration of justice, and others to other occupations."[8]

One motive for involvement in universities and their higher studies was further to extend the social impact of Jesuit education. Through the management of universities, the *Constitutions* noted, "this fruit sought in the colleges may be spread more universally through the branches taught, the numbers attending, and the degrees granted in order that the recipients may be able to teach with authority elsewhere what they have learned well in these universities of the Society, for the glory of God our Lord."[9] The strategic move into higher education, enabled by the patronage of civic and Church leaders who welcomed the practical value of higher education for cities, nations, and empires, flowed from Ignatius's insight that to change the world for the better—to achieve what he called the "more universal good"—one must engage with the powerful. Special attention was to be devoted to "universities, which are generally attended by numerous persons who, if aided themselves, can become labourers for the help of others."[10]

It would be anachronistic to read a contemporary concern with social justice into these passages. Service to the common good in the early modern era did not incorporate any commitment to social or political reform, for hierarchical societies were an unquestioned point of departure. The primary goal of education was the formation of the person and the helping of souls. The secondary goal of service to society incorporated both loyalty to the political order and acceptance of social divides. One was to serve the poor and alleviate their lot, but the existence of widespread poverty was generally taken for granted. A favorite humanist aphorism of the Jesuits, *Puerilis institutio est renovatio mundi* (The education of youth is the means to renew the world), referred more to moral and religious renewal within the social and political order than to any far-reaching transformation.

The civic mission of Jesuit education during the early modern phase of globalization also had a limited global character. For the most part Jesuit colleges and universities oriented students to particular cities and kingdoms and not to global humanity. Though the Society of Jesus was global in its reach, existing transnational communications and transportation technologies limited its social and political engagement. Moreover, in an era when international and not just national and local political hierarchy was accepted as normal—where the division of the world into empires of rulers and the ruled went largely unquestioned—the idea of a *global* common good was underdeveloped. As José Casanova points out in chapter 13 of this volume, some influential early modern Jesuit scholars, such as Francisco Suárez, did insist on the universal dignity of all humanity and did criticize the abuses of colonial domination in the Americas. But for the most part, the Jesuits and their educational network shared their contemporaries' axiomatic presumption of the cultural superiority of the West and its right to rule wherever it might prevail.

From Reestablishment through the Second Vatican Council

During the century and a half between the reestablishment of the Society of Jesus in 1814 and the Second Vatican Council in the 1960s, the relationship between the global and civic dimensions of Jesuit higher education began to change. Amid a renewed wave of globalization, the Jesuits reforged a higher education network particularly in the United States but also in Latin America and in the French and British empires in the Middle East and South Asia. In the era of intense nationalism and ideological conflict, their institutions were generally conservative in outlook, oriented to the political status quo, and opposed to the liberalism and socialism identified by the papacy as hostile to Christian civilization. Only with the emergence of Catholic social teaching in the late nineteenth century, to which Jesuit scholars and practitioners made significant contributions, did the Society's global educational enterprise begin to incorporate a civic dimension that went beyond dutiful national citizenship and local works of charity to encompass wider questions of social justice with an international reach.

A Global Network Reforged

While it never achieved its earlier levels of prestige and influence, the Jesuit educational network made an impressive global comeback during the nineteenth century. In Europe the Jesuits gradually constructed a network of schools and universities in response to a growing demand from the upper and middle classes for education. In the United States, a rapidly expanding immigrant nation, the growth was more dramatic; as John McGreevy notes in chapter 6 of this volume, twenty-two new colleges and universities were founded over the course of the nineteenth century, with

European-trained Jesuits dominating their teaching ranks. Over the same period, Jesuit missionaries and educators accompanied a second wave of Western colonial expansion, which was enabled by revolutions in military, transportation, and communications technology. For example, Spanish Jesuits founded what became Ateneo de Manila University in 1859, German Jesuits founded St. Xavier's College in Bombay in 1869, and French Jesuits founded St. Joseph University in Beirut in 1895.

As it had during early modern globalization, the expansion of this higher education network often entailed accommodation to local and national circumstances. The Jesuit Curia in Rome initially resisted two prominent trends—a greater use of the vernacular and a proliferation of more practical curricula. In 1832 Superior General Jan Roothaan (1829–53) convened a commission that reaffirmed the binding force of the *Ratio*, with its strong emphasis on philosophy and the use of Latin and Greek. By the end of the century, however, such strictures had loosened in practice. Most American Jesuit colleges were reorganized as four-year undergraduate institutions, with the lower grades cordoned off into freestanding high schools, a process completed by the end of World War I. While adjusting their structure and curricula in different ways, Jesuit institutions nevertheless sought to maintain the tradition's distinctive humanistic orientation, with its focus on the liberal arts and *cura personalis*.[11] Some grew into universities influenced by the new German model, with an emphasis on research alongside teaching, while others added new professional faculties of medicine, law, and business, extending a tradition of civic engagement under new circumstances.[12]

During the modern phase of Western imperial expansion, accommodation to local circumstances rarely translated into respectful engagement with other cultural and religious traditions. The superiority of Western culture, and of Roman Catholicism as the one true faith, was a point of departure for most of the Jesuits who moved around the world and administered, taught, and conducted research in institutions of higher learning. Jesuit leaders in Rome viewed the United States, with its Protestant majority and liberal institutions, with some suspicion and had even more for Latin America's newly independent states, often rife with anticlericalism. But the Americas were at least part of the Christian West, and Jesuit institutions operated there with some relative autonomy. The Society's European provinces typically set up and managed those institutions in colonial empires—for example, in Lebanon, India, or the Philippines. Some did employ a small but growing number of native-born Jesuits, but they too were trained in and taught a traditional Western curriculum. The Society of Jesus, like the Catholic Church as a whole, was not immune to the imperial mind-set of the age. In 1900, for example, Pope Leo XIII praised Jesuits for "settling amongst savage tribes in order to civilize them."[13]

Jesuit Education and the Common Good

The Jesuits' approach to their educational enterprise during the modern phase of globalization was related to the wider political and ideological constellation in Europe. The reestablishment of the order in 1814 took place after the defeat of Napoleon and in the context of reactionary efforts to shore up the alliance of throne and altar against the Enlightenment, liberalism, and the specter of renewed revolution. Pope Pius VII, in his Bull of Restoration, made this political context explicit. "Amidst these dangers of the Christian Republic," with the bark of Peter "tossed and assailed by continual storms," the pope hailed "the vigorous and experienced rowers, who volunteer their services."[14] Dependent on an embattled papacy and much less influential than in earlier centuries, the Jesuits fashioned themselves as a bulwark against modernity, which the Church identified with the rise of liberalism, socialism, and atheism.

This conservative stance shaped the horizon of Jesuit higher education into the twentieth century. Jesuit scholars at the Roman College—rechristened as the Gregorian University in 1887—were prominent drafters of major antimodern papal manifestos, with the most famous among them being Pius IX's *Syllabus of Errors* (1864).[15] In Europe the Society's colleges and universities gained a reputation for social and political conservatism. Jesuit educators, who were often dependent on patronage from the wealthy classes, saw in liberal individualism and socialist collectivism threats to Christian civilization. In this context the Jesuit mission to educate others for service to the common good upheld order and tradition. "The public and the press busy themselves much about the Society's attitude towards the various forms of government," Superior General Peter Jan Beckx noted in 1879. Its sole preference, he suggested, was "fulfilling loyally the duties of a good citizen and a faithful subject of the power which rules his country."[16] Leo XIII echoed a conservative view of the Society's educational role in 1900, emphasizing "the principles of religious virtue and duty, on which public peace and the welfare of states absolutely depend."[17]

The political complexion of Jesuit higher education, and its relationship with the wider society, varied considerably across countries and continents over this period. In the France of the Third Republic and in Otto von Bismarck's Germany, Jesuit institutions were periodically persecuted as extensions of clerical and papal power. In Italy, where national unification in the 1860s stripped the Church of its temporal power, anticlerical forces targeted the Jesuits and their institutions. And repeated expulsions from Latin America over the nineteenth century hobbled the Jesuit educational enterprise. Not surprising, this constellation reinforced a conservative siege mentality within the order. The environment was more favorable in the United States, where colleges and universities served immigrant communities in major cities including New York City, Chicago, Boston, and Washington, DC.[18] Confronted with an often anti-Catholic Protestant majority, Jesuit educators went out of their way to underscore their patriotism and insist on the compatibility between their tradition and American values and institutions.[19] By and large the strategy worked over time. At Georgetown University's centenary in 1889, for example, President Grover Cleveland lauded "an army of Alumni, learned, patriotic, and useful, cherishing the good of their country as an object of loftiest effort."[20]

The rise of the nation-state as a dominant frame for Jesuit education, most evident in the United States, reflected the competitive dynamics of globalization in the run-up to two world wars. At the turn of the twentieth century, Jesuits were caught up in the rising nationalism of the era; one apologist for the Society even insisted that "Jesuit students yield to none in ardent and self-sacrificing love of country."[21] By the time war broke out in 1914, and many Jesuits—and their students—enthusiastically served and died on both sides of the conflict, a gap had opened between Ignatius's original global vision and the social and political engagement of Jesuit institutions. The idea of serving the *global* common good made little headway in a nationalist era in which the most powerful form of internationalism on offer was one of the Church's avowed enemies, revolutionary socialism.

Catholic Social Thought and a Global Frame for the Common Good

Interestingly, when the Catholic Church and the Society of Jesus did begin to approach the common good in a more global frame, it was through the development of a social teaching that shared the socialists' concerns about the depredations of the Second Industrial Revolution. The start of Leo XIII's seminal encyclical *Rerum novarum* (1891), the founding document of modern Catholic social thought, placed the economic and social dislocations confronting humanity in a global context, referring to "the spirit of revolutionary change, which has long been disturbing the nations of the world."[22] In urging a program of social reforms to address the excesses of industrialization, Leo drew on the works of Luigi Taparelli, SJ (1793–1862), who had been rector of the Gregorian in Rome, one of his teachers, and one of the inventors of the term "social justice." As articulated by Taparelli and championed by Leo, the idea of social justice was not revolutionary; indeed, it focused less on class conflict than on how modern working conditions corroded the family and the wider social order. But by linking the idea of the common good to questions of economic and social inequality and exploitation, it broke new ground. While the body of *Rerum novarum* focused on problems internal to nations, it placed them in a transnational context, laying the groundwork for a more global understanding of the common good.

Jesuits and their institutions played a critical role within the Church in positioning issues of social justice and the common good within a more global frame. In response to Leo's new departure, the Society constructed a network of social institutes around the world to promote workers' education and linked some organizations to existing institutions of higher education. In France, for example, the Institut d'Études Sociales was founded in 1923, and a Catholic Workers' College was set up in the United Kingdom at Oxford in 1921. A decade later German Jesuit scholars helped to draft the second major encyclical on the social question, Pius XI's *Quadragesimo anno* (1931), which was more global in outlook than *Rerum novarum*. Pius noted that "with the diffusion of modern industry throughout the whole world, the 'capitalist' economic regime has spread everywhere" and has "invaded and pervaded the economic and social life of even those outside its orbit." The rise of a global economic system placed issues of social justice in a new light: "Public institutions themselves" were "to make all human society conform to the needs of the common good; that is, to the norm of social justice."[23]

After World War II, with the creation of the US-led United Nations system, the Jesuit superior general Jean-Baptiste Janssens began to connect the new world order with the social and educational mission of the Society. In his 1949 "Instruction on the Social Apostolate," he combined a strident anticommunism with a critique of "liberal materialism" that favored the wealthy and the "comforts and privileges they seek to promote rather than the common good of the whole human race."[24] A focus on the global common good, he argued, should inform solidarity with the world's poorest. "In regard to our missions," he wrote, "I cannot refrain from stressing not only the necessity of teaching the true social doctrine, but even more of promoting social works and a public order that is in conformity with justice and human dignity." Jesuit institutions of higher learning, through "the foundation of chairs or faculties dealing with social questions in our universities," should also be part of this orientation to a more global common good.[25]

Jesuit social institutes continued to expand around the world during the postwar decades. For example, an Institute of Industrial Relations was founded at Loyola University in New Orleans in 1947. The Institute of Social Order, created in Manila in 1946, later became part of Ateneo de Manila University. In 1951 the Jesuits founded the Indian Social Institute in Delhi, and in 1962 in Abidjan, Côte d'Ivoire, they created the African Institute for Economic and Social Development, which became the hub of a trans-African network. It is worth noting that much of this institutional innovation took place on the margins of the global Jesuit higher education network. Most Jesuit colleges and universities at mid-twentieth century were relatively traditionalist and conservative in orientation, with a humanist core centered on the Western canon, a national and anticommunist outlook fueled by the Cold War, and little institutional engagement with questions of social justice.[26] The 1960s would mark a turning point in efforts to connect the Jesuit educational enterprise with the promotion of the global common good.

Vatican II and a New Departure

Only in the fifty years since Vatican II have the global and civic dimensions of Jesuit higher education begun to fully converge. At the Council, several Jesuit scholars made decisive contributions to three declarations published in 1965 that marked a theological and political opening to the modern world.[27] The German cardinal Augustin Bea, former rector of the Pontifical Biblical Institute, was a driving force behind *Nostra aetate*, which opened the Church to dialogue with Judaism, Islam, and other religious traditions.[28] John Courtney Murray, an American at the theologate in Woodstock, Maryland, contributed to *Dignitatis humanae*, which abandoned the Church's traditional hostility to full religious freedom.[29] And Jesuit scholars who had led the development of Catholic social teaching between the wars, including Gustav Grundlach and John LaFarge, influenced *Gaudium et spes,* the Pastoral Constitution on the Church in the Modern World.[30]

Gaudium et spes most clearly captured the dynamics of a new era of globalization, driven by the diffusion of revolutionary transportation and communications technologies—at the time, passenger air travel and long distance telephony. "Never has the human race enjoyed such an abundance of wealth, resources and economic power," it noted, "and yet a huge proportion of the world citizens are still tormented by hunger and poverty." In the context of a "growing interdependence of men one on the other," the idea of the common good took on "an increasingly universal complexion and consequently involves rights and duties with respect to the whole human race."[31] *Gaudium et spes*, building on two of John XXIII's seminal encyclicals, *Mater et magistra* (1959) and *Pacem in terris* (1963), called for nothing less than a rethinking and redirection of Catholic identity and mission on a global scale.

The decade after the Council saw the Society's rapid, if contested, embrace of the global outlook of *Gaudium et spes*. Considerable Jesuit support for a new departure emerged with the election of the Spaniard Pedro Arrupe as superior general in 1965. Under his leadership Jesuits emerged as the most visible and influential advocates of a global turn within the Church, one toward a dialogue with other faiths and cultures and a global social justice agenda. As early as 1966 this new orientation was expressed by the Thirty-First General Congregation, which asserted that "dialogue in this pluralistic world is both possible and desirable" and which encouraged Jesuit educational institutions to "willingly cooperate with other organizations, even if these do not depend either on the Church or the Society . . . especially in the less developed countries."[32] The change in tone from the decrees of the Thirtieth General Congregation in 1957—they had still used the traditional language of "missions to the infidels"—was striking.[33]

The clearest expression of the reorientation of Jesuit education toward global social justice was Arrupe's July 1973 address "Men for Others: Training Agents of Change for the Promotion of Justice" to an international alumni gathering in Valencia. Speaking in Francisco Franco's Spain, Arrupe criticized the conservative political orientation of much Jesuit education in the past and up to the present. Arrupe posed a rhetorical question: "Have we Jesuits educated you for justice?" The answer, he suggested frankly, was, "No, we have not. If the terms 'justice' and 'education for justice' carry all the depth of meaning which the Church gives them today, we have not educated you for justice."[34] Two years later the famous Decree 4 of the Thirty-Second General Congregation of 1974–75 officially recognized the Jesuit mission as "the service of faith and the promotion of justice." On the educational front, Jesuits were to "help prepare both young people and adults to live and labour for others and with others to build a more just world."[35]

By the mid-1970s Arrupe had worked out his vision of what he called "Jesuit internationalism," which he traced back to Ignatius. It included not only a willingness to go around the world but also an openness to global issues: "According to this principle, *quo universalius eo divinius* [what is more universal is more divine], universal problems that affect the whole globe, or vast areas of it, have to be considered a top priority in the Society's 'mission.'" These problems, ranging from poverty and migration to humanitarian disasters and civil strife, demanded the intellectual and pastoral resources of the whole Jesuit network. The Society, he argued, "must be more and more conscious of these new international fields of labour, which—because of the vast and variegated zones affected by each problematic, and the complexity of the problems that have to be analyzed from different inter-disciplinary vantage points—require a world-wide and interdisciplinary collaboration."[36] The most tangible expression of this new internationalism was the creation of the Jesuit Refugee Service in 1980 as a response to the plight of the Vietnamese and Cambodian boat people.

This international reorientation continued under Peter-Hans Kolvenbach, who served as superior general from 1983 to 2008. The Thirty-Fourth General Congregation in 1995 formalized a new understanding of the university and its global social and civic mission. The new "Complementary Norms," a document expanding on the founding *Constitutions*, proclaimed, "Universities and institutions of higher learning play an increasingly important role in the formation of the whole human community, for in them our culture is shaped by debates about ethics, future directions for economics and politics, and the very meaning of human existence."[37] Kolvenbach deepened these themes in his 2000 address at Santa Clara University on the twenty-fifth anniversary of the Thirty-Second General Congregation. Drawing out the implications of the commitment to faith and justice in an increasingly global era, he concluded that "Jesuit universities have stronger and different reasons than many other academic and research institutions for addressing the actual world as it unjustly exists and for helping to reshape it in the light of the Gospel."[38]

Connecting the Global and the Civic at Jesuit Institutions

By the turn of the twenty-first century, most Jesuit universities had taken on a global and social justice orientation often reflected in their mission statements. The Gregorian, for example, referenced "the social sense of a faith that works for peace, truth and justice." St. Joseph in Beirut was "open to spiritual values and based on the principles of freedom, respectability, critical sense, peaceful initiatives and social solidarity," while students at the Ateneo de Manila were to "devote their lives to the service of others and, through the promotion of justice, serve especially those who are most in need of help, the poor and the powerless." Georgetown University referred to "our commitment to justice and the common good, our intellectual openness and our international character."[39]

It is not hard to find concrete examples of a global and civic outlook at these and other institutions across the Jesuit higher education network. In the curriculum and co-curriculum and through campus ministry and community engagement programs, most Jesuit colleges and universities introduce students to issues of social justice from a range of intellectual, cultural, and practical perspectives. The global dimensions of those issues are explored through teaching, research, and outreach, including study abroad and international summer programs. The avowed goal is what Kolvenbach called "a well-educated solidarity," an orientation to a global social justice that can accompany students wherever they go in the world and whatever their professional path. Progress in this direction, however uneven, has taken place through a deeper Jesuit-lay collaboration at the institutions of the Society as the number of Jesuits has declined from a peak of about thirty-five thousand worldwide during the early 1960s to about half that number today.

The turn toward global social justice has not gone uncontested in Jesuit institutions. Since the 1960s more conservative faculty and administrators have periodically warned against any politicization of the university that might detract from the core teaching and research enterprise. And in practice no institution has completely redefined its mission in the social justice direction that was advocated by Ignacio Ellacuría, a Jesuit theologian who was deeply influenced by liberation theology. In a much-cited address in 1982, Ellacuría insisted that "a Christian university must take into account the gospel preference for the poor" and work to "provide science for those without science; to provide skills for those without skills; to be a voice for those without voices; to give intellectual support for those who do not possess the academic qualifications to make their rights legitimate." In 1990, the year after Ellacuría's martyrdom at the hands of death squads in El Salvador, Jon Sobrino, SJ, one of his collaborators, extended this radical logic further: "If a Christian University never, never, never gets into some sort of serious conflict with those who have power in this world, it is not a Christian University."[40]

A radical orientation to the poor or a confrontation with the powerful is not a practical option for most Jesuit institutions. All depend to one degree or another on the patronage of the powerful—that is, governments, which provide political approval and legal frameworks, and those who cover operating costs and contribute other material resources through tuition and philanthropy. Given these constraints, which vary considerably between time and place, a university's option for the poor and the marginalized and its embrace of an activist social justice agenda risk undermining the political and material support upon which the academic enterprise depends. One can argue, of course, that Jesuit institutions have an impact on the common good precisely because they educate elites, those best positioned to serve the common good in practice. That was part of Ignatius's vision at the outset. But today it raises an uncomfortable question: What distinguishes Jesuit institutions from the rest of the higher education sector, in which the formation of global citizens and leaders for the common good is an increasingly commonplace mantra?

In a seminal speech in 2010 to Jesuit university presidents from around the world in Mexico City, Superior General Adolfo Nicolás addressed this question. He highlighted two distinguishing strengths of Jesuit higher education—a strong humanist ethos and a far-flung international network. Nicolás framed his argument about the importance of humanist pedagogy with a powerful indictment of the "globalization of superficiality" fostered by a combination of instant communications, consumer culture, and moral relativism. He called on Jesuit institutions to revitalize their commitment to *cura personalis* through attention to the deep spiritual, emotional, and social, as well as academic and professional, needs of students. A rich Jesuit education, he insisted, "integrates intellectual rigor with reflection on the experience of reality together with the creative imagination to work toward constructing a more humane, just, sustainable, and faith-filled world." And, he continued, "the experience of reality includes the broken world, especially the world of the poor, waiting for healing."[41]

Nicolás's invocation of the creative imagination, drawing on the *Spiritual Exercises*, highlights a distinctive contribution of Jesuit education to a global, humanistic formation. There is no shortage of articulate pleas, across the academy, for a more global liberal arts education that sensitizes students to cultural differences and complexities. And calls to link education with service to the community, both at school and after graduation, are prominent across a wide range of colleges and universities, whatever their religious or secular identity. To insist on the spiritual dimension of the human person, the infinite dignity and eternal destiny of every human being, gives the imperative of education for the global common good a greater depth. It links education with self-reflection and self-transformation through service to others. In the post–Vatican II era, few Jesuit educators describe the primary goal of the educational enterprise as "the salvation of souls." But the broader Ignatian formulation of "helping souls" is very compatible with Nicolás's call to arms against the "globalization of superficiality." "The times in which we happen to live are radically different from those lived by Ignatius of Loyola," Kolvenbach has argued in this connection. "But the 'help of souls,' the 'greater glory of God and the universal good' remain the fundamental motivation for the Society's commitment to education."[42]

Nicolás's address also emphasized a second comparative strength of Jesuit higher education in addressing the challenges of our global era: its international reach. Over the postwar decades Jesuit institutions have increased their regional collaborations, creating associations spanning Latin America, East and South Asia, Europe and the Middle East, and the United States. In 1995 the Thirty-Fourth General Congregation called for greater international collaboration, "in particular, to undertake common projects between Jesuit universities of developed and developing countries."[43] Pointing to the deepening of globalization since the turn of the millennium and to the emergence of a range of more interconnected economic, social, and political problems, Nicolás called on Jesuit institutions to develop more robust "international networks that will address important issues touching faith, justice, and ecology that challenge us across countries and continents."[44] One notable success since the Mexico City conference, highlighted by Peter Balleis in chapter 11 of this volume, is the Jesuit Commons: Higher Education at the Margins (JC:HEM), a collaborative effort that provides education to migrants in refugee camps around the world.

International collaboration is often difficult in practice for three main reasons. One is the decentralized character of the Jesuit higher education system. Since the 1960s Jesuit institutions have grown more independent of one another, with most now under the control of lay-majority boards. The Higher Education Secretariat, set up in the curia in 2006, has few resources with which to incentivize collaboration from the center. A second problem is the asymmetry of power and resources across developed and developing countries. It is difficult to collaborate as equals when wealthier institutions, concentrated in the United States, bring an oversized influence to partnerships. This point relates to a third problem—the diversity of political, cultural, and theological perspectives represented across Jesuit institutions worldwide. The experience of India, for example, home to more than twenty Jesuit colleges, is sharply different from that of Latin America or Europe. Collaboration on global issues from poverty to the environment that affect world regions so differently is inherently difficult.

These constraints are considerable. But if Jesuit institutions want to build on their global and civic traditions and maintain a position on the global frontiers of higher education, deeper collaboration is necessary. The most effective initiatives will likely emerge first out of compatible interests among a particular set of institutions after they reach a shared realization that collaboration around a particular global issue can strengthen their own teaching, research, and outreach efforts. Once initiatives have demonstrated their benefits to diverse internal stakeholders—in academic, material, and mission terms—they are more likely to attract other colleges and universities, thus further globalizing the basis of the collaboration. Proven success at scale then provides an opportunity to attract support from actors outside the network—international organizations, governments, and philanthropists—whose further investments can help to sustain the collaboration into the future. To date JC:HEM has followed this successful pattern regarding the refugees issue. This model might be applicable to a range of other international issues as well, ranging from economic development to just governance, peace and security, and the environment.

Conclusion

The juxtaposition of the global and civic dimensions of Jesuit higher education across three historical epochs reveals not only patterns of continuity and change but also some lessons for the present. Across all three periods of globalization—the early modern, modern, and contemporary—the Jesuits maintained an impressive international network of educational institutions aspiring to the service of faith and the promotion of the common good. Anchored in a Christian humanist tradition, Jesuit institutions have combined their global presence with a commitment to the care of the whole person and the cultivation of skills and knowledge to benefit the wider society. Over the centuries, however, links between the global and civic components of Jesuit higher education have changed significantly in response both to wider secular developments and to the internal evolution of the Catholic Church and the Society of Jesus. In the contemporary global era, more interconnected than any before it, service to the global, as well as the local and national, common good has emerged as a more salient imperative that is often difficult to realize in practice.

The rapid international expansion of the Jesuit higher education network, from the sixteenth to the eighteenth centuries, coincided with the early modern wave of globalization. As part of a wider missionary effort to spread Christianity to the ends of the earth and to strengthen the Church in Europe, the Jesuits developed a characteristic way of proceeding that was marked by adapting to local circumstances. Through an opening to intercultural encounter, particularly in Asia, India, and China, Jesuit education helped to transfer knowledge between East and West. And some Jesuit thinkers developed the idea of global humanity as a kind of extended community bound by mutual obligations. But over the early modern period such efforts to imagine and pursue the universal, global common good in missionary and educational enterprises were constrained by taken-for-granted assumptions about political and social hierarchies in European kingdoms and in new, world-spanning empires.

The Jesuit higher education network that was re-created during the second, modern wave of globalization, during the nineteenth and early twentieth centuries, also had extensive reach. It was carried by a new wave of European colonialism and, in the United States, flourished in a new and increasingly powerful immigrant nation. In a world more closely interconnected by the technologies of the Industrial Revolution, Jesuit educators were in many ways less accommodating of cultural differences than in earlier centuries. Most often closely allied with an embattled papacy opposed to revolutionary liberalism and socialism, they were generally conservative in outlook and did not distance themselves from the growing dominant imperialism and nationalism that arose before World War I. Only with the gradual emergence of Catholic social teaching from the 1890s did the idea of social justice and the global common good begin to shape the Jesuit higher education enterprise.

Vatican II and the acceleration of globalization since then have transformed the connection between the global and the civic at Jesuit colleges and universities. Under the leadership of Pedro Arrupe, the Society and its educational institutions redefined their mission in 1975 as the service of faith and the promotion of justice at the local, national, and international levels. In the intervening forty years, Jesuit institutions have sought, through curricula and co-curricular activities, to orient students to questions of justice and solidarity and to prepare them for lives of service to the global community. Adolfo Nicolás's address in Mexico City in 2010 initiated a deeper phase of reflection on what is distinctive about the Society's approach to humanistic education in a globalizing era. His call to Jesuit institutions around the world to collaborate around pressing global issues has met with some success to date, particularly regarding work with refugees. To answer the call going forward, Jesuit institutions will have to overcome obstacles posed by asymmetries of power and differences of perspective across their global network.

The selection of Jorge Mario Bergoglio as pope in 2013 marked a hopeful juncture for Jesuit higher education and its global mission. In his first two years in office, Pope Francis, himself a Jesuit, astounded the world with his call for a return to the simplicity of Gospel values. He reminded Catholic and Jesuit higher education institutions of their responsibility to educate the whole person and to accompany the marginalized. In the 2013 apostolic exhortation *Evangelii gaudium*, his warning to academics and other professionals—"No one must say that they cannot be close to the poor because their own lifestyle demands more attention to other areas"—was a stark challenge to both individuals and institutions.[45] Through his clear articulation of the connection between contemplation, love, and service, rooted in his own Ignatian spirituality, Francis has issued a call to conscience and to action for Jesuit colleges and universities worldwide. Their efforts to advance the global common good, at the centers and the margins of power, will require the further creative development of a living tradition.

Notes

1. For more on the origins of Jesuit education, see John W. O'Malley, SJ, *The First Jesuits* (Cambridge, MA: Harvard University Press, 1993). On early Jesuit universities in particular, see Hilde de Ridder-Symoens, ed., *A History of the University in Europe*, vol. 2, *Universities in Early Modern Europe (1500–1800)* (Cambridge: Cambridge University Press, 2003).

2. For an overview of Ignatius's understanding of the organization of university studies, see George E. Ganss, SJ, *Saint Ignatius' Idea of a Jesuit University* (Milwaukee: Marquette University Press, 1954), ch. 4.

3. The once-Jesuit University of Bamberg provides an illustration of this complexity. It began as a theological academy taken over by the Jesuits in 1611 and offered bachelor degrees starting in 1648. Faculties of law and medicine were added in 1735, but the title of "university" was only conferred later, in 1773, after the university was removed from Jesuit control. See Ridder-Symoens, *History of the University*, 2:69.

4. Ignatius of Loyola, *Spiritual Exercises*, trans. Louis J. Puhl, SJ (Westminster, MD: Newman Press, 1957), no. 106, 50.

5. Ignatius of Loyola and the Society of Jesus, *The Constitutions of the Society of Jesus and Their Complementary Norms: A Complete English Translation of the Official Latin Texts*, trans. Carl J. Moell, SJ (St. Louis: Institute of Jesuit Sources, 1996), 68.

6. Ibid., 67. I am grateful to Philip Endean, SJ, for pointing out the nuances between the 1540 and 1550 versions of the formula. See further Antonio M. de Aldama, *The Formula of the Institute: Notes for a Commentary*, trans. Ignatius Echániz (St. Louis: Institute of Jesuit Sources, 1989).

7. Reprinted in Ganss, *Saint Ignatius' Idea*, 319.

8. Ignatius to Antonio de Araoz, December 1, 1551, cited in ibid., 28–29.

9. Reprinted in ibid., 319.

10. Ignatius of Loyola and the Society of Jesus, *Constitutions*, no. 662.

11. In 1906 it was officially decided that each Jesuit province was free to adapt the *Ratio* to its particular circumstances. See Philip Gleason, *Contending with Modernity: Catholic Higher Education in the Twentieth Century* (New York: Oxford University Press, 1995). On the transition away from Greek and Latin, see Raymond A. Schroth, SJ, *The American Jesuits: A History* (New York: NYU Press, 2009), 110.

12. Professional schools were only officially endorsed by the Twenty-Eighth General Congregation in 1928.

13. Pope Leo XIII in his letter to the Archbishop of Paris, December 23, 1900, cited in Robert Schwickerath, *Jesuit Education: Its History and Principles Viewed in*

the Light of Modern Educational Problems (Woodstock, MD: Woodstock College, 1904), 277.

14. Pius VII, *Sollicitudo omnium ecclesiarum*, August 7, 1814, as cited in J. F. Maclear, ed., *Church and State in the Modern Age: A Documentary History* (Oxford: Oxford University Press, 1985), 120–21.

15. Pius IX, *The Syllabus of Errors*, December 8, 1864, http://www.ewtn.com/library/papaldoc/p9syll.htm.

16. *L'Univers*, Paris, January 20, 1879, cited in Schwickerath, *Jesuit Education*, 262.

17. Letter of Leo XIII to the Archbishop of Paris, December 23, 1900, cited in ibid., 277.

18. On the development of Jesuit higher education in the United States, see William P. Leahy, SJ, *Adapting to America: Catholics, Jesuits, and Higher Education in the Twentieth Century* (Washington, DC: Georgetown University Press, 1991).

19. One speaker at Georgetown University's centenary professed a conservative wariness of democracy that was more typical of European Jesuits at the time: "All free government, however democratic in theory, is necessarily aristocratic in fact. The few must always administer it; the few must always guide and control it." Martin Morris cited in R. Emmett Curran, SJ, "Georgetown's Self-Image at Its Centenary," in *Georgetown at Two Hundred*, ed. William C. McFadden, SJ (Washington, DC: Georgetown University Press, 1990), 10.

20. Cleveland quoted in Schwickerath, *Jesuit Education*, 261. The issue of how Jesuit institutions fit into American society was aired in an extended public controversy unleashed by Harvard president Charles Eliot's disparaging remarks about the quality of Jesuit education in 1899. Charles Eliot, "Recent Changes in Secondary Education," *The Atlantic Monthly* 84 (October 1899): 433–44.

21. Schwickerath, *Jesuit Education*, 256.

22. Leo XIII, *Rerum novarum* (Of New Things), May 15, 1891, https://w2.vatican.va/content/leo-xiii/en/encyclicals/documents/hf_l-xiii_enc_15051891_rerum-novarum.html.

23. Pius XI, *Quadragesimo anno* (On Reconstruction of the Social Order), May 15, 1931, http://w2.vatican.va/content/pius-xi/en/encyclicals/documents/hf_p-xi_enc_19310515_quadragesimo-anno.html.

24. Jean-Baptiste Janssens, SJ, to all Jesuit provincials, "Instruction on the Social Apostolate," October 10, 1949, http://www.sjweb.info/sjs/documents/Janssens_eng.pdf.

25. Ibid. The Twenty-Eighth General Congregation, meeting in 1938, had already insisted that "the principles of charity and social justice be carefully impressed upon the minds of the students in our schools, on both the higher and the middle levels." See "Decrees on the Social Apostolate," nos. 5–10, http://www.sjweb.info/sjs/documents/CG24-30_eng.pdf.

26. As late as 1941, for example, Fordham president Robert Gannon, SJ, warned: "In a cap and gown any one has the privilege of uprooting all the true foundations of life and of robbing the young of all the principles on which our

civilization rests." He continued, "All that he need do is hide behind academic freedom." Quoted in "Fordham's 100 Years," *New York Times*, September 14, 1941.

27. For more on the Jesuits' impact at the Council, see chapter 8 by David Hollenbach, SJ, in this volume.

28. Paul VI, *Nostra aetate*, Declaration on the Relation of the Church to Non-Christian Religions, October 28, 1965, http://www.vatican.va/archive/hist_councils/ii_vatican_council/documents/vat-ii_decl_19651028_nostra-aetate_en.html.

29. Paul VI, *Dignitatis humanae*, Declaration on Religious Freedom, December 7, 1965, http://www.vatican.va/archive/hist_councils/ii_vatican_council/documents/vat-ii_decl_19651207_dignitatis-humanae_en.html.

30. Paul VI, *Gaudium et spes*, Pastoral Constitution of the Church in the Modern World, December 7, 1965, http://www.vatican.va/archive/hist_councils/ii_vatican_council/documents/vat-ii_const_19651207_gaudium-et-spes_en.html.

31. Ibid.

32. Pedro Arrupe, SJ, *Pedro Arrupe: Essential Writings*, ed. Kevin Burke (Maryknoll, NY: Orbis Books, 2004), 231.

33. "A worldwide outlook, not only in the missions to the infidels but in every part of the vineyard of the Lord, demands that the apostle be adapted to the conditions of the region." Thirtieth General Congregation of the Society of Jesus, Decree 25, "On Aids to the Apostolate" (1957), in *For Matters of Greater Moment: The First Thirty Jesuit General Congregations*, ed. John W. Padberg, SJ, Martin D. O'Keefe, SJ, and John L. McCarthy, SJ (St. Louis: Institute for Jesuit Sources, 1994), 660—61.

34. Pedro Arrupe, SJ, "Men for Others: Training Agents of Change for the Promotion of Justice," in *Justice with Faith Today: Selected Letters and Addresses*, ed. Jerome Aixala, SJ (St. Louis: Institute of Jesuit Sources, 1980), 125. In addition to the Council's documents, Arrupe referenced Pope Paul VI's 1967 encyclical *Populorum progressio* and the 1971 Synod of Bishops in Rome, which famously concluded that "action on behalf of justice and participation in the transformation of the world fully appear to us as a constitutive dimension of the preaching of the Gospel, or, in other words, of the Church's mission for the redemption of the human race and its liberation from every oppressive situation." Cited in Kenneth R. Himes, ed., *Modern Catholic Social Teaching: Commentaries and Interpretations* (Washington, DC: Georgetown University Press, 2005), 341.

35. Thirty-Second General Congregation of the Society of Jesus, Decree 4, "Our Mission Today: The Service of Faith and the Promotion of Justice" (1975), no. 60, http://www.sjweb.info/documents/sjs/docs/D4%20Eng.pdf.

36. Pedro Arrupe, SJ, "Some Far-Reaching Vistas of Decree 4 of GC32," in Arrupe, *Justice with Faith Today*, 161.

37. Society of Jesus, "Complementary Norms, Part VII, 277–297," no. 289, http://www.sjweb.info/documents/education/Comp%20Norms%20VII,%20277-297.pdf.

38. Peter-Hans Kolvenbach, SJ, "The Service of Faith and the Promotion of Justice in American Jesuit Higher Education," conference on Commitment to Justice in Jesuit Higher Education, Santa Clara University, October 6, 2000, http://www.marquette.edu/mission/documents/TheServiceofFaithandthePromotionofJusticeinAmericanJesuitHigherEducation-Kolvenbach.pdf.

39. Pontifical Gregorian University Steering Committee, "Mission Statement," November 27, 2009, http://www.unigre.it/Univ/documenti/091127_PUG_dichiarazione_intenti_en.pdf; St. Joseph University, "Mission," 2007, http://www.usj.edu.lb/en/files/mission.htmlQ1; Ateneo de Manila University, "Vision-Mission Statement," http://www.admu.edu.ph/ateneo-de-manila-university-vision-mission-statement; and Georgetown University, "University Mission Statement," http://governance.georgetown.edu/mission-statement/.

40. Ignacio Ellacuría, SJ, Commencement Address at Santa Clara University, June 1982, http://www.scu.edu/Jesuits/ellacuria.html; and Jon Sobrino, SJ, Commencement Address at Regis University, May 6, 1990, http://academic.regis.edu/tleining/Word%20Docs/John%20Sobrino%20SJ%20commencement%20speech.doc For more on Ellacuría, liberation theology, and the struggle over higher education in Latin America, see chapter 9 by Maria Clara Bingemer in this volume.

41. Adolfo Nicolás, SJ, "Depth, Universality, and Learned Ministry: Challenges to Jesuit Higher Education Today," address to the International Conference on Networking Jesuit Higher Education: Shaping the Future for a Humane, Just, Sustainable Globe, Mexico City, April 23, 2010, http://www.scu.edu/scm/fall2010/upload/mexico-city-conference.pdf.

42. Peter-Hans Kolvenbach, SJ. "The Jesuit University in Light of the Ignatian Charism," address to International Meeting of Jesuit Higher Education, Rome, May 27, 2001, http://www.sjweb.info/documents/phk/university_en.pdf.

43. Thirty-Fourth General Congregation of the Society of Jesus, Decree 17, "Jesuits and University Life" (1995), no. 10, http://www.sjweb.info/documents/education/CG34_D17_ENG.pdf.

44. Nicolás, "Depth, Universality."

45. Pope Francis, *Evangelii gaudium*, Apostolic Exhortation on the Proclamation of the Gospel in Today's World, November 24, 2013, sec. 201, http://w2.vatican.va/content/francesco/en/apost_exhortations/documents/papa-francesco_esortazione-ap_20131124_evangelii-gaudium.html.

13

THE JESUITS THROUGH THE PRISM OF GLOBALIZATION, GLOBALIZATION THROUGH A JESUIT PRISM

JOSÉ CASANOVA

Each chapter in this volume has addressed two core questions from a specific thematic, historical, or regional perspective: What does the experience of globalization tell us about the Jesuits? And what does the experience of the Jesuits tell us about globalization? In this concluding chapter, my aim is to address the same two questions from a broader synthetic perspective, drawing upon some of the most important lessons offered across the chapters.

The Jesuits through the Prism of Early Modern Globalization

As a point of departure, taking what in the introduction we call the "subjective" dimension of globalization—the increased awareness of the unity of the world as a whole as a focus for human activities—one could argue that the Jesuits were the first organized group in history to think *and* to act globally.[1] What were the conditions for the possible emergence of such a nongovernmental organization (NGO) of global missionaries and global educators *avant la lettre*—that is, before the existence of global structures that could sustain such practices?

Of the small group of companions that gathered around Ignatius of Loyola at the University of Paris in the early 1530s, three interrelated historical developments shaped the opportunity structures that made possible its rapid transformation into a prodigiously successful global missionary, educational, and sociopolitical enterprise: the Iberian colonial expansion into the newly discovered "Indies," the early modern Catholic revival, and

Renaissance Christian humanism. All three evolving manifestations had been operative for more than half a century by the time Pope Paul III's bull *Regimini militantis ecclesiae* in 1540 certified, through the "Formula of the Institute" contained therein, the official foundation of the Society of Jesus. All three helped shape the institutional development and the global expansion of the new Society in the following decades, and the Jesuits, in turn, became primary global carriers of the three processes in the early modern phase of globalization.

The Iberian Colonial Expansion

The Iberian colonial expansion made possible the connection of the Old World and the "discovered" New World, linking the East and West Indies, thus forming for the first time one truly global world in novel transatlantic and transpacific exchanges. In this respect the early modern phase of globalization constitutes literally the "first globalization," a form of protoglobalization that can rightly be distinguished from earlier "archaic" and later "modern" forms of globalization.[2] In this newly connected world the Jesuits emerged to become pioneer globalizers. Indeed, no other group as eagerly took the entire globe as the focus of its activities. Jerónimo Nadal—one of Ignatius's closest collaborators and the man who, in the words of John O'Malley, "more than any individual . . . instilled in the first two generations their *esprit de corps* and taught them what it meant to be a Jesuit"—coined the famous phrase, "The world is our home."[3]

The Jesuits sailed around the world in the same ships with conquistadores, traders, migrants, and colonial administrators. António Vieira, the great Jesuit missionary of Brazil, put the matter most succinctly in his *História do Futuro*: "If there were not merchants who go to seek for earthly treasures in the East and West Indies, who would transport thither the preachers who take heavenly treasures? The preachers take the Gospel and the merchants take the preachers."[4] The vast Jesuit Portuguese Assistancy, which included not only the kingdom of Portugal and its maritime empire but also portions of the Indian subcontinent, Japan, China, Southeast Asia, and African territories, undoubtedly constituted the core of the global Jesuit enterprise in the sixteenth and seventeenth centuries.[5] That enterprise was largely sponsored by the Portuguese *padroado régio* and by the Spanish *patronato real* (royal patronage). It would thus be anachronistic to view the Society of Jesus as an NGO in the modern sense of the term. As Aliocha Maldavsky makes clear in chapter 4, Jesuit missions in colonial Ibero-America were irremediably embedded in colonial structures of coercion and political control.

From its inception, therefore, the Jesuit missionary enterprise could not avoid accruing a very "worldly" and secular connotation, that of being also an economic *and* political enterprise. The historian C. R. Boxer has claimed that the Jesuits could be considered "the first multinational corporation."[6] In chapter 5 Sabina Pavone's discussion of anti-Jesuitism shows how, from the beginning, the Jesuit order was not only viewed as political and as "a state within the state" but also maligned as the first and paradigmatic international secret organization bent on establishing "a world empire."[7]

Yet the Jesuit global salvific enterprise cannot be reduced to the economic imperatives of an emergent global capitalism or to the political dynamics of the new Westphalian system of nation-states in search of colonial domains. Its primary mission and its ultimate end was the universal salvation of "souls" *ad majorem Dei gloriam*. According to O'Malley, no other expression "occurs more frequently in Jesuit documentation—on practically every page—than 'to help souls.'"[8] To reduce the Jesuit mission to something else is not only to miss what clearly motivated Ignatius and the members of the Society he founded but also to misunderstand the very source of the globalizing dynamic of the Jesuit enterprise.

By "soul," however, Ignatius and the Jesuits meant the whole person; therefore, to help souls became a universal and global ministry practically without substantive or geographical limits. Without ever losing sight of their primary salvational mission, Jesuit ministries encompassed all kinds of activities and spheres that today may be considered secular but that they regarded as an intrinsic part of their religious mission.[9] The revised "Formula of the Institute" of 1550, after enumerating a long list of customary religious pastoral ministries to which the Jesuits ought to dedicate themselves, adds "according to what will seem expedient for the glory of God and the common good"—the first time in history that expedient consideration of the worldly *common good* appears in the foundational charter of a religious order.[10] Its inclusion was to have unforeseen consequences in the Jesuits' sustained professional dedication not only to the humanities but also to science, technology, and the arts. Following the Ignatian instruction, Jesuits were to find God in all things.

The Early Modern Catholic Revival

Ignatius's spiritual journey and the foundation and dramatic expansion of the Society of Jesus need to be viewed in the context of the broad and widespread manifestations of the early modern Catholic renewal that flourished in Italy and the Iberian Peninsula well before the Protestant

Reformation of the sixteenth century. In this context the Jesuits appear as contributors to a much broader reality going well beyond what the term "Counter-Reformation" suggests and to say nothing of the narrow Eurocentrism that the term connotes.[11] Whatever name we give to the changes in Catholicism during early modernity, in this era Catholicism attained its global reach from East Asia to North America, from the Philippines to South America. R. Po-chia Hsia has argued that "the centuries of Catholic renewal formed the first period of global history" in that the early modern era was shaped by "the encounter between Catholic Europe and the non-Christian world."[12] It was in this era, as Simon Ditchfield has shown, that Catholicism became a "world religion."[13]

The Jesuits were neither the only nor the first global missionaries. In fact, they followed literally in the steps of older Catholic orders—Franciscans, Dominicans, Augustinians, and others—that had preceded them in colonial Spanish America and in Portuguese India. In this respect the Jesuit global mission was part and parcel of the golden age of global Catholic missions that flourished throughout the sixteenth and seventeenth centuries and well before the global Protestant missions emerged toward the end of the eighteenth century. As was every Christian mission before and after, this global Catholic mission was a response to Jesus's "Great Commission" to his followers to "go and make disciples of all nations" (Matthew 28:19). Nonetheless, the Jesuit missionary expansion of the sixteenth century can only be understood properly if one takes into account that the global mission became the specific foundational mission or ministry of the Jesuits from the Society's inception and in a way that had not been the case of the mendicant or other Catholic orders.

Global mobility was culturally encoded, as it were, into the makeup of the Society of Jesus from its inception. Moreover, the Jesuit order's centralized hierarchic structure, which distinguished it from the older religious orders, implied that any Jesuit anywhere in the world had to be ready to be sent *ad missiones* anywhere in the world. Members of the Society who came from nations that did not have empires could be sent overseas by the general. Thus large numbers of Italian, German, Austrian, Bohemian, and Belgian Jesuits went on overseas missions, giving those missions their distinctive international character. The mission to "any heretics," to counter the Protestant Reformation, appears in the "Formula of the Institute" simply as one of the many particular forms of the Society's original global mission. The mission to the Turks probably appears first because the original intention of the first seven companions had been to travel to Jerusalem.[14] Once the journey to Jerusalem became unfeasible, they decided to put themselves at the service of the universal bishop of Rome and agreed to be sent anywhere in the world. The Jesuits were to become companions of Jesus in this universal salvific mission of early modern world Catholicism.[15]

Renaissance Christian Humanism

While the iconic image of the Jesuit as an itinerant global missionary has persisted, even more enduring has been the parallel image of the Jesuit as a resident schoolmaster. In fact, the Jesuits formed not only the first Catholic teaching order but also the first transnational professional organization of schoolmasters. Teaching had not been envisioned originally as a particular Jesuit ministry, but the establishment of the first Jesuit school in Messina, Sicily, in 1548 had immense repercussions on the character and development of the Society. O'Malley does not hesitate to call it "a crucial event in the history of schooling within the Catholic Church and in Western civilization."[16]

Indeed, what made the Jesuit college distinctive was precisely its global orientation, which was derived from the "Jesuit geography of knowledge."[17] On instruction from Ignatius himself, missionaries from the East and West Indies sent all kinds of novel information—natural, historical, geographic, demographic, ethnographic, linguistic, artistic—to the most important Jesuit colleges in Europe. There it was first processed into new scientific knowledge and then globally distributed in print form, eventually reaching Jesuit colleges and missions throughout the world. This virtuous feedback of global knowledge production between the global network of Jesuit colleges and the global network of Jesuit missions made the Jesuits into pioneer globalizers.

The development of Jesuit education in early modernity presents an interesting case, because the Jesuit college evolved at a time when the nobility and the emerging middle classes increasingly demanded education and well before the state assumed control over schooling. The Jesuits exploited a particular historical window of opportunity: They were the pioneer constructors of a model for an educational institution, which they themselves then reproduced isomorphically around the world.

The Stanford world polity school of globalization, led by John W. Meyer, has stressed the surprisingly isomorphic character of institutional and organizational structures worldwide: from constitutional and state bureaucracies, to universities and health systems, to normative scripts of economic development, environmentalism, and gender equality. The school emphasizes that "theories reasoning from the obviously large differences among national economies and cultural traditions have great difficulty accounting for these observed isomorphisms, but they are sensible outcomes if nation-states are enactments of the world cultural order."[18]

The central assumption is that all of these similarities derive from models embedded in an overarching world culture—or world society, as it were—that is exogenous to all the particular societies of the world and shapes those particular societies. The Jesuits, as pioneer cultural brokers and translators between North and South and East and West, were important actors in the early phases of constructing some aspects of such a world society.

The most important contribution of the Jesuits to the formation of a world society was their advancement of what Roland Robertson defines as two of the critical reference points of the global field—namely, *individuals* or *selves*, which in Jesuit-Christian parlance were called "souls," and *humankind* or global humanity.[19] As with so many other things, the Jesuits were not so much the originators but the effective carriers of a wider culture of universal Christian humanism that emerged from the confluence of Aristotelian-Thomist scholastic philosophy and Renaissance humanism and then crystallized in the Schools of Salamanca and Coimbra. The founding and leading figure of the School of Salamanca, Francisco de Vitoria, was a Dominican, as were the other leading theologians Domingo de Soto and Melchior Cano. At the School of Coimbra Francisco Suárez and Luis de Molina, two Jesuit theologians, became equally influential figures. In their encounters with the non-Christian Other, Jesuit global missions and colleges became the effective global disseminators of this culture of Christian humanism.[20]

Through the prism of globalization, one can view the Jesuits as a particular crystallization of the world-historical conjuncture of the three interrelated processes of the Iberian global colonial expansion, the early modern Catholic revival, and the culture of Renaissance Christian humanism. The Jesuits formed in response to the opportunity structures created by these processes and became paradigmatic carriers of the first globalization owing to their peculiar character as an inner-worldly, activist, and highly mobile transnational religious order that occupied an interstitial role between the Catholic imperial powers and the papacy from which they claimed to have received their global universal mission. Their interstitial role as a transnational and papal order was the source of their unique structural autonomy as a global organization in early modernity before the consolidation of the international Westphalian system of states. Further their role also gave rise to the persistent manifestations of anti-Jesuit animosity from many different quarters that led to their eventual suppression on the eve of the modern American and French Revolutions.

At the very moment when global Jesuit missions disappeared in the second half of the eighteenth century, a new era of self-confident global Protestant missions was initiated, this time riding the dominant waves of a renewed Western, global colonial expansion in which universal Christian missions, global capitalist exchanges, scientific rationalism, and secular humanism appeared intrinsically intertwined. When the Society of Jesus was restored in 1814 at the end of the Napoleonic Wars, the world-historical conjuncture had changed dramatically. The Iberian Catholic powers and their colonial empires were in tatters. They had been supplanted on the global stage by the expansionist North Atlantic Protestant powers that were the carriers of a different dynamic of modern globalization, which was fueled by industrial capitalism and liberalism. Some signs of Catholic revival still manifested in the proliferation of new male and female religious orders, many of which were dedicated to the two ministries that the Jesuits first pioneered—education and global missions. Throughout the nineteenth century, the restored Jesuits continued in the forefront of both missions. But the papacy and the world of traditional Catholicism appeared to be on the defensive, shaken by the accumulative shocks of the modern secular forces of the Enlightenment, the French Revolution, and liberal nationalism.

As the restored Society of Jesus began to operate in these new conditions, its transnational "catholic"—that is, universalist—identity and global mobility took on a new kind of significance, as John McGreevy makes evident in chapter 6. The Society's global missionary ethos now interacted with the two main structural dynamics of modern globalization. In the first place, the globalization of capital and labor produced a new European global colonial expansion, and in the mass migrations of European Catholics, the Jesuits accompanied them as pastors on their overseas journeys. But the globalizing dynamics of the nation-state and the global expansion of nationalism again pushed the transnational order into exile. For the nineteenth-century Jesuits, the United States became a safe haven from both dynamics of migration, a frontier missionary Society in its own right, a place where they could build new educational institutions more freely than anywhere else in the world, and a platform from which to start anew the building of global Catholic missions.

By the beginning of the twentieth century, Jesuits were found all over the world, but paradoxically their very institutional success had made the Jesuits in the United States and elsewhere more sedentary and more accommodating to the "national spirit" of the age. From the foundation of the order, Ignatius and succeeding superiors general had identified the national spirit as a constant threat from which the Society of Jesus had to protect itself deliberately to maintain its universal catholic identity and its transnational organizational structure in the face of the emerging Westphalian system. In the modern global age of nationalism, Jesuits everywhere were undergoing a new kind of "nativist inculturation" that made them more nationally local and less globally cosmopolitan. Nothing illustrates better the extent to which even the Jesuits had succumbed to the modern national spirit than the fact that French and German Jesuits, who had been expelled from their respective countries during the culture wars of the nineteenth century, returned to their "homes" during World War I to aid the national war effort. For Jesuits, as well as for Catholics everywhere, national solidarity proved stronger than Christian human solidarity or Catholic papal fidelity, although Pope Benedict XV was one of the few decrying the nationalist conflagration as "the suicide of civilized Europe."[21]

After accommodating the national spirit and becoming more sedentary, in the first half of the twentieth century the Jesuits seemed to lose much of the critical edge that had made them into a pioneering, controversial global force in the early modern phase of globalization. They became, instead, an antiliberal, antimodern, and still controversial though very much diminished force in the modern phase of globalization.

The cataclysm of the Second World War and the subsequent collapse of the great European empires opened a new phase in the history of Jesuit globalization. Furthering this global consciousness was the determination of world leaders to create international organizations such as the United Nations and the halting emergence of an international language of human rights, initially trapped within the rhetoric of the Cold War but then expanding through the work of such organizations as Amnesty International in the 1970s.

The Jesuits felt keenly the effects of decolonization—from French West Africa to the Philippines—and had already begun forming critiques of the imperial and nationalist projects of the nineteenth and twentieth centuries. Even more important was the impact of the Second Vatican Council and the emergence of a more pervasive sense of a "world church."

Viewed through the prism of a self-confident and globally hegemonic Western secular modernity, the Jesuits now appeared as a much subdued and insignificant phenomenon that did not elicit much scholarly or public attention. But in the 1960s a new conjunction of historical forces contributed to the global Catholic aggiornamento associated with the Second Vatican Council, to the renewal of the Society of Jesus under Superior

General Pedro Arrupe, and to the profound transformation of Latin American Catholicism. The Jesuits had once again become globally visible and controversial.

Western-centric social sciences were presenting the historical processes of modernization, secularization, and Westernization as interrelated and practically synonymous processes, with all of them converging into an increasingly homogeneous global order. Francis Fukuyama's thesis of the end of history as "the end point of mankind's ideological evolution" was just a radical expression of such a global cosmopolitan vision.[22] And yet, at that same moment, modern Western hegemony was yielding to a new and distinct third phase of globalization that differed from the early modern and modern phases. A new, more decentered, global age was emerging.

From the teleological prism of modern globalization, which viewed the future as having been reached already by the hegemonic, liberal, democratic, and capitalist West, the Jesuits and their contributions to early modern global history could easily be ignored as a rightly forgotten, religious idiosyncratic curiosity superseded by the progress of secular history and best left behind in historical archives. But as this third phase of globalization gathers strength, it may not be simply coincidental that today social scientists and global historians have rediscovered the Jesuits as a relevant contemporary global network and, more important, as a significant historical phenomenon that may offer some fresh insights into our understanding of the historical and contemporary processes of globalization.[23]

Globalization through the Prism of the Jesuits

Examining globalization through a Jesuit prism fosters a revisionist perspective that views modern globalization not as something universal and inevitable but as a particular phase of global history that was preceded by an early modern form of globalization before Western hegemony and that is being succeeded by a third new, open, and unprecedented form of globalization after Western hegemony. From this perspective, the patterns of intercultural and interreligious dialogical and dia-practical encounters of the early modern Jesuit global missions may offer some insights and some lessons, both positive and negative, for our contemporary global present. Currently global humanity is facing similar chronic and acute challenges of multicultural and multireligious mutual recognition in its construction of a more peaceful, just, and equitable global order. Moreover, the Jesuits' commitment to a worldwide open and solidaristic human civil society and their dedication to the pragmatic pursuit of a more universal common good remain an unfinished task and a catholic moral imperative.

Alternative Cultural and Religious Models of Globalization

The Jesuit catholic missionary impulse had naturally, as a matter of course, the hegemonic purpose of leading others to the universal conversion to the "true" Catholic faith. This aspect of the early modern Jesuit mission, based on the invidious theological distinction between "true" and "false" religion, at times seemed to justify even forced conversion with the help of secular coercive power, and it sounds repugnant today as one embraces the modern principles of individual religious freedom and religious pluralism. Nevertheless, what makes the Jesuits' global missionary practices still relevant is that, under certain circumstances, they adopted a controversial method of accommodation that today we would call "nativist inculturation." One should avoid, of course, anachronistic interpretations of early modern Jesuit practices from our contemporary global perspective of cultural and religious pluralism. Nevertheless, Alessandro Valignano's method of accommodation, analyzed in Antoni Ucerler's chapter 1, points to a formula of globalization that rejects unidirectional Westernization and opens itself to multicultural encounters and reciprocal learning processes.[24]

Significantly Ucerler's analysis stresses that European Jesuits did not invent the method of cultural accommodation to become effective missionaries; rather, the initiative was pressed upon them by their Japanese and Chinese interlocutors, particularly by Christian converts who often demanded that the Jesuit fathers engage the local culture *on its own terms*. In other words, the method emerged from the very practice of intercultural encounters. Notwithstanding the Jesuits' many limitations, Ucerler's conclusion is that "the rich cultural legacies of the early Jesuits in East Asia are worthy of renewed scrutiny in our own time . . . as an original paradigm or model of intercultural engagement."

Even in Spanish colonial America, where conquest, colonization, reduction of the indigenous peoples, and conversion to Christianity were so inextricably intertwined, José de Acosta already insisted that "hispanización" was not necessary to "preach the Gospel" to the Indians or to "procure their salvation."[25] This rationale was behind the simultaneous publication (i.e., translation from Latin) of the trilingual Lima Catechism (1583) in Spanish, Quechua, and Aymara. It amounts to a formula of globalization of Christianity through the particularization of the universal by going "local," "vernacular," or "native" through a process of reflexive inculturation and acculturation, which theologically amounts to a formula of ever-renewed Christian "incarnation."

This famous and controversial formula of Jesuit cultural accommodation led to the adoption of the Confucian habitus in China by Matteo Ricci, the Brahmin habitus in India by Roberto de Nobili, the Guaraní habitus in the Paraguyan reductions, and, less commendable for us today, the slaveholding habitus in the Jesuit plantations in Brazil and Maryland.[26] It was the differentiation of true universal *religion* and particular *culture*, as well as that between *civilization* and *idolatry*, first introduced by the Jesuits that allowed the various accommodating syntheses of supposedly Christian universalism and cultural particularism.[27] That other missionary orders, and even other Jesuits in India and China, attacked the method so vehemently before it exploded into the Chinese and Malabar Rites Controversies in Rome and Paris indicates the extent to which it challenged Eurocentric notions of a uniform Roman Catholic globalization.[28]

These early Jesuit missions made clear that, in some cases at least, what begins as a one-way mission of Christian evangelization that assumes both the exclusivity of Christianity as the "true religion" and the superiority of Christian European culture turns into a mutual intercultural and interreligious encounter that, under certain circumstances, transforms the missionary as much as it does the native. Of course, the Jesuit missions in Goa and Macau remained embedded within the Portuguese colonial establishments and were fundamentally different from de Nobili's mission to Madurai or Ricci's mission to Beijing. It seems, indeed, that the more the Jesuit missionaries were on their own and in the peripheries, without the support and protection of the Iberian colonial powers, the more favorable became the circumstances for an open-ended, nonhierarchical interaction and a genuine dialogue.

In Ibero-America, by contrast, the colonial circumstance and the assumed superiority not just of Christianity but also of European civilization and culture practically precluded a nonhierarchical interaction and open dialogue with indigenous religions and cultures. Yet even in Ibero-America there were fundamental differences between the Jesuit missions at the center of the viceroyalties of Peru and New Spain and their missions to the indigenous frontiers. Maldavsky's analysis, moreover, reiterates one of the central points of Ucerler's chapter: The method of accommodation was not an invention of European Jesuits applied to different non-European contexts; rather, it emerged from pragmatic interactions at the peripheries.

Jesuit missionaries in Ibero-America were not the only or even the major actors in shaping those intercultural encounters. Indeed, they found themselves constantly having to negotiate and accommodate the many tensions that arose from their position as crucial nodes in many of the interactional networks linking the local populations (natives and criollos, indigenous laborers and *encomenderos*), the urban colleges and rural parishes, the various levels of colonial and ecclesiastical administration and jurisdiction and the very different positions that Jesuits held under the Portuguese *padroado* and the Spanish *patronato real*, the multiple religious orders with their own transnational systems of governance, and the global jurisdiction of the superior general and the pope in Rome.

As indicated in the book's introduction, the Jesuits initiated their mission with the traditional and customary distinction between the true Christian faith, or Catholic religion, and all others: Christian "schismatics" and "heretics," Jewish and Muslim "infidels," and the remaining "pagans" and "idolaters." This classification was based on the "Mosaic distinction" between true and false religion, a distinction that exalts Yahweh, the God of Israel, as the one and only true transcendent God while degrading all other gods to the rank of false idols or demons and their worship to devilish idolatry.[29] Christianity, in its encounter with ancient paganism, had adopted a similar attitude. After the Constantinian establishment, it crystallized in Saint Augustine's eventual defense of state coercion and forced conversion and led to the destruction of pagan temples, the eradication of paganism, and the final establishment of the Nicene Creed as the state religion during the reign of Theodosius.[30]

The tribunal of the Holy Inquisition, which played a similar role of coercive persecution of heresy in the late Middle Ages, was only introduced in Spain rather belatedly by the Catholic kings at the end of the fifteenth century as an instrument of state making, religious confessional homogenization, and ethno-religious cleansing. Such a policy of religious confessionalization led to the expulsion of Jews and Muslims from Spain in 1492, the later expulsion of the Moriscos, and the protracted campaigns against Marranos and conversos, or the so-called New Christians.

It is in this context that we should understand the initial Jesuit missionary encounter with Amerindian religions in the New World, with Coptic Christianity in Ethiopia, or with the religions of Asia. The Jesuits at first continued, albeit somewhat reluctantly, the already established practices of the Portuguese Inquisition in Goa, the destruction of pagan Hindu temples, and the Catholic campaigns for the "extirpation of idolatry" in the Spanish viceroyalty of Peru.[31] But soon the Jesuits, or at least some of their prominent members, began to adopt a more ambiguous, open, at times even dialogical, but, more important, dia-practical relationship with the religious Other. The new praxis began, eventually and mostly unwittingly, to undermine the old religious taxonomy, thus initiating the long historical process of transformation in the direction of the still unsettled contemporary, pluralist global system of religions.

Indeed, what is striking is not that Jesuit missionaries in most respects behaved no differently from other Catholic missionaries but that, under certain circumstances, the Jesuit way of proceeding became peculiarly different, attracting in the process much controversial attention from all quarters, from friends and enemies. Particularly in their encounters with the multifaceted religions of Asia, the old catchall categories of pagan, heathen, or infidel began to collapse, and a new plural system of what later would be called "world religions" began to emerge.[32]

Without in any way attempting to settle the contested debate concerning the role of such colonial encounters and the later emergence of academic Orientalism in European universities, it is undeniable that the Jesuits served as pioneer interlocutors in the religious, cultural, scientific, and artistic encounters between the East and the West and between the Old and New Worlds. Pioneer Jesuits particularly in Japan, China, Tibet, Vietnam, and India played an important role in transmitting and mediating the first knowledge about the foundational texts, religions, cultures, and civilizations of the "Orient," knowledge that would later develop into full-fledged academic "Orientalism."[33]

Chapter 2 by Francis Clooney shows that Jesuit argumentative apologetics were not based on theological arguments proper or on the truth of revelation but on a supposedly universal human reason: They derived from Catholic medieval scholasticism and from the Renaissance humanist tradition. Clooney's critical analysis raises important questions not only about the universalist claims of Christianity but equally about the universalist claims of any cosmopolitan project, religious as well as secular, that envisions the building of a global human civilization as the global expansion of universally human rational principles without taking sufficiently into account the multiplicity of metaphysical, ethical, and civilizational presuppositions and the irremediable human religious and cultural pluralism that it entails. Clooney draws his critical analysis not from the perspective of a postmodern moral and cultural relativism but from the aspiration of what he calls "a truly universal religious rationality."

By contrast, Daniel Madigan's critical analysis of the Jesuit encounter with the world of Islam points to the important distinction between cultural and theological accommodation. In fact, Jesuits evinced a similar hostile and non-dialogical attitude in their encounters with Protestant heretics in Europe or with Eastern Christian schismatics in Eastern Europe, Ethiopia, and India. As Madigan points out, inculturation becomes more difficult when we engage with what we view as a heretical form of our own tradition. Only with the modern recognition of the principle of religious freedom as an individual right based on the sacred dignity of the human person was the old religious taxonomy based on the categorical distinction between true and false religion radically transformed.

The old proposition that "error has no rights" gives way to the proposition that individuals, not doctrines, have rights. Under such a premise, the conditions for interreligious dialogue are also transformed. The principle of individual religious freedom does not need to lead to relativism. It can also facilitate a new kind of interreligious dialogue that takes place between persons as a process of mutual recognition rather than between doctrines as a cognitive-theological disputation.

This does not imply that, in their method of accommodation in Asia during the early modern phase of globalization, the Jesuits anticipated the modern principle of religious freedom or religious pluralism. It only suggests that their openness to cultural pluralism within the premises of Christian universalism did contribute, through complex and mostly indirect ways, to the modern differentiation of religion and culture and to the process of dissociation between Christianity and the secular European culture of the Enlightenment.[34]

Alternative Political Models of Globalization

To understand both the favorable world-historical circumstances that allowed the Jesuits to become such successful pioneer globalizers in the early modern first globalization and the accumulation of hostilities that led to their final suppression on the eve of what the historian C. A. Bayly has described so persuasively as "the birth of the modern world," it is necessary to distinguish between those aspects of the Jesuit project of world evangelization that had elective affinities with the formation of the world-capitalist system and with the globalization of the Westphalian system of nation-states and those that appeared inimical, or at least in critical tension, with what became the hegemonic project of modern Western globalization.[35]

The Jesuit project of world evangelization was predicated on a vision of an open world system of societies in which the right to evangelize, and therefore open access, was taken for granted. It presupposed a global human civil society, and in this respect it had deep elective affinities with a world-capitalist system based on free trade. Ivan Strenski, in fact, has traced convincingly the modern legitimation of economic globalization back to its religious roots in the early modern Catholic project of world evangelization.[36] The right to evangelization and the right to commerce not only went hand in hand in practice but also appeared frequently interchangeably in early modern theological and political-economic texts. The discursive practice only reflected the intertwinement of missionary and colonial predatory practices. But the persistent religious humanitarian critiques of such abusive practices put forth by Dominicans, Jesuits, and members of other religious orders indicate that the project of world evangelization could also be in fundamental tension with the global capitalist project as well as with any project of a universal Christian empire that was indifferent to the dignity of the human person, to the pursuit of the common good, or to the right of indigenous people to protect their own culture from coercive colonization. Contemporary analyses of the theological development of jus gentium by the Schools of Salamanca and Coimbra as the first proto-articulation of an early modern conception of universal human rights in response to predatory colonial practices seem persuasive.[37]

That the religious orders, Jesuits included, were themselves deeply implicated in the Iberian imperial projects also explains how ineffective those critiques proved historically. But the Jesuits' protection of the Guaraní and other indigenous peoples from slave raiders and abusive *encomenderos* remained a persistent source of anti-Jesuitism in colonial Ibero-America. The Guaraní War of the Seven Reductions of 1756 and the unfounded accusation that the Jesuits had instigated the armed rebellion against the Portuguese and Spanish colonial empires served in fact as a critical catalyst for the expulsion of the Society of Jesus from the Catholic kingdoms of Portugal and Spain and put an end to the long history of royal Iberian patronage of the Jesuits.[38]

Pavone's chapter offers a compelling analysis of the intertwining of national and global dynamics that fed the various currents of anti-Jesuitism that led to the suppression. Standard accounts of globalization processes tend to view the dynamics of the expansion of the world system of capitalism as the primary globalizing logic. Yet the parallel and intertwined logic of the global expansion of state territorialization has been and still is, despite all the misleading talk about the end of nationalism or the fading away of the state, of equal relevance in the historical formation of our contemporary world system or world society, which now encompasses all peoples and all territories across the entire globe.

The process of state territorialization had from the beginning two intertwined dynamics—the *internal* dynamics of territorial nation-state formation within Europe that led to the consolidation of the Westphalian system of competing sovereign territorial states and the *external* dynamics of overseas colonial territorial expansion of the European states. The latter could be said to have been initiated by the 1494 Treaty of Tordesillas, whereby the competing Iberian colonial powers, in accordance with the legal fiction of papal jurisdictional *potestas* (authority) over non-Christian territories, accepted papal mediation in drawing the longitudinal meridian separating their future world empires. That other powers, Protestant and Catholic, such as the Dutch Republic, England, and France, did not take seriously the papal jurisdictional claims and initiated their own global colonial expansion, often at the expense of the Iberian powers, only confirms the dynamics of external colonial global territorialization.

The Jesuits were intimately implicated in both "political" processes—the internal European and the external colonial—and played ambiguous and relatively autonomous roles in both. For this very reason anti-Jesuitism—expressed as a critique of Jesuit "meddling in politics," of their operating as "a state within the state," and of the dread of a "Jesuit Republic" or a "global Jesuit empire" supposedly based on a secret Jesuit project of global domination—had so much traction and could persist for so long.[39]

Although particular grievances or concerns connected with specific Jesuit practices may explain any anti-Jesuit outburst at any one time, the persistence, recurrence, and broad character of the many accusations that fed into the "black legend" are only comprehensible if one takes into account the ambivalent, even contradictory location occupied by the Jesuits as a transnational and papal order in the early modern dynamics of globalization. Equally important was the ambiguous and equivocal signification, elicited by their peculiar way of proceeding, that the Jesuits, as a "hermaphrodite religious" order—as Étienne Pasquier labeled the Society—actively engaged in worldly secular affairs. Furthermore, their character as a highly centralized and hierarchical transnational organization with a highly flexible and mobile structure, with ambiguous and overlapping loyalties to various authorities and jurisdictions, and the capacity to accommodate the most diverse local contexts gave the Jesuits certain global structural advantages in the early modern phase of globalization that provoked much envy, dread, and competition from friend and foe alike.[40]

All the conspiratorial myths notwithstanding, there is no shred of evidence of a Jesuit global political project. What the Society clearly had was a project of "world evangelization."[41] But in the same way as the Jesuits adapted flexibly to different circumstances and to the various political structures in different countries in Europe and in overseas colonies, their method of accommodation in non-Western contexts also implied flexible adaptation to the most diverse sociopolitical and cultural systems they encountered. They adapted to the daimyo Warring States system in Japan, the centralized imperial mandarin system in China, the Muslim Mughal Empire in northern India, the Hindu Tamil kingdoms of southern India, and the tribal chiefdoms in Congo, among others.

While some individual Portuguese and Spanish Jesuits may have supported the competing imperial projects of their respective nations, in general the Jesuits were not the advocates of a universal Christian monarchy.[42] Prominent Jesuits often vehemently disagreed about all kinds of geopolitical, national political, and internal issues of Jesuit organizational policy.

The well-known and public polemics between prominent Spanish Jesuits José de Acosta and Alonso Sánchez, particularly their disagreements concerning the proposed Spanish military invasion of China from the Philippines, are a case in point.[43] If one may speak at all of a Jesuit political vision or ultimate political *ratio*, it is found in a rather conventional Thomist scholastic moral and political concern for justice and the common good—a topic Thomas Banchoff explores in chapter 12 of this volume—and for their defense of the early modern jus gentium in international affairs.[44]

Jus gentium or *derecho de gentes*—the moral laws and rights that allow and promote the peaceful coexistence and just interactions of the open world society of nations—was the basis for the Jesuit vision of a world society. Francisco Suárez, the Jesuits' most influential political theologian, wrote in *De Legibus* (1612) a passage reminiscent of Francisco de Vitoria's political theology:

> The human race, howsoever divided into various peoples and kingdoms, always has a certain unity, not only specific, but also as it were political and moral, which is indicated by the natural precept of mutual love and mercy, a precept extended to all, even strangers and of whatsoever reason. Therefore, although each perfect city, state or kingdom constitutes in itself a perfect community consisting of its own members, nevertheless each of them is also a member in a certain fashion of this universe, so far as it concerns the human race.[45]

This paragraph alerts us to the particular and contingent institutionalization of the isomorphic Westphalian world system of national societies. World society could have developed more in the direction of a system that accommodated the diverse preexisting civilizational forms and cultures and less in the isomorphic direction it took once the colonial imposition of Western hegemony forced all societies to follow the Westphalian territorial model. The Jesuit project of world evangelization was predicated on a vision of an open world system of societies. But the debate between Sánchez and Acosta concerning the evangelization of China indicates that their fundamental disagreement rested on the legitimacy or illegitimacy of the use of force (*jus belli*) to guarantee open access. Valignano's method of accommodation presupposed the missionary's need to adapt to the cultural habitus, civic customs, and political conditions of other civilizations, which were to be treated as equal to European civilization. Evangelization did not imply necessarily straightforward or unidirectional Europeanization.

Western colonial powers reserved for themselves the use of gunboats to guarantee their right to commercial open access. But just as globalization could have happened without imposing the Westphalian territorial state system, open world trade could have developed without the colonial imposition of unfair treaties that forced all Chinese walls to open. An analysis of the Jesuit story of globalization before the triumph of Western hegemony offers this most important lesson: Globalization did not need to happen through the imposition of Western modernization. Western modernity is a contingent historical process, not a functional necessity. It could have been otherwise. Thus, countering theorists of Western modernity such as Anthony Giddens, one may insist that globalization is not simply "a consequence of modernity," or "an enlargement of modernity, from society to the world," as if "modernity is inherently globalizing."[46] Globalization is neither Western "modernity on a global scale" nor necessarily Westernization.

But in the end, the Jesuit alternative vision of a global human society was clearly defeated. All the accusations and stereotypes about Jesuit conspiratorial politics, internal as well as external, converged and merged into the final suppression. The verdict was nearly unanimous: The Jesuits were supposedly guilty as charged. Anti-Jesuitism was shared not only by Protestants, Jansenists, and enlightened philosophes alike but also by Catholic sovereigns, national Catholic hierarchies, national bourgeoisies, Catholic religious orders, and even the papal curia. All four types of anti-Jesuitism so eloquently analyzed by Sabina Pavone had now merged into one. Ultimately nobody came to the Jesuits' public defense. Even the infamously polemicist Jesuits accepted their cruel fate silently and obediently *perinde ac cadaver* (in the manner of a corpse). Only by abandoning their hermaphrodite status and becoming *normal persons*—either regular clergy, secular clergy, or laity—and then abandoning their interstitial transnational status and becoming *normal subjects* of some sovereign territorial state could the Jesuits escape their fate of becoming stateless displaced persons and refugees.

Lessons from the Suppression of the Jesuits and Its Aftermath

The uncontested suppression of the Jesuits in the second half of the eighteenth century would seem to indicate that their global practices were in fundamental tension with all the ascending global forces: the triumphant structural forces of capitalist and Westphalian globalization that were being carried out by North Atlantic Protestant powers; the alternative secular cosmopolitan project of the Enlightenment, which thereafter would inform global educational systems; and even the two other Catholic models competing over the direction of global Catholicism—namely, plural national Catholic Churches under royal patronage (the equivalent to the Protestant Erastian Landeskirche) versus a uniform transnational Catholic regime under centralized Roman control. The latter project had been gaining traction since the establishment of the Sacred Congregation for the Propagation of the Faith in 1622.

After the papal restoration of the Society of Jesus in 1814, only the project of global Catholicism through centralized Romanization remained extant. The demise of the ancien régime had brought to an end the project of plural national Catholic Churches under royal patronage. From now on, neither the liberal, secular, national state nor the Vatican would countenance such a project. The Jesuits had lost any autonomy they originally had between their papal and royal patronage in the early modern era. Now they truly became a transnational papal order convincingly carrying the project of uniform, global Catholic Romanization and often against the emerging system of liberal democratic national states. As McGreevy documents in this volume, the restored Jesuits once again embraced global mobility, but they could hardly be viewed as pioneer globalizers any longer. The dominant dynamics of capitalist and nation-state globalization had taken a radical secular direction that the Jesuits most often resisted. The renewed Jesuit global mission was now perceived, even by many Catholics, as a reaction to the hegemonic global historical forces of political and economic liberalism, nationalism, and secularism.

As indicated before, this spirit of resistance still gave the Jesuits in the nineteenth century some critical edge. By the beginning of the twentieth century, however, the Jesuits seemed to have accommodated both the national and the bourgeois spirit. Leaving behind the pastoral frontiers, they had settled at the urban centers of national societies, running their prestigious upper-middle-class educational institutions. They also had lost much of the transnational mobility that had made them suspect to state power. They had largely accommodated to the establishment.

However, in the second part of this volume, the chapters analyzing contemporary perspectives make clear that since the 1960s the Jesuits have been undergoing a new global transformation that parallels transformations in global Catholicism that are in tune with the emergence of a new global age. As the chapters by Banchoff on higher education and by David Hollenbach on Vatican II and its legacies demonstrate, the Jesuits have again built an important global network with an active presence throughout the world, even though they are relatively much smaller, less central, and more removed from the current hegemonic economic, political, and ideological forces of globalization. While the order's presence and relevance are clearly declining in the West, it remains significant in Latin America and is growing in Africa and Asia. Today India has become the region with the largest number of Jesuits in the world. Though numerically small, they also have a symbolically relevant presence in East Asia and parts of Southeast Asia.

Most significantly Jesuits today find themselves increasingly at the peripheries rather than at the centers of globalization. Their mission has also been transformed and has become controversial again. In this connection, Maria Clara Bingemer's chapter 9 takes up the case of liberation theology and the struggle for social justice embodied in the life and martyrdom of Ignacio Ellacuría, SJ. In the next contribution to the volume, Joseph Puthenkalam and Drew Rau examine the experience of the Jesuit social apostolate in South Asia. And in chapter 11 Peter Balleis tracks the vital work of the Jesuit Refugee Service created by Fr. Pedro Arrupe in 1980. In these and other contexts, the writers show the mission of the Society of Jesus is being defined less by conversion and civilization—that is, bringing the people on the margins closer to the center—and more by being a witness and accompanying the people at the margins, or those who are being affected most negatively by contemporary processes of globalization. Their mission is, in this respect, anti-systemic and against the current. They have regained a critical edge.

Lessons for Today

In conclusion one may say that the story of the Jesuit project of early modern globalization might still hold important lessons for us. Undoubtedly the practical experiment in Christian inculturation that the Jesuits, following Valignano's instructions, were willing to probe in Japan, in China, and in the Madurai mission ultimately failed for a combination of geopolitical, civilizational, and ecclesiastical reasons. But if one takes seriously the argument that processes of globalization are contingent historical processes, not functionally necessary processes or consequences of modernity, then the most important lesson from the global story of the Society of Jesus is that different historical processes—that is, different outcomes in the Jesuit Christian encounter in Japan, China, and India—could have led to a different age of globalization.

One enters thereby into the highly problematic yet illuminating field of speculative "what-if" stories. The merit of such a theoretical exercise or thought experiment resides not so much in its ability to construct rational social structures freed from any particular practical constraint but rather in its facilitating the critical reflexivity that is required to free ourselves from what Charles Taylor calls "the unthought"—that is, to allow us to reflect critically upon the deep, taken-for-granted structures of our own epistemic and metaphysical presuppositions.

Every dialogical process of inculturation and every deep and open intercivilizational encounter create the possibility for such critical reflexivity. As we are entering a new, decentered global age after Western hegemony, the Jesuits' global story of dialogical inculturation and of deep intercivilizational encounters still contains valuable lessons for us. Most of the issues they grappled with and their attempts to find viable resolutions to the tensions between universality and particularity, and between the global and the local, are still with us.

Certainly one can easily hear echoes of the old Rites Controversies and of the anti-Jesuit diatribes in the following discourses: contemporary debates between cosmopolitan universalist globalizers and culturalist proponents of multiple modernities and of glocalization; discussions concerning the alleged universality, or the Western particularity, of human rights; calls for the establishment of an effective transnational global authority that enforces the right to humanitarian access to impede genocide; appeals for the transnational right to interfere in the internal affairs of countries to protect individuals and groups from their own regimes to the point of promoting regime change, or tyrannicide; and the assertions of the rights of refugees and immigrants to cross borders and to be guaranteed asylum.

How is the world system of societies to be regulated more fairly and more peacefully, with greater recognition of the irremediable civilizational and cultural diversity that characterizes humankind? How is the world-capitalist system to be regulated more equitably and more justly? How is one to protect the rights and the dignity of each and every individual person? How can we all best advance the more universal common good globally? These questions are and must perforce remain open for as long as the globalization of humanity remains an open, contingent, historical process. Besides the many concrete practical lessons, positive and negative, that one may draw from their global practices, the open and contingent character of world-historical processes is perhaps the most important theoretical lesson that one can gain from examining the Jesuit experience.

Notes

1. Roland Robertson, *Globalization: Social Theory and Global Culture* (London: Sage, 1992).

2. Cf. Geoffrey C. Gunn, *First Globalization: The Eurasian Exchange, 1550–1800* (Lanham MD: Rowman & Littlefield, 2003); C. A. Bayly, *The Birth of the Modern World, 1780–1914: Global Connections and Comparisons* (Malden, MA: Blackwell, 2004); and C. A. Bayly, "'Archaic' and 'Modern' Globalization in the

Eurasian and African Arena, ca. 1750–1850," in *Globalization in World History*, ed. A. G. Hopkins (New York: Norton, 2002), 45–73.

3. John W. O'Malley, SJ, *Saints or Devils Incarnate? Studies in Jesuit History* (Leiden: Brill, 2013), 147–64; and John O'Malley, *The First Jesuits* (Cambridge, MA: Harvard University Press, 1993), 12.

4. Quoted in C. R. Boxer, *The Portuguese Seaborne Empire, 1415–1825* (New York: Knopf, 1969), 65; and Luke Clossey, "Merchants, Migrants, Missionaries, and Globalization in the Early-Modern Pacific," *Journal of Global History* 1 (March 2006): 41–58.

5. Dauril Alden, *The Making of an Enterprise: The Society of Jesus in Portugal, Its Empire, and Beyond, 1540–1750* (Stanford: Stanford University Press, 1996). Also see C. R. Boxer, *The Church Militant and Iberian Expansion, 1440–1770* (Baltimore: Johns Hopkins University Press, 1978).

6. As quoted in Alden, *Making of an Enterprise*, 668.

7. See also Sabina Pavone, *The Wily Jesuits and the* Monita Secreta*: The Forged Secret Instructions of the Jesuits; Myth and Reality* (St. Louis: Institute of Jesuit Sources, 2005).

8. O'Malley, *First Jesuits*, 18.

9. Simon Ditchfield, "What Did Natural History Have to Do with Salvation? José de Acosta SJ (1540–1600) in the Americas," in *God's Bounty? The Churches and the Natural World*, ed. Peter D. Clarke and Tony Claydon (Woodbridge, UK: Boydell Press, 2010), 144–68.

10. Ignatius of Loyola and the Society of Jesus, *The Constitutions of the Society of Jesus*, trans. George E. Ganss (St. Louis: Institute of Jesuit Sources, 1970), 66–67.

11. New historiography in the last two decades has challenged traditional interpretations. Cf. John W. O'Malley, SJ, *Trent and All That: Renaming Catholicism in the Early Modern Era* (Cambridge, MA: Harvard University Press, 2000); Jean Delumeau, *Le Catholicisme entre Luther et Voltaire* (Paris: Presses universitaires de France, 1971); and Robert Bireley, SJ, *The Refashioning of Catholicism, 1450–1700: A Reassessment of the Counter Reformation* (Washington, DC: Catholic University of America Press, 1999).

12. R. Po-chia Hsia, *The World of Catholic Renewal, 1540–1770* (Cambridge: Cambridge University Press, 2005), 7.

13. Simon Ditchfield, *Papacy & Peoples: The Making of Roman Catholicism as a World Religion* (Oxford: Oxford University Press, forthcoming).

14. Emanuele Colombo, *Convertire i musulmani: L'esperienza di un gesuita spagnolo del Seicento* (Milan: Bruno Mondadori, 2007); Emanuele Colombo, "Jesuits and Islam in Seventeenth-Century Europe: War, Preaching and Conversions," in *L'Islam visto da occidente: Cultura e religione del Seicento europeo di fronte all'Islam*, ed. Bernard Heyberger et al. (Genoa: Marietti, 2009), 315–40; and Emanuele Colombo, "Jesuits, Jews and Muslims," *Archivum Historicum Societatis Iesu* 79, no. 158 (2010): 419–26.

15. Luke Clossey, "An Edifying End: Global Salvific Catholicism," in *Salvation and Globalization in the Early Jesuit Missions* (New York: Cambridge University Press, 2008), 238–57.

16. O'Malley, *Saints or Devils*, 199.

17. Steven J. Harris, "Mapping Jesuit Science: The Role of Travel in the Geography of Knowledge," in *The Jesuits: Cultures, Sciences, and the Arts, 1540–1773*, ed. John W. O'Malley, SJ, et al. (Toronto: University of Toronto Press, 1999), 212–40; and Mordechai Feingold, ed., *Jesuit Science and the Republic of Letters* (Cambridge, MA: MIT Press, 2003).

18. John W. Meyer et al., "World Society and the Nation-State," *American Journal of Sociology* 103, no. 1 (July 1997): 144–75.

19. Robertson, *Globalization*, 25.

20. Cf. Anthony Pagden, *The Fall of Natural Man: The American Indian and the Origins of Comparative Ethnology* (Cambridge: Cambridge University Press, 1982); and Guillermo Wilde, ed., *Saberes de la conversión: Jesuítas, indígenas e imperios coloniales en las fronteras de la cristiandad* (Buenos Aires: Editorial San Benito, 2011).

21. Benedict XV tirelessly denounced the war as a "scourge," a "horrible and useless slaughter" that was turning the world into "a hospital and a charnel house." See J. Derek Holmes, *The Papacy in the Modern World, 1914–1978* (New York: Crossroad, 1981), 1–19.

22. Francis Fukuyama, "The End of History?," *The National Interest* (Summer 1989): 3–18.

23. Simon Ditchfield, "Of Missions and Models: The Jesuit Enterprise (1540–1773) Reassessed in Recent Literature," *Catholic Historical Review* 93, no. 2 (April 2007): 325–43.

24. The literature on Valignano and the Jesuit method of accommodation is immense. Cf. Josef Franz Schütte, SJ, *Valignano's Mission Principles for Japan*, 2 vols. (St. Louis: Institute of Jesuit Sources, 1980–85); Adolfo Tamburello, M. Antoni J. Ucerler, SJ, and Marisa Di Russo, eds., *Alessandro Valignano S.I.: Uomo del Rinascimento, Ponte tra Oriente e Occidente* (Rome: IHSI, 2008); M. Antoni J. Ucerler, SJ, ed., *Christianity and Cultures: Japan & China in Comparison, 1543–1644* (Rome: IHSI, 2009); Charles E. Ronan, SJ, and Bonnie B. C. Oh, eds., *East Meets West: The Jesuits in China, 1582–1773* (Chicago: Loyola University Press, 1988); Jacques Gernet, *China and the Christian Impact: A Conflict of Cultures* (Cambridge: Cambridge University Press, 1985); Nicolas Standaert, SJ, *Methodology in View of Contact between Cultures: The China Case in the 17th Century* (Hong Kong: The Chinese University of Hong Kong, 2002); and Nicolas Standaert, *L'"autre" dans la mission: Leçons à partir de la Chine* (Brussels: Lessius, 2003).

25. José de Acosta, SJ, *De Procuranda Indorum Salute o Predicación del Evangelio en las Indias* (1588; repr., Alicante, Spain: Biblioteca Virtual Miguel de Cervantes, 1999).

26. On the Maryland plantations, see Thomas J. Murphy, SJ, *Jesuit Slaveholding in Maryland, 1717–1838* (New York: Routledge, 2001).

27. Joan-Pau Rubiés, "The Concept of Cultural Dialogue and the Jesuit Method of Accommodation: Between Idolatry and Civilization," *Archivum Historicum Societatis Iesu* 74, no. 147 (2005): 237–80.

28. On the internal Jesuit disputes concerning missionary methods in India, see Ines G. Županov, *Disputed Mission: Jesuit Experiments and Brahmanical Knowledge in Seventeenth-Century India* (New Delhi: Oxford University Press, 1999).

29. Jan Assmann, *The Price of Monotheism* (Stanford: Stanford University Press, 2010).

30. S. N. Balagangadhara, *"The Heathen in His Blindness . . .": Asia, the West and the Dynamic of Religion* (Leiden: Brill, 1994) offers a comparative analysis of the encounter of ancient Christianity with Hellenic and Roman paganism and the Christian-European encounter with the religious "Other."

31. Ines G. Županov, *Missionary Tropics: The Catholic Frontier in India (16th–17th Centuries)* (Ann Arbor: University of Michigan Press, 2005); Juan Carlos Estenssoro Fuchs, *Del paganismo a la santidad: La incorporación de los indios del Perú al catolicismo (1532–1750)* (Lima: Instituto Francés de Estudios Andinos, 2003); and Aliocha Maldavsky, *Vocaciones inciertas: Misión y misioneros en la provincia jesuita del Perú en los siglos XVI y XVII* (Sevilla: Consejo Superior de Investigaciones Científicas, 2012).

32. The literature on the colonial encounter, Orientalism, the emergence of the modern secular category of "religion," and the "invention" of the world religions is immense and controversial. Cf. Stuart B. Schwartz, ed., *Implicit Understandings: Observing, Reporting, and Reflecting on the Encounters between Europeans and Other Peoples in the Early Modern Era* (New York: Cambridge University Press, 1994); Richard King, *Orientalism and Religion: Postcolonial Theory, India and "The Mystic East"* (London: Routledge, 1999); Talal Asad, *Genealogies of Religion: Discipline and Reasons of Power in Christianity and Islam* (Baltimore: Johns Hopkins University Press, 1993); Tomoko Masuzawa, *The Invention of World Religions: Or, How European Universalism Was Preserved in the Language of Pluralism* (Chicago: University of Chicago Press, 2005); Peter Beyer, *Religions in Global Society* (New York: Routledge, 2006); and Peter van der Veer, *The Modern Spirit of Asia: The Spiritual and the Secular in China and India* (Princeton: Princeton University Press, 2014).

33. Urs App, *The Birth of Orientalism* (Philadelphia: University of Pennsylvania Press, 2010). A majority of the names—more than two thirds—on App's list of early modern European Orientalists are Jesuits. See also Lionel M. Jensen, *Manufacturing Confucianism: Chinese Tradition and Universal Civilization* (Durham, NC: Duke University Press, 1997); Paul Rule, *K'ung-tzu or Confucius? The Jesuit Interpretation of Confucianism* (Sydney: Allen & Unwin, 1986); D. E. Mungello, *Curious Land: Jesuit Accommodation and the Origins of Sinology* (Honolulu: University of Hawaii Press, 1989); Philip Caraman, SJ, *Tibet: The Jesuit Century* (St. Louis: Institute of Jesuit Sources, 1997); Trent Pomplun, *A Jesuit on the Roof of the World: Ippolito Desideri's Mission to Tibet* (Oxford: Oxford University Press, 2010); Peter C. Phan, *Mission and Catechesis: Alexandre de Rhodes and Inculturation in Seventeenth-Century Vietnam* (Maryknoll, NY: Orbis Books, 1998); Roberto de Nobili, SJ, *Preaching Wisdom to the Wise: Three Treatises by Roberto de Nobili, S.J., Missionary and Scholar in 17th Century India*, trans. Anand Amaladass, SJ, and Francis X. Clooney, SJ (St. Louis: Institute of Jesuit Sources, 2000); and Ângela Barreto Xavier and Ines G. Županov, eds., *Catholic Orientalism: Portuguese Empire, Indian Knowledge (16th–18th Centuries)* (New Delhi: Oxford University Press, 2015).

34. Rubiés, "Concept of Cultural Dialogue," 270–80.

35. Bayly, *Birth of the Modern World*.
36. Ivan Strenski, "The Religion in Globalization," *Journal of the American Academy of Religion* 72, no. 3 (2004): 631–52.
37. Peter Stamatov, *The Origins of Global Humanitarianism: Religion, Empires, and Advocacy* (New York: Cambridge University Press, 2013).
38. Barbara Anne Ganson, *The Guaraní under Spanish Rule in the Río de la Plata* (Stanford: Stanford University Press, 2003).
39. On Jesuit politics, cf. Dominique Bertrand, SJ, *La politique de Saint Ignace de Loyola: L'analyse sociale* (Paris: Les Éditions du Cerf, 1985); Robert Bireley, SJ, *The Jesuits and the Thirty Years War: Kings, Courts, and Confessors* (Cambridge: Cambridge University Press, 2003); and Magnus Mörner, *The Political and Economic Activities of the Jesuits in the La Plata Region: The Habsburg Era* (Stockholm: Victor Petersons Bokindustri Aktiebolag, 1953).
40. Pierre-Antoine Fabre and Catherine Maire, eds., *Les Antijésuites: Discours, figures et lieux de l'antijésuitisme à l'époque moderne* (Rennes: Presses universitaires de Rennes, 2010); Peter Burke, "The Black Legend of the Jesuits: An Essay in the History of Social Stereotypes," in *Christianity and Community in the West: Essays for John Bossy*, ed. Simon Ditchfield (Aldershot, UK: Ashgate, 2001), 165–82; and Susana Monreal, Sabina Pavone, and Guillermo Zermeño, eds., *Antijesuitismo y filojesuitismo: Dos identidades ante la restauración* (Mexico City: Universidad Iberoamericana, 2014). On the Jesuit organizational structure, see Markus Friedrich, *Der lange Arm Roms? Globale Verwaltung und Kommunikation im Jesuitenorden, 1540–1773* (Frankfurt: Campus, 2011); and Markus Friedrich, "Communication and Bureaucracy in the Early Modern Society of Jesus," *Zeitschrift für Schweizerische Religions- und Kirchengeschichte* 101 (2007): 49–75.
41. John Patrick Donnelly, SJ, "Antonio Possevino's Plan for World Evangelization," *The Catholic Historical Review* 74, no. 2 (April 1988): 179–98.
42. Franz Bosbach, *Monarchia universalis: Ein politischer Leitbegriff der frühen Neuzeit* (Göttingen, Germany: Vandenhoeck & Ruprecht, 1988).
43. Michela Catto, "Una cruzada contra la China: El diálogo entre Antonio Sánchez y José de Acosta en torno a una guerra justa al Celeste Imperio," in Wilde, *Saberes de la conversión*, 441–63; and Ana Carolina Hosne, "Lo deseable y lo posible: La visión y representación de China en la obra de José de Acosta," *Archivum Historicum Societatis Iesu* 81, no. 162 (2012): 481–514.
44. Harro Höpfl, *Jesuit Political Thought: The Society of Jesus and the State, c. 1540–1630* (Cambridge: Cambridge University Press, 2004).
45. Cited in Clossey, *Salvation and Globalization*, 254.
46. Anthony Giddens, *The Consequences of Modernity* (Stanford: Stanford University Press, 1990), 29, 63, and 177.

Contributors

Peter Balleis, SJ, is the international director of the Jesuit Refugee Service in Washington, DC.

Thomas Banchoff is vice president for global engagement at Georgetown University, professor in the Department of Government and the Walsh School of Foreign Service, and director of the university's Berkley Center for Religion, Peace, and World Affairs.

Maria Clara Lucchetti Bingemer is a full professor of theology at the Pontifical Catholic University of Rio de Janeiro, Brazil.

José Casanova is a professor of sociology at Georgetown University and a senior fellow at the university's Berkley Center for Religion, Peace, and World Affairs.

Francis X. Clooney, SJ, is the Parkman Professor of Divinity and a professor of comparative theology at Harvard Divinity School, as well as the director of the school's Center for the Study of World Religions.

David Hollenbach, SJ, is the university chair in Human Rights and International Justice in the Theology Department at Boston College.

Daniel A. Madigan, SJ, is an associate professor of theology and the Jeanette W. and Otto J. Ruesch Family Professor in the Department of Theology at Georgetown University.

Aliocha Maldavsky is a professor of history at Paris West University Nanterre La Défense.

John T. McGreevy is the dean of the College of Arts and Letters at the University of Notre Dame and a professor in its Department of History.

John W. O'Malley, SJ, is a university professor of theology at Georgetown University.

Sabina Pavone is an associate professor of modern history at the University of Macerata in Macerata, Italy.

John Joseph Puthenkalam, SJ, is the dean of the Graduate School of Global Environmental Studies and a professor in the faculty of economics at Sophia University, Tokyo, Japan.

Drew Rau is a research associate at the Berkley Center for Religion, Peace, and World Affairs at Georgetown University.

M. Antoni J. Ucerler, SJ, is the director and associate professor at the Ricci Institute for Chinese-Western Cultural History at the University of San Francisco, a research scholar and lecturer in Japanese history at the Oriental Institute at the University of Oxford, and a member of Oxford's Research Centre for Japanese Language and Linguistics.

Index

"Abrahamic faiths," 10, 80. *See also* Islam; Judaism
accommodation. *See* culture, accommodation of
accompaniment, 181–82
Acosta, José de, 10, 97, 103, 157–58, 270, 277
Acquaviva, Claudio, 29, 34, 120
Acquaviva, Rudolf, 71, 72, 87n9
Act of Supremacy (England), 115
Acts: 2:1-13, 31; 15:20, 30; 17:23-25, 36
adivasi, 216–17
Afghanistan, 21, 74, 214, 232, 235
Africa, 5, 14, 18, 132, 229. *See also specific countries*
African Institute for Economic and Social Development, 249
"Age of Discovery," 27, 131, 241
Ā'īna-i haqq-numā (The Truth-revealing mirror) (Xavier), 72. *See also Fuente de Vida* (Xavier)
Akbar (Mughal Emperor), 10, 70–75, 87n9, 88n24, 89n37
aldeamento system, 94
Alfaro, Francisco de, 99
Algeria, 132, 140
Amaladoss, Michael, 18, 179
American Revolution, 4
Americas, 10–11, 14–15, 102–5, 123. *See also specific countries*
Anderledy, Anton, 139
Anders, William, 17
Andes, missions in, 97–98
Andrés, Juan, 78
anthropology, 103–4
anti-Jesuitism, 1–2; after reestablishment of Society, 121–24; in Americas, 123; anti-Semitism and, 124; Black Legend in, 113–14; in Counter-Reformation, 116, 121; and cultural accommodation in missions, 118–19; currents of, 114–21; defined, 111; development of, 112–14; in Dostoevsky, 122; eclipse of, 124–26; in Elizabethan England, 115–16; in Enlightenment, 120–21; European revolutions and, 134–35; forms of, 112, 114–21; in Freemasonry, 123; in Germany, 116, 122–23; globalization and, 124; in India, 123–24; in Italy, 122–23, 130n42; Jansenism and, 118, 121; from Jesuits, 119–20; in literature, 127n17; magic and, 116, 127n17; missions and, 113, 123–24; in Montaigne, 113; origin of, 112, 114–15, 124; overview of, 112–14; pamphlets in, 116–17; papal loyalty and, 115, 122–23; in Pascal, 117, 118; Pope Francis and, 125–26; of Protestants, 116, 118, 123; religious, 115–18; Rites Controversy and, 118, 119, 123; Rodrigues, Simão in, 112–13; Russia and, 122; scholarship on, 143n11; social justice and, 112; Vatican II and, 111–12, 125; Vatican-Jesuit connection and, 122–23; women and, 116
anti-Semitism, 124. *See also* Judaism
Aoki Shūzō, 43
apologetics, 49–52, 72. *See also* rebirth
Aquinas, 137, 174
Araoz, Antonio de, 155
Arboleda, Julio, 134
Areopagus, 36–40
Argentina, 123, 196–97. *See also* Pope Francis
Arias de Saavedra, Hernando, 99
Aristotelianism, 29
Aristotle, 147, 150–51
Arrupe, Pedro, 17–20; education and, 161; globalism and, 250; and "Jesuit internationalism," 250–51; Jesuit Refugee Service and, 231; justice and, 125; Latin America and, 192, 193; leadership of, 194; on poverty, 176, 211, 213
Asia, 5, 7, 8, 14, 27–44, 98. *See also specific countries*
"Aspects of European Theology" (Rahner), 171
assassination, 178, 198, 204n35
assimilation, 190
astronomy, 35, 137, 157, 228
Ateneo de Manila University, 142, 245, 249, 251
Athalie (Racine), 159
Attappadi Adivasi Development Initiatives (AADI), 216–17
Audiencia de Charcas, 99

Augustinians, 264
Australia, 132, 229
Austria, 14, 134, 140, 240
Autobiography (Ignatius of Loyola), 182
Axial Age, 3

Badā'ūnī, 'Abd al-Qādir, 73
Balleis, Peter, 180, 280
Balmes, Jaime, 138
Banchoff, Thomas, 277, 279
Bangladesh, 214
baptism, 79–80, 84, 170
Bayly, C. A., 274
Bea, Augustin, 249
Beckx, Peter Jan, 139, 246
Beijing, 7. *See also* China
Beirne, Charles, J., 200
Bellarmine, Robert, 79
Benedict XIV, Pope, 40, 119
Benedict XV, Pope, 268
Benedict XVI, Pope, 192. *See also* Ratzinger, Joseph Cardinal
Bergoglio, Jorge, 141, 196–97, 256. *See also* Pope Francis
Bertrand, Joseph, 59–61, 67n16
Bhutan, 214
Bingemer, Maria Clara Lucchetti, 125, 177, 280
Bismarck, Otto von, 123, 135, 247
Blackfeet tribe, 135
Black Legend, 113–14
"boat people," 233, 251. *See also* refugees
Boff, Leonardo, 195
Bolivia, 240
Boscovich, Roger, 159
Bouchet, Jean Venance, 53, 58–59, 65n3, 67n14
Bouvet, Joachim, 35
Boxer, C. R., 263
Boxer Rebellion, 43
Brahma Purana, 59
Brazil: anti-Jesuitism in, 120, 123; economic growth in, 210; expulsion from, 228; migration to, 229; missions in, 93–94, 100, 102; schools in, 94, 162; social centers in, 193
Brito, John de, 158–59
Buddhism, 18, 28, 91n54; engagement with, 179; rebirth in, 51, 54–55, 60
Burke, Peter, 114

calendar reform, 34–35, 157
Cambodia, 230–31, 233, 251
Cameroon, 18, 177, 178
Campion, Edmund, 116
Campomanes, Pedro Rodrígues de, 121
Canada, 162
Candide (Voltaire), 121
Canisius, Peter, 116
Cano, Melchior, 266
capitalism, 5, 207. *See also* market
Cardiel, José, 103

Carta a las Iglesias (journal), 204n37
Casanova, José, 244
Catechisme des Jésuites (Pasquier), 112
Catechismus Christianae fidei (Valignano), 36–37
Cathay, 74–75, 76
Catherine II of Russia, 121
Catholic Reformation, 97, 98, 100. *See also* Counter-Reformation
Catholic social teaching, 15, 18, 142, 206, 247–49
"Catholic Theological Ethics in the World Church" (conference series), 177–78
Catholic Workers' College, 248
Center for Theological Reflection (University of Central America), 204n37
Central African Republic, 232
Centro Gumilla, 193
Cesarini, Ascanio, 112
Chad, 235
Characteristics of the Social Apostolate of the Society of Jesus, 212
Chardin, Pierre Teilhard de, 225
charity: in *Characteristics of the Social Apostolate of the Society of Jesus*, 212; common good and, 154, 242; in de Nobili, 57; education and, 242, 258n25
Charles V, Holy Roman Emperor, 96
Chiara, Giuseppe, 41
Chile, 96–97, 193, 196
China, 4, 5, 8, 9, 20, 28; American missions vs., 98; ban on missionary activity in, 43; Boxer Rebellion in, 43; calendar reform in, 34–35; cultural accommodation in, 30–31; de Góis in, 74; economic growth in, 210; education in, 34–35, 158; idolatry in, 40; Opium Wars in, 43; rebirth in, 55–56; Ricci's catechism in, 36–37; in Treaty of Nerchinsk, 7, 43
Chinchilla, Perla, 127n9
Cicero, 153–54, 161
cities, missions in, 94–95
civic life, education and, 242–44
Civiltà Cattolica, La (journal), 122, 137, 138, 140
Civil War (United States), 140
civil war, in El Salvador, 19
Clark, Helen, 209
Clavius, Christoph, 157
Clement XI, Pope, 40
Clement XIV, Pope, 12, 13, 121, 137, 159, 228
Cleveland, Grover, 247
climate change, 84–85, 216
Clooney, Francis, 83, 179, 214, 273
Coeurdoux, Gaston-Laurent, 65n2, 67n14
Cold War, 17, 172, 191, 249, 268
Colegio San Ignacio "El Bosque," 196
collaboration, 254
college, as term, 240
Collège de France, 134
Collège Louis-le-Grand, 159
College of Nobles, 159

colleges. *See* education
Colombia, 14, 123, 134, 193, 232
colonial encounter, 102–5
colonial expansion, 1, 3–4, 7–8, 14, 207–8, 262–63. *See also* imperialism
colonialism: assimilation and, 190; education and, 228, 245–46; "Jesuit system" and, 111; technology and, 226. *See also* decolonization; imperialism
colonial societies, missions and, 99–102
Columbus, Christopher, 226
Commentary (Monserrate), 70
common good, 2; Catholic social thought and, 247–49; charity and, 154, 242; in charter, 154; in Cicero, 153–54; education and, 151, 161, 164, 242–44, 246–47; as goal of Society, 154, 155; justice and, 15, 153–54, 161; missions and, 175; and organizational structure of Jesuits, 115; today, Jesuits and, 175–79; universalism and, 174–75; Vatican II and, 170, 171, 176, 249–55
communication: in contemporary globalization, 5; education and, 151; in *Gaudium et spes*, 249; in globalization, 224–26; Jesuit, 102, 227; missions and, 98; in modern globalization, 4; in objective dimension of globalization, 3; poverty and, 212
Confucianism, 9, 30–31, 37, 39, 118
Congo, 140, 232, 235
Congregation de Propaganda Fide, 39, 113, 119
Constitutions, 95, 114–15, 116–17, 118, 163, 175, 242
conversion(s): in Americas, 94; as assimilation, 190; colonial regime and, 103; idolatry and, 30; knowledge as tool in, 102; of Muslims, 74, 90n40. *See also* missions
Costa Rica, 14
Côte d'Ivoire, 249
Council of Jerusalem, 30, 40
Council of the Indies, 99
Council of Trent, 98
Counter-Reformation, 6, 7, 116, 121, 264. *See also* Catholic Reformation
Cristo Rey schools, 162
Cross of Christ, 30
Cuban Revolution, 191
culture: accommodation of, in missionary work, 28–31, 92–93, 118–19, 158–59, 208, 270–71; adoption of Christian, 104–5; adoption of native, in missionary work, 8–9; "pagan," 10
cura personalis, 20, 150, 219, 239, 245, 253
curriculum, 33, 101, 137, 155–56. *See also* education

Daniélou, Jean, 125
death threats, 198, 204n38. *See also* murder
Declaration on Religious Freedom, 172
decolonization, 123–24, 191, 268

De Legibus (Suárez), 277
democracy, 5, 138, 173–74, 258n19
Democratic Republic of the Congo, 140, 232, 235
De Officiis (On Responsibility for Others) (Cicero), 153–54
De rege et regis institutione (Le Paige), 117–18
Desideri, Ippolito, 53, 66n13
development. *See* human development
devotio moderna, 31–32
dialogue, interreligious, 18, 51, 69, 179
Dictamen fiscal de expulsión de los jesuitas de España (Campomanes), 121
Didier, Hugues, 73, 75, 76–77, 86n3, 89n39
Dignitatis humanae (Second Vatican Council), 17, 249. *See also* Vatican II
displaced persons, 231–32. *See also* refugees
Ditchfield, Simon, 264
Dogmatic Constitution of the Church, 44, 170
Dominicans, 118, 190, 241, 264
Dominus ac redemptor (Clement XIV), 121
Dostoevsky, Fyodor, 122

Earthrise (Anders), 17
economy. *See* market
Ecuador, 14, 134
education, 11–12, 20; accommodation in, 158–59; in Americas, 100–101, 195–96, 197–98, 200; in Brazil, 94; Catholic social thought and, 247–49; centralization in, 241; charity and, 242, 258n25; in Chinese missions, 34–35, 158; Christianity and, 148; Cicero and, 153–54, 161; civic life and, 242–44; colonialism and, 228, 245–46; common good and, 151, 161, 164, 242–44, 246–47; communication and, 151; contemporary, 161–62; Cristo Rey schools in, 162; curriculum in, 155–56; *devotio moderna* and, 32; Ellacuría and, 197–200; in El Salvador, 197–98, 252; emergence of Jesuit tradition of, 147–48, 240–44; ethics and, 150, 161, 163; expansion of, 155; Fe y Alegría system and, 162, 176, 195, 212; goals in, 149–51; humanism and, 148, 150–51, 153–55, 241, 243; Ignatius of Loyola on, 243; immigrants and, 229, 247; in India, 158–59, 162; institutions of schooling in, 149–51; in Japan, 9, 32–34, 155–56, 162, 228; Jesuit Refugee Service and, 180–81; in "Jesuit system," 111; justice and, 154, 161, 176–77, 239; languages in, 158; literary tradition in, 148, 150; in Middle Ages, 147; missions and, 148; modernity and, 265; in Mughal Empire, 71; Muslim, 71; Nicolás on, 224, 233–35, 253–54; online, 233–37; as overshadowing ministry, 218–19; poverty and, 197–98; professionalization in, 147; public, 134; *Ratio studiorum (Plan of*

education (*continued*)
Studies) and, 9, 15, 32, 136, 159–60, 227–28, 241, 243, 257n11; and restoration of Society, 136–37, 159–61, 244–46; social mission of, 197–200; *Spiritual Exercises* and, 151, 152–53, 163, 253; in United States, 162, 176–77, 244–45, 247; unity and, 241; universities in, 156–59; Valignano and, 155–56, 158; values in, 149; Vatican II and, 249–55
Ellacuría, Ignacio, 19, 177–78, 189, 197–201, 204n41, 252, 280
El Salvador, 14, 19, 178, 196, 197–98, 200
Emerson, Ralph Waldo, 136
empires. *See* colonial expansion; colonialism; imperialism
Endō, Shūsaku, 41–42, 47n29
Enlightenment, 120–21, 160, 267
Epictetus, 153
Erasmus, 153
Estenssoro Fuchs, Juan Carlos, 103
ethics: Confucianism and, 37; education and, 150, 161, 163; globalization and, 177, 206–7; in Murray, 173; poverty and, 201
Ethiopia, 10, 71, 272, 273
Eucharist, 170. *See also* sacraments
Evangelii gaudium (Francis), 220, 256
evangelization. *See* Gospel; missions
Exposcit debitum (Julius III), 184n14

faith: in Coeurdoux, 67n14; in de Nobili, 57; in Endō, 42; in Gregory XV, 39; justice and, 176, 177, 178–79; meaning and, 173; reconciliation of, with intellectual currents, 138; in Uchimura, 40–41
Fenicio, Giacomo, 53
Ferdinand, Franz, 140
Ferreira, Cristóvão, 41, 42
Fe y Alegría system, 162, 176, 195, 212
1 Corinthians 1:23, 30
First Jesuits, The (O'Malley), 178
1 Peter 3:15, 35, 44
First Vatican Council, 111, 122, 141
Flathead tribe, 135
Fonseca, Pedro da, 33
Fordham University, 61, 258n26
"Forgotten Ellacuría, The: What Must Not Be Allowed to Decay" (Sobrino), 198–99
"Formula of the Institute of the Society of Jesus" (Ignatius of Loyola), 7, 15, 174, 241–42, 262–63
Foyaca, Manuel, 192–93
France, 13–14, 123, 134, 140, 246, 248. *See also* University of Paris
Francis, Pope, 6, 20, 21; on accompaniment, 181–82; anti-Jesuitism and, 125–26; on globalization, 2, 206, 217; importance of poverty to, 220; on justice, 201. *See also* Bergoglio, Jorge
Franciscans, 118, 190, 241, 264

Franco-Prussian War, 140
Frankfurt Parliament, 135
freedom, 50, 55–56, 131, 138–39, 172–75. *See also* liberation theology
free market. *See* market
Freemasonry, 123
French Revolution, 4, 14, 122, 160, 267
From Evangelical to Catholic by Way of the East (Wallace), 62
frontier missions, 96–97
Fuente de Vida (Xavier), 72, 78, 84
Fukuyama, Francis, 268
Funai, Japan, 8, 32, 156, 242

Galatians 3:28, 30
Gannon, Robert, 258n26
Gaudium et spes (Second Vatican Council), 17, 170, 249–50. *See also* Vatican II
General Congregation: Thirteenth, 259n33; Thirty-Fifth, 179; Thirty-First, 250; Thirty-Fourth, 18, 178–79; Twenty-Eighth, 258n25; Twenty-First, 137; Twenty-Ninth, 192. *See also* Thirty-Second General Congregation
Georgetown University, 177, 247
Gerbillon, Jean-François, 35, 43
Germany, 6, 14, 140; anti-Jesuitism in, 116, 122–23; education in, 246; expulsion from, 135; religious segregation in, 133. *See also* Prussia
Gesuita moderno, Il (Gioberti), 123, 135
Ghost Seer, The (Schiller), 127n17
Giddens, Anthony, 6, 278
Gioberti, Vincenzo, 123, 135
Giudicelli, Christophe, 104
globalization: alternative models of, 270–78; anti-Jesuitism and, 124; contemporary, 5, 16–21; defined, 3, 82; dynamics of, 2–4; early modern, 1, 4, 6–13, 93, 261–69; emergence of term, 2; God and, 82–83, 241; historical setting of, 207–9; humanism and, 265–69; Jesuit engagement with, 211–13; modern, 4–5, 13–16; modernity and, 5–6, 278, 280; objective processes of, 3, 72; phases of, 4–6; pluralism and, 81–84; Pope Francis on, 2, 206; and restoration of Society, 141–42; Stanford world polity school of, 265–66; subjective dimensions of, 3, 5, 211; through prism of Jesuits, 269–80
God: accompaniment and, 182; Buddhism and, 28; in Chinese missions, 37–38; cultural accommodation and, 29–30; in foundation of Society, 174; globalization and, 82–83, 241; Hinduism and, 60; Islam and, 79, 80–81; partiality of, 199; unified vision of, 82–83; union with, meaning and, 173; Vatican II and, 170–71. *See also* Holy Spirit; Trinity
Góis, Bento de, 69, 74–77, 85
Golden Country, The (Ōgon no kuni), 42
Gómez, Pedro, 33

González de Santalla, Tirso, 69, 77–81, 84, 85, 90n40
good. *See* common good
Gospel: in China, Ricci and, 38–39; in East Asia, 35; globalism and, 189; Islam and, 84; in Jerome Xavier, 87n12; Jesuit Refugee Service and, 233; Pentecost and, 31. *See also* Jesus Christ; missions
grace, 31, 37, 170–71, 199, 200
Grande, Rutilio, 198
Grant, Ulysses S., 43
Greene, Graham, 41
Gregorian calendar, 157
Gregory XIII, Pope, 157
Gregory XV, Pope, 39
Gregory XVI, Pope, 14
Grienberger, Christoph, 157
Grundlach, Gustav, 249
Guaraní, 99–100, 103–5, 190, 200, 208, 228, 275
Guatemala, 14, 134, 155, 197
Guizot, François, 131
Gutiérrez, Gustavo, 194–95

Habsburg Empire, 116
Harris, Steven, 12
Harris Treaty, 42
Henry VIII of England, 115
heresy, 80–81
Hinduism, 9, 18; in Bertrand, 59–60; engagement with, 179; in Johanns, 62; rebirth in, 51, 58–59, 59–60, 66n12; romanticization of, 60–61. *See also* India
Hiroshima, 20
História do Futuro (Vieira), 262
Historia natural y moral de las Indias (Natural and Moral History of the Indies) (Acosta), 158
Hogar de Cristo shelters, 192
Hollenbach, David, 279
Holy Spirit: in Ricci, 38; in Vatican II, 44. *See also* God; Trinity
Hsia, Po-chia, 264
human development, 206, 209–11, 214–19
humanism, 11–12, 31, 100; education and, 148, 150–51, 153–55, 241, 243; globalization and, 265–69
humanities, 150. *See also* education
human rights, 17, 18, 172, 177, 185n25, 268
Hungarian Empire, 78
Hurtado, Alberto, 192

Idaho, 135
Idiot, The (Dostoevsky), 122
idolatry, 272; in China, 31; conversion and, 30; in Council of Jerusalem, 40; cultural accommodation and, 30–31, 271; in Peru, 98
Ignatius of Loyola, 7, 17, 124; on education, 243; Muslims and, 77; universalism and, 189; at University of Paris, 149. *See also* Autobiography (Ignatius of Loyola); *Spiritual Exercises* (Ignatius of Loyola)
Imitation of Christ (Thomas à Kempis), 6
Immaculate Conception of Mary, 137–38
immigrants: Catholic, from Europe, 133, 136; education and, 229, 247; United States and, 122, 247. *See also* migrants
imperialism, 4–5, 7–8, 14, 15, 140–41. *See also* colonialism
Incarnation, 30, 44, 84
Inchofer, Melchior, 119
India, 4, 8, 9, 10, 18, 19, 28; American missions vs., 98; anti-Jesuitism in, 123–24; economic growth in, 210; education in, 158–59, 162; human development in, 214–19; Japan and, 218; rebirth in, 56–59; rural vs. urban life in, 215; tribal groups in, 216–17. *See also* Hinduism; Mughal Empire
Indian Social Institute, 249
individual rights, 138–39. *See also* freedom; human rights
Indology, 49. *See also* rebirth
Industrial Revolution, 4, 15, 16, 192, 207, 247, 256
infallibility, 122, 138
Inoue Masashige, 42
Institut d'Études Sociales, 248
Institute of Industrial Relations, 249
Institute of Social Order, 249
Instituto Brasileiro de Desenvolvimento, 193
Instituto de Estudios para el Desarrollo, 193
Instituto Latinoamericano de Doctrina u Estudios Sociales, 193
Instituto Patria, 196
"Instruction on the Social Apostolate" (Janssens), 248
interdependence, 170, 180, 249
International Congress of the Social Apostolate, 212
International Federation of Fe y Alegría, 162
Internet, education via, 233–37
interreligious dialogue, 18, 51, 69, 179, 214, 233, 269, 274
Iraq War, 21
Ireland, 133
Islam, 5, 10, 17; attitudes on, 69–70; in contest with Christianity, 83–84; conversions from, 74, 90n40; de Góis and, 74–77; evangelization to, 75, 76–78; González de Santalla and, 77–81; heresy in, 80–81; Ignatius of Loyola and, 77; in Monserrate, 70, 89n37; negative view of, 69; Ottoman Empire and, 77–78; segregation in, 133; in Spain, 77–81; theological engagement with, by Church, 171–72. *See also* Mughal Empire
Italy, 6, 14, 130n42, 140; anti-Jesuitism in, 122–23; education in, 155, 246–47; expulsion from, 134; religious segregation in, 133
Iwakura Tomomi, 43

Jahāngīr (son of Emperor Akbar), 72, 73, 88n24
Jains, 60, 72
Jansenism, 118, 121
Janssens, Jean-Baptiste, 16, 192–93, 248
Japan, 8, 14, 28; American missions vs., 98; cultural accommodation in, 29; education in, 9, 32–34, 155–56, 162, 228; India and, 218; "primitive Church" in, 32; rebirth in, 52–53, 54–55; Ricci's Chinese catechism in, 37; torture of Christians in, 42–43; transition to modernity in, 40–43
Jaspers, Karl, 3
"Jerusalem compromise," 30–31, 44
Jesuit Centers of Social Investigation and Action (Centros de Investigación y Acción Social [CIAS]), 193
Jesuit Commons: Higher Education at the Margins (JC:HEM), 180–81, 233–37, 254
Jesuit Refugee Service (JRS), 20–21, 180–81, 186n37, 212, 224, 231–35, 251
Jesuits. *See* anti-Jesuitism; restoration, of Jesuits; Society of Jesus
Jesuit Secondary Education Association (JSEA), 176–77
Jesuits in Social Action (JESA), 19, 214–16
"Jesuit system," 111
Jesus Christ: in cultural accommodation approach, 30; in de Góis, 75; education and, 153; Ellacuría and, 199–200; in evangelization to Muslims, 75, 87n12; missions and, 227; and rebirth in Asian thought, 51; in *Spiritual Exercises*, 136
Jews. *See* Judaism
Jiaoyoulun (Treatise on friendship) (Ricci), 38, 158
Jnanopadesam (Catechism) (de Nobili), 56–57
Johanns, Pierre, 62
John III of Portugal, 7
John of Damascus, 80
John Paul II, Pope, 196
John XXIII, Pope, 170, 192, 250
Jordan, 180, 234, 235
Journal de voyage (Montaigne), 113
Joy of the Gospel, The (Evangelii gaudium) (Francis), 181–82
Judaism, 10, 17, 80, 81. *See also* anti-Semitism
Julius III, Pope, 154, 184n14
justice, 15, 18; anti-Jesuitism and, 112; Arrupe and, 125; Arrupe on, 250; in Cicero, 153–54; education and, 154, 161, 176–77, 239; faith and, 176, 177, 178–79; "from below," 201; in General Congregation decree, 194, 211, 218; income inequality and, 161; in Jesuit identity, 176; religious freedom and, 172; in *Rerum novarum*, 247–48
Justicia Social Cristiana (journal), 192–93

Kangxi Emperor, 35, 43
karma, 62. *See also* rebirth
Karuvelil, George, 83
Katha Upaniṣad, 61
Keenan, James, 177
Kenya, 180, 234, 235
Kerala, India, 216–17
Kerridge, Thomas, 88n24
Kolvenbach, Peter-Hans, 19, 195, 200, 212, 251, 252
Korea, 37, 162, 173
Kyushu, 29

LaFarge, John, 249
languages, 31, 98, 101
language study, 158
Lapide, Cornelius à, 153
Las Casas, Bartolomé de, 96
Latin America. *See* Americas; *specific countries*
Lebanon, 245, 251
Lechner, Frank, 72
Leo XIII, Pope, 132, 137, 138, 246. *See also Rerum novarum* (Leo XIII)
Le Paige, Louis-Adrien, 117–18
Lettres édifiantes et curieuses, 119
Lettres provinciales (Pascal), 118
liberalism, 1–2, 138, 229, 244, 246, 267, 279
liberation theology, 192, 194–97. *See also* freedom
Lima Catechism, 270
literary tradition, in education, 148
living standards, 209
Li Zhizao, 34
López, Luis, 99
Louis XIV of France, 35
Loyola, Baldassare, 90n40
Loyola University, 249
Lubac, Henri de, 125
Lumen gentium (Second Vatican Council), 44, 170. *See also* Vatican II
Luther, Martin, 116
Luxembourg, 132

Macau, 28, 240
Madagascar, 132
Madigan, Daniel, 273
magic, 116, 127n17
Magni, Valeriano, 118
Maharashtra Prabodhan Seva Mandal (MPSM), 215
Mahatma Gandhi National Rural Employment Guarantee Act, 215
Malabar rites, 118, 119, 271. *See also* Rites Controversy
Malawi, 180, 235
Maldavsky, Aliocha, 191, 262
Manuductio (Manual for the conversion of Muhammadans) (González de Santalla), 77–78, 80, 84, 90n40
market: in *Characteristics of the Social Apostolate of the Society of Jesus*, 212; Francis on, 220;

globalization and, 20–21, 207, 225; Jesuit criticism of, 211
Martín, Luis, 139
Mary, 137–38, 190
Masons, 123
Mataix, Anselmo, 218
Mater et magistra (John XXIII), 250
materialism, 219, 248
Matthew 28:19, 264
McGreevy, John, 122, 279
McLuhan, Marshall, 17
Medellín Conference, 125, 192, 193
MEGUKO, 218
Meliá, Bartomeu, 104
Mencius, 39
"Men for Others: Training Agents of Change for the Promotion of Justice" (Arrupe), 250
Mengzi, 39
Mensaje (journal), 192
Mercurian, Everard, 28–29
Mesquita, Diogo de, 33–34
Messina, 11, 152, 155, 240
metempsychosis, 65n1
Mexico, 14, 94; economic growth in, 210; education in, 162, 196, 253; expulsions in, 134; indigenous parishes in, 95–96
Meyer, John W., 265–66
Michelet, Jules, 134, 135
Middle Ages, 147
Middle East, 14
migrants, 229–30, 232–33. *See also* immigrants; refugees
Millennium Development Goals (MDGs), 210–11
Missio Moscovitica, 7
missions: anti-Jesuitism and, 113, 123–24; in Asia, 7–8; ban of Chinese, 43; in Brazil, 93–94, 100, 102; in Chile, 96–97; in cities, 94–95; colonial societies and, 99–102; common good and, 175; cultural accommodation by, 8–9, 28–31, 92–93, 118–19, 208; education and, 148; education as overshadowing, 218–19; frontier, 96–97; in Ibero-America, 93–98; in "Jesuit system," 111; in Paraguay, 97, 99, 102; in parishes, 94, 95–96; in Peru, 94, 96, 99; "primitive Church" and, 31–36; and restoration of Society, 136; rural, 97–98; types of, 93–98. *See also* Gospel
Missions Étrangères de Paris, 123
Mission to Tibet (Desideri), 66n13
Mitre, Bartolomé, 123
mobility, 72, 106, 224–26, 237–38, 249, 264
modernity: education and, 265; globalization and, 5–6, 278, 280; hostility toward, 14, 123, 246; interconnectedness and, 64; Jesuits in prism of, 268; transition to, in East Asia, 40–43
Mogrovejo, Toribio de, 99
Molière, 159

Molina, Luis de, 266
Monarchia solipsorum, 119
Monita, Protocatastasis seu prima Societatis Iesu Institutio restauranda Summo Pontifici (Pasquelin), 128n20
Monita Secreta Societatis Jesu, 116–17
Monserrate, Antonio, 70, 71–72, 89n37
Montaigne, Michel de, 113
Montana, 135
Montesquieu, 120
Montpersan, Louis de, 118
Morocco, 90n40
"Mosaic distinction," 272
Moscow, 7
Moura Carvalho, Pedro de, 87n12
Mughal Empire, 4, 10; conversions in, 74; education in, 71; encounters with, 70–74; Jerome Xavier and, 72–74. *See also* India; Islam
multipolarity, 5
Murad (son of Emperor Akbar), 71
Muratori, Ludovico Antonio, 120
murder, 178, 185n28, 198, 204n35
Murray, John Courtney, 17, 169, 172–74, 249
"Musalman," as term, 71, 86n3
Muslims. *See* Islam; Mughal Empire
Mveng, Engelbert, 18, 177, 178
Myanmar, 232, 235
mysticism, 198–99

Nadal, Jerónimo, 7, 194, 227
Nagasaki, Japan, 42
Naples, 134
Napoleon, 13, 246
Napoleonic Wars, 122, 267
nationalism, 124, 139–41, 229–30, 267
nation-state, emergence of, 134, 229, 247
Native Americans, 135
Natural and Moral History of the Indies (Acosta), 10
Navarrete, Domingo de, 119
Nepal, 214, 215
New Granada, 14, 134
New World, 4, 10–11, 229, 262
Nicaragua, 14, 134, 197
Niccolò, Giovanni, 156
Nicene Creed, 272
Nicolás, Adolfo, 142, 179–80, 224, 233–35, 253–54
Nicomachean Ethics (Aristotle), 150
Nirvana, 91n54
Nobili, Roberto de, 8, 9, 53, 56–58, 66n9, 158–59
Nostra aetate (Second Vatican Council), 17, 249. *See also* Vatican II
Novi Advertimenti (Cesarini), 112
Nussbaum, Martha, 209

Obara Satoru, 33
objective dimension, of globalization, 3, 72

O'Malley, John, 31, 120, 178, 182, 227, 240, 262, 263, 265
online education, 233–37
Opium Wars, 43
order, 173
Orientalism, 273
"Otherness," 10, 12; "Age of Discovery" and, 27; humility before, 182; openness to, 182; poverty and, 182; respect for, 169–74; Vatican II and, 17
Ottoman Empire, 4, 5, 77–78. *See also* Islam
"Our Mission Today," 161–62

Pacem in terris (John XXIII), 170
Padma Purana, 59
"pagan" culture, 10, 104
Pakistan, 214
Palafox y Mendoza, Juan de, 99, 118, 119
Pallavicino, Nicolò, 77
pamphlets, anti-Jesuit, 116–17
Pantoja, Diego de, 35
papal infallibility, 122
papal loyalty, anti-Jesuitism and, 115, 122–23
Paraguay, 97, 99, 102–4, 120, 190
Paris Foreign Missions, 123
parishes, 94, 95–96
Parisot, Pierre, 119
Parsons, Robert, 116
Pascal, Blaise, 117, 118
Pasio, Francesco, 35–36
Pasquelin, Guillaume, 128n20
Pasquier, Étienne, 112, 276
Pastoral Constitution on the Church in the Modern World, 17, 170, 249. *See also Gaudium et spes* (Second Vatican Council)
Paul, 30, 31, 36, 37
Paul III, Pope, 93, 112, 262
Paul VI, Pope, 196, 211, 259n34
Pavone, Sabina, 134, 263, 275, 278
Peace of Westphalia, 5, 113
People's Manifesto (South Asian People's Initiative), 215
Peramás, José Manuel, 103
Pereira, Tomás, 43
Père Norbert, 119
Perry, Matthew, 42
persecution, in Japan, 42–43. *See also* anti-Jesuitism
Peru, 14, 94, 96, 99
Peter, 30, 31, 35
Petitjean, Bernard-Thadée, 42
Petrarch, 150–51
pharmacy, 157
Philip II of Spain, 89n37, 94, 96
Philippines, 173, 218, 228, 235. *See also* Ateneo de Manila University
Piedmont, 134
Pieris, Aloysius, 18, 179
piety, 6, 31–32, 79, 95, 136

Pinto, Mendes, 52
Pioneer Column, 229
Pius IX, Pope, 122, 132, 137. *See also Syllabus of Errors* (Pius IX)
Pius VII, Pope, 13, 122, 160, 246
Pius XI, Pope, 16, 248
Pius XII, Pope, 40
Plato, 62
pluralism, 5, 81–84, 122, 172, 250, 270, 273–74
Polanco, Juan Alfonso de, 155, 227
Poland, 133, 155, 173
Polish-Lithuanian Commonwealth, 7
Politique des Jésuites (Montpersan), 118
Pope Benedict XIV, 40, 119
Pope Benedict XV, 268
Pope Benedict XVI, 192
Pope Clement XI, 40
Pope Clement XIV, 12, 13, 121, 137, 159
Pope Francis, 6, 20, 21; on accompaniment, 181–82; anti-Jesuitism and, 125–26; on globalization, 2, 206, 217; importance of poverty to, 220; on justice, 201. *See also* Bergoglio, Jorge
Pope Gregory XIII, 157
Pope Gregory XV, 39
Pope Gregory XVI, 14
Pope John Paul II, 196
Pope John XXIII, 170, 192, 250
Pope Julius III, 154, 184n14
Pope Leo XIII, 132, 137, 138, 246. *See also Rerum novarum* (Leo XIII)
Pope Paul III, 93, 112, 262
Pope Paul VI, 196, 211, 259n34
Pope Pius IX, 122, 132, 137. *See also Syllabus of Errors* (Pius IX)
Pope Pius VII, 13, 122, 160, 246
Pope Pius XI, 16, 248
Pope Pius XII, 40
Populorum progressio (Paul VI), 211, 259n34
Portugal, 7, 12, 97, 173, 208
poverty: accompaniment and, 181–82; Arrupe and, 176; in *Characteristics of the Social Apostolate of the Society of Jesus*, 212–13; "civilization of," 199; as continuing problem, 208–9; early Jesuits and, 178; education and, 197–98; Ellacuría and, 198–99, 204n41; Fe y Alegría and, 176; growth and, 208–9; human development and, 209–11; income inequality and, 161; in India, 214–19; John XXIII and, 192; justice and, 176; in Latin America, 195; liberation theology and, 198; in Medellín Conference, 125; Otherness and, 182; Pope Francis and, 220; solidarity with, 248; in *Spiritual Exercises*, 189, 202n5; Thirty-Second General Conference and, 176; universalism and, 189–90; in Vatican II, 125
praxis, 33
press, freedom of, 138–39
"primitive Church," 31–36

printing, 33, 34, 225
professionalization, of education, 147
Protestantism and Catholicity Compared (Balmes), 138
Protestantismo Comparado con el Catolicismo en sus Relaciones con la Civilización Europea, El (Balmes), 138
Protestant Reformation, 115–16
Protestants, 10, 116, 118, 123
Protocols of the Elders of Zion, The, 124
Prussia, 13, 135, 140. *See also* Germany
public education, 134. *See also* education
"public order," 173
Puebla Conference, 193, 204n38

Qing Empire, 4, 5
Quadragesimo anno (Pius XI), 16, 248
Quinet, Edgar, 134, 135
quinine, 157
Quintilian, 151, 153
Qur'an, heresy in, 81. *See also* Islam
Qu Rukui, Ignatius, 38

Racine, Jean, 159
Rafael Landívar University, 197
Rahner, Karl, 125, 141, 169, 170–72
Ramanuja, 62, 63
Ramos, Celina, 204n35
Ramos, Julia Elba, 204n35
Ratio studiorum (Plan of Studies). *See* education
Ratzinger, Joseph Cardinal, 196. *See also* Benedict XVI, Pope
Ravignan, Gustave de, 59–60
rebirth, 49–52; in Bertrand, 59–61; body and, 54; in Bouchet, 58–59, 67n14; in China, 55–56; in Coeurdoux, 67n14; in de Nobili, 56–58; in Desideri, 66n13; developments regarding, in 19th and 20th centuries, 59–63; freedom and, 55–56; in India, 56–59, 66n12; in Japan, 52–53, 54–55; in Johanns, 62–63; justice and, 57; origins of Jesuit argument against, 52–59; in Ricci, 55–56; romanticization of, by Christians, 60–61; sin and, 56–57, 60, 61, 62; soul and, 54, 57, 62; in Thébaud, 61; in Tibet, 66n13; in Valignano, 54–55; Xavier and, 52–53, 65n3
Reformation, 115–16, 138. *See also* Catholic Reformation
refugees, 20–21, 121, 180–81, 212, 224, 251. *See also* displaced persons
Regimini militantis (Paul III), 262
Regis University (Denver), 235
reincarnation. *See* rebirth
religious freedom, or liberty, 139, 169, 172
Renaissance, 11–12, 31, 151
Rerum novarum (Leo XIII), 15, 122, 192, 247–48
responsibility, moral, 50
restoration, of Jesuits, 13–14; anti-Jesuitism and, 111, 121–24; education and, 136–37, 159–61, 244–46; European revolutions and, 134–35; Immaculate Conception of Mary declaration and, 137–38; imperialism and, 140–41; individual rights and, 138–39; liberalism and, 138; missions and, 136; nationalism and, 139–41; new foundations after, 135–39; Reformation and, 138; Roothaan in, 135–36, 139; *Spiritual Exercises* in, 136; vs. before suppression, 131
Revista Latinoamericana de Teología (journal), 204n37
revolutions, European, 134–35. *See also* French Revolution
Rho, Giacomo, 35
Rhodes, Alexandre de, 53, 175
Rhodes, Cecil, 229
Ricci, Matteo, 8, 9, 27–29; as accommodative, 208; Chinese catechism of, 35–36; and Chinese converts, 34; education and, 158; and God concept in China, 37–38; and Gospel in China, 38–39; rebirth in, 53, 55–56
Rig Veda, 61
Rites Controversy, 12, 118, 119, 123, 271
Robertson, Roland, 3, 82, 266
Rodrigues, Sebastião, 41
Rodrigues, Simão, 112–13
Roman College, 32, 33, 156–57, 240, 246
Romans 2:13–15, 36
Romero, Óscar, 19, 198, 204n37
Roothaan, Jan, 122, 135–36, 139, 245
Ruggieri, Michele, 28–29, 38, 158
rural missions, 97–98
Russia, 5, 7, 13, 43, 228. *See also* Soviet Union
"Russian Jesuits," 121–22

Sacra Lega, 77
sacraments, 116, 170–71, 178
Sacred Congregation for the Propagation of the Faith, 39, 279
Sacred Heart, 132
Safavids, 78
Sahagún, Bernardino de, 102
Sahel zone, 232
St. Francis Xavier. *See* Xavier, Francis
St. Francis Xavier University, 240
St. Ignatius. *See* Ignatius of Loyola
St. John de Brito, 158–59
St. Joseph University, 245, 251
St. Paul's University, 240
St. Thomas Aquinas. *See* Thomas Aquinas
St. Xavier's College, 245
samsara, 62
samurai, 29
Sant'Ignazio, Enrico di, 118
Sarpi, Paolo, 117
Sattar, 'Abdus, 73
Schall von Bell, Johann Adam, 35
Schiller, Friedrich, 127n17

Scholasticism, 137
School of Coimbra, 266, 275
School of Salamanca, 266, 275
science, 137, 147, 156, 252. *See also* astronomy
Scotti, Giulio Clemente, 119
Second Industrial Revolution, 15, 207, 247
Second Vatican Council. *See* Vatican II
secularism, 1–2, 120, 123, 124, 279
Sen, Amartya, 209
Shangdi, 38, 39
Short Christian Doctrine (Bellarmine), 79
Sikhs, 72, 73
Silence (Chinmoku) (Endō), 41
sin, rebirth and, 56–57, 60, 61, 62
Sino-Russian Treaty of Nerchinsk, 7, 43
slavery, 18, 95, 99–100, 271
Sobrino, Jon, 198–99, 204n35, 252
Social Apostolate Congress, 213, 214, 218
social justice. *See* justice
society, colonial, 99–102
Society of Jesus: anti-Jesuitism within, 119–20; "Axial Age" and, 3; establishment of, 112, 174, 188; expansion of, 7; formation of, 6; globalization through prism of, 269–80; global outlook of, 189–91; mission of, 176; as nongovernmental organization, 262; reestablishment of, 13–14, 111, 121–24, 131–42, 239, 244–46 (*See also* restoration, of Jesuits); at Second Vatican Council, 169–74; as "state within a state," 13, 113, 117, 263, 276; suppression of, 1, 13, 69, 103, 111, 121, 133–34, 160, 239; in United States, 1, 14–15, 122, 244–45. *See also* anti-Jesuitism; restoration, of Jesuits
Sogang University, 162
solidarity, 15, 17, 171, 198, 219–20, 248, 251–52, 268
Sophia University (Tokyo), 218
Sōrin, Ōtomo, 29, 32
Soto, Domingo de, 266
soul, in criticism of rebirth, 54, 57, 62
Sousa, Tomé de, 93–94
South Africa, 210, 229
South Asia, 9, 10, 14. *See also* Asia; *specific countries*
South Asian People's Initiative (SAPI), 215
South Korea, 162, 173
South Sudan, 232
Soviet Union, 17, 20, 173. *See also* Russia
Spain, 6, 12, 14, 99; democracy in, 173; education in, 100–101, 154; Fe y Alegría in, 162; Islam in, missions with, 77–81, 89n37; in Treaty of Madrid, 208
"spiritual conquest," 12
Spiritual Exercises (Ignatius of Loyola), 6, 11; cultural accommodation in, 79, 90n42; education and, 151, 152–53, 163, 253; freedom and, 175; global orientation in, 241;

on interpretation, 183; poverty in, 189, 202n5; Roothaan and, 136; universalism and, 189
Sri Lanka, 18, 179, 214, 215, 232, 235
standard of living, 209
Stoicism, 37
Strenski, Ivan, 274
Suárez, Francisco, 244
subjective dimension, of globalization, 3, 5, 211
substance abuse, 216–17
Sudan, 232
Sumario de las cosas de Japón (Summary of Things Japanese) (Valignano), 35
Switzerland, 14
Syllabus of Errors (Pius IX), 14, 138, 246
Syria, 132, 180, 232

Taparelli, Luigi, 247–48
Tarahumara, 104
Taylor, Charles, 280
technology: in globalization, 17, 207, 225–26; in online education, 233–37
Teología de la liberación (Gutiérrez), 194–95
Tepehuanes, 104
Thailand, 210, 235
Thébaud, Augustus, 61
Third Council of Lima, 98
Thirteenth General Congregation, 259n33
Thirtieth General Congregation, 250
Thirty-Fifth General Congregation, 179
Thirty-First General Congregation, 250
Thirty-Fourth General Congregation, 18, 178–79
Thirty-Second General Congregation: justice in, 18, 161, 176, 194, 211, 218, 250; Latin America in, 194, 195, 196–97; poverty in, 211; progressiveness and, 125
Thomas à Kempis, 6
Thomas Aquinas, 137, 174
Tibet, 53, 64, 65n2, 66n13, 273
To Christ through the Vedanta (Johanns), 62
Toledo, Francisco de, 99
Torres Bollo, Diego de, 99
torture, of Christians in Japan, 42–43
Tours, François-Marie de, 119
trade, 212. *See also* market
transcendence, 3
transmigration, 62, 65n1. *See also* rebirth
transnational initiatives, in Asia, 217–19
transportation, 237–38, 249
Treaty of Madrid, 208
Treaty of Nerchinsk, 7, 43
Treaty of Tordesillas, 275
Treaty of Westphalia, 5, 113
tribal groups, in India, 216–17
Trinity, 44, 84, 87n12, 189–90
True Meaning of the Lord of Heaven, The (Tianzhu shiyi) (Ricci), 36–37, 55–56

"True Record of the Lord of Heaven" (Ruggieri), 38
Tupí, 93–94
Turkey, 4, 210
Twenty-Eighth General Congregation, 258n25
Twenty-First General Congregation, 137
Twenty-Ninth General Congregation, 192

Ucerler, Antoni, 155, 175, 214, 270
Uchimura Kanzō, 40–41
United Nations (UN), 16–17, 191, 248
United Nations Development Programme (UNDP), 209, 210–11
United Nations Millennium Declaration, 210
United States: Civil War in, 140; in contemporary globalization, 16–17; education in, 162, 176–77, 244–45, 247; in Jesuit renewal, 122, 244–45; Jesuits in, 1, 14–15; Native Americans in, 135
unity, 170, 171, 241
"universal common good," 170, 171. *See also* common good
Universal Declaration of Human Rights, 17
universalism, 119, 174–75, 188–90, 199, 273–74
Universidad Andrés Bello, 196
university, 149, 150, 156–59, 240–41. *See also* education
University of Bamberg, 257n3
University of Central America (UCA), 19, 177, 189, 197–200, 204n35, 204n37
University of Central America of Nicaragua, 197
University of Paris, 6, 149, 240
University of Rome, 157
University of Vienna, 240
Uruguay, 14, 120, 123, 134

Valdivia, Luis de, 97
Valignano, Alessandro, 8–9, 35; common good and, 175; cultural accommodation and, 27–28, 29; de Nobili and, 66n9; education and, 32, 33, 155–56, 158; Jerome Xavier and, 76; rebirth in, 53, 54–55; Ricci's Chinese catechism and, 37
Vatican II, 2, 6; anti-Jesuitism and, 111–12, 125;

Index 299

Areopagus model and, 44; common good and, 170, 171, 176, 249–55; in contemporary globalization, 17; education and, 249–55; freedom and, 172–74; Jesuits at, 169–74; justice and, 15; Latin America and, 193–94; Murray and, 169, 172–74; "Otherness" and, 17; "public order" and, 173; Rahner and, 171; Rahner in, 169; religious freedom and, 172; and restoration of Society, 141; universalism and, 174–75
Vélaz, José María, 162, 195
Venezuela, 193, 195, 196
Verbiest, Ferdinand, 35
Vieira, António, 262
Vietnam, 53, 140, 175, 230–31, 233, 251
Villanueva, Daniel, 180
violence, 178, 185n28, 198, 204n35
Vitoria, Francisco de, 266, 277
Voltaire, 121, 159

Wallace, William, 62
Wang Yangming, 37
Wilde, Guillermo, 104
women: and anti-Jesuitism, 116, 117; rural missions and native, 102
Woodstock Theological Center, 177, 185n25
World War I, 140, 230
World War II, 20, 208, 230, 232

Xavier, Francis, 7, 9, 27, 28, 35; as accommodative, 208; common good and, 175; education and, 152; John III of Portugal and, 93; rebirth and, 52–53, 65n3
Xavier, Jerome, 69–70, 72–77, 74–78, 85
Xu Guangqi, 34

Yang Tingyun, 34
Yemen, 70

Zahorowski, Jerome, 117
Zambesi mission, 229
Zhu Xi, 37
Zimbabwe, 229
Zoroastrianism, 72
Zubiri, Xavier, 199

www.ingramcontent.com/pod-product-compliance
Ingram Content Group UK Ltd.
Pitfield, Milton Keynes, MK11 3LW, UK
UKHW041925140426
5217IPUK00014B/324